The Norms of Nature

Can moral philosophy alter our moral beliefs or our emotions? Does moral scepticism mean making up our own values, or does it leave us without moral commitments at all? Is it possible to find a basis for ethics in human nature? These are some of the main questions explored in this volume, which is devoted to the ethics of the Hellenistic schools of philosophy. Some of the leading scholars in the field have here taken a fresh look at the bases of the Stoics' and Epicureans' thinking about what the Greeks took to be the central questions of philosophy. Their essays, which originated in a conference held at Bad Homburg in 1983, the third in a series of conferences on Hellenistic philosophy, propose important new interpretations of the texts, and pose some fascinating problems about the different roles of argument and reason in ancient and modern moral philosophy.

This book will be of interest to moral philosophers and to scholars of Greek philosophy too.

The Norms of Nature
Studies in Hellenistic ethics

edited by

Malcolm Schofield and Gisela Striker

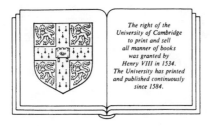

The right of the
University of Cambridge
to print and sell
all manner of books
was granted by
Henry VIII in 1534.
The University has printed
and published continuously
since 1584.

Cambridge University Press

Cambridge

London   New York   New Rochelle

Melbourne   Sydney

Editions de la Maison des Sciences de l'Homme

Paris

CAMBRIDGE UNIVERSITY PRESS
Cambridge, New York, Melbourne, Madrid, Cape Town, Singapore, São Paulo

Cambridge University Press
The Edinburgh Building, Cambridge CB2 8RU, UK

With Editions de la Maison des Sciences de l'Homme
54 Boulevard Raspail, 75270 Paris Cedex o6

www.cambridge.org
Information on this title: www.cambridge.org/9780521266239

First published 1986
This digitally printed version 2007

A catalogue record for this publication is available from the British Library

Library of Congress Cataloguing in Publication data

Main entry under title:
The Norms of nature.
Bibliography: p.
Includes index.
1. Ethics, Greek.   I. Schofield, Malcolm.
II. Striker, Gisela.
BJ192.N67   1985   170′.938   85–7917

ISBN 978-0-521-26623-9 hardback
ISBN 978-0-521-03988-8 paperback

Contents

Acknowledgements

This book contains the papers delivered to the third in a sequence of recent conferences on Hellenistic philosophy. It is the successor to *Doubt and Dogmatism* (Oxford 1980) and *Science and Speculation* (Cambridge 1982). In concentrating on ethics it takes up the central concern of philosophy in the Hellenistic period, and offers new explorations of the major preoccupations of the Stoics, Epicureans and Sceptics. For the convenience of the reader these have been grouped under two heads: first come a series of studies of the way reason and argument in Hellenistic ethics bear more directly on emotional attitudes and on moral belief than does most modern moral philosophy; then follow essays on the views on the foundations of ethics and on the conceptions of happiness and the goal of life which govern Stoicism and Epicureanism.

The conference was held from 17–25 August 1983 at the conference centre of the Reimers-Stiftung in Bad Homburg. The following scholars attended the proceedings: Julia Annas, Jonathan Barnes, Dieter Birnbacher, Jacques Brunschwig, John Cooper, Pierluigi Donini, Troels Engberg-Pedersen, Dorothea Frede, Michael Frede, David Furley, Malte Hossenfelder, Brad Inwood, Anna Maria Ioppolo, Terry Irwin, André Laks, Geoffrey Lloyd, Anthony Long, Mario Mignucci, Martha Nussbaum, Günther Patzig, Malcolm Schofield, David Sedley, Richard Sorabji, Jürgen Sprute, and Gisela Striker. The Reimers-Stiftung not only offered members of the conference warm hospitality but provided generous financial support. We are most grateful for their help and for the care they took of us in beautiful surroundings. We also thank the Deutsche Forschungsgemeinschaft for a handsome subvention to cover secretarial costs and the travel expenses of participants.

M.S.
G.S.

Preface
Günther Patzig

After two successful meetings in Oxford (1978) and in Paris (1980), the Third International Conference on Hellenistic Philosophy was held in August 1983 in Bad Homburg. The Reimers-Stiftung and the Deutsche Forschungsgemeinschaft made it possible for 25 scholars from seven countries to discuss under ideal conditions the nine papers presented to the conference. We were lucky in having unusually fine weather; all participants will, I think, gladly remember the friendly informal discussions in the open air which often went on until late into the summer night.

The present volume will provide further evidence that Hellenistic philosophy is not only historically, but also philosophically interesting. The arguments of the Hellenistic philosophers are here explained and critically discussed by experts who have contributed to the scholarly debates on the Presocratics, Plato and Aristotle and also on modern philosophers. The participants and contributors were also fully conversant with today's systematic discussions of the philosophical themes dealt with in Hellenistic times. It is, therefore, a reasonable hope that this volume will be of value not only to students of Greek philosophy, but also to those, whose main interests are in the field of ethics proper.

In this way, the present volume, as its two predecessors, may help to bridge the gap between historical and systematic work in philosophy, a gap which is, in itself, somewhat artificial, since historical studies without systematic guidelines tend to be lacking in vivacity, whereas systematic discussions without historical perspective seem often somewhat parochial.

G.P.

Part I
Argument, belief and emotion

1 Doing without objective values: ancient and modern strategies

Julia Annas

I

Before doing philosophy, we tend to think that people, actions and institutions are good or bad, praiseworthy or deplorable. That we are wrong to have these beliefs is a point on which ancient and modern sceptics appear to agree. Ancient sceptical arguments about proof, say, or perception, are different from modern analogues, and in important respects less radical.[1] But when we read the arguments that Sextus Empiricus retails to the effect that nothing is by nature good or bad, they appear familiar.

The appearance is misleading, however; ancient and modern uses of, and reactions to, sceptical arguments about value are profoundly unlike. If this is so, then pointing it out is of more than historical interest; it alerts us to a number of interesting possibilities about value, and moral value in particular.

I shall begin by looking at the ancient arguments (few and easily surveyable, it turns out) which try to undermine our confidence that people and actions really are good or bad. I shall also look at the ancient sceptics' account of the benefits of having been convinced by these arguments. Then I shall consider what seem to have been the standard ancient objections to moral scepticism, and the strength of the sceptic's defence. Doing so will, I hope, bring out the radical difference between ancient and modern attitudes to sceptical arguments about moral value.

Discussions of ancient philosophy often stress the continuity of ancient concerns with ours, and sometimes it is felt that if no such continuity can be established, then studying the ancient texts loses its point. In this area, however, the reverse seems to be true. Modern moral philosophy has been rejuvenated by study precisely of discontinuities in moral concern, and of different understandings of morality. Why this should be so is rather a mystery. One's understanding of an essentially modern sceptical problem, such as scepticism about induction, is not necessarily furthered by realising the extent of the gap between it and ancient analogous but different problems, such as sceptical arguments about 'signs'. But in the area of

---

[1] The importantly restricted scope of ancient scepticism is brought out in different ways by Richter (1902, 1904) and by Burnyeat (1982).

moral value the problematic nature of the concepts involved makes awareness of differences often more fruitful than awareness of similarities.

II

In Sextus' extended compilation, arguments for moral scepticism come right at the end of both the *Outlines of Pyrrhonism* (*PH*) and of the section of the *Adversus Mathematicos* (*M*) that we number as VII–XI. This position need not reflect lack of interest; it merely reflects the way that sceptics gave their destructive attention to topics methodically, in accordance with the ancient division of philosophy into logic, physics and ethics. (Cf. *PH* II 13; Diogenes Laertius IX 90; this seems to go right back to Aenesidemus.)[2] One of Aenesidemus' Ten Modes is also 'mostly concerned with ethics' (*PH* I 145) and since there is clear overlap between this Mode and some of Sextus' arguments (at least in *PH* III) it seems best to begin with it.

I call it the Tenth Mode, following Sextus' order (it is the fifth in Diogenes and the eighth in Philo).[3] Sextus gives the fullest and most organised version, but the outlines of an already ordered argument are visible behind all three variants.

Sextus carefully distinguishes five factors which are relevant to our beliefs about values. These are

(1)   Lifestyle (*agōgē*): the way one structures one's life either as an individual deliberately copying another individual, or as part of a community.
(2)   Customs or habits (*ethē*):[4] unwritten codes of behaviour that bring it about, for example, that even where there is no law about it, people just do not copulate in public (ancient writers seem obsessed with alleged public performance of this private act).
(3)   Laws (*nomoi*): conventions that are backed by definite sanctions against those who break them.
(4)   Mythical beliefs (*mythikai pisteis*) about various divine and fictional matters.[5]

---

[2]   In Photius' account (*Bibliotheca* 169–70) Aenesidemus' last three books were devoted to ethical matters. Three out of eight books does suggest a higher level of interest than we find in Sextus, whose account of ethics is decidedly thinner and slighter than his discussions of logic and ethics.
[3]   Sextus, *PH* I 145–63; Diogenes IX 83–4; Philo, *de Ebrietate* 193–205. See Annas and Barnes (1985) ch. 13 for translations and discussion of this Mode.
[4]   Diogenes' manuscripts omit this, and have the meaningless τεχνικὰς συνθήκας. Menagius' emendation to ἐθνικὰς συνθήκας seems obviously right. See Annas and Barnes (1985) Appendix E for further discussion.
[5]   Philo omits these, but this can be understood (without postulating a separate source or intermediary) given his concern to make the Modes relevant to exegesis of a Jewish theme; pagan myths would be out of place.

(5)   Dogmatic conceptions (*dogmatikai hupolēpseis*)[6] of which the examples
       are various abstract philosophical theories about the constitution of the
       universe and the providence of the gods.

How are these factors relevant to scepticism? None of our sources make
this explicit. Diogenes just lists examples of laws which differ, customs
which differ, and so on. Persians, he implausibly claims, marry their
daughters, Massagetae have wives in common and Cilicians shamelessly
enjoy piracy, but (we civilised) Greeks do none of these things. Why, however, should this lead us to any kind of scepticism, rather than to com-
placency, since we civilised Greeks seem to have got it right? Sextus
produces conflicts by systematically listing examples of a lifestyle clashing
with a custom, a lifestyle clashing with a law, a custom clashing with a
law, and so on, until we have gone through every possible combination of
the five factors. However, while such clashes do occur, they also get resolved, whether by compromise, prosecution or whatever; it is still not
clear how we get to scepticism.

The strategy of the Tenth Mode becomes clear from what we know
from elsewhere, and in particular the other Modes,[7] about ancient sceptical argument. The clashes Sextus points to are evidence for the conflicts
which do have sceptical import: conflicts in the way things appear good
or bad to people.

Take Sextus' third example (a hardy perennial in ancient sceptical texts,
despite its falsity, like the false belief that sufferers from jaundice see
everything yellow). Indians have sex in public, other nations not. This is a
conflict in that it implies that having sex in public appears acceptable and
good to Indians, and unacceptable and bad to other nations. This is a
clash between customs; we can generalise, if we use a generic term, say
'persuasion', for all five factors, and say that the Mode gives us material
with which to produce the following kind of conflict. One thing (action,
practice, etc.) appears to have positive value (to be good, praiseworthy,
etc.) to people of one persuasion. But the very same thing appears to have
negative value to people of a different persuasion. And obviously both
persuasions can't be right – the thing can't have both positive and negative value.

The sceptic proceeds this way in order to shake our beliefs, for these
often rest on our acceptance of our own persuasion. Having been brought

---

[6] Philo does not name these; but he clearly deals with them (198ff.), making the transition
   by a rhetorical flourish of his own. He alters the structure of the Mode somewhat by giving
   so much stress to philosophical disagreement and by introducing arguments of his own.
[7] See Annas and Barnes (1985) ch. 3 for an account of the structure and history of the
   Modes.

up in certain customs, I believe public copulation to be unacceptable. When I encounter people who, having been brought up in other habits, do not think it wrong, my belief that it is wrong is weakened. The sceptic aims to get us to the stage of *isostheneia*, 'equipollence', the state where I can find no more to be said for than against the belief that public copulation is wrong. For if I get to this point, I will suspend judgment about it; I will lose all commitment to any belief in its wrongness. It may still, of course, *appear* to me to be wrong; I will retain certain reactions to it. But I will have lost the belief that it is wrong – and equally, of course, be unable to acquire the belief that it is right. Suspension of belief is not a conclusion of any inference; rather, pointing out differences in persuasion puts us in a position where we are led to find no more reason to hold our beliefs about value than their opposites, and hence, as a matter of fact, to suspend judgment. Moral scepticism thus comes in as part of a wider sceptical strategy; differences of persuasion lead us to suspend judgment about values just as differences in distance, species, frequency and so on lead us to suspend judgment about other features of the world. The sceptic regards people who believe things to be good or bad as misguided, and in need of correction; but this is achieved not by altering their beliefs, but by putting them in a position where they lose them. To do this, all the weight, in Diogenes and Sextus, is put on establishing the 'conflict of appearances': I believe that public copulation is wrong, because it appears to me a certain way; but there are others to whom it appears differently, and it is pointing this out that brings me to lose the belief.

Philo has two different arguments, which are isolated in ancient scepticism and may be his own contribution. One (§ 202) is that dispute is, where persuasions are concerned, chronic and hopeless. It is not just that uneducated people disagree – philosophers, who have given all their time and talent to it over generations, are still locked in apparently insoluble disagreement over questions like providence and the meaning of life; and this strongly suggests that their disagreement is, in fact, insoluble.

The other (§§ 196–7, 199) is that people's habits and upbringing differ so totally that they are bound to find that things appear differently to them, and that they disagree. 'This being so, who is so senseless and idiotic as to say steadfastly that such-and-such is just or intelligent or fine or advantageous? Whatever one person determines to be such will be nullified by someone else whose practice from childhood has been the contrary.' Philo is not entirely clear here, but it is reasonable to see here at least a proto-version of the argument, popular with modern sceptics, from preferred explanation. Disagreements over value correlate strongly with differences in persuasions. The sceptic claims that it is reasonable to explain the disagreements, not as genuine disagreements about a real subject-matter, but as merely being the effects of the different persuasions. As Mackie puts it, 'Disagreement about moral codes seems to reflect people's adherence to and participation in different forms of life. The causal connexion seems to be mainly that way round: it is that people approve of monogamy because they participate in a monogamous way of life rather than that they participate in a monogamous way of life because they approve of monogamy' (Mackie (1977), p. 36).

Philo's two arguments are interesting in that they are more limited than the conflict of appearances argument. They lead to a piecemeal scepticism; they apply only where conflict *is* chronic, only if and where disagreement *is* best explained by differences in persuasion. In any case they do not form part of the standard ancient strategy for moral scepticism: their force was probably unappreciated.

In *PH* III and *M* XI Sextus retails a string of more elaborate arguments 'against the moral philosophers'. The Tenth Mode worked on the level of common sense; these arguments attack moral philosophy – the theories and arguments of Platonists, Stoics and Epicureans. But the same simple strategy applies, and only its application is more complex. Moral philosophers make claims about value, which recommend themselves to us *via* their arguments. The sceptic aims to get us to equipollence: both sides are equally convincing, there is nothing to tip the balance either way; and we find ourselves suspending judgment on philosophical claims about good, pleasure and value in general.

Sextus begins these arguments by taking the field of ethics to be demarcated by the division of things into good, bad and indifferent.[8] (This is, perhaps, a rather remote and boring way of beginning ethics, all too reminiscent of G. E. Moore's conviction that the fundamental question in ethics was the meaning of 'good'; but this is the fault not of Sextus but his targets.) In both books Sextus adds a long critique of the supposed 'art of living'; but his arguments here are all directed to notions like those of skill and learning, not to specifically ethical matters; and I shall pass them over here.[9]

In both passages Sextus points out that there is widespread disagree-

---

[8] *M* XI adds a rather stupid critique of the nature of this division considered solely *qua* division (3–20); this is irrelevant to ethics, and its inclusion perhaps an indication that Sextus himself was more interested in logic than in ethics proper.

[9] Sextus himself seems to regard this topic as an *addendum*: cf. *M* XI 167:ὅθεν περὶ ἀγαθῶν καὶ κακῶν ἀποδόντες, ἀφ ων αἱ ἀπορίαι ἐπὶ πάντα σχεδὸν τὸν ἠθικὸν διατείνουσι τόπον, φέρε τὸ μετὰ τοῦτο σκοπῶμεν εἰ ἔστι τις περὶ τὸν βίον τέχνη.

ment over the definition of 'good' (and so of 'bad' and 'indifferent' – *PH* III 169–78, *M* XI 21–41). He spends some time on particular definitions of 'good', notably the Stoics', and retails some *ad hominem* objections, but the general sceptical objection is to hold against *all* purported definitions (*M* XI 35); its form is clearer in *M* than in *PH*. These definitions cannot give the essence or nature of good. A definition that did, would put an end to controversy; but controversy has manifestly not ceased, so these definitions must have failed to make the essence of good clear. At most, claims that good is 'choiceworthy' or 'productive of happiness' and the like can tell us what happens to be true of good, its accidents or *sumbebēkota*. In fact, though, they can't make a decent job even of that; for we can't be told informatively even what a thing happens to be until we know its nature. Therefore, defining good as e.g. 'choiceworthy' tells us neither what good essentially is nor even what is contingently true of it. Therefore we should suspend judgment about our conception of good.

This argument is clearly exploiting the assumption that when a definition gives rise to disagreement, we have a conflict in the way things appear which cannot be rationally resolved. 'If what good is had been shown by the definitions mentioned, they would not have gone on fighting [*epestasiazon*] as though the nature of the good were still unknown' (*M* XI 37). Once we have started arguing over the definition, thinks the sceptic, we will either just carry on or end up suspending judgment because both sides have come to seem equally convincing.

Sextus goes on to claim that people disagree endlessly also over what things (people, actions) are good (bad, indifferent) (*PH* III 179–234, *M* XI 43–109). In both passages there are subsidiary arguments – what's good can't just be what we choose (*PH* III 183–90, *M* XI 79–89);[10] the Epicureans can't argue from animals to what is good for people (*PH* III 193–6, *M* XI 96–109). In *PH* III Sextus swamps us with a flood of examples, often overlapping with those of the Tenth Mode (199–234); in *M* XI he has got bored by all the publicly copulating Indians and incestuous Persians, and limits himself to typical examples (47–67, 90–5). But in both passages the core of the argument is quite simple (*PH* III 179–82, *M* XI 68–78): if anything were good by nature, as the philosophers claim, it should be good, and so positively motivating, for everyone. But in fact different people are differently motivated, and disagree over what is good. We can't accept all

---

[10] Richter (1902), pp. 281–4, discusses this argument, claiming that here ancient scepticism is (uniquely) committed to denying the existence of objective values, rather than suspending judgment about them. Sextus, he claims, does not introduce the argument as being merely one side of the discussion, but as one he agrees with. But the thesis, that the good is what we choose, is explicitly introduced as a view held by others (*PH* III 183), and Sextus then shows systematically that, of various interpretations of this, none is tenable.

the claims, because they conflict; and conflict cannot be resolved, either by intuition or by argument.

We can see the basic sceptical strategy at work. Every belief is countered, to produce a conflict, and argument *pro* is countered by argument *con*. The disagreement cannot be resolved; as a result, both sides end up appearing as convincing, and judgment is suspended; we cease to be able to commit ourselves to the original beliefs or to their denials. Diogenes brings this out economically at IX 101 (which derives from the same source as some of Sextus' arguments, since they share an example: pleasure appears good to Epicurus, bad to Antisthenes). People disagree about what is good; the arguments on either side are equally compelling; so we end up with suspension of judgment about the nature of the good.

In *M*, though not in *PH*, Sextus confuses this line of thought with another. In *M* XI 69 he introduces the idea that what is by nature good should be *common* (*koinon*) to all.[11] The denial of this is presented as a form of relativism: nothing is good in a way common to all, but things are good relative to particular agents' particular situations. And Sextus goes on to speak of the sceptic as holding just this: what is good is always relative, not absolute, and this is the sceptic's liberating discovery (78, 114–18). But this is a confusion. Moral absolutism, the belief that there are general rules or principles that apply to everybody without exception in all circumstances, cuts right across the issue of moral realism. The claim that 'this is good relative to me, though it might not be good relative to you' can be a perfectly good claim about moral reality.

Confusion of moral realism with moral absolutism is, apparently, endemic in moral philosophy. It probably gains some of its attraction from the fact that sceptics have often had to argue against opponents who were both moral realists and moral absolutists. (Hume is, in the third book of the *Treatise*, arguing against such opponents; hence the controversy over what his own position is.)[12] Sextus is by no means alone in failing to distinguish relativism from the rejection of realism.[13] The same failing dogs discussion of moral and political norms since the fifth-century sophists; often it is assumed that if norms hold at all they must hold absolutely. Anyone who teaches moral philosophy will find that pupils depressingly often make the same assumption.

[11] The word *koinon* occurs in Diogenes IX 101, which clearly derives from the same source (cf. the example of pleasure in both passages); but the confusion is absent. This might be just a lucky accident of compression, but it is absent from *PH* III too, and seems to have been imported by Sextus himself into his reworking of the argument in *M* XI.

[12] Cf. the discussion by Mackie (1980), which distinguishes various possibilities.

[13] The particular confusion in *M* XI may go back to Aenesidemus, if he is the source of the arguments against the existence of good and bad, as well as of the frankly subjectivist position ascribed to him at XI 42–4.

Still, it is a confusion, and one that Sextus could reasonably have been expected to avoid, for three reasons at least. Firstly, he goes on to argue that the offending belief (that there is a good common to all) is a source of troubling anxiety and perturbation, whereas the relativist thought that it's only *my* good brings relief and mental equilibrium (*M* XI 118). But this is *obviously* wrong; however relative to me, *my* good is still my *good*, just as real and troubling a part of moral reality as any universal good. Presumably the thought is: once I see that my belief that, for example, honesty is good is only *my* belief, held for various contingent reasons, it will lose significance for me, being now regarded in much the same light as my likes and dislikes, which I do not expect others to share. But the content of my belief that honesty is good has essential reference to the world and other people; it is still appropriate matter for concern however aware I am that it is only *my* belief. It should have been clear to Sextus that relief and detachment can supervene only on suspension of belief as to whether something really is good, not on the belief that it really is good, but only relative to me.

Secondly, it had already been clearly stated by at least one philosopher that even if values are relative to a group or individual they are just as real (and therefore just as troubling) as any non-relative items. Polystratus the Epicurean[14] had claimed that it is a mistake to think that 'good' or 'just', even if we concede that they are relative terms, refer to items that are any less real than the referents of non-relative terms.

Thirdly, relativism is, in ancient terms, not a form of *scepticism* at all, for it leaves the agent holding beliefs. And, however narrowed-down the content of those beliefs – 'this is good in certain respects for me here now in this situation' – they are still beliefs; the relativist is a dogmatist, not a sceptic, for the sceptic aims to shed his beliefs by suspending judgment. It is strange that Sextus should confuse two such utterly unlike positions; all we can say is that he does it elsewhere as well, in areas where there is even less excuse for confusing realism and absolutism.[15]

How good are the ancient arguments? Philo's arguments, being atypical, can perhaps be left aside. In any case their effectiveness will have to be made out for each case, for we should not be ready to accept ahead of time that *all* chronic disagreement is, just as such, insoluble; or that differences

---

[14] Polystratus *De contemptu inani*, chs. 6 and 7. Striker (1983b) points out the importance of this for the Modes as a whole. Indelli in ch. 5 of his Introduction to *De cont. in.* claims that the attack is directed at contemporary sceptics; if so, they missed the point of it.

[15] See Annas and Barnes (1985) Index of Topics, s.v. 'Relativism and Scepticism' for discussions of the various passages in the Modes (with reference to others passages in Sextus) where relativism and scepticism are, puzzlingly, confounded.

of persuasion will always be a preferred explanation of disagreement about value; or, indeed, that such explanation will render idle our initial assumption that the disagreement is genuine.

It is the conflicting-appearances argument which is the heart of ancient sceptical strategy; and here we may well raise queries at two stages. Firstly, do the appearances really conflict? Even if persuasions differ as the sceptic says they do (and much of the ancient material is transparently fictional), must this be because people have conflicting appearances of value? What look superficially like disagreements over value can often be better interpreted as consensus over value coupled with differences over what particular means are appropriate; thus the fact that Ethiopians tattoo their babies while Greeks do not reveals more community than difference in shared beliefs about attitudes to babies. Often the sceptic is at least taking a short cut.

But even where appearances do conflict, do we get to suspension of judgment? Only if we get to equipollence, if we are convinced that nothing tips the balance one way or the other, because either side is equally convincing. And here the ancient sources do let us down. As they stand, few of the examples piled up in the Tenth Mode and *PH* iii have the power to make us feel any uneasiness. Why should we care that Crates and Hipparchia copulated in public, or that the early Stoics thought that there could be situations where incest and cannibalism would be all right? The obvious response is not to be shaken, but to conclude that Crates and Hipparchia were being deliberately shameless, and that Zeno and Chrysippus were not prescribing for the sort of situations that it would be reasonable to worry about. Indeed, we can find a certain tension, at least in Sextus, who plainly enjoys retailing examples of shocking and upsetting persuasions. For the more shocking an example, the *less* likely it is to undermine our belief that we are right to believe the opposite. Many of Sextus' examples would be more likely to reinforce than to weaken his audience's moral beliefs. And even the blander examples can hardly on their own lead us to abandon our commitment to our own beliefs. We need more argument to convince us that there is nothing to choose between the alternatives, that neither is preferable. To this Sextus could certainly retort that there are certain general all-purpose sceptical arguments which he frequently uses for the purpose; but he could not appeal to anything relevant to ethics in particular, and that is what we need.

Why cannot argument settle matters in favour of one alternative over another? Where ethics is concerned Sextus simply retains his general confidence that no argument is immune, that an equally powerful counter-argument can always be found. He shows no interest in the idea that ethical argumentation might be in any way special to the field, or require careful attention. If anything he seems somewhat dismissive of ethical arguments: at *M* xi 77 he states as though obvious that arguments about the good convince only the committed within each philosophical school. Here he is just wrong; arguments do change people's positions in ethics, and ethical argumentation does require careful study. It is also disappointing to find Sextus, at *PH* iii 233–4, urging us to be moved by *possible* conflicts of appearances if no actual ones are available. This is not peculiar to ethics – Sextus when in straits urges merely possible examples in other fields also (*PH* i 34, 143) – but in ethics is particularly weak. Why ever should I be shaken in my belief that some practice, say, is bad because, although nobody *has* brought an objection to it, somebody *might*? And if this will not even shake my belief, still less will it ever get me to equipollence on the subject, to the state of seeing no more to be said for it than against. Just as Sextus exaggerates the impact on us of the clash of persuasions, so he exaggerates the ease of getting argument in ethics to balance out and leave us undecided. Even a moderately serious look at the subject shows us that some positions are such that equipollence about them would be extremely hard to obtain.

Nor is it clear why we should be shaken by the fact of continued disagreement about the meaning or definition of 'good'. Perhaps some progress has been made though disagreement remains – it makes a difference, after all, whether disagreement is widespread or limited, and some disagreement in a subject is a sign of healthy progress rather than of hopeless confusion. Or perhaps (and more likely) progress in moral philosophy was not to be found, in the first place, by trying to explicate the meaning or definition of 'good'. People are bound to disagree over a division as wide as that of good, bad and indifferent. They are not so likely to fall into chronic disagreement over the question of whether an action is generous, or a person cruel.

The ancient arguments are disappointing, then; they give up just where the discussion gets interesting, at the point where the sceptic has to cope with the opponent who thinks that there may well be a right answer in cases of moral disagreement, and that equipollence, and hence suspension of judgment, are not reached so quickly or so easily.

It should be obvious that, whatever they are worth, the ancient arguments are radically different from modern ones in the same area. To begin with, the point is to reach suspension of judgment about the objective existence of values. None of the arguments aim to show that there are no such things. For a conclusion that there are no objective values would be, not scepticism but negative dogmatism, the holding of beliefs, and this would be no improvement on the original common sense positive dogmatism. (Why this should be so will become clearer later.)

Modern arguments, by contrast, aim to show that when we assume that actions and people are really good or bad, we are making a discoverable and correctible *mistake*. No ancient sceptic claims this, and thus it is no accident that there are no ancient analogues to Mackie's 'error theory'. For ancient sceptics do not see themselves as preserving us from error by pointing out the true view; a project locating moral scepticism as part of a larger attempt to find out the truth about the world would be thoroughly dogmatic despite the negative nature of some of its conclusions. Ancient scepticism leads to suspension of judgment as the salvation from rashness and precipitancy; the enemy is not error but premature commitment to assertions that we have no warrant for (*PH* III 235, *M* XI 111).

Another important contrast is to be found in the absence, in the ancient sources, of any thought that scepticism about the existence of values is a healthy rejection of dubious items based on an equally healthy confidence in the reality of better attested parts of the world. Scepticism about values is part of a *general* sceptical approach to *all* beliefs, not a localised choosiness resting on the soundness of beliefs in other areas.

Thus we find no analogue in the ancient sources to the common modern assumption that there is something too *queer* about values for them to be genuinely existing items. Mackie, in a passage that has become notorious because of the openness of this crucial assumption, declares that differences in moral beliefs *must* be explained entirely by differences in people's upbringing, etc., and not as being differing views of something objective, for *that* would demand 'queer' entities, 'utterly different from anything else in the universe' (Mackie (1977), p. 38), and known in a similarly distinctive way. Of course the mere claim that objective values are queer has no force on its own; so are lots of things that we happily believe in.[16] The reason that this kind of claim is thought to have force by opponents of moral reality is that the 'queer' entities are taken to be dubious and unacceptable by the standards of a world-view that we all share which certifies other kinds of entity as real. It is thought to be so obvious as not to need argument, merely pointing out, that moral values show up badly by comparison with other, more solid parts of our familiar world.

---

[16] Cf. Platts (1980) p. 72: 'The world *is* a queer place. I find neutrinos, aardvarks, infinite sequences of objects and (most pertinently) impressionist paintings peculiar kinds of entities, but I do not expect nuclear physics, zoology, formal semantics or art history to pay much regard to that.'

It may be claimed that this assumption of an obvious contrast to the disadvantage of value *is* present in the ancient arguments. For in two places (*PH* III 179–82, *M* XI 68–78) Sextus presents the following argument: fire, which heats by nature, heats everyone alike, and snow, which chills by nature, chills all alike; nothing which affects us by nature does so in a non-uniform way. But what is good does not affect all similarly, as is shown by the fact of continued disagreement; so there is nothing good by nature. This certainly looks like an attempt to contrast things in the world of nature, whose existence we confidently assume, with values, which are rejected by contrast with these. But a closer look dispels any apparent similarity.

Firstly, the difference between fire and good is that the effects of the former but not of the latter are constant and common to all; and this raises the suspicion that the argument rests on the confusion mentioned above, between scepticism and relativism. And we find that in the *M* XI version this confusion is explicit: the rejected good is a 'common' one (69, 71), while a 'private' good (77–8) can be accepted.

Even the *PH* III version, which does not contain this confusion, hardly presents a strong case. Perhaps the variable effects of goodness are to be explained by our varying degrees of sensitivity to it, unlike our crasser responses to fire and snow. It has not been argued that they vary too much to allow the assumption of a core of common response 'by nature'. It is instructive that in §179 Sextus both admits that he will have to *establish* the fact of differing response, and reports the view that it is *obvious*; it is not clear just how much we do differ in our responses to goodness.

Secondly, even if it held up, Sextus' rejection of values as not being 'by nature' is not presented as part of a firmly established world-view unfolding the truth about natural objects. Such a view is dogmatism (cf. above, p. 13) and Sextus, the sceptic, is not in his own person committed to it. He uses its premises only to get us to be sceptical about values; thus he uses, for example, the notions of 'nature' (*phusis*) and 'by nature' (*PH* III 179) without commitment to this marking off a real division. Partly this is because the ancient sceptic always regards arguments as *ad hominem* and tailored to need (*PH* I 35 and III 280–1), so that even rotten ones will do provided that they have the desired effect; once you have got to suspension of judgment, the arguments that got you there can be kicked away or purged out along with the harmful beliefs they removed (cf. *M* VIII 481, *PH* I 206, Diogenes IX 76 and Aristocles *ap.* Eusebius, *Praep. Ev.* XIV 762a–b). But partly the sceptic's position results from the fact that ancient scepticism about values does not ride on the back of any commitment to the truth of beliefs in other areas.

Modern scepticism on this issue, however, does rely crucially on the sceptic's having a serious commitment to the reality of a contrast between values and some other preferred area of the world, and to there being a real basis for this preference.

This becomes clear from a (rapid) inspection of two kinds of ground commonly put forward for moral scepticism. One comes from the thought that moral values cannot be real because there is so much dispute about them and no clear way of resolving it. In morality we are always aware of the existence of alternative points of view; and unless we accept a very unrealistic theory like utilitarianism there is no decision-procedure for determining who is right. Moreover, there are no acknowledged experts in morality, and (connectedly) no cumulative and developing body of generally received results, no firm marks for what counts as progress in the subject. Someone impressed by these points will probably conclude that morality is a spurious enterprise, and that there is no real subject to be right or wrong about; morality has no genuine subject-matter, by contrast with subjects where there are clear guidelines for what constitutes successful argument and progress in discovery, and where accordingly there are acknowledged experts and received results. The reality of moral values is rejected because moral inquiry as an intellectual enterprise does not come up to the standards of those to which we unhesitatingly assign a genuine subject-matter.

It is not a necessary condition of accepting this line of thought that one be over-impressed by science (hence it is somewhat simplistic to blame the rejection of moral realism on 'scientism'). However, it is undeniable that the preferred paradigm will be the empirical sciences, since nothing else will in fact fill the bill. (Disconcertingly, the model of mathematics does not fit at all.)[17] The norms of objectivity which morality is deemed to fail are to be found, if at all, in the natural sciences. This comes out in the fact that the person who suffers loss of confidence in the objectivity of science loses *pari passu* their grounds for impugning the objectivity of the other term of the contrast, morality. If one is convinced that disputes in science are not definitely resolvable, because scientists are (for example) too committed to incommensurable background frames of thought, one is left with no convincing contrast with the alleged inadequacy of moral argu-

---

[17] In fact an influential modern school of *anti*-realists rests its arguments on the analogy with mathematics, though arguably this depends on an idiosyncratic view of mathematics. (For Plato the same analogy provides strong support for a *realist* view of morality.) My own view (which I merely state here, unargued) is that *any* view which assimilates moral reasoning to mathematical has got to be wrong; practical thinking is fundamentally different from theoretical.

ment. A firm conviction that moral values are, for the reasons suggested, not real requires a robust sense of the objectivity of the scientific world-view. If that crumbles, so does the crucial contrast which undermined the objectivity of morality. So one source of scepticism about values does require serious commitment to the objective nature of our inquiries into the natural world.[18]

Another source of modern moral scepticism springs from our conception of the subject-matter rather than our investigations of it. Values, it is claimed, are not real because they are not part of the world as that is independently of us. Values depend on there being people with various concerns, desires and so on; but anything so dependent cannot be what *really* exists. Values, on this view, are like secondary qualities such as colours. Given our physical constitution, it is understandable that we see things as coloured, and also that we think that colours are really part of the world that we experience; but in fact they are only projections on to the objective world of what appears to us to be so in virtue of our own sensitivities. Of course we think that people are good, and pillarboxes red; but an objective account of how the world really is will include neither values nor colours, though it will include explanations both of why we see things as good and as coloured, and why we project these features on to a neutral reality.

Values are not objective, then, *if* the world as it really is, is like that: as it would be described from the non-human, absolute viewpoint. Here the moral scepticism rests crucially on the confidence that there is such a viewpoint, even if it is one that we have not attained and never will. (And, again, it would be useless to deny that a part is played in this by the belief that this is what science actually or ideally aims at.) If one's confidence that this is the nature of reality is sapped, one has correspondingly less reason to exclude values from reality. If, for example, one comes to doubt that what actually does figure as explanatory in our accounts of the world is reality as seen from the absolute viewpoint, then one loses the corresponding reason to deny that values themselves can be explanatory of what we believe and do. Once more, the scepticism is local, and essentially local; the sceptical thought about values rides on the confidence, untouched by scepticism, about the objective part of reality from which values are excluded. If this conception of objectivity goes, then the needed contrast goes.

[18] It is relevant here that ancient science was so theoretical and speculative, with numbers of very general competing theories highly underdetermined by available evidence, and no accepted canons of empirical inquiry. It could strike no one as an example of the cumulative pursuit of secure results.

Modern moral scepticism, then, is essentially local, a part of a globally unsceptical world-view which is likely to be scientifically based, with claims to explain the nature of the world, including us humans as part of that world. But ancient scepticism never takes this partial form: as a systematic approach it undermines the claims in turn of 'the logicians', 'the physicists' and 'the ethical philosophers', fighting a total war over the whole range of philosophy, and, if from dogmatic premises, always regarding them as occupied only provisionally and *ad hominem*. For the ultimate aim is a rejection of all beliefs, not a dogmatic retention of some after preliminary sifting.

III

I turn now to Sextus' account (much fuller in *M* than in *PH*) of the sceptic's reaction to his arguments. Leaving aside, as he would do, questions of their soundness, and concentrating only on their supposed power to convince, why would it be preferable to be led by them to suspension of judgment than to act in the conviction that things really are good or bad?

The account of the benefits of moral scepticism is fuller in *M*, but unfortunately affected by the earlier confusion in *M* of moral realism with moral absolutism. Thus we find the claim that the sceptic, having given up the vain search for things that are absolutely good, good for everyone always, finds relief in the relativist position that his good is only good *for him* (114–18). But, as we have seen, this is not to the point; for he still believes it to be his good, and Sextus' main contention is that pursuing *anything* as being good is an evil which only suspension of judgment will release us from (112–13).

The main thought is: all unhappiness is produced by anxiety (*tarachē*). Happiness consists in the desirable state of relief from anxiety (*ataraxia*). But we will never be free from anxiety as long as we believe that the things we pursue and avoid really are good or bad – that there really is something about, say, a course of action which genuinely produces motivation to do it (112–13). The sceptic alone is happy because he lacks this belief. He suspends judgment as to whether anything really is good or bad, and relief supervenes on this state without being positively sought for (*PH* I 28–9, cf. Diogenes IX 107). The sceptic is pleased by good things and pained by bad insofar as these are of an unavoidable nature (hunger, physical pains and pleasures). These are feelings over which reason has no power; one can't be persuaded not to be cold or hungry (*PH* I 29–30, *M* XI 148–9). But what most people regard as goods or evils are not like this, but depend crucially on belief. Sextus implicitly though not very clearly distinguishes two ways in which this happens. Firstly, the belief that an object of pursuit is good will bring with it a lot of subsidiary beliefs. If, for example, I think wealth good, I will be harassed by many beliefs about its precariousness, my ability to get and keep it, others' desires to have it, and so on (cf. *M* XI 146–7). But also, and more fundamentally, the mere belief that an object is good brings with it an exposure to anxiety in its own right, consequences apart. Anxiety lurks in any commitment to an object's being good, as opposed to the agent's merely observing that it seems good to him.

Sextus never retails any argument for this fundamental point. And we may well say: why should detachment from values produce relief and commitment to them anxiety? Once we accept the claim, Sextus has no difficulty in showing us that no philosophical theory about value can help us. For to be persuaded that one type of behaviour is better than another is merely to have one's anxiety redirected, not removed, and to compare values is to compare degrees of anxiety without reducing it (*M* XI 130–40). Sextus points out acutely that from the sceptical point of view, the philosopher who recommends moderation of desires is not reducing anxiety but actually increasing it, since the agent now thinks his present aim *more* valuable than his previous one (*M* XI 137–8). But none of this meets the fundamental point, why belief in objective values should bring anxiety rather than, say, a sense of security. (We shall return to this point.) Sextus does claim that anxiety comes from pursuing goods intensely (*suntonōs* – *M* XI 112, *PH* I 28); the sceptic is happier because less keen, more relaxed. But this seems an illicit point: sceptical detachment, it will be claimed, does not preclude the agent from *acting* in a normal way, and the radical inner detachment from values that is recommended is presumably to be compatible with paying a normal amount of attention to one's aims. The sceptic is not claiming that in everyday life he will be conspicuously more laid-back or mellow than anyone else. Rather, he will be active in his profession (*PH* I 24). But then claims that he is free from the 'intensity' that torments the moral realist are just restatements of the claim that moral realism is *in itself* a source of anxiety, and therefore a hindrance to happiness.

Insofar as the sceptic has an argument, it is not one that is peculiarly relevant to morality, or to practice in general. The anxiety latent in moral realism must simply be the possibility that arises in any area, of conflicting appearances with no way to decide between them. Moral realism is more exposed to this kind of anxiety than realism in, say, physics, only in that it is (supposedly) easier to find conflicting beliefs in the former than in the latter. (And insofar as this is not true of ancient physics, the contrast is further weakened.)

The sceptic about values, then, is happy because in suspending judgment about values he is detached from them; he lives without the belief that anything is good or bad (*PH* III 235, *M* XI 144, 167 (which refer to *PH* I 23–30), *PH* II 246). He will act, both because some motives to action are unavoidable, and because in all matters something will always appear to be the better course, and will work on him accordingly. But 'he does not identify with the values involved'.[19]

This characterization of the sceptic already looks very unlike anything in modern moral scepticism. But to bring out its full strangeness I shall first face it with a typical attack in the ancient sources.

Aristocles, in his sustained attack on scepticism (*ap.* Eusebius, *Praep. Ev.* XIV 758c–763d) makes a particular objection to scepticism in the area of morality (761d5–762a0). What kind of citizen, he says, or judge or counsellor or friend can the sceptic be – in fact, what kind of person? What evil thing would he not dare to do, seeing that he thinks nothing to be really bad or shameful, just or unjust? It can't be said that sceptics can still be afraid of laws and penalties – how can they be when they claim to be so unaffected and unanxious (*apatheis* and *atarachoi*)?

The sceptic response to this attack, which is very obvious and must have been very frequent, is preserved most fully in Sextus (*M* XI 162–7, which refers to *PH* I 21–30).[20] The sceptic will act; following the way things appear good or bad he will behave accordingly. That is, he will follow 'the conduct of life' (*biōtikē tērēsis*). And there is no reason to think that it follows that he will act in a bad way when under pressure to do so – from a tyrant, for example. In such a case he will (perhaps) make his choice according to his intuitions, which are in accordance with the laws and customs he was brought up in.[21] The sceptic has adequate reason for acting in the fact that things appear good or bad to him. And he will have moral intuitions that are the result of his upbringing, so there is no reason to think that he will do wrong because of immediate pressure to do so. The tyrant's threats produce some effect, but not necessarily as much as that produced by his upbringing.

Aristocles has no patience with this. He retorts: when they come out with the clever point that one should live following nature and habits but

---

[19] Burnyeat (1980). Frede (1979) argues for a more restricted interpretation of the sceptic's detachment, but it seems to me that his arguments apply to theoretical rather than practical beliefs; he admits (p. 127) that in ethics the sceptic's attitude to his beliefs cannot be that of the ordinary person, who in this area is dogmatic. See also Barnes (1982).

[20] Diogenes IX 108 is essentially the same, but unfortunately the text is a mess.

[21] *M* XI 166 – τῇ κατὰ τοὺς πατρίους νόμους καὶ τὰ ἔθη προλήψει τυχὸν τὸ μὲν ἑλεῖται τὸ δὲ φεύξεται. While in general 'intuition' would not be an apt translation of πρόληψις, I think that the role allotted to it here answers rather well to that of intuitions in ethical theory. Diogenes IX 108 has κατὰ τὴν συνήθειαν ... καὶ νόμοις χρώμεθα.

not assent to any belief, they are just being silly. For one would have to assent to *that* (the belief that one should so live) if to nothing else. And, if one has no knowledge and no means of judging, why should one follow nature and habits rather than not?

Aristocles' first point begs the question: Sextus, for example, goes to great lengths in *PH* I to show that the sceptic is not someone who commits himself to the *truth* of scepticism, but someone to whom a certain attitude happens to recommend itself, so that he lives by appearances, not beliefs; scepticism is not a theory like others, but a detachment from all theory. It can of course be questioned whether this defence works; but it exists.

But the second point is not so easily dismissed. Why *should* the sceptic follow the moral intuitions he finds natural[22] because he has been brought up in them? The answer has to be: there is no *should* about it. He just does. They work on him and lead him to act in basically the same way as do feelings of hunger and cold. He regards himself as passive with respect to them in much the same way he does to hunger and other bodily feelings. This is certainly the picture we get from *PH* I 23–4, where the handing-down of customs and laws (and the learning of skills) is explicitly put on a level with the constraints arising from our nature as sentient beings with desires (for food, for example) that we can do nothing about.

But this is a disturbing answer, and one which casts doubt on the claim that the sceptic lives an *ordinary* life, unaffected by his philosophy (*M* XI 165, Diogenes IX 105). For such a response to the tyrant's command, even if it results in the right action (and it might not; even Sextus adds 'perhaps') is an essentially *uncritical* response. The sceptic *just does* what his intuitions tell him. He has no basis for considering alternatives, or for wondering whether this occasion might prove an exception. He might, of course, fail to follow his intuitions, because of the immediate fear, but this would not worry him, or present itself as a difficulty in decision, for he could not see it as his responsibility, something which concerns him because its origin goes back to his choosing self. The fear outweighed the moral intuitions – why should that be anything for him to worry about? For the intuitions themselves are only motives to action which happen to be there, like hunger or thirst – not to be ignored, but not the kind of thing that can sensibly be questioned, either.[23]

---

[22] 'Nature' does not, of course, imply a state of original nature uncorrupted by culture; one's nature includes one's education and cultivated dispositions, which leave one disposed to act and react in some ways rather than others.

[23] Cf. Hossenfelder (1968), p. 73: the sceptic's values 'werden sie überhaupt nicht durch ihn selbst gesetzt, sondern bestimmen sich durch die gänzlich aüßerliche Tatsache, in welcher Gemeinschaft er lebt. Wäre er woanders geboren, handelte er anders.'

We do not think of moral choice this way, because we do not think of our moral intuitions and principles this way, as just happening to be there and working themselves out one way or another while we, so to speak, look on. Whatever he or she actually does in the end, the person threatened by the tyrant will identify with his or her moral outlook and intuitions; moral motivation is seen as part of the self, not as something external to the self from which one might be detached.[24] Here there is an immense split between scepticism and ordinary life, given which it is unimportant that the sceptic will usually come out with the same action as the ordinary person.

The radical nature of this detachment emerges if we ask, can the sceptic retain the notions of *laws* and *moral* intuitions? The notion of a *law* one has been brought up to obey is precisely the notion of something with a justifiable sanction, something utterly unlike hunger or thirst. If the sceptic is right, my belief that something contrary to the law, say murder, is wrong is no more than a feeling that I happen to be stuck with as a result of my upbringing. But this is no good except as an initial move. It only pushes us back to the fact that the people who gave me that upbringing did not think of it that way; they thought that murder was *wrong*. They had a non-sceptical belief which was their basis for giving me my belief. The sceptic's response has to be: whether they realised this or not, their belief was no better grounded than mine is. It no more than mine can be relied on to correspond to anything in reality. But the problem here is obvious. If *their* belief is just a result of *their* upbringing, we push the question back again; and if we are never going to reach beliefs that are immune from the sceptic, we have to conclude that morality as a whole *is* a sham; for it presents itself as having a claim on us, while in reality it is just another appearance, like hunger or thirst, only perhaps more avoidable.

This *need* not be a reason for ignoring or despising morality; sophisticated moderns find biological or more likely sociobiological reasons why we say the moral things we do. All the same, this detached attitude to morality as a whole, while compatible with theoretical interest, precludes any half-way serious practical commitment to any moral project; and while the sceptic might accept this, he can hardly also claim that his conduct of life is 'non-philosophical' (*M* XI 165). If we really cannot hold our

---

24 It is possible (as has been suggested to me by T. Irwin) that the sceptic might simply come to lack the sense of self that we take for granted here, and thus not be so much detached as simply uninvolved in a continuing notion of his or her life. This is, of course, an equally unsettling prospect.

beliefs that there are values, then everyday moral life is not what we take it to be. For the moral world as it appears to us provides us with reasons of varying kinds for our moral responses, and we are engaged in our acceptance or rejection of those reasons. When we are led to suspension of judgment as to there being anything behind this appearance, we become detached both from the reasons and – more weirdly – from our own responses, which now become themselves nothing more than appearances: a desire to be generous, say, becomes merely a feeling that happens to present itself to me, but with nothing behind it. But then everyday moral life as it appears to us is indeed not what we take it for, and the sceptic is reduced to merely going through motions. Whatever the upshot of his motions, or the content of the utterances he produces, he is in an important sense not *in* them, not committed to them. Moral scepticism, then, is not, in its ancient version, a bland doctrine that can be held in insulation from everyday life; it is profoundly subversive of everyday life. Timon declared that he had not gone outside 'the customary' (*sunētheia*); but he was wrong (Diogenes IX 103).

It is interesting that both objection and response here can be seen as a special application of a more general objection: that scepticism, in leading the sceptic to suspension of judgment about the truth of his beliefs, and thus to detachment from their content (since he cannot assert them as being true), renders him unable to act, since action requires commitment to the truth of some beliefs. This objection, the *apraxia* or inactivity argument, is highly interesting in its own right,[25] and too complex to be discussed here. I mention it in passing only to point out briefly the ancient rebuttal (used by Arcesilaus: see Plutarch, *Against Colotes* 1122a–d). Action, the sceptic claims, does not require assent to the truth of any belief; it merely requires that the world appear to the agent in a certain way, and that movement be thereupon produced by an impulse in the agent. However, any impulse to action that is regarded by the agent as merely an impulse in him, detached from any beliefs, will leave it mysterious to him why that impulse should result in that action; he becomes the uncommitted spectator of his own actions and his own impulses. Moral scepticism merely gives us a special case of this; the agent notes his moral intuitions, their strength and their upshot in much the same way as he regards his hunger, or pains; they are all merely things that happen to and in him. What he does may look from the outside like what the ordinary person does; but on the inside it is completely different.

---

[25] The best treatment of the *apraxia* argument is Striker (1980).

This radical consequence of scepticism about value was recognised in the ancient world, though the response to it was inadequate and uncertain. All our accounts agree that Pyrrho, the prototypical sceptic, suspended judgment about the real existence of values. But one set of stories has him neglect the most obvious types of prudence and concern for others, being indifferent alike to falling off precipices and saving a friend from a bog (Diogenes IX 62, 63, 66; Aristocles *ap.* Eusebius, *Praep. Ev.* XIV 763a–b); whereas another set has him live the life of an honoured citizen and high priest (Diogenes IX 64–5).[26] There is no doubt that the sceptic will have radical inner detachment; the unsolved question is the extent to which this will show up in the life that is visible to others.

This ancient response to the experience of finding oneself convinced by arguments for moral scepticism is dramatically different from the modern one in at least three ways, all of which are illuminating for our understanding of either. The first two are perhaps more striking, but it is the third that is in the end philosophically fundamental.

The first emerges in the extreme oddity, to our minds, of the happiness that Sextus thinks will supervene on sceptical suspension of judgment. Sextus urges that moral scepticism is the only way to *ataraxia*, freedom from anxiety, and, as we have seen, assumes that commitment to moral realism is just in itself something that produces anxiety. But not only is this not argued for, it is the opposite of what modern sceptical theories find obvious. We have become used to the idea that assent to belief that things are good or bad by nature produces security, not anxiety; that it is responsible for moral laziness, not intensity and over-keenness; and that it brings about bad faith and refusal to face difficulties, rather than hazardous exposure to the conflicts in the world. For Sextus, the person who believes that his moral problem has an answer which is independent of his decision is foolishly letting himself in for all kinds of anxiety, whereas the person who realizes that no objective answer is available is able to relax into relief. For us the matter tends to be presented as being the other way round; it is the moral sceptic who is commonly put forward as the intense one, alert to the seriousness of his or her plight in the world where there are no objective values to fall back on. Moral scepticism is presented as a *rejection* of security – indeed sometimes as a course forced on one by mature consideration of the ways in which moral realism supposedly pre-

[26] If Elis really did relieve philosophers from taxation on Pyrrho's account, that suggests that they knew that philosophers would cause no trouble, make no waves. Cf. passages where the aim of scepticism is said to be gentleness (πραότης) – the sceptic can be relied on to fit in, not to query things (Diogenes IX 108; Sextus *M* I 6 (but this may be ironical)).

empts one's moral decisions. The favoured image that we find over and over again is that of the moral sceptic as the person who grows up, where this is taken to mean: who thoughtfully rejects comforting easy answers in order to grapple seriously and responsibly with the complexities of personal moral thinking. Undoubtedly this common picture is exaggerated, sometimes to the point of caricature, by naïve and limited views of moral realism, but the fact remains: whatever one's reasons for being a moral sceptic in the twentieth century, a search for security is not among them.[27]

Secondly, the ancient sceptical response is a programmatically *passive* one: suspension of judgment as to things being really good or bad is followed by the radical inner detachment from one's beliefs which involves taking up a passive attitude to them, and treating them as items which just happen to be there given certain conditions.

A common modern reaction to the abandonment of the belief in objective values has been the extreme opposite from passive detachment: the thought that if I do not discover value then I actively *create* it. Mackie's book, for example, is subtitled, '*Inventing* Right and Wrong'; the sceptic invents or creates where there is nothing to discover. In line with this is the immense stress that has been laid on our alleged *freedom* in moral matters if there are no objective values – a totally creative, unconstrained freedom stressed in traditions so otherwise different as those of Sartre and early Hare.[28] This goes with the view that morality is essentially a matter of choice and deciding what to do, not in the humdrum sense of choosing between alternatives whose practicability depends on external factors, but in the more exciting sense of choosing what is to be valuable, deciding what is to count as a moral reason.[29] Indeed, in an exact reversal of the ancient picture, the person rejecting moral realism identifies with the purely *active* self rather than the purely passive, with the freely choosing, totally creative will. (Both pictures leave it equally mysterious how this 'real' self is related to the tediously obtrusive empirical self and the constraints that that imposes.)

Such a view is unavailable to the ancient sceptic. And it is worth asking,

[27] See the end of Richter (1904) and the comments at the end of Striker (1981).

[28] Cf. Hare (1963), p. 2: 'We are free to form our own moral opinions in a much stronger sense than we are free to form our own opinions as to what the facts are.' Hare takes this freedom to be so strong as to set up a *prima facie* dilemma when coupled with the belief that 'the answering of moral questions is, or ought to be, a rational activity'. He thinks that this is just common-sense, talking of 'this conviction, which every adult has, that he is free to form his own opinions about moral questions'. (Note the image of adulthood and maturity.) For refutations of the claim that this is common sense, see C. C. W. Taylor (1970) and G. Warnock (1978).

[29] Charles Taylor (1976) discusses this idea of radical choice and its relation to the agent's self and his or her notion of the self.

what it is that makes the modern view not only available but so apparently compelling. Two quite different streams seem to me to have fed the current. One is the tradition which sees the alternative to the constraining existence of values as *personal* creation of value. The ancients were, after all, familiar with the idea that values might be the product of *society*, that justice might be rooted in political rather than natural fact. But this is quite distinct from the idea that *I* can unaided bring value into the world.[30] It is only in the last century and a half that we find such stress on the first person in ethics that we are frequently presented with the alleged dichotomy: either values are there in the world to make me act, or I decide what is to be a value. It is a further question, probably unanswerable, what brings into moral philosophy this stress on the isolated first person and the agent's ability to create from nothing.[31]

The other stream derives from twentieth-century analyses of moral terms as being 'non-cognitive' or involving a 'non-descriptive' element. Such analyses have usually not been motivated by a desire to understand moral language, but have been by-products of analyses of language that have concentrated on 'scientific' statements and have had a narrow conception of what a descriptive term could be. All the same, they have had appeal within moral philosophy. For if moral language is not straightforwardly descriptive, it is tempting to think of it as having the 'real' form of imperatives or commands (or, in the ultra-crude version, of exclamations like 'Boo!' and so on). And such analyses reinforce the thought that in making a moral judgment I am not reporting on anything that exists independently of me, but am performing a more creative act, bringing something about that was not there before. That thought is powerfully supported by theories like emotivism and prescriptivism, which are both formally the products of an analysis of the meaning of moral statements which allots them no, or only partial, descriptive meaning. That analysis is a twentieth-century one, and so it is no surprise that there are no ancient analogues of emotivism or prescriptivism. It also seems to me that though such meaning-analyses have been highly influential in the formation of twentieth-century moral philosophy, they are not as fundamental an element as is sometimes claimed. The basic debate between moral sceptic and moral realist is independent of whether moral language is judged to

---

[30] Interesting here is Timon fragment 70, quoted by Sextus at *M* XI 140. Anxiety about pursuit of things as being good or bad is to be allayed by the sceptic who conveys the lesson that there is nothing good or bad by nature – in Timon's words ἀλλὰ πρὸς ἀνθρώπων ταῦτα νόῳ κέκριται. Hirzel's emendation to νόμῳ has some appeal, but even if we reject it we do not find an appeal to the *individual's* mind; it is the thoughts of *people* that are in question, not *my* thoughts.

[31] See Midgley (1981), pp. 43–58, for pertinent comments on Sartre and Nietzsche.

be 'non-cognitive' or not. Non-cognitivist analyses of moral language have at most facilitated the development of an existing tendency to see morality as creation rather than discovery, and I suspect that in future their rôle in the debate will be seen as a minor one.

The third major contrast can be seen in the fact that modern versions of moral scepticism do not so much as recognise the possibility of any *apraxia* argument.[32] There is not felt to be any conflict between accepting arguments that render one sceptical about morality, and yet acting on firmly held moral beliefs. Mackie, indeed, after an initial chapter claiming that 'there are no objective values' goes on to produce a book-length theory of ethics. Why is this assumed to be so unproblematic? If moral reality really is 'queer' and unacceptable, how can one continue to feel confidence in the commitment to values that everyday life requires?

Those modern forms of moral scepticism which avoid the cruder versions of the idea that moral judgment is merely sounding-off or expressing one's feelings are explicitly *insulated* from moral practice in a way that no ancient variety is. Insofar as the sceptic retains the forms of everyday life (making what look like moral judgments, instead of explicitly prescribing or emoting), these are compartmentalised in a way insulating them from his philosophical judgments on them. There are two ways in which this happens, and they tend to reinforce each other: one from the side of scepticism in general, one from that of moral philosophy in particular. On the one hand, modern scepticism itself is not taken to have any practical consequences; the sceptic about time, for example, does not regard himself as refuted by Moore's point that he knows that he had breakfast *before* lunch; this is taken to be simply irrelevant to the philosophical question.[33] Scepticism is taken to be neither established by everyday beliefs nor refuted by them. Hence the moral sceptic regards it as a confusion to challenge his consistency in holding that there are no objective values while passionately claiming that honesty is the best policy; this is a special case of a philosophical sceptical theory being insulated from everyday beliefs, answerable to them neither for support nor disproof.

This is reinforced by the (distinct) tendency to distinguish 'meta-ethics' from 'normative', common or garden ethics. Sceptical questions are taken to be questions about the meanings of ethical terms, and our conclusions here are on the 'meta-level', and have no effect on our employment of the terms in actual use. On different grounds we get the same result: there is

---

[32] Though see recent work by Platts (1980) and Brandon (1980).

[33] See Burnyeat (1984), to which I owe both the terminology of insulation and much in the way of understanding of the fundamental differences between ancient and modern forms of scepticism.

nothing odd about committedly campaigning for the *best* candidate whilst giving an analysis of the meaning of 'good' revealing it as a mere vehicle for the agent's sounding-off; these activities are supposed to take place at different levels.

It seems to me that neither of these insulating moves has the self-evident merits that are often assumed. But obviously I cannot argue that here; I am concerned only to show that it is the assumption of insulation that forms a large part of the difference between ancient moral sceptics, who took the *apraxia* argument seriously, and modern ones, who seem unaware of its force, who avoid it by analysing it as a confusion either between the philosophical and everyday levels, or between meta- and normative ethics.

Two positions in particular are, by virtue of insulation, open to the modern moral sceptic but inconceivable to the ancient sceptic, who has no logical room for them.

One is that of the philosopher who holds a substantive moral theory but is comparatively indifferent as to whether it comes in a realist or a non-realist form. Two utilitarians, for example, can agree that they hold the same theory, discuss details and so on, although one holds that it is a fact that I ought to maximise utility, while the other holds that 'I ought to maximise utility' merely expresses the way I happen to feel about things. They regard themselves as having clearly more in common than either does with a deontologist. Here moral scepticism has become insulated at a level which cuts across different moral theories; it has in effect become a purely metaphysical theory about the basis of a moral theory, not a moral theory in its own right. The ancient sceptic, by contrast, regarded moral scepticism as a theory in its own right, with its own conception of the end that is desirable (freedom from anxiety) and of the means to get there.

The other position is that of the 'quasi-realist'.[34] This is the person who rejects moral realism on the grounds that there can be no such things as objective moral values or moral facts bringing about, and explaining, our moral beliefs and actions. Nevertheless he does not see himself as forced to reject all the ideas that normally are held to depend on realism: he does not see moral thinking as unconstrained free choice, or moral language as essentially imperatival or expressive of feeling. He thus feels free to regard moral judgments as being such that we can say that they are true or false, discussable rationally, correctible and improvable by reflexion and so on

---

[34] Quasi-realism is defended and developed by Blackburn (1971, 1980, 1981). It is, I think, the implicit view of many people who are anti-realists but turn out to wish to retain at least some of the intellectual attitudes associated with realism, rather than jettisoning them in favour of a totally 'creative' view of moral statements.

– in fact, we can make free with all the intellectual attitudes and commitments of the realist. But we can not only have our cake, we can eat it too; for we can do all this while rejecting the actual existence of objective values which is the hallmark of realism.

Such a view clearly depends on insulation; for it takes the question 'Are there really objective values (moral facts, etc)?' to be isolable; it answers it negatively while taking this to leave unaffected the questions, 'How can I act on what appear to me to be moral values?', 'How can I be seriously committed to my practical beliefs?' Indeed, insulation has to be regarded by the quasi-realist as one of the *strengths* of his position. For he has to demarcate that position against the realist, who points to our irresistible feeling that values present themselves as really being there; and also against the kind of anti-realist who insists that the only alternative to accepting the existence of objective values is the view that moral language is, despite appearances, nothing but a vehicle for sounding-off. The quasi-realist accepts neither position; for he thinks that we can *both* reject the existence of values *and* be as serious as we ever were about our moral commitments. But this position is achieved only by insulating the question of moral values and our acceptance of them from practical moral concern – paradoxically, given what the quasi-realist wants to achieve. Once again the question about values has been transformed into a purely metaphysical question, with no intrinsic moral repercussions.

Quasi-realism is thus a position unavailable to the ancient sceptic, who refuses to separate moral beliefs from their practical import. For him, there can be no third way like quasi-realism, because, if we can no longer assent to our beliefs about values, those beliefs lose the rôle they used to play for us; we are reduced to reporting the way values appear to us, and this makes a real difference.

This is important, both because some form of quasi-realism is the implicit view of most thoughtful people who reject extreme 'creative' views of moral language; and because of the depth of the disagreement. For the ancient sceptic is not putting forward a *recommendation*, which one might accept or reject; he is not saying that, if we come to find realism false, we *should* cease to assent to the truth of our moral beliefs. Rather, he takes himself to be pointing to a *fact* about human nature: once we come to see that there is no more reason to think realism true than to think it false we *will in fact* cease to assent to our moral beliefs. For he takes it as a deep but obvious fact about human nature that there is *no way* we can be motivated to go on acting according to moral beliefs once we have ceased to believe in the existence of values for those beliefs to be beliefs about; once that goes, our practical commitment, which depends on it, will simply wither. The possibility just does not occur that this might be avoided by insulating the rejection of realism and confining it to a harm-less level with no practical effect. This is surely not due to lack of imagination or ingenuity. Rather, it comes from a conviction that this is not a human option, not a viable way of living. Thus a whole tradition of moral scepticism took it absolutely for granted that its upshot could not be conveniently avoided by insulating the effects of scepticism to a practically ineffective level. This makes it all the more remarkable that modern theories take the opposite for granted, assuming without defence that such insulation is not only a possible, liveable option, but easily available to all who reflect on the foundations of their moral convictions but want to go on having them.

IV

So both the sceptical arguments against the objective existence of values, and the response to those arguments, are quite different for the ancient and the modern, who perceive a different range of alternatives. It would be easy, and useless, to draw simplistic morals by siding with one or the other. We might dismiss the ancient lines of thought simply because they do not perceive the possibility of insulation, or the distinction of normative from meta-ethics; if these distinctions are themselves thought to constitute a philosophical advance, then philosophers who do not employ them will seem crude and blundering. On the other hand, it is equally possible to see the contrast as revealing the extent to which twentieth-century forms of moral scepticism have been formed by comparatively parochial twentieth-century concerns; and if so, one will be less inclined to think that now, at last, as never before, we have the definitive answers to these problems. Certainly, if it is a fact that we can live with a position like quasi-realism, whereas the ancients thought it obvious that we could not, this is a deeply mysterious fact, and one that needs consideration, rather than just being taken for granted.

We cannot, of course, straightforwardly choose between these options, or give them comparative marks; it is not open to us to take on the ancient way of thinking, as though we could forget our own philosophical history and habits. But we can see both negative and positive ways in which it clarifies the modern approaches we find familiar; and what we need is not a ready-made alternative, but a deepened understanding of the options that we can and cannot make real to ourselves.[35]

---

[35] An earlier version of this paper had the benefit of discussion and comments from Myles Burnyeat, Tony Long and Gisela Striker. I am also very grateful to Terry Irwin for comments and discussion, and to Jonathan Barnes for helpful joint work on the Modes, and the Tenth Mode in particular.

2   Therapeutic arguments: Epicurus and Aristotle

Martha Nussbaum

With incantations a certain man has even made
life's toil painless.

Pindar, *Nemean* 8 49–51

Epicurus said, 'Empty is that philosopher's argument, by which no passion of a human being is therapeutically treated. For just as there is no use
in a medical art that does not cast out the sicknesses of bodies, so there is
no use in philosophy, if it does not throw out passion from the soul' (Us.
221 = Porph. *Ad Marc.* 31 p. 209, 23 N). He also said, 'What produces
unsurpassed jubilation is the contrast of the great evil escaped. And this is
the nature of good, if one applies one's mind correctly and then stands
firm, and does not go walking about [*peripatēi*] chattering about the good
in an empty fashion' (Us. 423 = Plut. *Non Posse* 1091b). The conjunction
of these two utterances, the second of which is clearly a swipe against Aristotelian (Peripatetic) ethical argument, suggests the following criticism.
Aristotelian ethical arguments are empty and useless because they are not
single-mindedly dedicated to the only proper task for philosophical argument, namely the therapeutic treatment of the human soul. It is my aim
here to establish that this is in fact Epicurus' view and to investigate his
charge. I want to ask what it means for an argument to be therapeutic in
the Epicurean sense, and what sort of *argument* a therapeutic argument is:
how an analogy between philosophy and medicine is used in Epicureanism to develop a distinctive picture of the nature and function of arguments and of the proper contribution of philosophy to ethical matters.
This will require us to place this medical analogy in its historical context
and, above all, to show to what extent Epicurus' use of the analogy is developed in reaction to Aristotle's ethical-medical analogies, both continuing and criticising them. Out of this will emerge, I hope, the outlines of a
rich and complex debate about the proper procedures and functions of an
ethical philosophy and some perpetually urgent questions about the practical usefulness of moral philosophising, the proper relation of philosophy
to the expectations and needs of human beings.[1]

---

[1] In April 1986 I shall have given the Martin Classical Lectures at Oberlin College on the
subject of Therapeutic argument in Greek ethics, especially in the Hellenistic period.

It will be useful to begin the historical investigation in reverse order, by characterising, briefly, Epicurus' general view about the rôle of philosophy in treating disturbing *pathē*, and then by going into some detail about the nature of therapeutic argument, as practised in accordance with the medical analogy in the Epicurean community. We can then situate these arguments in a long tradition of regarding *logos* as a form of medical treatment. I shall then argue that Aristotle is an opponent whom Epicurus has continually in view in this area, and I shall sketch Aristotle's conception of the practical rôle of ethical *logoi*, showing how the analogy between ethics and medicine is both developed and criticised in his metaphilosophical remarks. With all this in place we can explore the confrontation between the two philosophers, asking how Aristotle would defend the practical value of the non-therapeutic elements in his arguments and how Epicurus would respond to that attempt; asking, finally, what the relationship is between the normative ethical conceptions of each philosopher and his views about proper philosophical method and procedure.[2]

I The Epicurean diagnosis

We begin with a brief – and, I hope, relatively uncontroversial – account of some well-known facts, in order to set the scene for the operation of therapeutic argument. As Epicurus sees it, human beings are troubled and driven creatures. Their bodies are vulnerable to numerous pains and diseases. This assault of worldly contingency we can do little to control, except insofar as the medical art has found sufficient remedies; but bodily pain is, in his view, not especially awful as a source of general unhappi-

---

These lectures and the ensuing publication will give me an opportunity to enter much more fully into the background of therapeutic argument in pre-Aristotelian Greek culture and in Plato, and to compare Epicurus' approach to the medical analogy with other uses of it during the Hellenistic period. For certain matters touched upon by this article – for example the possible rôle of a recognition of unconscious desires in Epicurus' defence of his procedures – I cannot, for reasons of space, give an adequately full statement of the issues here. I therefore hope that the reader will regard my brief remarks as promissory notes, to be redeemed on that occasion. Here I shall also keep references to the literature to a minimum, citing only those works that have influenced the development or statement of my argument.

[2] There will be an apparent asymmetry in my procedure, in that I shall be concerned, in the case of Epicurus, to characterise the entire range of therapeutic arguments, which include, clearly, many arguments in natural philosophy; in the case of Aristotle, only with ethical arguments, which are for him in important ways different from arguments in natural philosophy. The reason for this is that my starting point is the practical effectiveness of argument in the human search for the good life: I investigate, in both cases, all and only those arguments for which a practical benefit is claimed.

ness. Worse by far is the disturbance of the soul. And human souls are, most of them, quite needlessly in a state of painful disturbance, a state comparable to a violent tempest (*Ep. Men.* 128). Needlessly, because the causes of the disturbance can be removed. These causes are false beliefs about the world and about value – or, more immediately, the 'empty' desires that are generated by these false beliefs. Epicurus sees people rushing about after all sorts of objects of desire: wealth, luxury, power, love, the immortal life of the soul. It is his conviction that the central cause of human misery is the disturbance produced by the apparently 'boundless' demands of desire, which will not let us have any rest or stable satisfaction. But quite fortunately, as he sees it, the very same desires that cause anxiety, frenetic activity, and all sorts of trouble by their insatiable boundlessness are also the desires that are thoroughly dependent upon false belief, in such a way that the removal of the belief would effectively remove the desire and hence the trouble. What he needs, to make out this position clearly and to propose a cure, is, first of all, a procedure for separating good desires from bad, healthy from sick; then, a diagnosis of the genesis of bad desires that will show that and how they are based upon false belief; finally, a therapeutic treatment for false belief that will show us how, through belief, to get rid of bad desire.

Epicurus' procedure for separating healthy from sick desires is of interest to us: for we shall much later see to what extent the values embodied in this procedure influence the choice of a therapeutic method. He selects a creature who would seem to be a reliable, uncorrupted witness, and asks what that creature goes for. Any desires not found in this creature are somehow suspect; there is a *prima facie* case for regarding them as corruptions or diseases. The desires that are present in this healthy creature are themselves taken as healthy. The creature chosen is the natural creature, the creature living in and as a part of nature and not corrupted by any influence that is not from nature: that is to say, the animal, or, alternatively, the child not yet corrupted by language and education (*DL* x 137, Cic. *Fin.* I 30ff., 71ff.). The testimony of this witness is taken to be the only uncorrupted and reliable testimony we can get (*neque depravate judicant neque corrupte*, Cic. *Fin.* I 71); it is taken as criterial of the end or final good.[3] But this creature does not pursue wealth, luxury, power, love,

---

[3] We must be careful to say what this does and does not imply. It does imply: (1) that anything that cannot be seen and desired as good by the child is not a part of the real final good; thus, if the child does not pursue mathematics, mathematics will be shown to have, at best, an instrumental value. (2) It implies that no faculties or procedures not possessed or used by a child are necessary for recognising the final good: thus, if the child does not employ philosophical reason, this must be non-necessary for getting a view of the correct end. However, Epicurus' position does not imply that we should live the life of untutored

the immortal life of the soul; it neither desires these things nor ascribes to them any value. When it has secured the removal of pain all of its wants are satisfied. In case the example of the pre-linguistic child is not altogether convincing as a norm for adult human desire, Epicurus adds a further thought experiment. If we can really get ourselves to imagine a human being for whom all disturbances and pains are removed – for whom the child's natural desires are truly (and stably) satisfied – we will, he claims, recognise that this person lacks nothing and has no need to go after more:

When once this [sc. freedom from pain and disturbance] comes to be for us, the entire storm of the soul is undone, in that the animal does not have to go off as if in search of something that is lacking and to look for something further with which to fill up the good of the body and soul.[4] (*Ep. Men.* 128; cf. the thought experiment in *Fin.* 1 40, and the test for desires in *VS* 71)

The child is a reliable witness in part because when we most seriously reflect we find ourselves endorsing this figure as our witness.

Using this picture of the natural as a guide, Epicurus now divides human desires into two broad groups, the natural and the empty (cf. *Ep. Men.* 127, *KD* 15, 26, *VS* 21, 33, 35, 59; Cic. *Fin.* II 26ff., etc.). The natural are those whose appropriateness is witnessed by their presence in the uncorrupted creature; the empty are those which, being absent in the uncorrupted natural condition, are diagnosed as the products of teaching

---

children, or that this life is best for us now. It is not best for two reasons: (a) As we are, we are products of our culture; we are full of fears and desires that need continued therapy (cf. infra, p. 35ff.). (b) The child, while capable of seeing the constituents of the end, is not necessarily best at devising instrumental means to it. Even supposing he or she has no anxieties caused by false belief, he or she will still be subject to bodily pains and diseases. An instrumental use of reason can help the adult to avoid these pains in the first place, by providing for a stable source of food and drink; it can help to banish them by finding medical treatment when necessary; and, as Epicurus emphasises, it can employ happy memories to balance or counteract the disturbing force of bodily pains that cannot be banished. If Epicurus had been childlike, he would not have been able to be happy on his deathbed, as he claims to be. Thus though the child gets the end correctly, the adult is far more self-sufficient with respect to the end.

I have been very much enlightened by Jacques Brunschwig's treatment of this material, pp. 113–44 below. It will be evident that I am in agreement with him in insisting that Epicurus does not propose a simple return to the life of nature. But I would emphasise more than he does the importance, for Epicurean philosophical theory and practice, of the fact that the child is taken to be a reliable and sufficient witness to the end. If we do not return to the childlike life, that is not because this life is taken to be impoverished in its sense of intrinsic value; it grasps everything truly good.

[4] It is significant that Epicurus sees no problem in replacing 'us' (*hēmas*) with 'the animal' (*to zōion*): our entire final good is also the good for us as animals. We are at the *telos* when all the needs of which our animal nature is aware are stably satisfied.

and belief. The natural desires turn out all to be easily satisfied; the 'un-limited' character of human longing, which causes so much pain in our lives, turns out to be the result of belief. For example, the natural desire concerning food is easily satisfied with what is in most cases ready to hand; the craving for unlimited quantities of food, or for gastronomic lux-uries and delicacies, is something that comes from our education. 'It is not the stomach that is insatiable, as the many think, but the false belief that the stomach needs an unlimited amount to satisfy it' (*VS* 59; cf. *Ep. Men.* 130, *KD* 15, 30, *VS* 25, 33, 67, 68, *DL* x 11, Stob. *Flor.* 17 34 = Us. 181). The longings associated with love are the result of a belief-based corrup-tion of sexual desire; sexual desire itself is easily satisfied, and painlessly ignored if it is not.[5] The desire for immortality – like all the other complex human pursuits that can be diagnosed as stemming in one way or another from this desire – derives from false beliefs concerning personal survival and the soul.[6] In short, nature is well designed: the natural desires are just the ones that are reliably easy to satisfy; and all of our pain comes from our own corrupt ways of thought.[7]

The nature of the relation between empty desire and false belief is a very intimate one. The belief, Epicurus holds, is the basis and essential necess-ary condition of the desire. Its presence generates the desire in the first place, and its removal removes not simply the justification or rationale for the desire, but the desire itself. If we really remove the belief thoroughly and effectively, the desire will not persist; it will depart along with the belief. For example:

Correct apprehension of the fact that death is nothing to us makes mortal life enjoyable, not by adding on some limitless time, but by taking away the passion-ate longing for immortality. For nothing is fearful in life to the person who is genuinely convinced that there is nothing fearful in not living. (*Ep. Men.* 124)

---

[5] Here much of the evidence comes from Lucretius: compare the account of the happy and easy sexual behaviour of the natural creature in I with the therapy for the disease of love in IV. Natural sexual desire is gentle, benign, and joyful, easily satisfied, aimed at reproduc-tion; love is painful, conflicted, frequently severed from its procreative end. Epicurus (Us. 483) defined *erōs* as 'an intense desire for intercourse, along with madness and anguish'; cf. also D.L. x 118, *VS* 18.

[6] This hardly needs documentation, since it is the central Epicurean teaching. Below I shall suggest, however, that some of the beliefs in question here may be exerting their influence beneath the level of conscious awareness.

[7] Epicurus seems to have omitted the desire for truth and knowledge from his list of the child's natural desires. Thus he gives a picture of natural psychology very different from Aristotle's in *Metaphysics* A 1, where the child's love of seeing and distinguishing gives evi-dence of the naturalness of the desire for understanding. For this omission he is repeatedly criticised by his opponents – most vividly, perhaps, by Plutarch, who gives a moving account of the strength and naturalness of the love of reasoning (*Non Posse* 1093dff.).

Similarly, *KD* 20 tells us that 'Reason ... by driving out fear of eternity, makes life complete.' *VS* 21 speaks even more boldly of an *elenchos*, a refutation, of painful desires.

All of this means that there is a job of great urgency to be done. And since belief is the root of the illness, the cure must work through a treatment of belief. The curative art must therefore be an art that is equipped to challenge and conquer false belief. It must, then, be an art of reasoning:

> It is not drinking and continual feasting, nor is it enjoyment of boys and women, nor of fish and the other things offered by a luxurious table, that make the pleasant life; it is sober reasoning [*logismos*] that searches out the causes of all pursuit and avoidance and drives out the beliefs from which a very great disturbance seizes the soul. (*Ep. Men* 132)

Since false belief is an illness with which we are all in one way or another afflicted, this art will be *necessary* for a good life for each of us (cf. for example Cic. *Fin.* 1 63–4, *KD* 22, *VS* 54). Since the removal of false belief by reasoning is thoroughly effective in driving out disturbing desire, an art that effectively treats belief will also be *sufficient* for securing the happy life (e.g. *Ep. Men.* 135, and cf. below, the end of section II).

This art uses reasoning as its tool. It also deals with many of the traditional concerns of philosophy: nature, the soul, the value of ends. It therefore seems to Epicurus appropriate to give this saving art the name of philosophy; and, furthermore, to insist that this saving art is what, properly understood, philosophy *is*. Sextus tells us that Epicurus defined philosophy as 'an activity that secures the happy life by means of arguments and reasonings' (*tēn philosophian energeian einai logois kai dialogismois ton eudaimona bion peripoiousan*, M xi 169 = Us. 219; cf. Us. 227 = Schol. Dion. Thr.: *methodos energousa tōi biōi to sumpheron*).

II Therapeutic arguments in the garden

If that is what philosophy is, there remain the questions, what sort of discipline is it, how does it approach its recipients, and what sort of arguments does it use? To answer these questions, Epicureanism relied heavily on an analogy between philosophy and medical science, between philosophical arguments and types of medical treatment. We have already seen one striking example of Epicurus' use of the analogy to make the point that the only proper mission of philosophy is the curing of sick souls. And in fact medical imagery permeates the Epicurean tradition, as a guiding metaphor – and more than a metaphor – for the philosophical endeavor. As medicine deals with the body, so philosophy with the soul. The *Letter to Menoeceus* begins with the parallel: 'Let nobody put off doing philosophy when young, nor get tired of doing it when old. For no one is too young or too old to secure the health of his or her soul [*pros to kata psuchēn hugiainon*, 122].' *VS* 54 uses the same language: 'We must not make a show of doing philosophy, but really do philosophy: for what we need is not the appearance of health, but real health.' A number of other passages employ the language of sickness, therapy, and doctoring for the philosophical endeavour (*VS* 64, *Ep. Hdt.* 35, Cic. *Fin.* I 59, Us. 224 = Florilegium Monac. 195, Us. 471 = Porph. *Adv. Marc.* 27, p. 208 Nauck).

But we know that the medical analogy was far more prominent and more pervasive in the garden than these explicit words of Epicurus alone would make clear to us. The first four of the *Kuriai Doxai* were known to pupils as the *tetrapharmakos*, or four-fold drug. And in the writings of Philodemus, especially the *Peri Orgēs* (hereafter O) and the *Peri Parrhēsias* (P), medical imagery abounds; despite the notorious difficulty of working out the substance of these lacuna-laden fragments, we can extract a complex account of the Epicurean view of therapeutic *logos*.[8] Philodemus not only uses the image of doctoring as his primary and guiding image for the philosophical endeavour throughout both of these texts; he also develops the analogy with painstaking detail, comparing different types of arguments to different types of medical procedure, different problems faced by the working philosopher to analogous problems faced by the doctor.[9] The appropriateness of the analogy is assumed from the start: this is why reference to medicine can be used, as it so frequently is, to justify some element in the Epicurean practice of argument that at first appears questionable. This fascinating material is not likely to be original with Philodemus, since he constantly refers to the authority and practice of Epicurus, cites known writings of Epicurus as exemplary of the sort of therapeutic *logoi* he has in mind, relates anecdotes of life in the garden, and in general represents himself as giving a picture of the way things go in the well-functioning Epicurean community. In Diogenes of Oenoanda as well – another not very original writer – the point and purpose of the whole enterprise of 'publishing' his huge philosophical *logos* is described in terms of the medical parallel: the sickness of false belief is rapidly spreading, people are dying 'like sheep', only the therapy of *logos* can save them. (At the end of this section we shall be examining that passage in more detail.)

[8] Except where noted, I rely on the editions of the *Peri Parrhēsias* by Olivieri (Leipzig 1914) and of the *Peri Orgēs* by Wilke (Leipzig 1914).
[9] See the excellent treatment of this material in M. Gigante (1975), with extensive references to both ancient texts and modern literature.

What, then, is philosophical argument when practised in the Epicurean medical way, and how does the medical analogy influence, express, or justify a distinctive attitude to the practice of arguing? Let us ask this question by imagining a young person full of empty desires: ambitious for renown, prone to passionate love, fond of exquisite food and other luxuries, deeply afraid of death. Since this is our only clear opportunity in this part of our profession to imagine, with historical accuracy, a female philosopher, I hope that I shall be forgiven if I call this imaginary pupil 'she', and give her the attested Epicurean name of an otherwise unknown courtesan-pupil, Nikidion.[10] (Philodemus tells us that women offer more resistance to therapeutic argument, on the whole than men, in that they dislike receiving the sort of 'frank criticism' of belief, or *parrhēsia*, that was Epicurus' stock in trade (*P* col. XXIb). So choosing a woman will also give us a chance to speak of the therapeutic techniques that are applied to the recalcitrant pupil, an especially fascinating part of our subject.)

Nikidion arrives, then, at the garden. (I shall not address myself to the problem of initial recruitment, recently attacked in challenging fashion by B. Frischer (1982), for it is only after she is interested enough to go there that argument proper begins.) She is not yet fully convinced of the seriousness of her problems, and is in consequence relatively half-hearted about the cure. Let us suppose that her primary teacher is the master doctor himself. She begins her study of philosophy. What sorts of arguments does she encounter, and what makes them therapeutic? I shall now specify nine characteristics which these arguments must, it appears, possess, in order to escape being, by Epicurus' standards, empty. For reasons that will become apparent only later, I shall divide these characteristics into two groups, A and B.

Group A. (1) *Practical causal efficacy.* The first, most general, and most essential characteristic of the arguments to which Nikidion will be exposed is that they are effectively designed to achieve a practical goal: specifically, to effect a change in Nikidion's psychological condition *vis-à-vis* happiness. If the argument is a good one, she will be better off, closer to the leading of a good Epicurean life than she was before it. Arguments do not simply provide her with *reasons* to live thus and so; they may do this, but this, strictly speaking, is irrelevant to their function, hence to the

[10] Since the other female names given (D.L. x 7) are Mammarion and Hedeia – roughly, Tits and Sweetie-Pie – it will be clear why I have made this choice. The authenticity of all the names is highly questionable, clearly; and we see that the beginnings of female philosophising went hand in hand with the beginnings of sexist 'humour' about the character of the women concerned.

assessment of their quality. Their task is to act as *causes* of good living. Each argument, each day of argument, should put her a little closer to the good of *ataraxia*. Any argument that does not do this will have failed in its therapeutic task. A valid, simple, elegant, non-causally effective argument is of no more use in the art of philosophy than a nicely coloured, fragrant, but ineffective drug is in the art of medicine. The promise of therapeutic argument to Nikidion is the promise made to Menoeceus: 'Practise these things ... and you will never be disturbed, waking or sleeping, and you will live like a god among humans' (135). If the course of treatment is a good one we shall expect her to write home to her parents what Epicurus wrote to his mother: 'O mother, be of good cheer ... Consider that each day I advance towards greater happiness, acquiring some further helpful benefit.' Arguments and reasonings are 'useful' items (cf. *chrēsima ta dialogismata, Ep. Pyth* 85) which 'will continuously come to the aid' (*sunechōs boēthēsei, Ep. Hdt.* 83) of the aspiring pupil.

(2) The arguments used towards Nikidion must also, if they are therapeutically sound, be *value-relative*. I mean by this that although they may give her new information and alter her beliefs in important ways, they must have a close and fruitful relationship to her antecedent beliefs and, especially, desires. An argument in pure science (at least as an Epicurean would conceive of it) might lead the pupil anywhere at all. The desires and wishes of the scientists do not, in any obvious way, constrain what they can find. A certain conjecture is either proved or disproved; the desire of the mathematician that it should turn out true (or false) should not influence his enquiry into its status or his choice of methods of proof. Some ethical enquiries behave as if this is so in ethics as well: we dispassionately inquire as to what the human good is, as to whether a certain picture of the good is true or false; and we will not allow our antecedent wishes, or the sort of life we *want* to live, to influence the result. A therapeutic argument cannot be like this. The medical analogy informs us that argument must deliver as its conclusion something that the pupil will accept gladly as health, or as progress towards health. The doctor cannot say, 'See this condition of body that I've put you in, which you find intolerably painful and crippling? Well that's what health is, as I've discovered through pure scientific enquiry.' Such a doctor would quickly lose his practice. He must and should hook up with the patient's antecedent ideas of health sufficiently well that the patient will recognise the cure as a cure. So much is true of Epicurus' treatment of Nikidion. However much he will alter her beliefs, his challenge is always to get her to see that what he delivers to her *does* in fact fulfil her desires, at least her deepest and most central desires. She may in the therapeutic process alter her ideas concern-

ing what her desires are and which of them are deepest; but in the end the therapist must establish the connexion, or nothing has been accomplished. Philodemus makes it clear that this was a much-discussed problem in Epicurean therapy: for often, especially at the beginning of treatment, the pupil will refuse to admit that her 'empty' desires are in fact bad, and in consequence may not be disposed to accept the result of therapeutic argument as an improvement in her condition. Nikidion may *enjoy* being in love; she may be quite attached to her wardrobe, to her fine wines. It is quite essential, Philodemus tells us, that the therapeutic teacher should at an early stage do what a good doctor similarly does for a patient who refuses to acknowledge her physical illness. Just as the doctor will try, through vivid description of the disease in frightening language, to make the patient *see* its danger and enormity, so the philosopher must present the pupil's current condition to her in language that 'causes a great shudder' and place the 'size' of the illness 'before her eyes' in an unavoidably clear way (O col. III–IV). For only that shudder and that vision show Nikidion that the end of therapeutic argument does after all hook up with what she really wants and thinks good for herself; only then will she 'turn round and get herself ready for treatment' (IV). An alternative Epicurean technique for convincing the pupil that the arguments are leading to a place that has the right sort of connexion with where she wants to be is positive. The teacher holds up, as in Cicero, the picture of the happy godlike sage or the carefree child, as a sign of the good things in store. He tries to get the pupil to *recognise* that image as one to which she has a deep antecedent attraction; nostalgia for the uncorrupted bliss of childhood will frequently provide the connexion between her current predicament and the therapeutic outcome.

Characteristics (1) and (2) already make the notion of truth in argument begin to look a little strange to us – particularly if we are approaching the text with the expectation that ethical or practical truth should look like truth in the sciences or in mathematics (where these are construed on a realist model). Although the teacher insists that the illness is one of *false* belief and that argument is substituting *correct* or *true* beliefs for false, one cannot help feeling that the demand for practical effectiveness and the connexion of the practical end with deep antecedent desires make the notion of truth in question quite unlike truth in our mathematical example. It is, we feel, no coincidence that all and only the disturbing beliefs are false. At any rate, we have no confidence that the Epicurean teacher has a standard of truth that is altogether independent of the therapy's practical aims. Nikidion will not be taught that the business of ethical argument involves following the quest for truth anywhere it may lead; she and the teacher will be in antecedent agreement, at least in a general way, about where they are going. Truth would not be permitted to distract them from that journey; it looks as if it is defined in some more pragmatic manner – at least in part, in terms of that journey. But to expect of the Epicurean a value-neutral and desire-neutral standard of the ethical truth would not only be quite anachronistic – in that very likely no Greek thinker up to this time, including Aristotle, as we shall see, conceived of the goal of ethical enquiry in this way; it would also, more significantly, be a philosophical impoverishment of the text. For one of its most challenging contributions to our ethical reflexion – whether we ultimately accept it or not – is its articulation of the idea that expectation and discovery, value and fact, are thoroughly interwoven and mutually illuminating. We may question the *way* in which Epicurus presses this claim – as we shall when we study Aristotle's subtly different version of the same point. We would be wrong to say that his pragmatism is foolish, manipulative, or without profound philosophical interest.

(3) The first two characteristics of Epicurean therapy lead the school to insist upon a third: therapeutic argument, like good doctoring, must be *attentive to the particular case*. It cannot proceed in a monolithic or fixedly rule-governed way. The philosophical teacher, like a good doctor, must be a keen diagnostician of particulars, making a specific prognosis and devising a specific course of treatment for each pupil. If Nikidion had gone to some other philosophical school, she would have found that there were certain established canons of reasoning and arguing: for example, the sceptical modes and tropes, which were learned by all pupils alike. The Epicurean teacher does, of course, put out some common teaching and even require some common homework, as we shall see. Human beings are all ill in roughly similar ways, and to some extent the false beliefs of all will be set right by the same materialist/hedonist teaching. Epicurus is convinced that a systematic teaching about nature is far more causally effective than *ad hoc* devices such as those used by the sceptics: for it gives the pupil something solid to hold on to. But at the same time the Epicureans pride themselves on the responsiveness of their ethical arguments to particular cases and situations. This is common sense, given the medical analogy: for any decent doctor will want to see how and how far this particular patient is ill before prescribing treatment.

And this is, in fact, the subject on which Philodemus makes his most extended use of medical imagery. Some arguments, like some drugs, are 'bitter' or 'biting'; some are gentle. Epicurus will treat Nikidion as gently as he can in curing her of her bad desires – for such a teacher is 'the mildest and most even-handed of people' (O XLIV); Pythocles is mentioned as a person whom Epicurus addressed with mild critical therapy (*P* 6). The doctor will, then, 'do therapy with moderate discourse' (*P* 20) insofar as this works; but he also has at his disposal harsher and stronger remedies. If he uses a 'bitter' argument, Philodemus stresses, it is not from bad temper or ill will, as some people think (*P* 54); it is good contextual medical judgment. Operating like a doctor who decides 'through plausible signs' that a certain patient needs a purgative, he will administer an argument that has a similarly evacuating effect – presumably a devastating or sarcastic critique of Nikidion's former values and ways of life. (I think, for example, of Lucretius' scathing attacks upon love.) And if the purge does not work the first time, he will try his harsh treatment 'again and again' (*P* 63–4), so that if it does not accomplish its *telos* one time it may the next (64). (So Lucretius IV piles argument upon argument, beating down the resistance of even the most stubborn devotee of that virulent disease.) Epicurus said: 'Let us altogether chase out our bad habits, like evil men who have long done us great harm' (*VS* 46). Purgative arguments, repeatedly applied, are the doctor's remedy of choice for deeply entrenched habits of believing and valuing. At the same time – since the teacher is not a one-sided character and his 'devotion to his *technē* is many-coloured' – he will 'mix in' with his harsh medicine some good-tasting stuff, for example some 'plentiful words of praise'; and he will 'encourage her to do good things' (*P* 86). (Even so Lucretius 'mixes in' some helpful accounts of non-disturbing procreative sex.) So young Nikidion will find herself swallowing a heady mixture of praise, protreptic, and caustic reproof, designed and mixed especially for her – and, we now add, administered by a doctor who knows how to spot the critical moment (*kairos*) for its administration (*P* 22, 25), as he takes note of the *akmē* of her *pathos* (*P* 65).

Now it may turn out that Nikidion, being a woman, will prove resistant even to the strongly purgative or abrasive sort of medicine. Even words that are analogous to wormwood in their power have no effect (*P* 68). Then, says Philodemus, the teacher/doctor has no choice but to opt, very reluctantly, for surgery. Like 'a wise doctor', he will operate at just the right time, and 'out of well-wishing' (*O* XLIV, *P* col. XVII, cf. Gigante). It is a little hard to know what the surgical form of argument would be. Philodemus calls it 'reproof' (*nouthetein*). He also, however, records the following words spoken by a student who protests that he does not deserve criticism this time, though he did before. About the 'before', he says, 'I fell of my own will into the ignorance of youth and on account of that he had to give me a beating [*mastigoun*]' (*P* 83). We have no other evidence that suggests that corporal punishment was an acceptable part of Epicurean therapy; so it is likely that this is a highly coloured metaphor, as 'surgery' is, for some sort of very stern reproof-cum-dissuasion. But stern the reproof certainly could be. It is likely that Epicurus was not averse to 'mixing in' such incentives as the threat of isolation from the *philia* of the community. Take for example the ominous letter written by Epicurus to an anonymous child: 'Know well, that the reason why both I and all the others love you so much is that you are always entirely obedient to them (Us. 176).' This letter, called 'charming' by Bailey for reasons that are incomprehensible to me, seems to contain a veiled threat. If *the reason* for love is obedience, then disobedience will bring about the withdrawal of love. And that would be surgery indeed.

We seem to be in danger of losing touch with *argument*. For our account has led us into areas of psychological interaction that do not look much like the give and take of philosophical discourse. It is tempting at this point to imagine that we have in some of this material interesting information about the *extracurricular* life of the garden, but that the real hard-core philosophical activity was something else. (For after all, the extant writings of Epicurus look like philosophical arguments of the recognisable kind; they are detailed, systematic, frequently sophisticated in their strategies against the opposition.) We must resist this temptation. First, all this therapy is conducted through argument. Just as the illnesses Epicurus decries are illnesses of belief, frequently taught and nourished in philosophical doctrine, so the cure must of necessity come through philosophical arguments, such as those preserved in the extant letters. All this elaborate apparatus of medical imagery is illustrative of the variety of ways in which the philosopher practises his distinctive activity, 'using reason and discourse'. Philodemus repeatedly cites actual writings of Epicurus as examples of the therapeutic practises he has in mind. The doctor will need to teach a complex system, since only this will calm the patient's anxiety, giving her a way to account for everything in the universe. The doctor will frequently need detailed and traditional-*looking* refutations of opposing doctrines, to prevent these from troubling the patient's soul. In this sense therapy must be good philosophy. Furthermore, we must equally well insist that what all argument *is*, in this community, is therapy. Purgation and drugging are not ancillary to philosophy; they are what, given its practical aim, philosophy must become. Whatever parts of the traditional philosophy are omitted are just those parts that are taken to be empty of practical usefulness. Thus we should not be surprised that there seems to be a thoroughgoing interpenetration of philosophical activity and daily human interaction in this community; for interaction is mediated above all by philosophy, and philosophy is aimed entirely at the amelioration of daily practice. Epicurus insists upon this intermingling in the strongest terms: 'We must at one and the same time laugh and do philosophy and do our household tasks and use our other faculties, and never leave off proclaiming the sayings of the correct philosophy' (VS 41). We are not to imagine Nikidion (like one of *our* pupils) going to class for several hours and then living the rest of the day as if the class did not exist. Her life is suffused with philosophy, as the philosophy she learns is suffused with life. While she eats, walks, dresses, talks with her friends, she should never entirely stop going over therapeutic arguments. Nor do these arguments have a place to stand, apart from their rôle in her daily life.

But if (from our modern perspective, which has been shaped in a fundamental way by Aristotelian practices) we feel that there is something more than a little odd about calling the whole of this therapeutic interchange *philosophy*, and its tools *arguments*, we will not be wrong. Our uneasiness can be further explored and rendered concrete if we now turn to our second group of attributes, pursuing the implications of the medical model.

B. (4) Nikidion's arguments are not just suited to her concrete situation: they are in every way *individual-relative*, that is to say, directed at the end of health for her as an individual rather than at any communal end. The end and point to which argument is a means can be specified thoroughly without mentioning other people, as can the end of the medical art. The community, and doctrinal agreement in the community, is important as a supportive *means* to her health; it is no part of what her health *is*. Her health is a condition of her own single body and soul; and this, not attunement or interpersonal agreement, is what ethical argument aims to secure.

(5) In these arguments *reason*, like community, plays a merely *instrumental* rôle. This is brought out very clearly in the medical model. An argument is really a kind of drug. If there had been an amnesiac or otherwise psychotropic drug for false beliefs, we have no reason to think Epicurus would not have used it (provided that it would also perform, or at least not impede, the other instrumental functions of practical reason, such as the provision of distractions from bodily pain). Therapy must go its arduous and difficult course through argument and intellectual practice only because no such drug exists: our only access to the ills of the soul is through its rational powers. But these powers and the *logoi* that work through them have no intrinsic value. Epicurus makes this explicit: 'If we were in no way burdened by our superstitious fears concerning the heavens and by things about death ... and by not recognising limits to pains and desires, we would have no further need of argument about

nature' (*KD* 11). We are never altogether safe from bodily ills: thus we need reason around continually to counter them should they arise. Nor, very likely, can false beliefs be permanently put to rest, so deeply are they fixed in people who have grown up in a conventionally religious culture: so we need to counter them continually by rehearsing the arguments of Epicurean teaching. But reason is with us as a handmaid only: useful and even necessary, but not valuable in herself.

(6) It goes with this that the Epicurean teacher has *no intrinsic respect for the standard virtues of rational discourse*, such as consistency, validity, clarity in definition. Nikidion will be taught to hold logic and the study of definition in contempt, as an empty matter. If a certain degree of clarity makes an argument more causally effective, for example in refuting other powerful arguments, the teacher will seek such clarity. Again, if simplicity and schematic structure aid memory and hence causal effectiveness, Epicurus will give Nikidion, as he gave others, a simple outline of his difficult teaching. There are many ways in which our traditional philosophical virtues come in by the back door, as aids to communication and causal efficacy. This must be stressed, since it is obvious that in many of his writings Epicurus appears to argue in a familiarly careful and cogent way. But these virtues function as domestic servants only. If Nikidion shows daily progress towards *ataraxia*, the fact that she cannot distinguish a valid from an invalid argument, a clear from an ambiguous definition, is altogether beside the point – just as an effective medical procedure will be praised and followed regardless of the lack of sophistication of its theoretical underpinnings. No recipient of an Epicurean letter is ever reproved for lack of logical acumen or definitional precision; nor does Philodemus mention this problem as one that troubled the Epicurean teacher. (We have no reason to suppose that this is because they were all above reproach.)

At this point, a comparison with sceptical 'therapy' will prove illuminating. The sceptic, claims Sextus, will argue in exactly the way suited to the nature of the pupil's disease. In the fascinating section of *Outlines of Pyrrhonism* entitled 'Why the sceptic sometimes deliberately puts forward arguments that are weak in cogency' (III 280–1), he argues that a good doctor never gives a patient an overdose: he carefully calibrates the dose to the magnitude of the disease. Even so the sceptic will carefully gauge the degree to which the pupil has been affected by dogmatic beliefs, and will choose the weakest and mildest remedy that will knock out these obstacles to *ataraxia*. Sometimes, then, his arguments will be 'weighty'; but sometimes 'he does not shrink from propounding those that are evidently less forceful'. According to my account Epicurus will at bottom agree with the sceptic about the goal of argument, about the purely instrumental value of argument and the virtues of argument, and about the importance of selecting arguments that are appropriate to the pupil. There is, however, a salient difference, well described by Sextus. The sceptic thinks that any systematic teaching is bound to leave the pupil prey to uncertainty, since he believes that no philosophical system can stably protect you against the anxiety-producing assault of conflicting appearances. Try for completeness and you will be frustrated. You hit on the end only when, like the painter Apelles who had failed by effort to produce the effect of foam on a horse's coat, you 'throw in the sponge' (*PH* I 25–9). The Epicurean denies this: you will get rest only within the security of an all-embracing system of beliefs that has an answer for everything. But this means that the system will need, instrumentally, to have a certain degree of order and elaboration; it really will need to have an answer for everything, if it is to give you the shelter you desire. Epicurus will presumably not give Nikidion the same teaching he gives Herodotus: more sophisticated diseases require more elaborate remedies, and if she shows no sign of worry about minimal parts there is no reason why she ought to be taught such a recondite part of the doctrine. But the whole of the system is there waiting in the wings, should the pupil's state require it. This is indeed an important difference. It is, however, just exactly the sort of difference Sextus says it is, namely, a difference about instrumental means to *ataraxia*, not about intrinsic human value.

(7) The procedure of therapeutic argument is essentially and fundamentally *non-mutual* and *asymmetrical*. The medical model creates a sharp distinction of rôles: doctor and patient, active and passive, authority and obedient follower of authority. It was part of Epicurean doctrine that everyone is sick; and Philodemus stresses that the teacher must continue to work, and to receive criticism – presumably from self or fellow teachers. But nonetheless the pupil is encouraged to follow the example of medicine and to put herself entirely in the power of the doctor. She must 'give [herself] over to', 'put [herself] into the hands of' the teacher (cf. *O* IV, *P* 40). She must even, says Philodemus, explicitly citing the medical parallel, 'throw [herself], so to speak, into the hands of the leaders and depend on them alone' (*P* 39).[11] Before embarking on the course of therapy, he continues, the pupil might recite to him or herself the tag from the *Iliad* that goes 'with him at my side'; this passage is one in which Diomedes asks to have Odysseus as his protector on the night expedition: 'With him at my side, both of us could come back from the blazing of fire

---

[11] Here see Gigante's discussion and revision of Olivieri's text.

itself, since his mind is best at devices' (x 246–7). Philodemus says that the pupil, reciting this, acknowledges the teacher as the 'only saviour', the 'one correct guide of correct speech and deed'. All ancient portraits of Epicurus and Epicureanism agree in depicting an extraordinary degree of devotion and deferential obedience towards the master. The pupils, from Lucretius to Cicero's Torquatus, concur in revering him as the one saviour of humanity. Plutarch even reports that one day, while Epicurus was arguing about nature, Colotes fell at his feet, seized his knees, and performed a *proskunēsis* – an act of obeisance appropriate to a divinity or a self-deifying monarch (*Non posse* 1100a, *Adv. Col.* 1117b); and he quotes a letter from master to pupil in which Epicurus recalls the incident with approval, stressing that Colotes 'lay hold of (him) to the whole extent of the contact that is customarily established in revering and supplicating certain personages' (*Adv. Col.* 1117bc = US. 141). Epicurus makes the vague claim that he would like to 'revere and consecrate' Colotes in return – presumably a wish that Colotes should eventually attain his god-like condition. But this just further underlines the asymmetry of the give and take of argument: either you are a god or you are not, and if you are not your proper response to the arguments of the one who is, is acceptance and worship. In this context, it is in no way surprising that the salient virtue in a child is obedience. Philodemus tells us that the student's fundamental attitude is: 'We will obey the authority of Epicurus, according to whom we have chosen to live' (*P* 15).

(8) Had Nikidion gone to other philosophical schools, she might have been exposed to a number of alternative positions on a topic and taught to examine their merits with her critical faculties. From the time of Parmenides, it was at least one tradition in Greek philosophy that the pupil should follow dialectically all the available 'routes' and perform 'by reason' the judgment between them. Nikidion's education, by contrast, will be marked by a total *lack of interest in alternative views*. To put it more strongly, she will as much as possible be kept away from alternative views – except, of course, for an interest in refuting them. The 'correct philosophy' is all that it is important to know; and the fact that the whole process of argument is frequently called *diorthōsis*, 'correcting', shows us how little concern there is for any sort of dispassionate even-handed scrutiny of the opposition. This flows naturally from the medical analogy: for the good doctor will be concerned to get the patient immersed in the treatment; and we can easily see that experimenting with rival treatments would be a distraction, rather than an aid, in this process. No doctor tells you to take three medicines simultaneously and see which one works; their effects would block one another. Even so, Epicurus will encourage

Nikidion to avoid competing influences, both from the general culture and from other philosophical schools. He writes to Apelles, 'I congratulate you, o Apelles, because you have embarked on philosophy pure of all *paideia*' (Us. 117 = Athenaeus XIII p. 588).[12] He writes to Pythocles, 'Happy man, hoist sail and flee from every form of *paideia*' (Us. 161 = D. L. x 6). These images of purity and isolation give us a good idea of what Nikidion could expect.

These features of therapeutic argument (especially features 5, 7, and 8) lead to the establishment of certain practices associated with arguing that mark off the Epicurean school from all other schools of the day. These practices are: memorisation, confession, informing. Nikidion's relation to the teaching of Epicurus is submissive and accepting: she wishes the teaching to rule her life and soul. Because reason is only instrumental, she does not insist on using reason for herself, working out her own understanding of the teaching. And Epicurus will have told her that the stubbornness of her bad habits can be overcome only by daily repetition of the therapeutic treatment. She will, then, be content to follow the school's great emphasis upon memorisation and regular repetition of doctrine. The *Kuriai Doxai* were to be learned by heart; the surviving letters are brief compendia of doctrine aimed at memorisation and repetition (*Ep. Hdt.* 35–6, 83; *Ep. Pyth.* 84, 116; *Ep. Men.* 135); the *Letter to Menoeceus*, for example, ends by enjoining the recipient: 'Practice these things and things similar to these night and day, saying them to yourself and to someone similar to yourself.' We have already imagined Nikidion going about her daily tasks saying to herself the sayings of the correct philosophy; we can now add that she will spend time with companions such as Hedeia and Mammarion, rehearsing more complex arguments on a variety of topics. This emphasis on practice and repetition is neither fortuitous nor peripheral in Epicurean practice. For, as Epicurus sees it, the beliefs and desires that impede *ataraxia* are very deeply rooted in the soul; they are too deep to be eradicated by one-time rational persuasion. In fact, it is likely that Epicurus believed that the fear of death and its grounding beliefs frequently operated beneath the level of consciousness, causing unhappiness in a way not directly accessible to rational argument.[13] This impressive discovery lends force and dignity to his claim that practice and repetition must supplement the work of dialectical reason.

---

[12] Wachsmuth's text; others conjecture *aikia*, but Plutarch's paraphrase (*Non Posse* 1094d), which uses the word *mathēmata*, supports Wachsmuth's choice.

[13] This is suggested by Lucr. III 873–8; cf. also 1056ff. I must defer to a later time the full examination of this important material; for stimulating discussion on these points at the meeting, I am indebted to Myles Burnyeat.

But the pupil who has put her life into Epicurus' hands seeks, as well, a more intimate form of communication. The teacher/doctor will always be seeking, as we said, to treat her with regard to her own concrete situation. But for this to happen the pupil must reveal her situation. When the disease is bodily, the symptoms are frequently perceptible; the doctor has access to them independently of the patient's report. When the disease is a disease of thought and desire, the symptoms are not available to the doctor unless the pupil makes them available by telling the doctor her desires and her thoughts. In consequence, we find in Epicureanism the first record of an institution of confession. The importance of this fascinating section of the *Peri Parrhesias* was first seen by Sudhaus in 1911, although he did not print all the relevant fragments, and although he assimilated the practices in question too closely, I think, to Christian practices from which it is important to distinguish them. Philodemus tells us that Epicurus 'praised Heracleides, because he considered that the reproaches he would receive on account of what he was going to bring out into the open were less important than the help [*ōphelias*] that he would get from them; and so he divulged his errors [*hamartias*, wrongly rendered "Sünden" by Sudhaus] to Epicurus (*P* 49)'. Philodemus concurs with his teacher in judging that Epicureans should 'become accusers [*katēgorous*] of ourselves, if we err in any respect' (51). And in a passage we have already mentioned, he gives the point of the practice in terms of the medical analogy: 'The pupil must show him his failings without concealment and tell his defects in the open. For if he considers him the one guide of correct speech and deed, the one whom he calls the only saviour and to whom, saying "with him at my side", he gives himself over to be therapeutically treated, then how could he not show the things in which he requires therapeutic treatment, and receive his criticism?' (*P* 39–40). This passage, not noticed by Sudhaus, shows us that notions of sin and absolution have nothing to do with Epicurean 'confession', which is a common-sense application of the medical analogy. It is simply a matter of getting the symptoms out into the open, so that the cure can be effectively begun. It has far more in common with practices of modern psychiatry than with any superficially similar Christian custom.

Nikidion, however, is, we have supposed, a recalcitrant pupil who does not like to receive criticism. So we can imagine that this practice will not be one into which she will enter with alacrity. She may make a habit of concealing erotic fantasies, a craving for oysters, regret for the silk dresses she left behind. Epicurus is ready for this problem. For if Nikidion is weak, there are always her devoted friends Hedeia and Mammarion to look out for the well-being of her soul. Philodemus reports that there was a certain Polyaenus who, seeing that Apollonides was 'slackening' in his pursuit of Epicureanism, 'went' (or: 'wrote': the text is corrupt here) to Epicurus. The next fragment continues the saga: 'For if a person desires his friend to attain correction, Epicurus will not consider him a slanderer, when he is not this; he will consider him a person who loves his friend [*philophilon*]: for he knows the difference well' (*P* 50). Another fragment reports that on account of the activity of friends, 'the person who doesn't come forward is clearly seen to be concealing, and . . . not one thing has escaped notice' (*P* 41). We can see how these remarkable practices, once again, get their support from the medical model. For an undeclared non-evident symptom cannot be therapeutically treated; and it is not outrageous, although it is controversial, to hold that a friend ought to tell a doctor of the patient's symptoms – especially in the case where the patient is actually unable, by reason of her disease, to describe them.[14]

(9) The final property of therapeutic argument that I want to mention here is its *self-praising* character. The arguments heard by Nikidion do not simply go about their business of being arguments. They are always commenting upon their own efficacy. The pupil is frequently reminded, in the course of argument, that these arguments are both necessary and sufficient for saving her. It is hardly necessary to illustrate this feature, which makes itself felt in every piece of Epicurean writing. To explain it, we can turn, again, to the medical analogy, reminding ourselves of Philodemus' view that the good doctor must mix encouragement with his painful remedies. Epicurean practice is rigorous; it involves surrender of much that was previously valued, and a kind of disciplined study that would have been unaccustomed for most of Epicurus' pupils, many of whom had not received much formal education. Therefore, to encourage them to keep with philosophy, an argument must mix exhortation and self-advertisement with its reasoning.

Now we have a glimpse of Nikidion's philosophical education. We can see that she is engaging in *logoi* of a distinctive kind, and we can see how their distinctive features all flow from, are influenced by, the guiding analogy with medical treatment. The features are not all equal in their importance. Dominant is always the keen sense of drastic illness and the

---

[14] This practice would seem less unusual in Greek culture, where informers were a common, if not always welcome, political reality, and where there is no general agreement as to the importance of a right to privacy. A full investigation of these issues would require setting them against this social background.

need for cure. Feature (1) is what gives the medical analogy its purchase and motivates the other more specific features of the therapy. We can see, for example, that at times a conflict arose between (1) and (3): to cure effectively all the sick who need cure, the doctor cannot always take the time to make a careful individualised prognosis for each patient. In an epidemic, the urgency of need dictates less finely calibrated and more general remedies. Epicurus himself, confining his teaching to the immediate community, had little to say about this tension. But Diogenes of Oenoanda is surely in the true spirit of the medical analogy when he insists that the epidemic nature of the belief disease in his time requires the erection of a single, non-specific, and permanent *logos*:

If it was one only, or two or three or four or five or six or however many more than that you want, o human being, but not a very large number, who were in a wretched condition, then calling them one by one... But since, as I said before, most people are sick all together, as in the plague, of false opinion concerning things, and since they are becoming more numerous – for, because of their reciprocal emulation, they get the disease from one another like sheep – and since it is also right to come to the aid of those who are going to live after us – for they too are ours, even if they have not yet been born – in addition to the fact that it is *philanthrōpon* to help strangers who pass by the way – since, then, the aid of this piece of writing goes out to many, I have decided, using this stoa, to put out in public for all the drugs that will save their lives [*pharmaka tēs sōterias*]. (III–IV, Chilton)

This shows us very clearly to what extent the practical needs expressed in (1) are, for the good Epicurean, dominant over all other considerations concerning the nature and structure of arguments. Philosophy is the discipline whose business it is to cure the ills of the soul by *logos*. If a spoken and individualised *logos* does not speak to the patients' needs and an inscription does, then that inscription, and not the give and take of argument, is what philosophy in those circumstances *is*. Concrete personal precision, dialectical mutuality, these are at best instrumental; what is always essential is to establish saving contact with the soul.

We now want to ask where, historically, this picture comes from; and how, in particular, it responds to and criticises the Aristotelian picture of ethical argument. For we shall see that Aristotle shares with Epicurus the view that philosophy about human conduct is worth doing only insofar as it is practically effective; and he shares, and is the source of, much of Epicurus' interest in the medical analogy. But once we see his reservations about some ways in which the medical analogy might be pressed, we will be in a better position to grasp the critical force of Epicurus' wholehearted endorsement.

III *The therapeutic tradition*

The Epicurean picture of the therapeutic *logos* is no invention of the master's; nor does it derive, except in detail, from recent advances in medical science. Indeed – ironically, given Epicurus' professed disdain for poetry and the other parts of a traditional *paideia* – the analogy between *logos* and medical therapy is one of the oldest and best-entrenched traditions concerning *logos* in all of Greek culture. From Homer on, we encounter, frequently and prominently, the central idea of the Epicurean position: that *logos* is to illnesses of the soul as medical treatment is to the illnesses of the body. We also find the claim that *logos* is a powerful or a sufficient remedy for these illnesses; and often that it is the *only* available remedy. To an Achilles whose heart is 'swollen up' with the 'bile' of anger (*Il.* 9 946), Phoenix tells the story of the Prayers, divine *logoi* that go behind strife and exercise a healing function (*exakeontai opissō*, 9 503). Pindar writes of his own poetic discourse as a 'charm' (*epaoidē*) that can effectively bring about freedom from disturbance in the troubled soul (*Nem.* 8 49ff., cf. *P.* 3 51, *P.* 4 217). The Chorus of Aeschylus' *Prometheus Bound* tells the hero, as a piece of well-known information, that 'for the sickness of anger, *logoi* are the doctors' (377); to which Prometheus replies by giving the detail of a theory of timely (*en kairōi*) application of remedies. A fragment of Euripides contains a rather complex analogy between different sorts of therapeutic *logoi* and different types of medical treatment, which strikingly anticipates Philodemus' Epicurean imagery. Empedocles speaks of his discourse as providing *pharmaka* for human ills (B111,112). Gorgias' *Helen* famously developed the comparison between *logoi* and drugs, insisting upon the great causal power of *logoi* to 'stop fear and take away grief and engender joy and increase fellow-feeling' (14). Democritus, in a fragment that has been linked to Epicurus, but whose traditional character has perhaps not been sufficiently seen, argues: 'Medicine heals the sicknesses of bodies; but wisdom [*sophiē*] rids the soul of its *pathē*' (68 B 31). Isocrates places himself in this tradition of discourse when he says – again, as if alluding to a commonplace: 'For sicknesses of the body, medical men have discovered many and varied forms of therapeutic treatment; but for souls that are sick ... there is no other drug but *logos* that will forcefully strike those who are in error' (*Peace* 39). He continues with an elaborate analogy between medical cuttings and burnings and harsh or grating forms of argument: to get well, people are going to have to hear arguments that will give them distress (40).

We can say that fifth- and fourth-century Greeks found it increasingly easy to think of ethical/political *logos* on the analogy of medicine and to look to it for healing when confronted with seemingly intractable diseases of the soul. What we would also expect to find sooner or later, however, in a culture already deeply committed to argument and to critical discourse about the quality of arguments, a culture in which a lot of activity is being devoted to forging canons of *rational* argument and working out a distinction between superstitious and rational uses of *logos*, would be an attempt to delineate, for ethics as well as for science, some criteria of acceptable and appropriate procedure when applying a *logos* to a soul: criteria that would enable the ethical practitioner to distinguish between *logoi* that were merely causal forces and *logoi* that were in some sense truly rational. We might expect this delineation to take place through a criticism or at least a delimitation of the medical analogy: for Gorgias' comparison of *logos* to drug is intended to alert us to the delusive and irrational potential of discourse, which can exercise great causal power independently of truth, validity, clarity, and in general rationality. We would, then, expect someone to say, in reply, that we want, in discourse about the good human life, *logoi* that are therapeutic in the sense of practical, but not therapeutic in the way that drugs are therapeutic; *logoi* that exercise their practical effect in a way that conforms to certain standards of critical rationality; *logoi* that work by not just being *causes*, but by giving us *reasons*. This would be an especially important task for a philosopher who was anxious to distinguish his professional activity as ethical *logos*-giver from that of the rhetorician or the practitioner of mere eristic; he would have to do it, if he wanted to win respectability for his philosophical art in a culture grown enormously suspicious of the uses and abuses of argument in the ethical and political sphere.

IV Aristotle: the positive use of the medical analogy

This task was taken on in different ways by both Plato and Aristotle. I have chosen to omit Plato's contribution to the debate.[15] But I think it can be fairly said that in this area, as with the validity of argument generally, Aristotle's characteristic explicitness and fullness made him the first really to *set out* the standards of proper and improper argument, as he gives an account of the rôle and the limits of the medical analogy in ethics to which any subsequent philosopher would have to respond. With his character-

---

[15] I have discussed Platonic therapy in Nussbaum (1979), reproduced as chapter 6 of my *The Fragility of Goodness* (Cambridge, 1985); chapter 4 on the *Protagoras* also contains extensive discussion of the medical analogy.

istic fondness for distinguishing and qualifying, he takes the medical analogy apart, arguing that in some ways it is a good analogy for ethical purposes, but in other ways a seriously misleading one that could lead the philosopher to ignore essential virtues of good ethical arguments. In the process, he defends as appropriate the characteristics of therapeutic argument that we have discussed under section A of the Epicurean therapeutic model; but severely criticises and rejects those we have listed under B.[16]

(1) The philosophical study of ethics, the giving and hearing of philosophical *logoi* about the good human life, is, Aristotle repeatedly stresses, a practical and not simply a theoretical matter. Unlike other discourses in which a philosopher might engage, this one has as its goal not simply theoretical understanding, but also the improvement of practice (*EN* 1095 a5, 1103 b26ff., 1143 b18ff., 1179 b35ff.; *EE* 1214 b12ff., 1215 a8ff). These *logoi* must be *chrēsimoi* (*EN* 1143 b18, *EE* 1217 b25, 1218 a34, 38), have an *ophelos* (*EN* 1103 b29). And ethical arguments are appropriately criticised as *useless* if (like many of Plato's) they have no bearing on this practical end (*EN* 1096 b33, *EE* 1217 b25–6, 1218 a33–4, 1218 b1–2, 9–10). In *EE* I 5, he uses the medical analogy to underline this point about the practical goal of ethics. Some sciences, he writes, for example astronomy and geometry, have only knowing and understanding as their proper ends (1215 b15–17). There are, on the other hand, other forms of enquiry whose proper end is something practical over and above the knowledge gained through inquiry: such studies are medicine and politics. 'For we aim not to know what courage is but to be courageous, not to know what justice is but to be just, just as we aim to be healthy rather than to know what health is, and to be in a good condition rather than to know what good condition is' (1216 b22–5). Aristotle is not saying that the practical sciences should not acquire knowledge or that the natural sciences cannot have practical application; he explicitly asserts the latter point (1216 b15–18), and the former he clearly believes. What his talk of the *telos* of a discipline seems to mean is that this is the primary thing we are going for in pursuing the discipline, the thing that gives that discipline its point and importance in our lives. We would, and do, as he insists in *Metaphysics* A, pursue the study of astronomy and mathematics with alacrity for the sake of understanding alone. We do not demand of mathematicians that they improve our lives. Although they might incidentally do so, our assessment of them as mathematicians is based solely

---

[16] For discussion of several related Aristotelian issues, see chapters 8, 10, and 12 of *The Fragility of Goodness*. The positive use of the medical analogy was well discussed by Jaeger (1957). By failing to bring out Aristotle's criticisms of the analogy, however, Jaeger underestimates the complexity of Aristotle's position.

upon their contribution to the advancement of understanding. The same is not true of medicine: we assess doctors as good doctors, not on the grounds that they are knowledgeable or get theoretically elegant results, but on the grounds that they are good at curing; we give their science as a whole its place of respect in the community because of its relation to health, a practical good. So much, he is claiming, is true of the philosophical study of ethics: if it makes human lives no better, it will be deservedly ignored; and intellectual sophistication alone does not make a practitioner a good one. To say this is not to say that the contribution of ethical study must be simply instrumental to an end that can be completely specified and aimed at apart from the study; any more than it is to say that the medical science cannot tell us more concretely what our vague end of health *is*, as well as give us its instrumental means. We shall see that the further specification of the end is one of the main practical contributions of ethics, as it is of medicine.

(2) So far we know very little about the ways in which ethics should go about yielding its benefits. But this positive use of the medical analogy leads Aristotle to make two more claims about ethical argument that bring him into close connection with the Epicurean conception of *therapeia*. First, ethics, like medicine, cannot start its enquiry in a void: it must set itself in some fruitful relation to the antecedent hopes and expectations of the human beings who engage in it. It has, then, the element of *value-relativity* that we have noticed in Epicurean therapeutic procedure. What will count as an acceptable and even a *true* outcome is constrained, though it is not fully determined, by what human beings antecedently want and hope to find. Aristotle is quite open about the fact that the notion of truth in ethics is expectation-relative in a way that the best notion of truth in science is not. In the same passage of the *EE* in which he advances the medical analogy, he tells us that ethical inquiry ought to be made 'with reference to our hope of good things in each area' (1215 a11–12). He follows this with an example that also figures prominently in the *EN*: we reject the view that the good life simply comes by luck or by nature, we reject this view as *false*, on the grounds that it would make good life 'unhoped for to many, in that it is not secured by effort and does not rest with people themselves and their own activity'. We will favour a view that makes the good life 'more generally available, in that it is possible for more people to partake in it' (1215 a16–17). Below, shortly before the medical passage, he puts the point even more graphically: a life in which the most important things are delivered entirely by external agencies is a life that would not be chosen as worth the living (1215 b27ff.). Although the medical analogy is not explicitly deployed inside

this passage, its presence in the context certainly makes us notice that Aristotle is in fact making ethics resemble medicine in the nature of its engagement with human hopes and desires. In both cases it is certainly open to the 'doctor' to offer an account of what health/*eudaimonia* is that will go beyond and even seriously revise the pupil's antecedent conception. But the results in both cases, unlike mathematical results, are restricted by our sense of what is good for us, what we can live with. In Aristotle as in Epicurus, then, the philosophical practitioner by his practice is bringing the pupil closer to the end; in both cases he must satisfy the pupil that it is a worthwhile end. There are important differences in the ways these constraints operate in the two cases. For Aristotle's constraints permit of continued enquiry as to the best specification of the end, while Epicurus' do not. But to see this point we must wait until we examine Aristotle's criticisms of the medical model.

(3) There is one final way in which ethical inquiry is like medicine; and it is in this connection that Aristotle makes his most extensive positive use of the parallel. Most of the sciences deal with the universal, and with what is so always or for the most part. Medicine, however, on account of its practical commitment, must subordinate the general rule to a keen perception of particular cases. Aristotle first of all makes the point that ethics, like medicine but unlike mathematics, is species-relative: it gives an account of the end relative to the particular sort of creature it is dealing with. 'Both the healthful and the good are different for human beings and for fish, whereas the white and the straight are the same in all cases' (*EN* 1141 a21–5, 31–3; cf. 1097 a11ff., *EE* 1214 b14ff.). But he goes still further: within the species, the good ethical *logos*, like good medical diagnosis, will attend to the particular, giving it precedence over the general rule. The doctor's primary responsibility is 'the health of this person – for he treats one by one [*kath'hekaston*]' (1097 a12–13). The same is true of ethical *logoi*, which are *truer* the closer they are to the particular case and should fit themselves to it the way an architect's rule flexibly fits itself to the particular stone before him (1107 a29–32, 1137 b13ff., cf. 1180 b7ff.). In a well-known passage Aristotle compares the appropriate procedures in ethical enquiry to the procedures of both medicine and navigation:

Matters of practice and questions of what is advantageous never stand fixed, any more than do matters of health. If the universal *logos* is like this, it is even more true that a *logos* concerned with the particulars does not have precision. For such cases do not fall under any science [*technē*] or precept, but the agents themselves must in each case look to what suits the occasion, as is also the case in medicine and navigation. (1104 a3–10)

Both ethics and medicine, unlike, for example, mathematics, concern themselves with mutable particulars; Aristotle seems here to want to point both to mutability and to particularity as reasons for the deficiency of general *logoi* in both areas. (Here he is presumably criticising the 'precision' of a *logos* that allegedly covers a whole group of particulars, not a particular *logos*: for just below he insists that the concrete particular *logos* will be 'more true' than any general *logos* (1107 b30ff.); and this is a position he consistently defends in related passages (e.g. 1137 b13ff.).) A system of rules set up in advance can encompass only what has been seen before – as the medical treatise (however compartmentalised) can give only the recognised pattern of a disease. But the world of change confronts agents with ever new configurations, surprising them by going beyond what they have seen. A doctor whose only resource, confronted with a new assortment of symptoms, was to turn to the text of Hippocrates would surely provide woefully inadequate treatment; a pilot who steered his ship by rule in a storm of unanticipated direction or intensity would be, quite simply, incompetent at his task. Even so, the person of practical wisdom must be prepared to meet the new with responsiveness and imagination, cultivating the sort of flexibility and perceptiveness that will permit him (as Thucydides appropriately articulates a shared Athenian ideal) to 'improvise what is required'. In several important contexts, Aristotle speaks of practical wisdom as involved in an enterprise of *stochazesthai* at the correct. This word, which originally means 'to take aim at a target', comes to be used of a kind of improvisatory conjectural use of reason. For Aristotle, 'the person who is good at deliberation without qualification is the one who takes aim [*stochastikos*] according to reason at the best for a human being in the sphere of things to be done' (1141 b13–14); he associates this norm with the reminder that practical wisdom is concerned with particulars and not universals (1141 b14–16). We shall see that the target image is a central one in Aristotle's characterisation of his own practice as teacher; the medical analogy gives us an idea of the sort of responsiveness that good ethical teaching both stresses and exemplifies.

The passage invoking the medical analogy also stresses that the concrete ethical case may simply contain some ultimately particular and non-repeatable elements. He says that such cases do not fall under any *technē* or precept, implying that in their very nature they are not, or not simply, repeatable. Just as the good doctor suits his prescriptions to the concrete situation of this human being, noticing even what is not mentioned in any general treatise, so too good ethical discourse will be attentive to non-repeatable contextual features of each person's history and situation.

Both mutability and particularity make the ethical teacher acknowledge the deficiency of general accounts, and make us wish to have teachers who have wide experience of cases, not simply a grasp of general rules. Like doctors (cf. 1181 b2) they must have the keenness of perception and the capability for seizing the occasion (*kairos*, cf. 1096 a32, where the medical example occurs again) that only experience yields. Like Epicurus, he uses visual imagery to characterise the good and responsive person's grasp of his situation.

V Aristotle: criticism of the medical analogy

Aristotle has used the medical analogy to develop a picture of an ethics that is practical, committed to and fruitfully related to our hopes and expectations, responsive and perceptive in its fine-tuned concern with particular cases. In all of this, he and Epicurus appear to be hand in hand. But nobody who reads the two philosophers can help feeling that rarely have two ethical discourses written in roughly the same period been so far apart in style and intention. The *Nicomachean Ethics* is sober, balanced, calm, cautious, committed to clarity in argument and definition; the *Letter to Menoeceus*, for example, is highly coloured, almost violent, strident in its criticisms, without much in the way of detailed linear argument, in no way preoccupied with definition. The social picture presents equally striking differences. Aristotle gives his students research projects in political history, while Epicurus, teaching a disdain for history and for all elements of *paideia*, sets them to memorise his words. We cannot imagine that any student of Aristotle's would have responded to a lecture such as those that became the *Nicomachean Ethics* with an act of obeisance; his style positively discourages these intense emotions. Nor can we imagine Aristotle soliciting confessions, listening to informers' private reports about friends. That would not be the way in which he would want the practical reason of the student to be occupied. I shall now try to show that these differences are linked to differences in the two philosophers' attitude to the medical analogy; that Aristotle's conception of the proper practical rôle of ethical discourse causes him to turn away from that analogy at a crucial point, so that he rejects what we have called the B group of therapeutic characteristics as inappropriate for ethical argument.

We can begin with two passages in which Aristotle explicitly breaks with the medical analogy and then use other related passages to bring out the view of ethical argument on which this criticism relies. In *EE* I 3, 1214 b28ff., Aristotle gives argument for excluding children and insane people from the range of those whose ethical opinions will be surveyed. He says that such people have many beliefs that no sane person would pause to consider seriously. Then he adds what appears to be an argument not only for omitting these opinions, but also for omitting the holders of the opinions from the procedure of scrutiny of opinions in which teacher and audience are now engaged: 'They are in need not of arguments [*logoi*], but, in the former case, of time to grow up, and in the latter case, of either political or medical chastisement – for the administering of drugs is a form of chastisement no less than beating is.' Here Aristotle seems to assimilate medical treatment to the use of other forcible causal techniques for the manipulation of behaviour; he dissociates it sharply from the giving and receiving of argument among reasonable men. Similarly in *EN* x 9, he speaks of irrational types whose *pathos* yields not to *logos* but to *bia* (1179 b28–9). Medical treatment, he implies, is a form of *bia*; argument is something else, something apparently gentler, less violent, and more mutual. The former is suitable for young and/or seriously irrational types, the latter for reasonable adults. We shall return to this contrast shortly; but we must first examine his other explicit criticism of the medical analogy.

In *EN* vi 13, Aristotle confronts an opponent who charges that the intellectual element in ethics is useless. If practical knowledge aims not at theory but at practice, then someone who is already good in character has no need, the objector charges, of any further intellectual study of goodness. The objector uses Aristotle's own characteristic parallels from the practical arts. The *study* of medicine does not improve the health of the patient; the *study* of gymnastics does not improve gymnastic performance. 'If we want to be healthy we do not learn medical science' (1143 b32–3). So too in virtue: if you *are* good you don't need the study; if you are not good, it won't help you become so. In either case, then, study and intellectual grasp are useless from the practical point of view. Aristotle does not dispute the opponent's point about medicine; he implicitly grants that medicine has an intellectual asymmetry about it. Its practical benefits require that the doctor should know, but not that the patient should know; its *logoi* are authoritative and one-sided. He does, however, go on to dispute the claim vigorously for ethics, arguing that study and the application of intellect have a practical value for *everyone* in this area, in ways that we shall shortly examine. Ethics appears to be less one-sided, more 'democratic', than medicine: the benefits of its *logoi* require each person's active intellectual engagement. (We can now observe that even the positive use of the medical analogy at 1104 a was strained: for it compared what each person ought to do with what the good *doctor* does.) This observation fits well with the contrast, in the *EE* passage, between force and argument: ethical *logoi* are unlike medical treatment in that they involve a reciprocal discourse in which the pupil is not ordered around by an authority figure, or manipulated by coercive tactics, but is intellectually active for herself. But in order to understand the view of argument and its benefits that lies behind this contrast, we need to turn to some related material in which the medical contrast is not explicitly present.

First, Aristotle repeatedly claims that the proper recipient of ethical argument and ethical lectures (for example the *EN* or *EE*) must already be a person of a certain maturity, who is both experienced and has his passions relatively well under control. The need for experience flows, we can see, from the positive side of the medical analogy: ethical *logos* deals with particulars, and only experience can deliver a good grasp of these. Therefore a young inexperienced person who might already do very well at mathematical *logoi* should not study the *EN* (1095 b4–5, 1094 b27ff., 1179 b23ff.; cf. 1142 a12ff.). Passional control is necessary for the reasons already suggested in the first criticism of the medical analogy: uncontrolled people are unable to listen to *logos*; their passional disorder ill fits them for the give and take of argument, and they will 'listen badly'. Their *pathos* requires something more compelling – the element of 'force' supplied by punishment and discipline – to bring it into order (1179 b23ff.); thus a study of ethics will be of no use to such a person (1095 a4, 9–10).

This claim is easy enough to understand if we think of the *EN* or *EE* as our model of an ethical *logos*. We can agree with Aristotle that a very disorderly person, either young or older (cf. 1095 a6–7, 9), will not get much out of a study of this book. But, as Epicurus knows, and his tradition before him, there are many kinds of *logoi*. We might say that for any *pathos* we can always find *some* sort of therapeutic *logos*. If Nikidion proves unable to attend to the *EN*, she may well do better with the *Kuriai Doxai*. The real question is, why Aristotle opts for the sort of *logos* that is gentle, complicated, reciprocal, and quite unlike force and drug treatment. On what grounds does he insist, as he repeatedly does, that there is an important sort of practical benefit to be gained from the very sort of *logos* that does not therapeutically treat the passions, but requires their antecedent ordering? Why, in other words, should ethical philosophy not be altogether like medicine? For if we can discover this we can begin to understand how he would deal with the Epicurean charge that his ethical arguments are empty and useless chatter.

Aristotle repeatedly insists that the study of ethical arguments such as those contained in the *EN* and *EE* is helpful: even 'very helpful' (*poluōpheles*, *EN* 1095 a11), 'making a great shift in the balance where life is concerned' (*EN* 1094 a23). The help offered is, it appears, of two kinds, closely related to one another; we might call these individual clarification of ends and communal agreement concerning ends. These two goals go together – indeed, they are usually conflated in Aristotle's ways of speaking – in that what the individual comes to see more clearly is a conception of the good that he receives from society and according to which he intends to live in a society; the communal agreement is arrived at as a result of the reciprocal scrutiny and clarification of different individual proposals. Aristotle assumes that what individuals *are* in terms of ethical values comes so much from the society of which they are members that any 'target' each scrutinises for himself is really a shared target; he also assumes that fundamental among the desires of the individuals engaged in ethical enquiry is a deep need to move out of the wide-spread disagreement and confusion that characterises our talk of ends to a larger measure of agreement (cf. for example 1095 a17–22 with 1097 b22–4; *EE* I 6, to be discussed below). This noted, we shall consider Aristotle's two ends together, as he does. In the *EN*, he uses an image from archery to illustrate the practical contribution of his arguments: 'Won't the knowledge of it [sc. the good] make a great shift in the balance where life is concerned, and won't we, like archers with a target before us, be more likely to hit on what is appropriate?' (1094 a22–4) Ethical inquiry is presumably not *supplying* a target where one was previously altogether absent. The use of the same language in Book VI (1144 a7) suggests that adults trained in the virtues are already aimed at some target (1214 b 7ff.); what is, it seems, lacking is a clear *view* of the target, an articulation of *eudaimonia*, our shared end, into its component parts. Aristotle's claim is that a philosophical treatise can help us to see more clearly what our ends are and how they relate to one another. This will improve practice in the way that a clear view of a target makes it easier to hit: we become more discriminating, more confident, more reliably accurate in choice. Book VI repeats the visual image. Aristotle answers the opponent who compared ethics to medicine by stressing, once again, the practical value of getting a clearer view of the constituents of the end. We do not go after health by studying medicine, but we do go after goodness by considering things intellectually, because we get through intellectual scrutiny of our ends a clearer *vision* of that which pertains to the end, i.e. of the constituents of the end and how they stand to one another. He insists that although virtue alone may aim us at the target, we need intellect and teaching to get it correctly articulated (1144 a7–8); practical wisdom, an intellectual virtue, is the 'eye' of the soul. We know of course that practical wisdom requires experience and moral education. What *EN* I insists is that it is also importantly developed by philosophical discourse.

The task demanded of *logoi*, being one of clarification and articulation, requires clarity and articulation in the *logoi* themselves: 'We will have spoken sufficiently if we make things clear as far as the subject matter permits' (*diasaphētheiē*, 1094 b11–12, cf. *diasaphēsai*, 1097 a24, *dioristhōsi*, 1098 b6, *enargesteron*, 1097 b23). The *EE* makes this requirement even clearer. To live well, we must have our lives ordered towards some end of our choice (1214 b7ff.). But then, 'it is most especially important first to demarcate within oneself [*diorisasthai en hautōi*], neither hastily nor carelessly, in which of the things within our power living well consists' (1214 b12–14). This careful clarification is contrasted with the 'random talk' (*eikē legein*) in which most people usually indulge on matters ethical (1215 a1–2). Then, in a most important passage, Aristotle tells us that this enterprise, and its related goal of communal attunement, are best served by a cooperative critical discourse that insists upon the philosophical virtues of orderliness, deliberateness, and clarity:

Concerning all these things we must try to seek conviction through arguments, using the appearances as our witnesses and standards. For it would be best of all if all human beings could come into an evident communal agreement with what we shall say, but if not that all should agree in some way. And this they will do if they are led carefully until they shift their position. For everyone has something of his own to contribute to the truth, and it is from these that we go on to give a sort of demonstration about these things. For from what is said truly but not clearly, as we advance, we will also get clarity, always moving from what is usually said in a jumbled fashion [*sugkechumenōs*] to a more perspicuous view. There is a difference in every inquiry between arguments that are said in a philosophical way and those that are not. Hence we must not think that it is superfluous for the political person to engage in the sort of reflexion that makes perspicuous not only the 'that' but also the 'why': for this is the contribution of the philosopher in each area. (1216 a26–39)

Aristotle here accepts, once again, a part of the medical analogy: for he insists that the touchstone and standard of ethical argument must be the appearances, i.e. the particulars of human ethical experience. But he shows us very clearly his reasons for breaking with that analogy. The ends of personal specification of ends and communal agreement concerning ends require a progress beyond the hasty and confused modes of ordinary discourse, towards greater clarity and perspicuity. But this progress requires the sort of argument that sorts things out and clarifies, that leads people to shift their alleged ground by pointing to inconsistencies in their system of beliefs, that makes evident not only the fact of our commitments, but also their 'why', i.e. how they contribute to one another and to the good life in general. He tells us unabashedly that to give this sort of *logos* is the business of the professional philosopher, and that this is why the philosopher is a useful person to have around and to emulate. After this passage he goes on to warn the reader that clarity and elegance are not by themselves *sufficient* for practical value in ethical argument. You have to be on your guard, he says, against the sort of philosopher who argues clearly but is lacking in the proper connectedness to human experience. And some pupils are led astray by such people, thinking that 'to use arguments and to say nothing at random is the mark of the philosopher' (1217 a1–2); they thus allow themselves to be influenced by jejune and irrelevant glibness. Clarity, deliberateness, and logical consistency are not enough: arguments must also be medical in the good way, rooted in the particulars and attentive to them. But we should not let the empty glibness of some philosophers give ethical philosophy a bad name. We should not disdain the specifically philosophical contribution to ethics or think of the moral philosopher as a superfluous person. He is useful both because of his similarity to the doctor and also because of his difference from the doctor. Unlike the doctor, he engages you actively in discourse, taking your view of things seriously; and he leads you on through the interchange of calm and clarifying argument to what he hopes will be an articulated picture of a shared view of the good.

We can sharpen the contrast by returning to the B features of Epicurean *logos* and seeing how, and on what grounds, Aristotle has dissociated himself from them.

(4) Aristotelian ethical argument is not individual-relative but thoroughly *communal*. The criterion of success is that we find a specification of the good life that we can endorse as a group, one that is the best adjustment of *all* the appearances. Unlike Nikidion, Aristotle's pupil will be working towards agreement with her fellow pupils; this is so because the end sought is not satisfaction for each taken separately, but a communal convergence.

(5) Reason in Epicurean argument was instrumental and in a sense incidental to the benefits derived. In Aristotle's conception, the practical ends sought cannot be described without mention of reason: we seek a clearer grasp of ends, a more perspicuous apprehension of the relationships among ends. Reason is both a means to and a constituent of the end.

(6) The logical virtues of consistency and clarity, relegated to instrumentality, at best, by the Epicurean, are absolutely central to the Aristotel-

ian enterprise. We move beyond the muddle of daily life only by ferreting out inconsistencies, striving for clarity in definition and in the rest of our discourse. And a perspicuous grasp of the end is a valuable end in itself.

(7) The activity of argument here involves authority in a sense, for the professional philosopher claims that his superior experience in the criticism of argument and in giving perspicuous accounts gives him a claim to be heard by the political person. But the denial of the medical analogy in *EN* VI shows us that the pupil will not be a passive recipient of this expertise. He must emulate the philosopher, entering actively into the give and take of criticism, being not subservient but independent and active. The teacher and the pupil are engaged in the very same activity, each as an independent rational being; it is only that the teacher has done it longer and can therefore offer a kind of experienced guidance. It is no accident that near the beginning of the *EN* Aristotle gives an example of how to regard the authority of one's teacher: it may be difficult to criticise the views of those dear to us, but we must put the truth first, all the more since we are philosophers (1096 a11ff). No pupil of Epicurus was ever encouraged to think such thoughts.

(8) A central part of the Aristotelian procedure is a respectful survey of alternatives. What we are after is to find out more clearly what we share; and this requires a patient and non-hasty working-through of the available accounts on the subject. Our attitude is that each person has something to contribute to the ethical truth. As Aristotle remarks of some of the alternatives he is examining: 'Some of these things have been said by many people over a long period of time, others by a few distinguished people; it is reasonable to suppose that none of them has missed the mark totally, but each has gotten something or even a lot of things right' (1098 a28–30). (Here we find another source of the teacher's claim to teach: for the Aristotelian philosopher knows more political history and more history of ethics than most people, and therefore can bring these to bear on the project in the most perspicuous way.) The Aristotelian pupil will study critically and respectfully many books in philosophy and history. The Epicurean procedure of ridiculing the opposition would be inimical to the Aristotelian's whole enterprise.

We can see that the Aristotelian would have no interest at all in practices such as confession, informing, and even memorisation; for these would short-circuit the work of critical reason, which has been claimed to be of high practical value, both instrumental and intrinsic.

(9) The Aristotelian argument is characteristically self-deprecating, rather than self-praising. For given the positive use of the medical analogy, the sort of discourse embodied in lectures like the *EN* must be incom-

plete, not more than an outline or *sketch* of what is to be done. Furthermore, given the respectful attitude to the views of others, Aristotle is willing to claim that his own discourse must, like all discourse, be subject to future criticism and correction: 'It would seem to be open to anyone to take things further and to articulate the well-done parts of our outline; and time is a good discoverer or partner in these matters' (*EN* 1098 a22–4).

VI *Epicurus is attacking Aristotle: a philological digression*

We have at hand the materials of a fascinating confrontation. An implicit confrontation between the two figures there surely is. An explicit confrontation between Peripatetics and Epicureans on some of these points was certainly reported by Cicero; and we can easily use our imaginations to stage this one for ourselves. But there is in fact strong evidence that the confrontation was, on Epicurus' part, more than implicit: that he was familiar with Aristotle's position on the medical analogy and consciously constructed his own claims in opposition to Aristotle's. In recent years it has become increasingly evident through scholarly work that Epicurus was thoroughly familiar with the *EN* and had it in view in many parts of his writing. Work by P. Merlan, J. M. Rist, and especially David Furley has brought us to the point where we can safely invite ourselves to look for a relationship between the two thinkers on an ethical topic, even in the absence of more concrete evidence of a connexion. There is, however, also, in this case, some concrete evidence.

(1) The fragment with which we began this paper clearly shows that Epicurus had Aristotle's ethical arguments in mind when he spoke about empty arguments. It also suggests that the particular source of their emptiness was in their failure to be thoroughly therapeutic, i.e. dedicated to the assuagement of distress.

(2) Epicurus' word for the process of medical treatment is *iatreia* (*VS* 64, fr. Ar. 29 13) – a word which, as Gigante correctly pointed out, is Aristotle's word of choice, but is never used by Plato, who instead uses *iatreusis* (*Rep.* 357c). We can add to Gigante's argument the fact that Aristotle is the only pre-Epicurean writer to make use of this word. So there is good reason to think of Epicurus as taking his medical vocabulary from Aristotle and therefore as being familiar with the Aristotelian use of the medical analogy.

(3) Philodemus seems to show detailed knowledge of Aristotle's use of the medical analogy, and in general of the Aristotelian conception of ethics as, like medicine, concerned with the *kairos* and with *stochazesthai*.

He also links medicine and navigation in much the same way that Aristotle did in *EN* 1104 a; he may be referring to this very passage. Philodemus also refers to related aspects of Aristotle's view of ethical inquiry: for example, the idea that it speaks of what is non-evident using the evident as evidence (1104 a12). But Philodemus' work in this area seems to be heavily derivative from Epicurus, and to have as its aim the description of Epicurean practice. If Epicurus and Philodemus know Aristotle's positive use of the medical analogy, it is hard to imagine that they are unaware of Aristotle's qualifications concerning it. Then when they defend as necessary for human good living a form of therapy that is explicitly said to be similar to drugging, and even to beating, it is hard to suppose that they are not doing this in conscious reaction to Aristotle's distinctions.

(4) Finally, and perhaps most significant, Aristotle is the only thinker, so far as we know, who both used the medical analogy in ethical discourse and denied that the proper job of the moral philosopher was anything like 'throwing out' the *pathē*; who defended the practical value of a purely intellectual use of ethical argument. Therefore it is reasonable to suppose that Us. 221, which attacks the uselessness of non-therapeutic arguments, is directed not only against mathematicians and logicians, but, closer to home, against the very ethical arguments that Us. 423 declares to be empty. Epicurus would then be explicitly saying to Aristotle that although his use of the medical analogy might be in other ways admirable, his arguments are not thoroughly therapeutic enough. They do not escape the charge of emptiness.

VII *The nature of the debate*

We have two opposing conceptions of the practical value of ethical argument. Each of them continues and develops the tradition of the medical analogy; but Aristotle also breaks with the tradition. (For we need to emphasise that it is Aristotle, who looks familiar to us, who is the more radical figure in the Greek tradition.) He demands, for ethics, arguments that are genuinely practical in their effect, responsive to our hopes for ourselves, and flexibly attentive to the nuances of concrete cases. He agrees with Epicurus that the art of the ethical philosopher, like that of the good doctor, must involve flexible improvisation, a responsive seizing of the occasion. But at this point he parts company with the medical analogy. The practical benefit of ethical argument is, he claims, inseparable from even-handedness, deliberateness, mutual critical activity, and an attention to what seem to him the proper philosophical virtues of consistency, clarity, and perspicuous ordering. To be sure, this activity of argument presupposes a previous quasi-medical treatment of the *pathē*; but it is not identical with that treatment, nor would it deliver its own special practical benefits if it were.

We are now in a position to describe Epicurus' reaction, interpreting his cryptic assault upon the emptiness of peripatetic ethical argument. First, he clearly finds this conception of moral philosophy impossibly élitist, effete, and impotent against the real pains of human beings. For one thing, it begins by assuming that the pupil has the *pathē* in good order as a result of *paideia*. But this, the Epicurean knows, is just about never so. *Paideia* is selective and aristocratic; it does not speak to the practical needs of the poor, the female, the slave. (Epicurus would remind us that it is no accident that Nikidion is in his school and not in Aristotle's.) And to those who receive it is not effective; for bad *pathē* abound everywhere, and the false beliefs that feed them are taught and encouraged in *paideia* itself. In short, there is a deep need for the intervention of *logos* that is not being met in the culture; it is a need that can be met by a philosophy that devises the right, moving sort of *logoi*. If philosophy ignores this need, it shows itself to be callous towards human suffering. A compassionate philosophy will make itself over into whatever answers that need. Any holding back is a moral defect in the philosopher: at best, squeamishness; at worst, cruelty.

Second, the task of assuaging human suffering is the *only* proper task for philosophy. Aristotle not only starts too high up, neglecting an urgent task; he starts where the real job *stops* and nothing else of serious importance remains to be done. If *paideia* really worked, then the *EN* and the *EE* would add to that well-ordered life nothing of value. Clarity and system are no use on their own. These books look like empty chatter, of no more use than mathematics. The intellectual contribution to ethics is empty except insofar as it improves the heart.

Aristotle would reply, first of all, by defending the efficacy of *paideia*; and this is not simply an uninteresting difference about empirical fact, as we shall see. He would have to concede, as I think he does, that as things contingently are, this *paideia* and the ensuing training by *logos* requiring leisure as they do, cannot be distributed to everyone who is by nature suited to receive them. They cannot be given to the craftsman, the 'artificial slave'. But he would insist that this political problem is not solved by pretending that some other form of *logos* that *can* be distributed to all and sundry, say *via* an inscription, is the sort that human life requires. He has argued that his own ethical arguments have a distinctive practical contribution to make to human good living, one that is neither useless nor replaceable by Epicurean strategies. We can easily imagine his objections to these. First, he would argue that in the search for therapy Epicurus has treated adult people in a way not suited to human adults, neglecting their own capability for choice and dealing with them as extensions of someone else. He would certainly object to the rôle played by secrecy, informing, and so on, as violations of the dignity of citizens and incompatible with the bonds of personal and civic *philia*. He would object to the way in which the Epicurean therapeutic community fails to be a community of 'free and equal people, ruling and being ruled by turns'. He would object, too, to Epicurus' disdainful handling of alternative views as insufficiently respectful of the ethical standing of each. In short, Epicurus, in his search for an effective cure, has trampled on important ethical values.

But this is not all. He has, further, given up an important part of what ethical arguments properly ought to contribute to practice, namely those virtues that we associate with their being good as *arguments*. The professional concerns of the philosopher are not just empty frills; they help us to choose well singly, and to come into agreement in community.

VIII Procedures and values

We cannot avoid noticing at this point how thoroughly each philosopher's views about the content of the good human life influence his view of acceptable philosophical procedure. This influence appears, first, in the area of therapeutic *outcome*. What each will be disposed to accept as a reasonable practical outcome of argument depends very much upon what each thinks a good human life is like. Aristotle would not tolerate an outcome that makes us passive with respect to our practical rationality, because he is convinced that any good human life involves the active exercise of practical reason. Aristotle, again, would not tolerate an outcome that leaves us isolated from one another, with no progress made towards social and political agreement – because, unlike Epicurus, he is convinced that political activities are ultimate ends in any good human life. Epicurus, on the other hand, will not tolerate an outcome or argument which, like Aristotle's, leaves the human being quite far from *ataraxia*, subject to many of the world's disturbances and vicissitudes. Getting clear about a plurality of ends does not go far to deliver us from fear or conflict. The only outcome Epicurus will find acceptable is one that effectively secures freedom from disturbance and doubt – because, unlike Aristotle, he holds freedom from disturbance and from doubt to be an essential condition of good human life. Each finds that the other's arguments go too far and/or not far enough, because of what each one thinks concerning the destination of human life.

And the element of circularity appears in an even more interesting light if we consider how each man's view of the good influences his conception of appropriate and acceptable procedure. Because Epicurus believes that the best human judge is the child uncorrupted by *logos*, and that the human end contains nothing that this child cannot see and value, he has no objection to treating a pupil like a child in the course of the therapeutic process. What is slighted is nothing of intrinsic value, nothing crucial to getting the right view of the end. Aristotle's objection to this form of procedure is not separable from the value he attaches to dialectical practical reason as essential to a grasp of the end, and also an intrinsically valuable constituent of human good life. Because Epicurus wants human life to be maximally defended against the incursions of *tuchē*, he wants the procedures of therapeutic argument themselves to be rightly controlled, subject to no disturbances, securely supervised by an authoritative leader. Wisdom, he insists, has nothing in common with *tuchē*. Because Aristotle, on the other hand, thinks that a certain degree of vulnerability to chance is, if not *per se* good, at least inseparable from certain interpersonal and social goods, he is able to opt for a procedure of critical argument that is subject to many influences and that never closes itself off from further criticism and revision. Again, because Epicurus thinks of the good life as an individual and not a communal matter, to which interpersonal goods of all sorts, even the vaunted good of *philia*, are only instrumental, he is free to design a procedure which altogether neglects our political nature and which subordinates *philia* to the ends of individual therapy (as in its tolerance of informing). Because Aristotle holds both political exercise and friendship to be intrinsic goods he designs dialectical procedures that embody a commitment to these values.

Does all of this make the debate between the two conceptions of argument no real debate, the choice a merely irrational matter? Not unless we demand that a rational choice of an ethical method be made from some external point and using value-free criteria. The contrast between Aristotle and Epicurus shows us, however, how thoroughly even such apparently value-free questions as questions of method and procedure are infused with the thinker's conception of ethical value. The method, in each case, models an ideal of ethical community and ethical interaction that is a seamless part of the thinker's normative conception of the good life. This does not mean that there is no such thing as a rational choice between the two; it just means that rational choice cannot be the same thing as value-free choice. Our attitude towards the two views of argument will inevitably and properly be shaped by our response to the conceptions of ethical value that they express.

And we notice one thing further. Any procedure we ourselves use to choose between these methods will, like the methods themselves, reflect our ethical values and express a normative conception of rationality. It will escape nobody that I have tried to write an Aristotelian paper about this choice between Aristotle and Epicurus. That is, I have presupposed an audience of mature people with sufficient experience of practical matters to use their own experience as a guide, and sufficient self-discipline to read thirty pages of unemotional and rather colourless prose, without being distracted all the time by the forces of appetite. I have, again, made some attempt to give a perspicuous description of these two alternative contributions to the issue, a description which is attentive to their history, and which sets them beside one another, letting them argue with one another with some semblance of fair play. In doing this, I have addressed myself to the active critical faculties of the reader, hoping that he or she will help to revise and to fill out the sketch I have offered. I have written this way in the belief that this sort of procedure best reflects my own view about the way to treat an audience, and also offers the best hope of progress towards ethical ends that I, like Aristotle, believe important. An Epicurean writer would assail this paper for its elitist professionalism, for its dry and non-moving character, for its lack of engagement with the most urgent needs of human beings. In short, for emptiness and arrogance. The Epicurean would not be here in a conference room in the first place, talking to other professional philosophers. She would be working, somewhere, with the sick in soul; or erecting a billboard by the side of one of the larger highways.

IX Aristotle's contribution: and a note about modern parallels

Now that I have acknowledged the Aristotelian bias that was apparent all along, I shall, in characteristic Aristotelian fashion, say a little more to clarify my preference. (If I were an Epicurean I would be thinking instead of ways to give each one of you the sort of 'frank criticism' that would be best calculated to make you submissive adherents of my view of things. I would be using harsh verbal surgery on some, terrifying others with vivid descriptions of their errors, applying soothing and encouraging discourse to others.) I want to say, then, that I believe the distinctive contribution of Aristotle's metaphilosophical discourse on this point to be his subtle com-

bination of criticism with acceptance of the medical analogy. It has sometimes been supposed – and is, I believe, supposed in some ethical circles in
our culture today – that we have two choices only in ethics: to work for
systematic order and clarity, conceiving of ethics on the model of a natural science, or to conclude that philosophical argument and the characteristic professional concerns of the philosopher have no distinctive
contribution to make. If we opt (as most modern philosophy does) for the
scientific model, ethics ceases to have the right sort of practical engagement with real human lives; if, however, we opt for a more practical connexion, we must give up on our fond idea that there is a separate subject
called moral philosophy that has any special contribution to make to our
discourse about ethical matters. This idea arises in several different contexts. It was Russell's idea, when he decided that the way to 'cure' human
unhappiness was to turn away from the methods and the style of the professional philosopher to write that remarkably Epicurean therapeutic
work, *The Conquest of Happiness*, a work that abandons clear and sober
argument in favour of simple practical recipes for the banishment of
superstitious fear.[17] It is the idea of some, though by no means all, propon-
ents of the study of 'applied ethics' in American universities; for example,
the writers of the first draft of the Harvard University Core Curriculum,
in which it was held that ethics was to be studied with a view to practical
improvement, *and* that this meant *forbidding*, for these purposes, the historical study of ethical views *and* the systematic study of the foundations
of ethical theory. In a different way, it is an idea urged by some recent
American philosophers, who believe that professional philosophy, in its
aspiration to become a science, has cut itself off from the practical
discourse of human beings; Richard Rorty, for example, certainly holds,
both in writing and in choice, that the return to human discourse leaves no
distinctive contribution for the professional philosopher, as such, to

[17] This strange and fascinating book has as its epigraph the passage from Whitman's *Song of
Myself* that begins, 'I think I could turn and live with animals, they are so placid and self-
contain'd...' Its Preface begins as follows: 'This book is not addressed to highbrows, or
to those who regard a practical problem merely as something to be talked about. No profound philosophy or deep erudition will be found in the following pages ... All that I
claim for the recipes offered to the reader is that they are such as are confirmed by my own
experience and observation, and that they have increased my own happiness whenever I
have acted in accordance with them. On this ground I venture to hope that some among
those multitudes of men and women who suffer unhappiness without enjoying it, may
find their situation diagnosed and a method of escape suggested.' The central thesis of the
book is that superstitious fear and guilt taught us by religion are robbing us of our joy in
living. A particularly unpleasant feature of Russell's rhetoric is his tendency to use black
people as the analogue to Epicurus' child: they alone have the childlike ability to enjoy the
simple pleasures of the body, worrying about nothing else.

make.[18] All these are very different people, motivated by different concerns. What all of them share is the view that philosophy has somehow failed in its practical engagement with human lives, *and* that to do better it must, in effect, give up being philosophy, or at least move away from the traditional philosopher's commitment to consistency and clarity in argument.

What Aristotle shows us, I claim, is that our alternatives are more numerous and more subtle by far. We do not have to choose, as it were, between non-practical mathematics and Epicurean medicine as models for ethical theorising. We can insist that we want an ethical discourse that is like medicine in subordinating systematic elegance to concrete human truth; in being immersed in the messy world of human experience; in being attentive and responsive to particular mutable things. We can insist upon these values and still maintain that philosophy and philosophers have a distinctive practical contribution to make that is thoroughly connected with their professional training in assessing arguments, detecting inconsistency, describing the historical alternatives in a clear, thorough, and perspicuous way. Now of course one can have these virtues without being a professional philosopher; and the professional philosopher might, like the nameless people criticised by Aristotle, have these virtues while lacking the equally essential medical virtues of perceptiveness and responsiveness. But it is not accidental that the character who contributes to the improvement of practice through discourses that survey the alternatives is a character who puts in a lot of time practising the critical assessment of arguments. The activity of the professional philosopher, he would argue, has practical value because it contributes in a particularly helpful way to a result we all want. It also *is* of practical value, in that it expresses and exemplifies to a particularly high degree some of our deepest ethical commitments.

X *Two questions and a warning*

I have said that we can have the best of the medical analogy and also avoid its irrational dangers; that we can imagine, with Aristotle, a philosophy that is still recognisably philosophy, dedicated to clarity and rigour, and yet is also responsively engaged with human daily life in all of its contingent complexity. How are these features of ethical discourse to be combined? The *EN* gives us the clarity and simply informs us that the wise person would give responsive particular *logoi*. For obvious reasons, it

[18] See especially Rorty (1982).

does not try to give those *logoi*. So we are left to wonder about the implications of the Aristotelian proposal for the teaching and practice of moral philosophy. Is there, in fact, a way of putting together all the pieces of the Aristotelian project? And how, exactly, would its medical and non-medical pieces fit together? Aristotle tells us, in effect, that the way to do 'applied' or 'practical' ethics is not to give up on ethical theory, but to use it to inform and clarify experience, as it is itself built upon experience and informed by it. How will this go in a real case? How are we to combine general discourse with rich and complex particular examples? Aristotle leaves us a large challenge here.

Then, how deep *is* our commitment to the Aristotelian values in ethical argument? How far might we be willing to sacrifice them, or at least to relax them, in order to achieve a less élitist and more broadly distributed result? This is the deepest question posed by the confrontation I have described. Its importance was seen at the time. It is urgent once again in our contemporary culture, which, rather like Greek culture of the fourth century, combines, uneasily, these Aristotelian commitments with a deep desire for salvation. This question can be approached in the conference room through calm discourse among professional colleagues; or on the streets of a city, in interaction with the angry, the embittered, and the poor; or in some third, more Epicurean, setting. No setting is neutral, clearly, as to the answer. And I do not claim to know that I would express this sympathy for Aristotle had I not grown up in privilege and leisure, had I not spent my adult life to date in the sheltered environment of our remarkably benign profession. Epicurus would charge my choice with smugness and callousness; it would be difficult to answer his charge. It is probably good for the Aristotelian to be deeply torn about this question, so that the clarity and rigour of professional philosophy will not be allowed to slip too readily away from their practical commitment, into a self-congratulating elegance.

I offer, however, one final cautionary note in favour of the Aristotelian choice. The history of Epicureanism suggests that a relaxation of the commitment to argument is a move not to be taken lightly or unreflectingly. For we can always, and all too easily, turn *from* calm critical discourse to some form of therapeutic procedure, as Epicurus himself turned from Nausiphanes to his own way. But once immersed in therapy it is much more difficult to return to the values of Aristotelian critical discourse. The passivity of the Epicurean pupil, her habits of confession and veneration, become habitual and spoil her for the active critical task. (Nor does the individual encouraged to be obsessed with her own health easily return to an Aristotelian mutuality and concern with agreement.) Diogenes Laer-

tius reports that someone once asked Arcesilaus why it was that many
people moved from other schools to the Epicurean school, but no Epicurean pupil ever moved to another school. Arcesilaus replied: 'Because men
can become eunuchs, but eunuchs never become men.'[19]

[19] For stimulating criticisms at the Bad Homburg conference, I am indebted especially to
Myles Burnyeat, John Cooper, Geoffrey Lloyd, Malcolm Schofield, David Sedley, and
Richard Sorabji; I am sure that I have not answered all of their questions. This paper was
also presented at the Chapel Hill Philosophy Colloquium and at the Greater Boston Philosophy Colloquium. On the former occasion I had the benefit of excellent written comments by Gary Matthews; on the latter by Arthur Madigan, S. J. I am grateful to them and
to those present for their assistance. I would also like to thank the members of the Welles-
ley College philosophy department, for valuable comments made when this paper was
presented to a departmental colloquium.

3   Nothing to us?

David Furley

The second of Epicurus' *Kyriai Doxai* puts the case in a few words:[1] 'Death is nothing to us, since a decomposed thing is insensate [*anaisthē-tei*], and whatever is insensate is nothing to us.' It is expanded somewhat in the *Letter to Menoeceus*:

Make yourself familiar with the belief that death is nothing to us, since everything good and bad lies in sensation, and death is to be deprived of sensation. Hence the right recognition that death is nothing to us makes the mortality of life enjoyable, not by adding infinite[2] duration to it but by removing the desire for immortality. For there is nothing to be feared in living, for one who has truly comprehended that there is nothing to be feared in not living. So one who says he fears death, not because it will hurt when it is here, but because it hurts when it is coming, talks nonsense, since whatever does not hurt when it is present[3] hurts for no reason when it is expected.

So that most fearful of all bad things, death, is nothing to us, since when we are, death is not present, and when death is present, then we are not. So it is nothing to the living and nothing to the dead, since with regard to the former, death is not, and as to the latter, they themselves no longer are. (*Ep. Men.* 124–5)

I have translated the key phrase in these passages 'death is nothing to us'.

---

[1] For all quotations from Epicurus I refer to Arrighetti's second, revised edition (1973), with a note whenever the reading seems to need defence.

[2] I read ἄπειρον for the MS ἄπορον, a common emendation since the Renaissance (Aldo-brandinus). The MS text has to be translated thus: '[...] by not adding intractable time to it but removing the desire for immortality'. So Jean Bollack (1975), pp. 104–6 ('un temps impracticable') following Traversari ('non ambiguum adjiciens tempus') and Gassendi ('non quidpiam incerti temporis'). It is far from clear what this might mean: perhaps something like the following. The belief that death *is* something to us adds to our mortal life a time, after death, that is 'untrackable' – i.e. incomprehensible, unfathomable ('le temps auquel nous n'avons pas accès, c'est à dire le vide', says Bollack: the last clause introduces an equation that we need not pursue). But this involves an idea that has made no previous appearance – the idea that erroneous belief destroys our enjoyment of life because of some thought about *time* after death. This is an unnecessary complication, and it is unlikely to be what Epicurus meant. The emendation makes much better sense. If someone is troubled by the thought that life is finite, there are in principle two ways to comfort him: to persuade him that it is after all not finite, or to show him that its finiteness should not trouble him. Epicurus just says that he is rejecting the first course and taking the second.

[3] I read παρὸν for the better attested παρών, adopted by Bollack. The reading παρών is translatable, if one takes ὂ to be an internal accusative: 'the pain that it [sc. death] does not inflict when present hurts for no reason when expected'. This makes a difference in two respects: there is no direct antithesis between 'present' and 'expected', since they are attached to different subjects, and the sentence applies only to death and not to all pains.

It is best to avoid the expression 'death does not concern us', which is common in English versions. 'Concern' is often applied to what one thinks or believes or fears. But *ouden pros hēmās* means 'it *is* nothing to us'. Epicurus wants to infer from this that it *should not concern us*, i.e. we should not worry about it.

The structure of Epicurus' argument appears to be as follows:

I.   Nothing is good or bad for a man except what stimulates his feelings (of pleasure or pain).
II.   The dead feel nothing.
III.   Hence nothing is good or bad for one who is dead.
IV.   Hence his state of being dead is not (good or) bad for one who is dead.
V.   But if a thing is not bad when it is present, there is no rational ground, at any previous time, for fear of its future presence.
VI.   Hence no living person has any rational ground for fear of his future state of being dead.

Lucretius expands the argument and bolsters it up at various points. The most famous of his arguments is that which rests on a symmetry between past and future. Before he and his readers were born, the Carthaginians waged horrid war on Rome, and nearly won: 'we felt no pain [*nil sensimus aegri*]'. 'Just so, when we shall not exist, when body and soul, / of which we are fashioned into one, shall be sundered, / nothing at all will be able to affect us / who then will not exist, nor stir our sense' (III 832–41).

It must be observed that this argument is intended to reinforce the inference from I and II to III in the structure outlined above: it is not directly concerned with V, as is sometimes claimed. That is to say, Lucretius does not argue here from the observation that we are not *now* concerned about what happened in the Punic Wars to the claim that we should not *now* be concerned about anything that may happen after our death. He argues that we felt no pain in the past, when the Carthaginians came: so we shall feel no pain in the future, when we are dead. The tenses of the verbs are conclusive about this; there is no statement at all about our present emotions. E. J. Kenney, to take just one example, is therefore a little off the mark in commenting 'these events were, when they occurred, world-shaking [...] – but what are they to us now?'[4]

Lucretius continues with two appendices (843ff.) addressed specifically to those who have read the earlier part of Book III: that is to say, to those who know something about the Atomist account of man's nature. He has just concluded that nothing can happen to us after our own death – and this, he adds now, is true even if you consider two possibilities left open by

[4] Kenney (1971), p. 193.

his own earlier analysis of soul and body. Perhaps the soul has sensation, after being separated from the body. But that is nothing to *us*, because *we* are a union of soul and body (843–6). Secondly it may be that the precise collection of atoms constituting our present soul and body may chance to be reassembled one day after our death – all possible combinations may recur in infinite time and space. But even that would not affect *us*, when once the continuity of memory is interrupted (847–51).

At this point, he introduces something very like, although not exactly like, the symmetry argument attributed to him by Kenney and others with regard to the earlier passage. The argument is this (852–61). If we suppose our own collection of atoms may be reassembled in the future, we shall have to concede that it is just as likely to have been assembled in the past, before our birth. But we feel no pain *now* about such past identities. So, he infers, our reassembly in the future should not concern us; the inference is not explicitly made, but it seems plain enough. And this time the present concern is unmistakeable:

> And *now* nothing concerns us about the 'us' who were
> before, and no pain *now* afflicts us on their behalf.
>
> et nunc nil ad nos de nobis attinet, ante
> qui fuimus, neque iam de illis nos adficit angor.

Whether Lucretius, if pressed, would want to stand by his designation of those former persons as 'us' is questionable. Perhaps he wants to make his point by conceding the maximum. Even supposing those former persons are to be identified with our present selves, yet their experiences are nothing to us now, because of the interruption of continuity.

The lines that follow, 862–9, are a summing up of the whole section, rather than a comment on the immediately preceding argument. If there is to be pain in the future, the person must exist at that time, to feel the pain. Death prevents this. So there is nothing for us to fear in death. A non-existent person feels no more pain than one who has never been born.

At this point it will be convenient to interrupt Lucretius, and look at the rather mysteriously similar arguments in the pseudo-Platonic *Axiochus* – a dialogue of uncertain date, included in the Platonic canon in antiquity in the category labelled 'forgeries'.[5] We find Socrates summoned to give comfort to old Axiochus, who has hitherto put a brave face on the thought of death, but has taken a sudden bad turn and is consequently terrified. Socrates rebukes him for his childish folly – 'you, a man so advanced in years and a master of arguments – and an Athenian to boot'. Axiochus

---

[5] See Hershbell (1981), Introduction.

replies that this is all very well, but 'now that I am right up against the fearful thing, my brave and clever arguments imperceptibly expire', and he is left with the fear of being deprived of 'this light, and the good things' (365b–c).

You are contradicting yourself, says Socrates, in complaining about lack of sensation (anaisthēsia) and at the same time about deprivation of pleasures, as if you were going to die away into another life rather than into non-sensation. He follows up with a Greek version of the argument we have seen in Lucretius III 832–42:

As in the time of the government of Dracon or Cleisthenes there was nothing bad for you [οὐδὲν περὶ σὲ κακὸν ἦν], because you did not even exist, for whom it might have been bad [ἀρχὴν γὰρ οὐκ ἦς, περὶ ὃν ἂν ἦν], so there will not be anything bad after your death, because there will not be a 'you' for whom it will be bad [σὺ γὰρ οὐκ ἔσῃ, περὶ ὃν ἔσται]. (365d–e)

Like the Punic War argument in Lucretius, this makes no further point than that the future, after our death, will be as indifferent to us as the past was. Nothing is said directly about our present attitude to past or future.

Socrates continues with the same concern that comes next in Lucretius, but to a very different purpose. Lucretius argued that the soul, freed from the body, might have sensation – but this would be nothing to us who are a combination of soul and body. Socrates on the other hand says that the body, apart from the soul, is not the man: we are the soul; so to be freed from life is a change from bad to good.

Now, the introduction into the argument of the immortal soul, a personality that survives death, throws the whole of the Axiochus into irredeemable confusion. As Isnardi-Parente commented, the dialogue represents a low point in the intellectual spirit of the Academy.[6] In Plato's Apology, Socrates had consoled himself at the prospect of death with a disjunction: either death is like an indefinitely prolonged sleep, or else the soul survives to continue philosophical conversations with even more interesting people. The Socrates of the Axiochus wants to have it both ways: death is total unconsciousness (anaisthēsia) and moreover it is the release of the soul from a life of pain into 'a purer enjoyment of good things' (τῶν ἀγαθῶν ... εἰλικρινεστέραν τὴν ἀπόλαυσιν, 370c). This phrase occurs near the end of the dialogue. 'You have turned me around by your argument', says poor old Axiochus, hearing it; 'there is no longer any fear of death in me.'

After his first introduction of the immortal soul, Socrates continues in the same vein, quoting from Prodicus, the fifth-century Sophist. He at-

[6] Isnardi-Parente (1961), pp. 46–7.

tributes to Prodicus something astonishingly like Jaques' famous speech in *As You Like It*, with the difference that Prodicus stresses the misery and pain of life in all its stages, whereas Jaques is arguing for its futility. This is not directly relevant to the Epicurean theme.[7]

Socrates returns to Prodicus a page or two later in the *Axiochus* and attributes to him what we have already seen as Epicurus' main argument:[8]

s. I once heard Prodicus say that death is nothing to the living nor to those who have passed on [οὔτε περὶ τοὺς ζῶντάς ἐστιν οὔτε περὶ τοὺς μετηλλαχότας].
A. What do you mean, Socrates?

7

Axiochus	*As You Like It*
What part of a lifetime is Without its portion of griefs?	At first, the infant Mewling and puking in the nurse's arms.
Doesn't the infant cry out at the first moment of birth?.. When he reaches the age of seven [...] tyrannizing tutors. elementary school teachers, and physical trainers set upon him.	Then the whining schoolboy, with his satchel And shining morning face, creeping like snail Unwillingly to school.
When he is enrolled among the Ephebes [...]	Then the lover.. Then a soldier, Full of strange oaths.. And then the Justice In fair round belly [...] The sixth age shifts unawares [...] Into the lean and slippered pantaloon.
Then old age creeps upon him, and unless one quickly repays the debt of life, nature stands by like a money lender, taking security – [...] sight from one, from another hearing, and often both [...] in mind they become children for a second time. (366d–367b)	Last scene of all Is second childishness and mere oblivion, Sans teeth, sans eyes, sans taste, sans everything. (II 7, 143–66)

The *Axiochus* was well known in the Renaissance, and there was an English translation of it attributed to Edmund Spenser – now lost. It seems reasonable to guess that this was known to Shakespeare.

8 Some have believed that the citations from Prodicus in the *Axiochus* are genuine: for example, Taylor (1911), p. 102, and Fred D. Miller (1976), p. 171. Most scholars follow Diels (*Vorsokratiker* II 318n) in supposing that the attribution to Prodicus is fictional, or at least in being sceptical about it. It seems to me that the demonstration of the misery of life might perhaps be from Prodicus, although the similarities with Cynic ideas are hard to ignore. 'Death is nothing to us', on the other hand, is a theme associated particularly with Epicurus in antiquity. The *Axiochus* is the only source that attributes it to Prodicus, and it constitutes only a weak bit of evidence. Pseudo-Plato could not attribute the argument to Epicurus without anachronism; he could not give it to Socrates, because too many readers were too well informed about Socrates by Plato; if Prodicus was a plausible author of the 'misery of life' speech, he would make a plausible source for the 'nothing to us' theme.

s. It is nothing to the living, and the dead themselves are nothing. Hence it is nothing to you now, since you are not dead, nor will it be anything to you, if anything happens to you, since you will be nothing. So the pain is futile, for Axiochus to be grieving over what is and will be nothing to Axiochus. (369b–c)

We are clearly back in the Epicurean Garden again, after our trip to the Platonic heaven. Isnardi-Parente suggests that Prodicus is produced as spokesman because of the embarrassment of giving Epicurean arguments to Socrates.[9] But this can hardly be the whole story, since the first Epicurean argument *is* given to Socrates (365d–e) and the first release-into-a-better-world argument is given to Prodicus (366c ff.).

But Axiochus responds to Socrates this time with an objection that we have been waiting to hear: what pains him, he says, is the deprivation of the good things of life (369d).

Socrates replies:

You are illogically attaching to deprivation of goods, Axiochus, a corresponding perception of bad things, forgetting that you are dead. What pains one who is deprived of goods is the corresponding perception of bad; but one who *is* not is not even aware of the deprivation. So how could he feel pain if he is not to be aware of what will cause him pain? (369e–370a)

We have now followed Axiochus to a point in the discussion beyond where we left Lucretius. The argument about deprivation of goods is found also in Lucretius, although its function in the argumentative structure is usually overlooked because of its striking poetry. Instead of making a statement of abstract propositions, as Socrates does, he lists some of the good things of life of which the dead man will be deprived:

> No longer will you happily come home
> to a devoted wife...
>   'Poor wretch', men tell themselves
> 'One fatal day has stolen all your gains.'
>
> iam iam non domus accipiet te laeta, neque uxor
> optima [...]
>   misero misere, aiunt, omnia ademit
> una dies infesta tibi tot praemia vitae. (894–9, trans. Humphries)

So say the voices of unreason. But they ought to add, says Lucretius, that there will now be no desire left in you for these good things:

---

[9] Isnardi-Parente (1961), pp. 43–4.

> nec tibi earum
> iam desiderium rerum super insidet una. (900–1)

Lucretius' answer is thus the same as Socrates' answer to Axiochus: deprivation of goods can be a source of pain only to one who can feel the pain of loss: and the dead feel no pain. This argument is where the crux of the matter lies. We may be ready to concede to Lucretius that the stories of hellish punishments are false fantasies, and that the state of actually being dead will not incommode us in any way. What troubles us nevertheless is the thought of the loss of the good things of life.

At first sight, the argument of Lucretius seems to miss the point in some way. It might be countered rather easily, it seems, just by pointing out that if these *praemia vitae* are good for a person, then more of them will be better than fewer, and since death prevents one having more of them, death must be worse than continued life (other things being equal).[10] The Epicurean answer to this is that pleasure is not the kind of thing that accumulates: so it simply is not true that more is better. The voice of nature says in Lucretius (III 944–5): 'there is nothing new that I can devise for you beyond the goods that you are already enjoying: *eadem sunt omnia semper*'. 'Infinite time', says Epicurus (*KD* 19), 'contains the same amount of pleasure as finite time, if you measure its limits by calculation.' Cicero sums it up in *De finibus* II 87:

Epicurus denies that length of time adds anything to living happily, and that less pleasure is felt in a brief span of time than if it were everlasting [...] He denies that in infinite time pleasure becomes greater than in finite and bounded time... He denies that time brings increment to the highest good.

But this is just dogma, without argument, and the surviving Epicurean texts offer nothing in the way of argument. Diano suggests a comparison with Aristotle *EN* 1174a14;[11] pleasure is there compared with sight, in being complete (*teleia*) at any moment you like to take. 'For pleasure is a whole, and at no time could one get a pleasure whose form would be perfected with the elapse of more time.' But the comparison with sight reveals what is wrong about the Epicurean doctrine. Sight may indeed be complete at any moment in its duration, but one is not therefore content with seeing just one thing. Why should one not want a second, third, fourth ... pleasure, each of them perfect?[12]

Perhaps health would be a better analogy for Epicurus than sight. Cer-

---

[10] This answer is discussed by Bernard Williams (1973), pp. 84–5.
[11] Diano (1974), p. 122.
[12] Fred D. Miller explores the relation between Epicurean pleasure and Aristotelian activity in his article (1976), pp. 174–6.

tainly we want to be healthy so long as we are alive. But there is something odd about wanting to go on living because one wants more health; if we are in perfect health on Monday our health is not increased if it continues for a whole week. If we regarded health as the supreme good for man, would we have to alter these statements? What seems to be needed is a simple distinction between 'more' and 'greater'. It may be irrational to want greater health, or pleasure, if we already enjoy them completely and to perfection; but there is surely nothing irrational in wanting more of them.

This does little to help the argument, however. If we want more good health or pleasure, we want it for ourselves, and the Epicurean case claims that there is no self after death.

The question remains, then, whether we can say that there is anyone who is deprived of good things by being cut off by death. Before considering this at more length, there is one further argument in Lucretius that deserves a look (there is of course much more than this point in the last part of Book III, but the rest is more rhetorical, poetic, or satirical than philosophical). Right at the end of the book he makes the point that prolonging life does not take away anything from the time one spends in death:

> proinde licet quot vis vivendo condere saecla;
> mors aeterna tamen nilo minus illa manebit. (1090–1)

> Suppose it possible to live as many centuries as you wish:
> that same everlasting death will await you none the less.

Bernard Williams[13] finds this to be in contradiction with the 'death is nothing to us' argument, since it implies that dying *would* be an evil if it entailed being dead for longer – i.e. that death is a bad thing. But it does not actually contradict anything that the Epicureans said: it is perfectly consistent with the proposition that death is nothing to us. It is, however, a dialectical argument, in that it has a point only against one who rejects the Epicurean proposition.

The fear of death is of course a fear concerning the future. It is appropriate, therefore to raise some questions about the treatment in Epicurean ethics of concerns about the future, and also of memory of the past. Does his insistence that 'everything good and bad lies in sensation' mean that only the pleasures and pains due to one's immediate sensations are relevant to happiness? He is quoted by Aelian as saying that he would be ready to contend with Zeus with regard to happiness if he just had bread

---

[13] Williams (1973), p. 84.

and water.[14] But what if he knew it was the end of the loaf and the well was dry?

Epicurus' position is not altogether clear. There is plenty of evidence that he recognised the existence of the pleasures and pains of anticipation and memory, and that Aelian's report is therefore oversimplified. So the problem is to decide on what grounds he claimed that our feelings concerning our own future death are unwarranted, whereas other feelings about the future are not.

Up to a point the evidence is unambiguous and no problem arises. It is almost certain that Aelian's report is an oversimplified recollection of one of the aphorisms contained in the Vatican manuscript of Epicurus:

Voice of the flesh: not to be hungry, not thirsty, not cold. For one having these, *and expecting to have them*, might fight [with Zeus] for happiness. (*VS* 33)

(The manuscript does not contain 'with Zeus'. Most editors insert it, and it is strongly confirmed by Clement of Alexandria's statement about Epicurus, which is very similar to Aelian's but contains the same examples as the Vatican Saying, as well as the words 'might fight with Zeus'.[15] Without the mention of Zeus the aphorism must mean that the absence of hunger, thirst, and cold are necessary but not sufficient conditions for happiness.) The condition of happiness, then, includes some expectations for the future.

Several of Epicurus' own sayings reveal a concern for the future, none more pointedly than his remarks about justice in the *Kyriai Doxai*. It is fear of future discovery and punishment that makes men just.

Injustice is not itself bad, but in the fear that is attached to the apprehension that he will not escape those appointed to punish such things. (*KD* 34)

It is impossible that one who secretly violates the mutual compact not to harm or be harmed should be confident of escape, even if for the time being he escapes a thousand times. For right up to the end it is uncertain that he will escape. (*KD* 35)

Justice, which Epicurus approves of, depends on one's fears for the future.

Diogenes Laertius records some differences between Epicurus and the Cyrenaics on the subject of feelings. One of them is that the latter held physical pains to be worse than psychical ones, whereas Epicurus thought psychical ones were worse, because the flesh is distressed only by what is present, the soul by the past, the present, and the future.[16]

---

[14] Aelian *Var. Hist.* IV 13 = Usener fr. 602.
[15] Clemens Alex. *Strom.* II 21 p. 178,41 = Usener fr. 602. J. Bollack nevertheless retains the MS reading (1975), p. 469.
[16] Diogenes Laertius X 137.

If we take these thoughts together with the ban on being afraid of death, there is enough to suggest that Epicurus worked with a distinction between true and false feelings rather like the distinction between true and false pleasures in Plato's *Philebus* 37–41. A feeling of anticipation, according to this line of thought, would be a feeling arising from the belief that one will experience a similar feeling in the future; and the feeling would be true or false according to whether the belief is true or false, or at least well grounded or not. Thus the criminal's present fear of future punishment is a true one, because his belief that he will experience the pain of punishment in the future is well grounded. But one's fear of death is a false fear, because the belief that one will experience pain when dead is false, since when dead one experiences nothing at all.[17]

This distinction appears to be confused in a passage of the inscription of Diogenes at Oenoanda. This gives a classification of causes as antecedent, simultaneous, or posterior (*prōtochronein, synchronein, metachronein*). Interestingly enough, the example given for the latter is apparently (the inscription is broken) the pleasure afforded by a good posthumous reputation. The text reads '[...] for although men feel pleasure *now* because after them their memory will be a good one, nevertheless that which causes the pleasure comes later'.[18] But if it is irrational to fear death because one has no experiences after death, then it should also be irrational to take pleasure in the anticipation of being remembered kindly after death. This classification of causes seems to belong to a period somewhat later than Epicurus. It may be that later Epicureans failed to notice the discrepancy with Epicurus' doctrine about death.

Before we can assess the merits of the Epicurean case, it is necessary to say something in general about the logic of fear.[19] What exactly does Epicurus need to show, in order to persuade us that fear of death is irrational?

There is one sense in which fear may be rational that can be left out of account here. Fear has in certain circumstances an evolutionary function: certain types of fear, by stimulating men (and animals) to take avoiding action, contribute to survival. Fears may have this function even if they are unjustified in the sense that they are based on a false belief. To cultivate such fears may be a rational course of action for a man or a society to take. But this is plainly not a point at issue here, because it does not touch the proposition that death is nothing to us.

[17] Epicurus usually prefers the term 'empty' to 'false' in this context.
[18] Diogenes of Oenoanda fr. 27 col. IV Chilton
[19] In the paragraphs following, I am drawing on the analysis of the logic of fear by Richard M. Gordon (1980).

The relevant kind of rationality is something different from this. We must first distinguish two possible reasons why one might be afraid of dying: (1) because what may follow a man's death may be unpleasant or in some other way bad for him; (2) because although nothing follows upon death, death will deprive him of the good things of life. The Epicurean case against the first reason seems to be very strong, if one is committed to denying survival after death; if there is no experiencing subject after death, then nothing can be unpleasant for one who is dead. It is still worth considering, however, whether things may in some other way be bad for the dead. In the case of the second reason, we must first of all note that 'fear' is an inappropriate name for the emotion felt when there is no uncertainty. So for the sake of completeness we must distinguish two cases: (2a) S fears that he may die prematurely (being uncertain when he will die), because he will then be deprived of the good things of life; (2b) S is angry that he will die (knowing that he will die), because he will then be deprived, etc.

Epicurus' formula 'nothing to us' is equally effective against fear or anger. Words meaning 'fear' are most usual in the context, but not invariable: Axiochus, for example, is first described as 'taking painfully' (*aniarōs pherei*, 364b) the prospect of death. But this is not important: Epicurus' polemic is surely directed against all negative feelings about the prospect of death. The question we have to examine is whether being deprived of the good things of life is a good reason for a man's feeling fear or anger at the prospect of death. Epicurus tries to conflate (2) with (1), on the ground that deprivation is nothing if it is not felt as pain, and hence case (2), like case (1), presupposes an experiencing subject after death. But he may be wrong.

First it may be useful to consider whether Epicurus was right to claim that nothing can be good or bad for one who is dead. His argument depends on the premises of hedonism – premiss I in the structure set out on p. 76. If it is true that nothing is good or bad for a man except what gives him pleasure or pain, then the case is settled. Epicurus could concede that things are good or bad in general according to whether they are *such as* to give pleasure or pain, and still claim that nothing is good or bad for a particular subject S except what *does* give him pleasure or pain.

But for one not committed to Epicurean hedonism, there is a case to be made against this proposition. It is one that had already given some trouble to Aristotle, and it may be worth while to recall the main points of his rather puzzling discussion in *EN* I 10–11.

He raises Solon's question: 'should no one be counted happy [*eudai-*

monisteon] so long as he is alive?' Obviously, he says first, it is not the case that a man is actually happy at the time when he is dead – and an Aristotelian must be among the first to deny it since he reckons happiness to be an *energeia*. So perhaps Solon meant only that when a man is dead it is then safe to call him happy (if his life warranted it), because he is beyond all evils and misfortunes. But this raises some doubts in Aristotle's mind from the opposite direction, so to speak. 'It appears that there *is* some good and bad for the dead man, as for a man who is alive but unaware [sc. of what is happening to him] – for example, honour and dishonour, prosperity and misery of one's children or posterity in general' (1100a18–21).

Aristotle gives only moderate weight to this last consideration. Happiness, as we know, consists in activities of the psyche in accordance with virtue, and the winds of change in fortune have only a small effect, for better or worse, on the steady course of the happy man's psyche. So while it is hard to deny that posthumous dishonour or the disgrace of a grandchild have some effect on one's *eudaimonia*, just as it is hard to claim that a man is perfectly *eudaimōn* if his partner is successfully and secretly cheating him, nevertheless the damage is relatively slight. In these cases, when all is known, we say 'Yes, he was a happy man although, of course, there was that disaster that he knew nothing about . . .'

Now this is troublesome. Aristotle appears to be claiming both that *eudaimonia*, being an activity of the living psyche, is unaffected by anything after it ceases to be living, and that it is somewhat affected by certain posthumous disasters. Two ways of excusing him have appeared in the recent literature, but they seem to me not to work. Joachim[20] claims that he is considering 'the legitimate problem as to our estimate of the objective value of a man's life [. . .]' not 'whether what happens after a man's death will affect his own well-being'. But this lets Aristotle off too lightly. Joachim needs a distinction between 'the objective value of a man's life' and 'his own well-being', but Aristotle is discussing just the man's *eudaimonia* all the time – nothing else. And his distinction is just that between an enduring state and the mere fluctuations caused by external fortunes. A second line of defence is tried by Kurt Pritzl.[21] The essence of this is that Aristotle is here finding some merit in popular opinions about the continued existence of the dead: 'The dead, no longer capable of activity, according to the common opinions on the subject, may nevertheless be happy or unhappy in the land of shadows [. . .]' (pp. 108–9). Hence 'the rather odd idea that a person's happiness can be affected by something of

[20] Joachim (1951), p. 59.
[21] Pritzl (1983).

which he or she is never aware need not be read into the passage' (p. 106). But this solves a rather minor difficulty at the expense of introducing a greater one – that of attributing to Aristotle a doctrine about the psyche that flatly contradicts the *De anima*.

It seems to me that Joachim is right to distinguish two senses of *eudaimonia*, but wrong in claiming that Aristotle distinguished them in this passage. In the sense defined by Aristotle in *EN* I, *eudaimonia* is a function of the individual psyche, and everything that happens to us, except with regard to relational properties, must happen within the limits set by birth and death. But we can also speak of a man's *eudaimonia* when we mean something like the overall achievement of his life, and in this sense it is affected by relational properties that may not fall within the limits of life. Solon's question concerns *eudaimonia* in this sense.

An idea that has something in common with Aristotle's approach is employed by Thomas Nagel in his article 'Death'.[22] He explores the position that 'most good or ill fortune has as its subject a person identified by his history and his possibilities, rather than merely by his categorical state of the moment – and that while this subject can be located in a sequence of places and times, the same is not necessarily true of the goods and ills that befall him' (p. 5). To illustrate the idea, he imagines an intelligent person reduced by a brain injury to the mental condition of a contented infant. We pity this person, and the one we pity is not the contented infant but the intelligent adult, 'though of course he does not mind his condition – there is some doubt, in fact, whether he can be said to exist any longer'.

Nagel goes on from this example to claim that 'a man's life' (*sic*) 'includes much that does not take place within the boundaries of his body and his mind, and what happens to him can include much that does not take place within the boundaries of his life. A man is the subject of good and evil as much because he has hopes which may or may not be fulfilled, or possibilities which may or may not be realised, as because of his capacity to suffer and enjoy. If death is an evil, it must be accounted for in these terms, and the impossibility of locating it within life should not trouble us' (pp. 6–7).

This is an argument that seeks to meet Epicurus on the second of the two cases distinguished above. To the man who rationalises his fear of death on the ground that he will be deprived of the goods of life, Epicurus replied that such deprivation is an evil only if one can feel the loss. Nagel counters him with a claim that might be put this way: to fail to achieve X is an evil for S, if (1) X would have been good for S, and (2) S might have achieved X if he had lived.

---

[22] Nagel (1979), pp. 1ff.

Are there any arguments that can contribute to a solution of this question? The move that makes Nagel's claim possible is to regard the person as identified not by 'his categorical state of the moment', but 'by his history and his possibilities'. It is hard to regard this as a final answer. Of course we can identify a person by his history, and having done so we can comment on his possibilities, with some hope of being rational about it. If such a person is deprived of his possibilities by death, we are landed straight back in the Epicurean net: who is it that is suffering from a state of being deprived? Some possible but not actual person? This seems dangerously vague. Who can say what the possibilities are? Even if there were some way of limiting the possibilities for a given person – statistically, perhaps, as the Life Insurance Companies do, or through some sophisticated development of biochemistry – this would hardly meet the Epicureans' concern, which refers to a person's attitude to his own death. He must consider what possibilities his death would deprive him of – that is to say, he is invited to define himself by his own assessment of what he might do. Perhaps that is acceptable; but if it is acceptable at all, it would seem to make everyone liable to an infinite quantity of damage from dying, such that no one would have any hope of living a good life.

A different approach seems to me more promising – one more like that of Bernard Williams in his article 'The Makropoulos case'. The title comes from a character in a story who lived to be 342, having been given an elixir of life, but then became bored and refused to take any more of the elixir. And Williams is mainly concerned with exploring the thought that even if we refute the Epicureans, we should not therefore want to be immortal. He offers some arguments, however, in refutation of the Epicurean position, and it is one of these that I want to focus on.

His starting point is the idea that the satisfaction of desire is a good thing; hence it is rational to plan for a future in which we get what we want, and hence to avoid death, as being one kind of future in which we don't get what we want. But perhaps all desires are conditional on being alive at the relevant time: in that case, Epicurus wins. Death is nothing to us. So Williams argues that it is not the case that all desires are conditional. It is possible for instance to weigh the case for suicide against the prospect of continuing life; to opt for continuing life is to manifest an unconditional desire (at least, not conditional on continuing to live), since it resolves the question of whether life continues or not.

Such unconditional desires Williams calls categorical desires, and he bases his case against the Epicureans on the claim that we have categorical desires. It is rational to prefer a future in which our desires are satisfied to one in which they are not, and for categorical desires this preference is not cancelled but frustrated by death. Hence it is rational, if not to fear death, at least to avoid it.

There are some difficulties with this argument, however. Williams does not develop the notion of categorical desires as far as one would wish (at least, in the article referred to). We are, of course, concerned with self-regarding desires, not with desires concerning the future state of the world. So a case can be made for making most of them conditional on continuing to live. We desire the pleasure of eating dinner tomorrow, to avoid the pain of hunger: dead, we shall feel no pain. We desire the pleasure of your company on Tuesday at 8: dead, we shall not miss you. Which of our personal desires are categorical? A colleague, learning that he had cancer, feared that he might not be able to drink all of the wine he had laid down in his cellar. Another desires to finish such and such a book. Are these categorical desires? Does the badness of death depend on our having such desires? There is something unsatisfactory (as Williams observes himself) in making it thus dependent on the contingency of our having desires of this kind.[23]

We might perhaps do better by considering how desires are conditional on continuing life, and developing that idea more fully. Consider the case of a terminally ill man who is ignorant of his condition, although his family and friends know the truth. Conversation in his presence is an elaborate pretence. He talks about his return to work, next summer's vacation, reserving library books, booking opera tickets, how to improve the layout of the kitchen; and they all do their painful best to keep up the fiction. In this case, the embarrassment of the situation is due to the inequality of knowledge. But suppose none of them knows the medical truth: the conversation is no longer a pretence, but it is still in some sense unreal or vain.

The formation of plans, formulation of hopes and desires, depend for their meaning on the possibility of fulfilment. We know what fulfilment is. If there were a world in which desires were never fulfilled, it is difficult to see what a desire could be. We understand what fulfilment is because we are familiar with the distinction between frustration and fulfilment. A case could surely be made for saying that the distinction is at the heart of

---

[23] Another, more complex approach to the problem has been tried by Harry S. Silverstein (1980). This depends on the notion, derived from W. V. Quine, of treating time as a fourth dimension of objects. 'In brief, A's death coexists with A ("in an eternal or timeless sense of the word"), and is therefore a possible object of A's suffering, and is therefore an intelligible A-related evil' (p. 420). This needs a good deal of technical underpinning, and there is insufficient space here either to summarise or to criticise it adequately.

I am grateful to Alison McIntyre, of Princeton University, for drawing my attention to this article, and for showing me her own (unpublished) critique of it.

moral education and psychological development. As part of the structure of our interpersonal conversation, and more fundamentally of our intentions, the distinction is necessary to our lives as rational human beings.

It seems to me that the essential element in a rational fear of death is the fear that our desires and intentions are unreal, in the sense that they have no possibility of fulfilment.[24] Plato's Cave might be adapted as an illustration. The prisoners are not now being deceived by mere shadows of the images of the things that are, and imagining that these shadows are the *ontōs onta*. They are being deceived (because they do not know that they are about to die) into thinking that their hopes, desires, and intentions have a normal chance of fulfilment. In the world outside the Cave, desires and intentions are related in well known ways to their goals: they are not always fulfilled, of course, but they provide the model from which we learn what it is reasonable to desire or hope for or intend. If someone fears that he is unknowingly living in this Cave, and that his desires and intentions are vain and unreal, it seems to me that his fear is a rational one.

The desires about which we are concerned are present desires, and our concern is to do with their meaningfulness. I do not think it is necessary to extend the concept of personal identity, as Nagel wishes to do, so as to include future possibilities in it. The objection to that idea is that identity becomes an undefined and open ended concept. But we do not need to claim that a person has any particular possibilities, but only that it is not the case that all possibilities are ruled out for him. I am suggesting that the fear of death is the fear that there are no more possibilities, and that Epicurus' argument does not succeed in making out that this is irrational, because it is a fear concerned with our present state, not about our future (or timeless) state.

To eliminate fear of death it would be necessary to be in a state in which future possibilities were of no concern. This is indeed the state of one who follows to the letter Epicurus' advice to confine one's desires to the bare essentials for avoiding present pain. If Epicurus' case that death is nothing to us is to be persuasive, one must accept the hedonist premiss of Epicurean morality in its fullest strength. I think the best argument against Epicurus is that the human mind has desires and intentions that go beyond those limits, not contingently but necessarily, and that he himself, in

---

[24] On re-reading some work by others, I see that this is a development of a point in Amelie Rorty's paper (1983). Her point is not quite the same, however. It is that on realising, and in a sense regretting, that the world will go on well enough without us after our death, we come to fear that 'all our efforts to live well [...] were in vain. The fear is a terror that death shows our significant projects were meaningless.'

recognising the strength of pleasures of the mind, including anticipatory pleasures, found it impossible to maintain his position strictly enough to support his argument.

4 The Stoic doctrine of the affections of the soul

Michael Frede

According to Stoic doctrine the wise man is *apathēs*, free from *pathē*, free from affections. We have some notion of what the Stoics have in mind when they say this. After all, the equanimity of the Stoic sage has become so proverbial that the adjective 'stoic' (or 'stoical') has become part of our various vernaculars.

But it is also well known that, if we try to say what this freedom from affect is supposed to amount to, we face a difficulty. We may think that the Stoics mean to say that nothing will move the wise man, that he is entirely free from any emotion. This, in fact, is a view which often has been taken. But, given this view, one will be inclined to criticise the Stoic sage as somehow inhuman, as unfeeling, as having no feelings, when this not only would be entirely natural, but indeed, we think, the only appropriate human response. Hence we might rather think that the Stoics, for all their radicalism, cannot really have meant to assert that the sage is free from any emotion. Fortunately, there can be hardly any doubt on the matter. For it is well attested that the Stoics ascribe to the sage a variety of emotional states, the so-called *eupatheiai*, e.g. joy, which they characterise as a certain kind of elation (cf. D.L. VII 115, *SVF* III 431).

But, if we thus try to defend the Stoic sage against the charge of insensitivity, and claim that the Stoics, in denying their sage any affect, by no means deny him any feeling, we face another difficulty. In claiming that the wise man is free from affect, the Stoics seem to want to deny the view, held by Plato, Aristotle and their followers, that at least some of the *pathē*, some of the affections of the soul, are natural and appropriate, even for the wise man, namely those which it is reasonable to have, those which in their degree and their manner constitute a reasonable emotional response to the situation which gives rise to them. That the Stoics, in saying that the wise man is free from affections, mean to contradict the Platonists and the Peripatetics seems to be confirmed by the fact that the Platonists and Peripatetics, in turn, make a point of claiming that the wise man will be *metriopathēs*, i.e. measured or moderate in his emotional response, rather than free from any affect altogether (cf. D.L. V 31; Albinus *Isagoge* p. 184,24). In making this claim the Platonists and the Peripatetics seem to want to deny the Stoic claim that the wise man is free from any affect. But, if this is so, it would seem that the Stoics must be denying that the sage has any feelings. For if, in claiming that the sage is free from affect, they just meant to claim that nothing will move the sage unduly, beyond the limits of moderation, there would be no disagreement with the Platonists and the Peripatetics, who hardly would take issue with this claim. For the claim to be controversial, it seems, we have to deny the Stoic sage even the measured emotional response which the Platonists and the Peripatetics expect from their wise man. Hence we seem to be thrown back on the first assumption, namely the assumption that the wise man will be free from any emotion. But we have already seen that this assumption is unacceptable. Hence we seem to face a dilemma.

How do we find our way out of this apparent dilemma? Roughly speaking, the solution of the problem seems to me to be the following. As is well known, the Stoics assume that the human soul does not consist both of a rational part and an irrational part, as Plato, Aristotle (at least in his moral psychology), and their followers claimed, but only of a mind or reason. Hence, for the Stoics, all emotions are motions, inclinations and disinclinations, of reason, since, according to them, there is no irrational part of the soul they could be motions or affections of. But some of these emotions they take to be rational, some to be irrational. It is these irrational emotions which are called affections of the soul. The rational emotions are those of a perfectly rational reason whose sentiments are not coloured and intensified or weakened by any false assumptions, assumptions, e.g. concerning the value of the things we are attracted or repelled by. Only the emotions of the wise man will be rational, because only the reason of a wise man is perfectly rational, undistorted by any false beliefs. Since none of us is wise, all the emotions we have, and all the emotions we are familiar with, are irrational and thus affections of the mind. Thus, if by 'emotion' we mean the kinds of emotions we are familiar with, the Stoic sage will, indeed, be free from emotion. But the Stoics allow for the possibility of purely rational emotions, and these they do not want to deny their sage when they claim that he is free from affections.

The Platonic–Aristotelian tradition has a theory of those emotions which we ordinary human beings actually have, and, naturally enough, it goes on the assumption that all human emotions are like the ones we are familiar with. Thus the Stoics and the Platonists and the Peripatetics agree in what they call 'affections of the soul'. But they disagree in the way they conceive of them. For the Platonic–Aristotelian tradition assumes an irrational part of the soul and it identifies the emotions as the motions, inclinations and disinclinations, of this irrational part of the soul. It then proceeds to distinguish among them between reasonable and unreasonable emotions. Those emotions are reasonable which are in the line of reason. If I have good reason to be afraid, then it is reasonable for me to be afraid. Those emotions are unreasonable which are out of line with reason and might even interfere with its exercising its proper functions. If I know very well that there is no reason to be afraid, but nevertheless do feel fear, my emotion is unreasonable. The reason why some emotions are natural and reasonable is that their objects are good or bad. Hence we have every reason to be drawn to or to be repelled by them, to be satisfied when we have obtained what is good and managed to avoid what is bad, and to be dissatisfied in the opposite case. But the Stoics think that all this rests on a terrible confusion. The objects of our so-called reasonable emotions, e.g. life, health, beauty, honour, wealth, and death, illness, ugliness, shame, poverty, all these things in truth are neither good nor bad (D.L. VII 102, *SVF* III 117), but entirely indifferent, and hence it is utterly irrational to be moved by them as if they were goods or evils. Hence all these emotions, including the supposedly reasonable ones, are to be rejected, because even they presuppose that their objects have a value which in fact they do not have.

Thus, when the Stoics claim that the wise man is free from affections, they do mean to deny him all the emotions we are familiar with, and they do in particular mean to deny him, without exception, all the feelings which the Platonic–Aristotelian tradition calls affections of the soul and locates in an irrational part of the soul. But they do not mean to deny him any feeling whatsoever, because they assume that there are purely rational emotions of reason, which none of us, though, is familiar with, because we have not learnt to acquire the right attitude towards the objects of our feelings. This, in rough outline, is the solution of the problem which I want to propose and to clarify in this paper.

Obviously, to understand the Stoic position, we first of all have to understand why the Stoics take issue with the way the Platonic–Aristotelian tradition conceptualises the affections of the soul as motions of an irrational part of the soul. We may assume that all philosophers were agreed that there are irrational motions of the soul, that at times we get upset or excited without there being a reason which would warrant our upset or excitement. We also may assume that philosophers were primarily interested in those cases of such irrational motions of the soul, in which somebody does something, or fails to do something, against all reason, and in which we think that we can only explain his behaviour by assuming that it is not guided by reasons, but determined by some irrational factor. Finally we may assume that they regarded those cases as especially interesting and as somehow paradigmatic in which a person not only quite obviously behaves quite unreasonably, but in which the person himself is aware that he is acting unreasonably, cases in which it seems that the person is moved by some irrational motion of the soul to act irrationally against his own better judgment. It was such irrational motions of the soul which one called '*pathē*' or 'affections', and perhaps the term '*pathos*' originally was restricted to such flagrantly irrational emotions, and only later came to refer to the emotions quite generally. In any case, when Democritus (Clemens Alex. *Paed.* 1 6, DK B31) says that wisdom frees us from the *pathē* of the soul, just like medicine heals the ills of the body, there is no reason to suppose that Democritus thought that wisdom frees us from all emotion.

But however this may be, it was agreed by all that there are such irrational affections of the soul which move us to act irrationally, often, it seems, against our own better judgment. What one could not agree on was how these cases were to be explained. There is reason to believe that Socrates thought that there is no such thing as acting against one's own better judgment. What does happen is that reason in certain circumstances gets confused and, instead of holding on to its better judgment, follows some other judgment. If reason knew the truth, it could never get confused in this way. Thus, according to Socrates, such cases reveal nothing but a failure of reason which in its weakness does not hold on to the true belief, but accepts a false one and acts on it. Plato, Aristotle, and their followers, on the other hand, believed that such cases could not be explained as purely intellectual failures, that one had to assume that besides reason there is an irrational part of the soul with its own needs and demands which may conflict with the demands of reason and which may move us to act against the dictates of reason, if reason has not managed to bring the irrational part of the soul firmly under its control. Thus the irrational behaviour in question first of all reveals a failure of the irrational part of the soul, namely the failure to produce an emotional response to the situation which is adequate to it. Only secondarily do such cases reveal a failure of reason, namely the failure to control the emotions. And this failure ultimately involves a cognitive failure. For one can only be practically wise, if the irrational part of the soul has been conditioned in such a way as to invariably produce the emotional response which is in line with reason, which reason finds appropriate. Though such responses are irrational in the wider sense that they do not have their origin in reason, but seem to arise spontaneously, there is also a sense in which we may call them reasonable or rational, to distinguish them from the emotions which are irrational in a narrower sense. These emotions not only do not have their origin in reason, they also are not in conformity with reason.

Though it is only irrational motions in the narrower sense which cause the kind of irrational behaviour in question, and though there is reason to suppose that originally only these irrational motions were referred to as '*pathē*', following Aristotle all irrational motions in the wider sense of the word 'irrational' come to be called '*pathē*' or 'affections of the soul'. The reason for this is perhaps the following. In calling all irrational motions of the soul 'affections', attention is drawn to the presumed fact that the irrational motions which cause irrational behaviour do not differ in kind or in origin, but only in intensity, from ordinary quite unobjectionable emotions. It is not the emotion itself which is objectionable. Indeed, in this tradition, it seems, the very word '*pathos*' or 'affection' is taken to indicate that the irrational motions of the soul quite generally, not just those which are irrational in the narrower sense, are a thing which we suffer, which comes over us without our active participation, which is not directly in our control, which is not something we can make up our mind to have or not to have, as we please. It is for this reason that in this tradition the term '*pathos*' takes on the connotation of '*passio*', 'affect', 'purely passive affection'. What we have control over is not the affect itself, but at best the disposition or character which, depending on the circumstances, produces a certain kind of emotional response. At least to some extent we are in a position to change ourselves in such a way that the circumstances no longer evoke an emotional response which is quite unreasonable and by which we may get carried away so as to act unreasonably. But there is not the slightest suggestion that all emotional responses ought to be suppressed or even entirely eradicated. They rather are taken to be an essential part of human nature and to fulfil a positive function, a function, though, which they can only fulfil, if the disposition which produces them has been conditioned so as to produce responses which are in line with reason.

The way the Stoics conceive of the matter is radically different. Cicero reports (*Ac.* 1 39): 'whereas the ancients claimed that the commotions are natural and have nothing to do with reason, and whereas they located desire in one part of the soul, and reason in another, he [sc. Zeno] would not even agree with that. For he thought that these commotions were equally voluntary and arose from a judgment which was a matter of mere opinion [. . .]' This report seems to capture the salient features of the Stoic position and of what was at issue between the Stoics and those who followed the ancients, i.e. the followers of Plato and Aristotle. In the Platonic–Aristotelian tradition one opted for the position that the affections are commotions which are quite independent of reason and have their origin in an irrational part of the soul. But, in taking this position, one consciously rejected the Socratic position, that the affections of the soul which lead us to behave irrationally, are nothing but aberrations of human reason. And it is obviously this Socratic position which the Stoics try to defend. They want to claim that, as Socrates had said, such cases reveal nothing but an intellectual failure. Reason in its weakness abandons the correct belief and espouses a false one (Galen, *De dogm. Hipp. et Plat.* IV 6, p. 380 M, *SVF* III 473). If there seems to be internal conflict or if it even seems that we act against our better judgment, this is because reason may be wavering and now endorse one belief and then the other, it might oscillate between the two, and this so rapidly that we might not even be aware of the fact that for a moment we had changed our mind (Plutarch, *De virtute morali* 7 446f., *SVF* III 459). To defend this view they take the position that irrational affections of the soul which lead us astray themselves are nothing but the mistaken judgments which take the place of the true judgments which we abandoned (cf. e.g. Cicero, *Fin.* III 35; cf. *SVF* III 456ff.). But in order to be able to say this they have to say that all affections of the soul really are affections of reason, to be more precise irrational mistaken judgments of reason. And to say this is to deny the existence of an irrational part of the soul. For the irrational part of the soul with its irrational motions only was introduced in order to avoid the conclusion that the affections of the soul which lead us astray have their origin in nothing but a failure of reason.

But why should the Stoics have been attracted by such an extreme view? Cicero's brief remarks quoted above give us a first clue. Obviously it is assumed, by both parties in the debate, that the behaviour of reason is directly in our control, voluntary. Whether we agree to accept a belief or not is up to us. We can make up our mind whether we want to believe something or rather to suspend judgment. But one removes the affections from the immediate control of reason by placing them in an irrational part of the soul with a life of its own, as it were; and in doing so one is also denying any direct and immediate responsibility for these affections and the behaviour they produce. And to the extent in which one is inclined, as Plato, e.g., sometimes seems to be, to identify one's true self with one's reason, one also is inclined to regard one's affections as something which is not one's own, as if it were an animal one has to tame and not oneself who displayed these affections. But it is not just that one thus denies immediate responsibility for one's affections and to some extent disowns them. According to the Stoics, one also encourages irrationality and immorality by providing it with a theoretical excuse. For, if one assumes that an irrational part of the soul with its motions, inclinations and disinclinations, is part of human nature, then it is only reasonable if one also assumes that some of these motions, inclinations and disinclinations, are natural; that we are naturally constructed in such a way as to be inclined towards things which are good for us and to be disinclined towards things which are bad for us. Thus it seems that, if one assumes an irrational part of the soul with its own inclinations and disinclinations, one also is committed to the view that some of the objects of these inclinations and disinclinations are goods or evils. This, in fact, is what Platonists and Peripatetics teach, following in this the view of common mankind; however much they may stress the higher goods of the soul, and the relative unimportance of the goods of the body and of external goods, they nevertheless do recognise them as goods, and hence legitimise an inclination towards them which would be appropriate if they, indeed, were goods. Even if they do tell us that health is only a good of the body, they do acknowledge it as a good and hence help us to justify the great upset which we feel when we have lost our health, as if we had lost a good. But this is a thorough and fundamental confusion. None of the objects of the so-called natural and reasonable affections is a good or an evil. Wealth and poverty, health and illness, youth and old age, beauty and ugliness, honour and shame, and whatever else may be claimed to naturally repel or attract us, are neither good nor bad, but entirely indifferent.

For, if they were good or bad, reason should be able to recognise them as such, and if reason recognised them as such it would incline us to seek them out or shun them. Thus there would be no need for nature to endow us with an irrational part of the soul which, if it functions properly, inclines us towards what is good for us and disinclines us from what is bad for us. Reason itself would suffice to produce a behaviour conducive to our survival and our well-being.

It is for such reasons that the Stoics cannot accept the Aristotelian concept of the affections of the soul and insist, instead, on treating them as voluntary, but irrational motions of reason. If one did not, of one's own choice, subscribe to the frivolous and arbitrary belief that health is a good, but instead realised that health is completely indifferent, one would not be upset if one lost one's health. The upset is a result of the confusion of one's reason, and of nothing else. Hence they also think that it is grossly misleading to think of the affections of the soul as *pathē* in the sense of passive affections. They rather are *pathē* in the sense of illnesses, diseases. Indeed, they are the diseases of the mind which we have to cure. Thus Democritus was quite right when he said that wisdom frees the soul from its affections just like medicine cures the diseases of the body.

The Stoics, then, claim that the affections of the soul are voluntary, but irrational, motions of reason. To be more precise, they claim that the affections have their origin in a judgment of reason, or even that they themselves are judgments of reason, namely misjudgments to the effect that something is good or bad when, in fact, it is neither, but completely indifferent.

But before we turn to this more specific thesis, that the affections are nothing but judgments of reason, let us first consider the more general thesis that the affections are motions of reason, form part of the life of reason. For one difficulty which we have in trying to understand the Stoic theory clearly is that we find the mere suggestion that there are motions, inclinations or disinclinations, of reason which by themselves might suffice to account for our behaviour, very difficult to understand, if not unintelligible. The reason for this is simply that we tend to look at rationality as a formal ability or capacity, or perhaps rather as a set of abilities or capacities which allow us, ideally in accordance with logic, to draw certain conclusions and to decide on certain courses of action. But, in order to be able to do this, we think, reason has to be supplied with the appropriate premises from the outside. It can only draw inferences, if it is supplied with the data from which to draw inferences. And it can only figure out which course of action we should adopt, if it is supplied with the necessary information concerning our preferences. Thus reason for us is purely instrumental. The ancient conception of reason, on the other hand, and in particular the Stoic conception of reason, is radically different. The Stoics, but also the Platonists and the Peripatetics assume that reason in its natural, mature, completed state is a reason characterised by wisdom. It is assumed that it is part of rationality itself that reason disposes of a certain specifiable knowledge, that it does form certain notions, and that it does come to make certain assumptions concerning the objects of these notions, unless its natural development is thwarted, derailed, perverted. For it is assumed that reason cannot fulfil its natural function without having these notions and these assumptions. It also, correctly, is assumed that perception or sensation would never provide us with a sufficient basis for what we would count as a reasonable way to look at the world. Hence it is, presumably wrongly, assumed that our reason must be constructed in such a way that, given a normal environment, it will form the notions and assumptions which are necessary to arrive at a reasonable view of the world. In any case, rationality is not just characterised by certain formal abilities, but also by certain notions and assumptions about the world.

Moreover, most ancient philosophers, at least since Socrates, do assume that reason itself has its own preferences, inclinations and disinclinations, and that it is part of fully developed reason or rationality to have the right kind of preferences. Reason is supposed to be able not just to cognitively grasp what is true and what is good, but also to be naturally inclined to what it has recognised as good. Thus the recognition that something is good is supposed to provide not just a sufficient reason, but also a sufficient cause for action. Reason by itself, because of its natural inclination to what is good, can move us to act. Socrates in the *Protagoras* (352bff.) is made to argue that reason is not, as people commonly assume, the slave of the passions. Plato and Aristotle go on the assumption that reason has its own form of desire and is in a position to assert itself against the irrational affections. Plato in the *Republic* (IX 580d) ascribes a special form of desire to each of the three parts of the soul he distinguishes there. Aristotle follows Plato in this regard and repeatedly distinguishes three forms of desire, *epithumia*, *thūmos*, and *boulēsis*, of which boulesis is identified as the desire of reason (*MM* 1187 b36–7). Already in the *Topics* he had said that *boulēsis* is to be located in the reasoning part of the soul (126 a13). And this view is by no means peculiar to antiquity. It is to be found throughout the Middle Ages. As late an author as Eustachius a Sancto Paulo, whose Summa served as a standard textbook in Descartes' time, talks as if it were completely uncontroversial to claim: '*est autem in superiori animae portione facultas duplex, altera adprehensiva seu cogno-scitiva, diciturque intellectus, altera appetitiva, diciturque appetitus rationalis seu voluntas*'. (III 2, disp. 1, 9.1) This text not only shows that even at the end of the Middle Ages reason still was regarded as having a desiderative or appetitive aspect, a form of desire of its own, but also gives us a clue as to how it came about that we think of reason as something to be contrasted with desire and quite generally the passions of the soul. The latter Middle Ages, in part due to reflections on divine omnipotence which came to be an ever increasing concern, attribute such an import-ance to the will that the will comes to be seen as something opposed to reason or intellect. Instead of being regarded as another function of the intellect, it comes to be seen as a separate faculty of the rational part of the soul contrasted with the intellect. But, given the notorious problems which the doctrine of the will raises, it is not surprising that subsequent philosophers were ready to discard it and to assume instead that reason is purely cognitive and that it is the affections of the soul, rather than some mysterious will, which move us to act.

Upon reflection one might think, though, that the notion that reason has its own desires and inclinations is not quite as strange as it, at first sight, appears. If we are willing to talk about parts or faculties of the soul and to ascribe to them desires, it is not clear at all why we should not ascribe our desire for truth, consistency, clarity, rationality to reason itself, why we should not say that reason itself is not contented with a given solution of a certain problem and hence continues to think about it till it is satisfied. Admittedly it is easy enough to find other explanations for such desires, satisfactions, or frustrations, but the point is that the notion that reason has its own needs and desires is not in itself absurd, and only appears so implausible because we have become so used to a very different kind of theory.

But, however this may be, it is not the Stoics alone who take the view that there are inclinations and disinclinations of reason which can account for our behaviour. Their view rather is shared by most of our tradition, and what needs to be explained rather is why we no longer share this view. What distinguishes the Stoics from the rest of the tradition is their assumption that all motions of the soul are motions of reason and, ultimately, judgments. We already have seen why the Stoics think that they have to insist that even those irrational affections which, because of their utter irrationality, do not seem to have their origin in reason, nevertheless have to be understood as motions of reason itself. How they can say this will become clearer, if we now consider their more specific thesis that all motions of the soul are judgments or opinions of reason.

It will be easier to understand this, if we make an assumption as to the truth of the matter which seems to be shared by the Stoics. As Aristotle already before them, so the Stoics, too, quite rightly assume that for each affection there is a corresponding perceptible change in the state of the person. If we are afraid or in pain, we quite literally feel anxious, depressed; there is a sense of constriction and withdrawal into oneself. If, on the other hand, we desire something or are pleased, there is a sense of expansion and elation. The Stoics, moreover, assume that we are aware of our state. Thus Chrysippus talks of the changes in the region of the heart which occur when we are sad, and which we become aware of in feeling a certain kind of pain (Gal. *De dogm. Hipp. et Plat.* III 7; p. 302f. M). It seems, then, that we have to distinguish three things, (i) the affection, (ii) the physiological state which corresponds to it, and (iii) a characteristic feeling which we have when we are aware of this physiological state. Let us, e.g., assume that we are afraid that the rain is ruining the crops. In this case there are three things which we have to distinguish: (i) it is one thing to be afraid that the rain is ruining the crops; (ii) it is another thing to be in the physiological state which corresponds to this fear; (iii) it is a third thing to have the kind of feeling which we have when we are afraid, anxious, concerned, a feeling which is produced by our physiological state. Obviously, all three things are so closely related to each other that we tend to conflate them. Thus, ordinarily we tend to speak of our feeling as if it were the fear itself. The Stoics themselves sometimes talk as if 'fear' referred to the whole complex of belief, physiological state and awareness of this state. This may explain why they sometimes talk as if the affection of the soul were a judgment, but at other times say that the affection has its origin in a judgment. It still seems important to make the distinction. For when one does feel afraid, one just has the feeling which one characteristically has when one is afraid. It does not yet follow from the fact that one does have the feeling that one actually is afraid. For this feeling can also be induced artificially, e.g. by drugs. In this case there is no fear which produced the feeling of anxiety, there is only the feeling of fear. The person in question may in vain try to identify the fear which produced this feeling of anxiety. Exactly because of the close connection between being afraid and feeling anxious, the person may be driven to mistakenly identify some fear as the source of his anxiety.

Given such a distinction, it seems much easier to see how the Stoics can argue that the affection is just another judgment of the mind. They have to argue, e.g. in the case of fear, that they do not claim that feeling afraid is just a judgment, but rather that being afraid is just to make a judgment and that feeling afraid is only the natural consequence of such a judgment. It still will be difficult enough to see how being afraid could just be a matter of making a certain judgment, but at least the claim now no longer sounds outright counterintuitive, given that feelings clearly are not judgments.

Now, to understand how the Stoics might claim that to be afraid is just to make a certain kind of judgment, to have a certain kind of belief, we have to have a closer look at the Stoic theory of judgment. When we talk about a judgment or a belief, we primarily think of the explicit or implicit assertion of a proposition. The judgment or the belief has a certain propositional content, and to judge, we think, is just to assert this proposition. Now, if we think of judgments in this way, it is difficult to see how being afraid could be just a matter of making a certain judgment. It might very well be the case that to be afraid is to be afraid that p, and that in order to be afraid that p we have to assert, at least implicitly, a proposition. But being afraid seems to involve more than just asserting a proposition. But it is telling that, though the Stoics were the first to put us into a position to conceive of a judgment in this way by introducing the notion of a *lekton*, and though they were familiar with the view of judgment referred to, they nevertheless seem to have rejected it. For already Arcesilaus criticised the Stoics for saying that a judgment consists in an assent to an impression, rather than saying that it consists in an assent to the corresponding propositional content, to the *lekton* or *axiōma*, to use Stoic terminology (cf. S.

E. *M* VII 154). What is the difference? According to the Stoics the impressions of rational beings are characterised by the fact that they are articulated by reason in such a way as to invariably have a propositional character. They always are impressions to the effect that something or other is the case or is not the case. But this should not mislead one into thinking that an impression already is sufficiently characterised if we specify its propositional content. For, obviously, one and the same proposition that p can be thought in many different ways, and hence the thought, or the impression, that p will differ correspondingly, depending on the way in which it is thought that p. Hence it is not just the propositional content, but also the way it is thought, which has to enter into a complete characterisation of the impression, and which is relevant to the question whether we ought to give assent to the impression or not. It is for this reason that assent is not a matter of just accepting the proposition, but rather a matter of accepting the impression, since it also does matter how the proposition is thought in the impression. That this is the Stoic view seems to me to be clear because of the following. The Stoics distinguish between clear and distinct impressions, on the one hand, and obscure and confused ones, on the other. They also claim that the wise man will only assent to clear and distinct impressions. But the difference between these two kinds of impressions is not a difference in propositional content. Two people may entertain a thought of the same proposition, e.g. the proposition that two lines which cut lie in the same plane. But the impression which the average person will have when he is asked to entertain this thought will be obscure and confused. The geometer, on the other hand, in thinking that two lines which cut lie in one plane will think of all the relevant properties of lines which cut and of a plane, and it will be because of this that his impression will be clear and distinct, indeed so clear and distinct that it will be obvious to him that two lines which cut lie in one plane.

Now, if the Stoics had thought that judgment and belief were just a matter of assent to a propositional content, it would, indeed, be difficult to see how they could maintain that fear is just a certain kind of judgment. But, given that they think that a judgment also involves a certain way of thinking of a proposition, we can now pursue the possibility that on the Stoic view fear is a matter of the way in which we entertain certain propositions. If assent to the impression that Socrates is going to die is not just the assertion of the proposition that Socrates is going to die, but also involves the acceptance of the way in which one entertains the thought that Socrates is going to die, then perhaps one's fear that Socrates is going to die, after all, is the belief that Socrates is going to die, it now being understood that the belief essentially involves not just a certain propositional content, but also the way this content is thought of.

The reason, or at least the major reason, why thoughts of the same propositional content can differ enormously from each other is that the objects one's thought is a thought of can be represented in one's thought in the most diverse manner without affecting the propositional content of the thought. It is not that the blind man and the seeing person affirm a different proposition when they stand at a traffic crossing and correctly say that the light is on red. But it is likely that the seeing person in his thought represents the colour in a quite different way from the blind person. If one says that a certain book which one is looking at is green one is saying the same thing as one would be saying if one said that this book is green because one knew that all books in this series are green and that hence this book, too, which one had never seen, must be green. But the way this book and its colour are represented in one's thought that the book is green are likely to be quite different.

Now let us assume that two of Socrates' acquaintances, one a friend and one an enemy, agree that Socrates is pale. They assert the same proposition. But one of them, in addition to being a friend of Socrates, also is a doctor. He thinks of Socrates' paleness in a much more distinct way. He also knows from experience that this kind of paleness is the symptom of a fatal disease and represents it accordingly. He thinks of a fatal disease as something bad, because he thinks of death as something bad. All this enters into his thought that Socrates is pale by modifying the way he thinks that Socrates is pale, without though affecting the propositional content. Being told that Socrates is curiously pale, he might respond by saying 'I am afraid that this is so', not to indicate that he is switching the topic and talking about himself now, instead of talking about Socrates, but to indicate that he, too, thinks that Socrates is pale in this curious way, but to also indicate that he thinks in a certain manner of Socrates' being pale in this way, namely a manner which fills him with fear if he assents to, or accepts, the proposition thought in this way. For if, on closer inspection, he decided that Socrates after all did not have the symptomatic paleness there would be no assent and hence no fear. And if he did not think of the symptomatic paleness as a fatal symptom and of death as an evil, and did not assent to the thought thus thought for that reason, there would be no fear either. Hence his fear that Socrates is pale in this way is entirely a matter of his assent to a proposition thought in a certain way and thus depends both on the propositional content and the way this content is thought.

Similarly, if he is afraid that Socrates is going to die his fear is entirely a matter of his assent to the thought that Socrates is going to die, or the thought that there is some chance that Socrates is going to die, thought of in a certain way. If he did not think in the first place that Socrates was going to die, or that there was some chance that Socrates was going to die, he would not be afraid that Socrates is going to die. But he would not be afraid that Socrates is going to die, either, unless he thought this thought in a certain way, namely by thinking of Socrates' death as an evil, rather than as a blessing, as Socrates' enemy might well do. But, though he may fail to be afraid that Socrates is going to die for either reason, the reason for his fear lies in the way in which he thinks of Socrates' death. To put the matter differently: the doctor has the impression or the thought that Socrates is going to die. It is crucial that this impression or thought is not just characterised by the propositional content that Socrates is going to die, but also by the way this proposition is thought or entertained. Depending on the way it is thought or entertained, there might be, as we say, something frightening or anxiety-producing in the mere thought that Socrates is going to die. But just to have the thought occurring to one is not yet to be afraid that Socrates is going to die. To be afraid that Socrates is going to die is to accept the thought, or the impression, not just in its propositional content, but in the way in which this propositional content is thought.

This seems, indeed, the kind of view the Stoics adopt. For they assume that fears, like all affections of the soul, are excessive impulses, inclinations and disinclinations (Stob. *Ecl.* II, p. 88 10ff. W., *SVF* III 378). And they think of impulses in this way: they assume that among the impressions which we have some are impulsive (the so-called *phantasiai hormētikai*, cf. Stob. *Ecl.* II, p. 85 18W), namely those which are characterised by the fact that if we accept them, if we assent to them, we have a motion or an impulse, an inclination or a disinclination towards something. They insist, though, that the impression is just the antecedent cause of the impulse, the inclination or the disinclination. It, in each case, depends on the mind whether there actually is an impulse, an inclination or a disinclination. For in each case it will depend on the mind whether it gives assent to the impulsive impression, even though it is true that there would be no impulse without an impulsive impression (cf. Seneca *Ep. mor.* 113 18). All these impulses will be judgments. For the impressions which give rise to them, being the impressions of rational beings, will be propositional in character. Hence assent to them will amount to the assertion of a proposition. Nevertheless they will be impulses because of the special impulsive character of the impressions. This character is due to the fact that the impression represents something as to be gone after or to be avoided. We might have the impression that there is a spring of fresh water. Under the appropriate circumstances we might think of the water as something very appealing. Under these circumstances the mere thought that there is a spring of fresh water, if thought of in this way, might stir us. But it is only when we give assent to the thought thus thought that we desire, are impelled to go after, the water and feel appropriately pleased and satisfied when we have managed to reach it. Similarly the thought that Socrates is going to die may be impulsive if we think of Socrates' death as something to be averted. The mere thought might stir us. But, only when we are moved to accept the thought, will we be afraid and try to avert it, or be sad when Socrates' death no longer is to be averted. But whether we accept it or not, depends on our reason. If it is strong, it will accept only those thoughts which are appropriate, and refuse to accept those which are inappropriate.

Now, there is an appropriate and reasonable way to think about fresh water, death and the like; and one's impulse will depend on the importance one attributes to these things which will be reflected by the way one thinks of them. But, as we saw earlier, the affections are characterised by the fact that their objects are thought of as goods and evils. To think of something as good or evil is to attach to it the highest importance that can be attached to anything and which should only be attached to virtue, since, compared to virtue, nothing else is of any importance. But since people think of the objects of our 'natural' impulses as goods or evils they give assent to the impulsive impressions which represent them as good or bad, and hence feel impelled towards them or away from them, with an intensity which stands in no comparison to their real value, and which hence is excessive. Thus the Stoics can define the affections of the soul as excessive impulses.

In this way, then, we may be able, after all, to make some sense of the fact that the Stoics think they can claim that all our impulses, including the affections of the soul, are judgments of reason, without denying the impulsive or affective character of the affections.

It is easy to see now why the wise man is free from affections. All affections ultimately involve a wrong evaluation of things, the assumption that something is good or evil, when in fact it is neither. But it does not follow from this at all that the wise man has no impulses and emotions at all. In fact, in general he is inclined and disinclined towards the same things towards which we are inclined and disinclined, except that he attaches no particular value to them, and hence also does not particularly care whether he manages to obtain what he is inclined towards and to avoid what he is disinclined towards. For the only thing he really is attached to is the one thing which actually is good, namely virtue or, what according to the Stoics amounts to the same thing, perfect rationality. So he will be inclined towards something if this is the virtuous or rational thing to be inclined towards. Hence he will represent it in his thought as the rational or virtuous thing to be inclined towards. But it is a confusion to think that something has to be good in order to be the rational or virtuous thing to be inclined towards. The food offered by my hosts may be absolutely indifferent. Nevertheless the thought might occur to me that this is food offered by my hosts, and in this thought the food might be represented as the rational or virtuous thing to be inclined towards. If I were wise I would accept the thought and thus be impelled towards the food. But I would not think that the food was good, nor would it really matter to me whether I got it or not. What would matter to me is that I go for the thing it is virtuous and rational to go for. And this I can achieve, whether I manage to obtain the food which I do not really care for, or not. This is the attitude which, according to the Stoics, the wise man takes towards all the objects of the so-called natural affections, towards the objects of fear and pain, desire and pleasure.

To understand this more fully, something needs to be said about the Stoic account of the genesis of this attitude on the part of the wise man. The Stoics believe that we are born as animals, except that we are constructed in such a way as to become perfectly rational beings, unless the natural process of maturation is interrupted. By nature we are, as children, inclined towards those things which are conducive to our survival as animals; hence we desire them, when we do not have them, and are pleased, when we do obtain them. Similarly we are by nature averse to those things which are detrimental to our survival; we fear them, when they threaten us; we are dissatisfied or pained when we do not manage to avoid them. If all goes well, we learn to avoid what is detrimental and to go after what is wholesome. But as we become rational, a radical change takes place. It is this change which is misdiagnosed by the Peripatetics and the Platonists. They think that the change consists in the fact that the rational part of the soul comes, or at least should come, to exercise its rule over the irrational part of the soul with its natural animal impulses. The fact, according to the Stoics, is that the irrational animal soul of the child has disappeared and turned into a human reason. And with this change the functions of the soul have changed. Thus perception and impulse have become something radically different. Both have become judgments of a certain sort, namely a matter of assent to a certain kind of impression, here a perceptual impression, there an impulsive impression. The child acts on instinctive impulses. It neither has impulsive impressions, nor the reason to assent to them. For, not having a reason, it also does not have rational impressions, i.e. impressions of essentially propositional form. And hence, *a fortiori*, it does not have impulsive impressions in the sense in which rational beings have such impressions. Conversely, the grown-up, the animal soul having disappeared, does not have any instinctive impulses (though we might be tempted to think so, to avoid responsibility for our impulses). The only way for him to be moved is by assent to impulsive impressions. But impulsive impressions presuppose an evaluation of the objects of our impulses. And at this point ordinary human beings in ordinary human societies can hardly fail to make the mistake which even philosophers like the Platonists and the Peripatetics make. They think that since nature from birth has endowed us with certain natural inclinations and disinclinations the objects of these natural impulses must be goods and evils. Hence their behaviour comes to be motivated, not by instinctive impulses, but by affections of the soul, namely their assent to impulsive impressions in which the objects of the natural inclinations with which we are born are represented as good or bad. But little do they realise that not everything which is conducive to the survival of something, even be it one-self, for that mere reason is good. Nor do they appreciate the fact that the natural instinctive impulses of animals are meant to help them to maintain their existence as animals. But since we no longer are animals, but are rational beings now, it seems even more absurd to think of the things which were of importance for our survival as animals as goods or as evils. What we should now be concerned with is what is conducive or detrimental to our rationality, to our survival as rational beings.

As we become rational we are supposed to realise that there is a natural, rational order of things of which we are just a part, that we from birth have been constructed in such a way as to help to maintain this natural order and to maintain it by means of reason, once we have become rational, and that it is hence the most rational thing for us to do to try as well as we can to maintain this order, since, given that everything is fated, we cannot act against its design anyway. But it is part of the natural order that, other things being equal, beings which need food should obtain it, that beings which are ill should regain their health, and quite generally that beings should obtain what they naturally feel impelled towards. And hence these things, though they are not good, are of some value, insofar as, in general, they are conducive to the maintenance of the general, natural, rational order of things.

Thus the Stoic wise man will, after all, by and large be inclined towards the very things Peripatetics and Platonists regard as goods, but not because he regards them as goods, but because he has realised that these in general are the rational things to go after, though in any particular case there might be overriding reasons not to go after them. Thus there might be overriding reasons not to continue one's life. Hence the impulses of the Stoic wise man will be directed towards things which he, given his understanding of the order of things, thinks are the rational things to go after. But if he does not obtain what he is impelled towards this will be a very minor loss; a loss, because, other things being equal, the world would be a more reasonable place, if he did obtain what he is impelled towards given that it is not due to any failure on his part that he fails to obtain what he is after; a very minor loss, since the value of what he failed to obtain does not even begin to shift the balance if compared in weightiness to the rationality he maintained in being impelled towards the object he failed to obtain; moreover, the very fact that he did not obtain what he was after, just reveals that in this case other things were not equal, that there were overriding reasons for his lack of success, that the world is a more reasonable place because he failed.

It is for this reason that he can go about things with the proverbial equanimity of a Stoic sage. For it does not really matter to him which way the things he does turn out. For, whether he succeeds or fails, it will be for the best for the world in either case. And since this is what he was aiming at in the first place when he felt impelled towards what he failed to obtain, he succeeds even in his failure.

Thus the Stoic sage does not gain his equanimity by shedding human concerns, but by coming to realise what these concerns are meant to be, and hence what they ought to be, namely the means by which nature maintains its natural, rational order. And we have to realise that in this order our concerns play a very, very subordinate rôle, and are easily overridden by more important considerations, though we may find it difficult to accept this. But it does not follow from the fact that they play a very subordinate rôle, that they play no rôle whatsoever. Nature is provident down to the smallest detail. Hence it must be a caricature of the wise man to think that he has become insensitive to human concerns and only thus manages to achieve his equanimity. Things do move him, but not in such a way as to disturb his balanced judgment and make him attribute an importance to them which they do not have.

Part II
Ethical Foundations and the *Summum Bonum*

5   The cradle argument in Epicureanism and Stoicism

Jacques Brunschwig

'All the ancient philosophers, in particular those of our school, turn to cradles [*ad incunabula accedunt*] because it is in childhood [*in pueritia*] that they think we can most easily recognise the will of nature [*naturae voluntatem*[1] *cognoscere*].' Piso, disciple and mouthpiece of Antiochus of Ascalon in Cicero's *De finibus*, is perfectly correct in this assertion (v 55): the moralists of the Hellenistic period, of whatever school, made frequent use of what might be called the *cradle argument*, that is, a procedure which consists first in describing (or in claiming to describe) the behaviour and psychology of the child in the cradle (usually in conjunction with young animals) and then in drawing (or in claiming to draw), more or less directly, certain conclusions which, in one way or another, lead to the formulation and justification of a moral doctrine. Piso himself is aware that this argument is well worn: he apologises for 'returning too often to this type' of consideration. Perhaps we too should share his scruples, before embarking on a few remarks on the same subject.

Every reader of the *De finibus* is struck by the fact that in all the exposés of teachings that it contains the cradle argument is given pride of place. This is true for Epicureanism (i 30; cf. ii 31-2) and also for Stoicism (iii 16); as for the representatives of the academico-peripatetic tradition, they emphasise the fact that their starting-point is the same as that of the Stoics (iv 15, 16, 19, 25, 32, 34; v 23), and they set about things in much the same way as they do (v 24); this, however, does not prevent them from resorting to Epicurean phraseology when need arises (v 61, cf. ii 32).

The text that appears here is a considerably revised version of the paper I gave at the Bad-Homburg conference. I tried to take into account the comments put forward during and after the conference, in particular by Gisela Striker, Pierluigi Donini, Brad Inwood, Mario Mignucci, and Richard Sorabji, whom I should like to thank most warmly. My thanks go also to Pierre-Yves Chanut, my colleague at Nanterre, for his Latin expertise, and to Jennifer Barnes, who has kindly translated the paper into English.

[1] *Voluntatem* here is a very plausible correction by Lambinus for *voluptatem* in the MSS. A malicious fate seems to have encouraged confusion between these two words, but has decreed that Lambinus in particular should allay it. More famous (and more problematical) is the example in Lucretius ii 257-8.

These similarities have been picked up by all the commentators, even if they draw different conclusions from them;[2] and those who have studied individual doctrines among them have naturally been zealous in discussing the meaning and the place of the cradle argument in these doctrines as a whole. It seems, however, that there is nonetheless scope for many questions. What are the different versions of the cradle argument? How do they differ and how can this be explained? What do their premisses owe to observation, to experience, to current opinion, to anticipating their conclusions? What have these premisses to tell us about the image of the child, about the conflicts that assail it, and about the transformation it undergoes? How are their claims to objectivity expressed, justified and defended against actual or possible objections from contemporary schools of moral thought? Did moral controversies enable philosophers to refine and develop their child psychology, both in its content and in its method of justification? How was the alleged evidence from child psychology employed and exploited for other purposes than those of objective scientific study of the matter in hand? What investigative paths led, or were believed to lead, to moral consequences? Does the cradle argument, in all its many guises, remain a clear and characteristic expression of ethical naturalism? Does it recklessly steer by that transition from 'is' to 'ought' which traditionally risked the shipwreck of any naturalistic ethics? I should like to attempt an approach to just some of these questions.

I must point out straight away that there will be two gaps in this article. Firstly, I thought it best to leave aside almost entirely the association, recurrent though it is in the texts, between children and animals: Piso's remark, which I quoted at the beginning, seemed justification enough. However, I have deviated from his recommendations on another point. He claims for 'those of his school' – that is to say, for Antiochus' Academy – a very special interest in child psychology; he is right to do so, to judge from the eloquent and colourful descriptions that he scatters throughout his text (v 42, 48, 55, 61); and doubtless this wealth of observation is linked to specific elements of the theory he is defending. Yet these texts are dealing with the child at various stages of his development, distracting us from the cradle proper; besides, anything to do with Antiochus of Ascalon bristles notoriously with huge historical and doctrinal problems.[3] I have

---

[2] Cf. among others Dirlmeier (1937), pp. 47 sqq.; Giusta (1964–7), *passim*, notably I pp. 124ff. and 209ff.; Goldschmidt (1982), p. 311.

[3] On the problems that arise from the relationship between the exposé of Antiochus' ethics in *Fin.* v and the summary of peripatetic ethics by Arius Didymus in Stobaeus II, pp. 116–52 Wachsmuth, cf. most recently Görgemanns (1983), who begins with a résumé of previous studies.

therefore confined myself to the study of the two great moral philosophies of the Hellenistic period, namely Epicureanism and Stoicism.

I

It is in the Epicurean tradition that we come up against some of the simplest and most direct forms of the cradle argument. This is not to say that the same is true of Epicurus himself. The argument does not occur in what survives of his works. The *Letter to Menoeceus* (128–9) identifies pleasure as 'the principle and end of the happy life'; 'the first congenital good [*sungenikon*]', 'first and connatural (*sumphuton*)', because of its 'appropriate nature (*phusin oikeian*)'. The feeling (*pathos*), which acts as a *kanōn* to measure all good and all bad (cf. Diogenes Laertius x 3 1, 3 4) is what makes us 'end up' (*katantōmen*) at these identifications. But there is absolutely no reason to interpret the predicate 'first' in a chronological way, as if he were saying that pleasure is the first good we encounter and identify as such in the course of our life, and that this temporal pre-eminence imposes on it the stature of a mentor to advise us how to live the rest of our lives. What, indeed, is the subject whose feeling serves here as a rule for determining what is good? The passage I have quoted contains a large number of verbs in the first person plural; in some cases it is perfectly plain that he is talking about not just 'us, human adults' but 'us, Epicureans'; and the interplay of the connecting particles is consistent enough for us to extend this interpretation to cases which are less obvious.[4] It was the Epicureans who intellectually 'recognised' (*egnōmen*, 129) that pleasure is the 'first congenital good', adopting as their criterion an emotion that everyone feels without necessarily elevating it to the status of a rule; and it was also they who, working from the pre-eminence of pleasure, were rationally capable of directly inferring the conclusion that we should not take every pleasure, and that certain pleasures should be resisted because of their painful consequences.[5] In all this, the rational adult reflects on his own experiences, draws the rational conclusions they suggest, and does not seem to need any 'naturalist' observation to realise that pleasure is his 'connatural' good; there is no mention of child or of animal in this context. All the same, there is no precise justification of this predicate to be found, nor is there any answer to the possible objection that the adult predilection for pleasure is conditioned by the education he

---

[4] Cf. *legomen* at the end of 128, followed by the statement of a basic Epicurean dogma.
[5] The choice of the negative reading *ou pāsan hēdonēn hairoumetha*, in 129, seems dictated by the repetition, a little further on, of *ou pāsa mentoi hairetē* (despite Bollack (1975), p. 72 and p. 121).

has received and by the system of values in the society he lives in.[6] Thus the *Letter to Menoeceus* confirms two things: firstly, that Epicurus felt capable of producing an authoritative résumé of his ethics without using the cradle argument; secondly, that his argument does in fact leave a gap that would be well filled by this argument.

There is therefore no reason to doubt the truthfulness of Torquatus, the Epicurean in the *De finibus*, when just before he has recourse to the cradle argument, he asserts the fidelity of his explanation to Epicurus' own way of teaching (I 29), even if it is true that Cicero, for his part, is only claiming to conform to the ways of the Epicurean school (I 13), and makes Torquatus refer to groups of Epicureans distinct from the master himself (I 31). Did the cradle argument play a part in Epicurus' *Peri telous*, one of the most complete exposés of his ethics?[7] Such a hypothesis should neither be accepted nor rejected out of hand.[8]

In Torquatus' exposé, the object of his investigations is first defined as the sovereign good (*extremum et ultimum bonorum*, I 29): the criterion for identifying it is a concept of the *telos* accepted 'by all the philosophers', so that the other goods must relate (*referri*) to it while it does not relate to anything else.[9] This criterion allows us to identify pleasure with the sovereign good, and its opposite, pain, with sovereign evil. Epicurus 'undertakes to teach' this double dogma 'in the following way' (*idque instituit docere sic*):

(T1) Every living being, from birth [*omne animal, simulatque natum sit*] seeks [*appetere*] pleasure and enjoys it [*gaudere*] as sovereign good; it shuns [*aspernari*] pain as sovereign evil and rejects it [*repellere*] as far as possible; this it does at a time when it is still not depraved [*depravatum*], nature itself, incorruptly and impartially, being the judge. (I 30)[10]

Before examining the conclusions the Epicurean draws from these assertions, we should note that they are put forward, in fact, as assertions, in

---

[6] Cf. in particular Calcidius *in Tim.* 165 = SVF III 229.

[7] Cf. Cicero, *Tusc.* III 41–2; *Fin.* II 20; Diogenes Laertius x 30.

[8] Usener (1887), p. 119, attributes to the *Peri telous* a version of the cradle argument that we shall return to later and which is reported by Diogenes Laertius x 137; but Arrighetti (1973), pp. 187–9, no longer takes this view.

[9] Arius Didymus in Stobaeus II, p. 46, 18 Wachsmuth, credits the Epicureans with a peculiar definition of 'the notion of the *telos*,' which seems to exclude them from this general agreement (τὸ οἰκείως διατιθέναι ἐξ ἑαυτοῦ πρὸς αὐτὸ χωρὶς τῆς ἐπ' ἄλλο τι ἁπάσης ἐπιβολῆς). Whatever its exact meaning may be, this definition certainly seems to suggest that its *definiendum* is not the *telos* as such, but rather the state or the disposition which the Epicureans identified with the *telos*. This particular concept of the *reference* of the term *telos* does not therefore imply a deviation from the general philosophical agreement on the *meaning* of the term.

[10] Compare *Fin.* II 31–2, which distinguishes the case of infants (*a parvis*) from that of animals (*a bestiis*), but groups them both under the heading of *specula naturae*.

the infinitive (*appetere, gaudere, aspernari, repellere*), or, in a parallel passage, in the indicative (*gaudet, appetit, aspernatur,* II 31). There is no attempt to decide whether they are the result of direct observation, or of an inference drawn from directly observable evidence, and in this second case, whether this inference is legitimate, or even necessary. There is no trace of hesitation when he tells us what an infant feels and desires, still less does he stop to wonder whether it actually has feelings and desires. It is all a long-standing tradition: the child is governed by a principle of pleasure.[11] This was a commonplace whose acceptance called for no particular originality, and whose various possibilities had all been fully explored during the psychological and moral controversies over pleasure on the stage of the old Academy; certain philosophers, like Eudoxus, thought that the desire that visibly (*horān*) attracts all beings to itself, rational or not, is the sign (*mēnuein*) that it is the best for everybody (Aristotle, *EN* 1172 b9). Others, however, like Speusippus, saw in it sufficient grounds for maintaining that pleasure is not a good (1152 b19). Nonetheless, the Epicurean statements are not entirely trivial, as is illustrated by the care with which two verbal nuances are juxtaposed, and implicitly distinguished: the vocabulary of emotive states, with verbs like *gaudere*, and those of tendency or disposition to act in whatever way, with verbs like *appetere* or *repellere*.[12] But neither the order of the words nor any other perceptible sign indicates a precise relation between states and tendencies; we cannot say (I shall return to this point later) whether the child seeks pleasure because he has experienced its enjoyment, or whether he pursues it instinctively before he has had any experience, and its enjoyment just reinforces this tendency. Nor do we find the merest hint of any discussion of the truth-conditions of a description of a state and of a description of a tendency, nor of their possible differences. Does the observation of the new-born child enable us to be sure that he feels subjectively a sensation of pleasure that is only manifested to the observer by expressive signs? Is this observation sufficient to convince us that the child is seeking pleasure rather than (for example) the things, activities or states whose consummation, effectuation, or realisation are accompanied by pleasure? These questions are never asked. The silence with regard to the first question is probably quite normal; the 'mentalist' interpretation of other people's behaviour and, more generally, of other living beings', was not, as far as I

[11] Cf. in particular Aristotle, *EN* II 1105 a2ff., X 1172 a20ff.

[12] It is possible that *aspernari* corresponds here to *gaudere*, as *a se repellere* corresponds to *appetere*; this is not certain, because in I 31 *aspernandum* is contrasted with *appetendum*. In II 31, *aspernari* stands alone against *gaudere* and *appetere*. G. Striker has drawn my attention to the vocabulary Diogenes Laertius uses in a passage (X 137) that I shall return to later; there there are only the verbs of emotion *euaresteisthai* and *proskrouein*.

know, questioned in ancient thought.[13] But Epicurus' blithe indifference to the second question is more peculiar. We might well think, indeed, that he had to prove, in one way or another, that the pursuit of pleasure is *primary* for the child: pleasure had often figured as the accompaniment or by-product of this or that state or specific activity,[14] so that the question naturally arose whether the truer, real object of the tendency is pleasure as such, or rather the state or activity that accompanies it. Yet nobody seems to have thought of conducting a decisive experiment;[15] nor did it occur to them to resort to observation, even of the most everyday nature. I imagine, for example, that Greek children sucked their thumbs; the Epicureans could have used this as evidence that they were doing this for pleasure, independently of the satisfaction of their alimentary needs; but I have not found a single text among those ancient texts I have read that deal with children which refers to this well known phenomenon. Where this was concerned, Epicurus probably considered that the *onus probandi* was on those who were questioning the traditional interpretation of infant behaviour in order to replace it by a more elaborate reading that might seem to have been dictated by moralistic undertones.

The most noticeable and pregnant characteristic of the Epicurean description is the emphasis laid on the precocious nature of the child's emotive and practical hedonism: it appears 'from birth', and this is important not because this is the earliest period and the impressions we receive then are fixed for ever, influencing all the rest of our existence[16] (Epicurus does not put forward the adult pursuit of pleasure as a legacy from childhood), but because this discovery allows *the adult* to assert the purely 'natural' character of this emotion. Without having recourse to etymological

---

[13] The theory of animals as machines does not appear to have had adherents in antiquity. Rather than anyone else, the Cyrenaics would have felt drawn to tackle the problem of 'other minds', because they claimed that we can only understand our *pathē*, emphasising that we cannot understand other people's *pathē* or compare them with our own. But they never seem to have doubted for a moment that other people exist and that they experience *pathē*; cf. Sextus, *M* VII 196–8. The existence of other minds is no more doubted than that of the external world: cf. Burnyeat (1982).

[14] Cf. Aristotle, *EN* II 1104 b4; X 1174 b33 (*epigignomenon*); the word recurs in Chrysippus, in the form *epigennēma* (D.L. VII 85).

[15] See the famous experiment set up by the King of Egypt, Psammeticus (Herodotus, II 2), who brought up two children so that they never heard a word of human speech, with the aim of discovering in which language they would express themselves. (This experiment, incidentally, was not intended to discover what is the 'natural' language, but to find out which was the first race to have appeared on earth.) Ethics, I fear, cannot boast a Psammeticus.

[16] A theory emphasised in Plato (*Leg.* VII 792 e1–2), and linked to the traditional view of the child as an essentially adaptable being, physically as well as morally (789 e2–4). On the occurrence of this theory in texts on medicine, see J. Bertier's rewarding work (1972), especially pp. 118–26.

pedantry, Epicurus identifies what is natural with what is native, which appears before any experience of the outside world, before any influence of the family or of society as a whole. The *parvus* is something which nothing has yet depraved, or made *pravus*; the use of the notion of 'depravity' (which does not necessarily imply a moral judgment, but rather a view of culture as a distortion of nature) shows that this type of nature is not that of the child as such, which does not survive infancy, but that of the human (or living) being itself, just as it is found, even in a distorted form, in the educated child and then in the adult.

It is here that we may probably see Epicurus' true originality. To appreciate it, we have only to remind ourselves briefly of Aristotle who is also concerned to discover the nature of beings by distinguishing corrupt specimens (*en tois diephtharmenois*) from those in a state of nature (*en tois kata phusin echousi*, *Pol.* 1254 a36–7);[17] when it is time to apply this criterion, however, he identifies the natural state with adulthood: 'that which each thing is when its growth is completed [*tēs geneseōs teleistheisēs*] we speak of as being the nature of each thing' (1252 b32–3). The things that differentiate the adult from the child, language, reason, citizenship, are constitutive elements of human nature. Lacking these benefits, the child also lacks even the ability to be happy, nor can he be considered as exhibiting human nature, unless we allow him to do so 'potentially', or even, more dramatically, unless we envisage birth itself as the violent conjunction of a human soul with a body that it does not immediately control, and which temporarily inflicts on it its disorder and restlessness; this is what happens in Plato.[18] Epicurus' originality lay not so much in that he gave a normative meaning to the idea of nature (which had already been done before him, both in the name of an immoralism that had sophistic connexions[19] and, as a reaction to this, by certain moralists who had

---

[17] Cf. the Latin translation of this passage, which Rousseau put as rubric to his *Discours sur l'Origine de l'Inégalité*: *Non in depravatis, sed in his quae bene secundum naturam se habent, considerandum est quid sit naturale.*

[18] Aristotle often states that a child cannot be happy, and that no one in his senses would tolerate returning to childhood. Cf *EN* II 1100 a2, *EE* I 1215 b22, and many other quotations cited by Gauthier and Jolif (1959), II 1, pp. 75–6. We may, however, disagree with the latter when they assert that this abhorrence of childhood is peculiar to Aristotle, 'an intellectual who married late, a stranger to cradles until too late in life'; and there is no lack of texts that denigrate the state of childhood (cf. Plato, *Leg.* VII 792 a; Ps. Plato, *Axioch.* 366 d; Teles in Stobaeus, *Flor.* 34 72 Wachsmuth-Hense; Lucretius V 222–7; Augustine, *Conf.* I 8). On the fundamental disturbance produced, according to Plato, by the incarnation of the soul at birth, cf. *Phaed.* 81 c.83 d; *Tim.* 44 a; in *Leg.* VII 790 e, Plato brings out the fear that rules supreme at the roots of the childish state, born of 'a sort of evil disposition of the soul'. Marrou (1948), p. 202, puts forward an over-idyllic view of Greek childhood which could perhaps be qualified on this point.

[19] Cf. *Gorg.* 483c–484a, *Leg.* X 888e–890a.

attempted to counter this immoralism with a renewed summons to conform to nature),[20] as that he shifted the subject of the identification of what is 'natural'. Tell me what you were like in your cradle, and I will tell you what you are by nature: we can well imagine that this new criterion seemed shocking.[21]

Is the hedonist scandal a direct result of this first one? To help us decide, let us return to Torquatus' exposé. Immediately after describing the 'natural' pursuit and enjoyment of pleasure in the new-born child, he goes on to say:

(T2) Thus [*itaque*] he says there is no need to reason or dispute (to show) why [*quam ob rem*] pleasure should be sought [*expetenda*] and pain should be avoided [*fugiendus*]. He thinks these things are felt [*sentiri*] as fire is felt to be hot, snow to be cold, honey sweet; none of these things needs to be confirmed by subtle arguments: it is enough simply to point them out [*admonere*].

In contrast to (T1), which described infant behaviour in the indicative, (T2) at once catches our attention by introducing propositions in the gerundive (pleasure is *expetenda*, pain *fugiendus*). We notice at once that the verbs affected by this change are only the verbs of tendency, not the verbs of state. This allows us safely to assign a clear-cut imperative character to these gerundives: if, when he said that pleasure is *expetenda*, the Epicurean simply meant that it is desirable (susceptible of being an object of desire), nothing would stop him from saying also, in one way or another, that it is susceptible of being an object of enjoyment; if he did not do so, it is because he was giving an imperative meaning to his pronouncements, and he thought that it would be just meaningless to say that pleasure must be enjoyed, whereas it is not meaningless to say that it must be pursued.[22]

Having said this much, we realise next that it would be incorrect to say (whether in a critical way or just in a descriptive one) that the Epicurean claims to deduce, from a statement in the indicative (A), a statement in the imperative (B): he is careful to make clear that what follows from (A) is not (B), but is that (B) does not need to be demonstrated; and he adds that (B) is the object of an immediate intuition, identical to or comparable with sensory intuition.

---

[20] Cf. Speusippus in Clement of Alexandria, *Strom.* II 22 133 (=frag. 57 Lang, 101 Isnardi-Parente); Polemo in Cicero, *Fin.* II 34, IV 14. See also Dirlmeier (1937), pp. 22–5.

[21] Cf. *Fin.* II 33. A comment from Richard Sorabji helped me to a fuller appreciation of this point.

[22] The Greek texts Cicero used certainly had *haireton* (cf. the parallels in Sextus, *PH* III 194, *M* XI 96); but the Epicureans do not, it seems, draw the fine category-distinction that the Stoics developed between *haireton* and *haireteon* (*SVF* III 89, 91).

We might wonder if this does not contain a redundancy or a contradiction. Indeed, if (B) is the object of an immediate intuition, the direct result is that it need not be proved, and it is pointless to turn to (A) to convince yourself of the fact; conversely, if (A) is necessary to show that (B) does not need proof, (B) cannot be the object of an immediate intuition, which would remove this necessity.

The solution to this dilemma is to be sought in the rules of Epicurean canonics. The remarks of the Epicurean are addressed to a rational, civilised adult (this is shown by the simple fact that we may wonder if, in order to convince him of (B), we should put forward a rational argument, or whether a simple *admonitio* is enough); it is he who is thought to 'feel' that pleasure should be pursued, as he feels that fire is hot, and to conclude that this really is the case. Nevertheless, he cannot ignore his adult status; if he were inclined to forget it, the mere fact that his 'feeling' is expressed in linguistic terms, in the form of a judgment (*doxa*), would suffice to remind him. From that point on, without even having to query the reliability of the 'feeling', as criterion, he may ask if it is really the feeling that is expressed, pure and unadulterated, in his judgment. The notion of feeling unites (and assimilates) emotion (*pathos*), the criterion of value, and perception (*aisthesis*), the criterion of truth; now perception owes its value as a criterion to the fact that it is *alogos*, dumb and irrational;[23] the same is true of emotion. When it is expressed, is it really expressing itself? Perhaps the judgment pronounced by those who feel it is conditioned by the education they have had, by the influences in their lives so far, and by the society in which they live? The voices of authority are all around them, suggesting that hedonist convictions are the outcome of the relentless workings of a whole series of perverting forces ranging from nurses and teachers to poets and playwrights who take turns to impress these convictions first on the child, then on the adolescent, and finally on the adult.[24]

An observation of the new-born child enables us to eliminate precisely the hypothesis of a distortion of *pathos* in its conscious expression. Its function is not to base the authority of *pathos* on external evidence, which cannot play such a rôle, because it is quite without any emotive character[25] and because it refers to beings that, numerically and specifically speaking, are different from the being that feels this *pathos* and which is invited to trust it; it allows us to verify that raw impressions are not distorted by the judgment that expresses them. In the field of perception,

---

[23] Cf. Diogenes Laertius, x 31.
[24] Cf. Calcidius, note 6 above.
[25] Except in the special case of friendship, the sight of a being feeling pleasure does not seem to have been seen by Epicurus as a source of pleasure.

'close inspection' allows us to confirm a judgment that is 'awaiting confirmation';[26] in the field of practicalities, observing the child provides us with the equivalent of this experiment, because judgment plays no part in the child's make-up. If the adult has the same feeling as one he can attribute to the child, going by its behaviour, he is justified in seeing in it the product of a natural mechanism, and need not fear the intervention of some adventitious element in the genesis of his *doxa*. The indicative statement is therefore not the foundation of the imperative statement; it is confined to defining it and to authenticating its origins; it invalidates an attempt at invalidation by establishing that the *doxa* expresses unadulterated *pathos* and that it shares its source with practical truths.[27] Thus the Epicurean argument is free from redundancy or contradiction: observation of the child is not necessary to justify the value of emotion as criterion (so there is no contradiction); but it is necessary to see in the allure of pleasure, as felt by the adult, a legitimate application of the emotive criterion (so there is no redundancy).

II

In one sense, as we see, there is no 'cradle argument' in Epicureanism; the identification of pleasure with the sovereign good is founded not on any observation of the new-born child, but on adult feelings. Yet, in another sense, cradles do provide an 'argument'; thanks to them, the adult is justified in accepting the force of his feelings. This position sets up a delicate balance between a summons to intuition and a return to reasoning. It is hardly surprising that such a balance should have proved unstable, as we shall see if we investigate its subsequent history with both the partisans and the opponents of Epicureanism.

According to Torquatus himself (1 3 1), there are two distinct groups of Epicureans who consider that the justification of his ethics, as he has just presented it, is not satisfactory. The first group, disapproved of by Torquatus, do not think it sufficient to say that good and evil can be judged by perception (the fact that this is the only conclusion they retain from the preceding speech confirms that in their view the only rôle of the summons to the cradle is to be an auxiliary to perception). Their intention was not, however, to replace sensory intuition by a discursive proof; it was rather

---

[26] Cf. Epicurus, *Ep. Herod.* 38, KD 24; Diogenes Laertius, x 34.

[27] While the Cyrenaics thought that '*pathos* that affects us shows us nothing more than itself' (Sextus, *M* VII 194), Epicurus numbers *pathos* among the criteria *for truth* (D.L. x 3 1, quoting the *Kanōn*); pleasure is the judge of the objective good (cf. *Ep. Men.* 129), not of itself.

to replace sensory intuition by rational intuition. Making good use of the second criterion of Epicurean canonics, that is, *prolēpsis*,[28] they maintained that 'our souls contain, as if implanted in them by nature, a notion [*quasi naturalem atque insitam* [...] *notionem*] which makes us feel [*sentiamus*] that pleasure should be sought and pain rejected'. The object of this preconception is not clearly stated;[29] but its effect indicates that it plays the same part as perception did in the previous discussion, since it lets us grasp the same propositional truth as *pathos*, with the same immediacy. What benefit did the authors of this suggestion hope to gain? One might suppose that they were intent upon strengthening the intuitive character of hedonist principles. On one hand, preconception (at least as they see it) seems independent of any live experience of pleasure, in contrast to perception. On the other hand, more importantly, by emphasising the rational and intellectual nature (*animo etiam ac ratione*) of the criterion they are using, they are restricting its application to rational adults, and thus they are trying to convince us that there is no need to venture out on philosophical by-ways to justify our own intuition and no need to wonder if it is supported solely by our own natural sensibility or if it embodies traces of our cultural background; we are equipped with everything necessary to justify it. The cradle argument becomes pointless and vanishes; doubtless it introduced an element of discursiveness that seemed too powerful for the attempts to justify hedonism.

On the other hand, the second group of Epicureans that Torquatus mentions (and indeed approves of) consider that the argument sins by lack of discursiveness, thus preventing a successful reply to the opponents of Epicureanism: 'Others, with whom I agree, seeing many philosophers saying a great many things about the reasons why we must not reckon either pleasure among goods or pain among evils, think that we must not rely too heavily on the excellence of our cause and think that we must argue and expound with exactness and discuss pleasure and pain with carefully elaborated arguments.' Cicero does not reveal how they satisfied these requirements: Torquatus, in fact, reverts somewhat unexpectedly to Epicurus himself, whom he covers with praise ('inventor of the truth and, so to say, architect of the happy life'), instead of telling us how his disciples filled those gaps that they saw in his arguments. It seems that, to him, Epicurus' work was able to satisfy them, in the sense that he had given an explanation of how the anti-hedonist error arose, and that this explanation provided the most acceptable means of refuting this error.

---

[28] Cf. Diogenes Laertius x 31, 33–4.
[29] It may be the preconception of pleasure or (more likely) the *appetendum*.

Anti-hedonism works from this claim: in certain circumstances, rational adults avoid indulging in certain pleasures, and everyone approves of them for doing so. Epicurus allows this, but he denies that there is any reason to conclude that pleasure is not a good. A pleasure is never rejected because it is a pleasure, but because it brings with it painful consequences, consequences that can be foreseen rationally. If pleasure should not always be taken, *assumenda*, this does not mean that it should not always be sought, *expetenda*; quite the contrary, it is through hedonism that an adult refuses a pleasure. Certainly this argument does not establish that pleasure is the sovereign good; but it is understandable that it could appear more 'exact' (*accuratē*) than the cradle argument, in so far as it succeeded in reinterpreting in hedonist terms rational adult behaviour, which the opponents of pleasure attempted to muster on their side, and which they were well placed to put forward as the only pertinent factor when the character of the adult good was under discussion.

The two groups of Epicureans that Torquatus quotes had a symmetrical effect on the basic hedonist method, one favouring a purer intuitionism, the other a more rigorously argued discursiveness, and thus they confirmed the ambivalence of the initial position that they were trying to complete. Other diversions occur in the doxography, some connected with the method of argument, some with the empirical basis for the cradle argument.

On the first point, we might expect to see the complex version we have analysed ('(A) proves that (B) never needs demonstrating') being abbreviated and simplified to the point where it became something like: '(A) proves (B)'. This development can be traced in two stages. According to Diogenes Laertius (x 137): 'As a proof [*apodeixei*] that pleasure is the goal, Epicurus adduces [the fact] that animals, as soon as they are born, rejoice in [*euaresteisthai*] pleasure and dislike [*proskrouein*] pain, naturally [*phusikōs*] and independently of reason [*chōris logou*]. Thus it is purely emotionally [*autopathōs*] that we avoid pain.' In this version, the elements of Torquatus' version are readily recognisable, but juxtaposed and to some extent disconnected: the first statement presents the normative statement as if it were deduced directly from the descriptive statement;[30] the second restores to *pathos*, in all its purity, its rôle as a criterion;[31] but it is hard to see how the appeal to the cradle can be recon-

---

[30] The use of only the verbs of emotion *euaresteisthai* and *proskrouein* (cf. n. 12 above) doubtless mirrors his intention of avoiding a teleological interpretation. What indicates that pleasure is the end is not, basically at least, that living beings incline towards it rather than towards everything else, but rather that experience tells them that they enjoy it more than anything else.

[31] The adverb *autopathōs*, according to Usener (1977), p. 129, is only attested here.

ciled with the invocation to *pathos*. This last element disappears in the next stage, which can be illustrated by a doxographical passage in Sextus (*PH* III 194), which credits the Epicureans as a whole (without any apparent contrast with Epicurus himself) with the following argument: 'Hence also the Epicureans suppose themselves to have proved [*deiknunai nomizousi*] that pleasure is naturally choiceworthy [*hairetēn*]; for the living beings, they say, as soon as they are born, when still unperverted [*adiastropha*], seek after [*hormān*] pleasure and avoid [*ekklinein*] pains.' It is only at this level of extreme simplification that the argument moves openly from 'is' to 'ought'.

If the line of argument, subtle at first, grows simpler, the empirical basis of the argument, succinct at the outset, grows more elaborate. As I mentioned above, Epicurus does not seem to have made a close connection, on the causal and on the chronological levels, between the experience of pleasure and the pursuit of pleasure. Does the experience come first, and does it constitute a basis on which a behavioural system may gradually be constructed? Or is the pursuit of pleasure, rather, instinctive, preceding all actual experience? Here as in other areas, Epicurus does not feel it incumbent on him to distinguish between the innate and the acquired.[32] He was in any case in no position to do so, because he was borrowing from Democritus the idea that the embryo is fed by the mouth, in the mother's belly, taking nourishment from some form of teat present in the womb: 'That is why, from birth, the child takes the breast with his mouth' (Aetius V 16 1=Usener fr. 332). Its behaviour outside the womb, apparently spontaneous, derives from its experience inside the womb of oral sustenance and of, we may assume, the concomitant pleasure;[33] but whether this behaviour in the womb is itself innate or acquired is lost in the mists of a time and place inaccessible to us. This uncertainty seemed a hurdle to 'some members of the Epicurean school', if we are to believe Sextus (*M* XI

[32] We are familiar with the disputes aroused by the conflict between the empiricist theory of the genesis of *prolēpseis*, which is put forward in D.L. x 33 and widely accepted by commentators, and the apparent adherence to the innate theory in Cic. *ND* I 43–4, taken as gospel by DeWitt (1954), pp. 142–50. This inconsistency seems to demand a choice; the Epicurean doctrine, however, does in fact ignore or deny its terms (cf. Kleve (1963), pp. 23–4, and my review of this work in Brunschwig (1964), pp. 352–6).

[33] The continuity between the child's life in the womb and his first moments of life outside it is a basic theme of Greek view of childhood (cf. for example Aristotle *GA* v 778 b20ff.). The idea is both realised and supported by the customs of child-rearing, which leave the child for his first seven years of life inside the house, in the care of women, mother, wet-nurse (*titthē*), or nurse-maid (*trophos*). There are, it is true, some quite lively descriptions of what today we should call birth-trauma (cf. Philo, *De opif. mund.* 161; Sextus, *M* II 96; Calcidius *in Tim.* 165=*SVF* III 229); but these texts also bear witness, with or without approval, to the attempts of accepted methods of upbringing to minimise this trauma, in particular by warm or hot baths.

96): in order to counter any objections of a sceptical nature, they recast the cradle argument by inserting into it an observation drawn from a behavioural phenomenon, the first cry of the child, which takes place in the very first moments of life outside the womb and which cannot owe anything to an earlier preparation, because it is the result of encountering a cold environment quite foreign to the experience of the new-born child. These Epicureans, Sextus says, 'are wont to argue that the living being avoids pain and pursues pleasure naturally and without teaching [*phusikōs kai adidaktōs*]; thus when it is born, and is not as yet a slave to opinions, it cries and screams as soon as it is smitten by the air's unwonted chill. But if it naturally has an inclination for pleasure and a disinclination for pain, pain is a thing naturally avoided by it and pleasure a thing desirable.' The citing of this immediate reaction to a new stimulus allows us to eliminate not only the cultural factor, but also that of discovery by trial and error; here we are as close to the notion of instinctive behaviour as we can get. But this bonus on the side of observational precision and relevance is outweighed by a disadvantage: the information we can glean from the instinctive behaviour of the infant loses its relevance when we come to the adult, moulded not only by society but also by his own experience. The text shows traces of this redress of balance: Sextus' Epicureans stress that it is for the new-born child itself (*autōi*) that, by nature, pain is to be avoided and pleasure to be pursued. All in all, they probably lose more than they gain by the change.

In principle, however, they were right to believe that the Epicurean version of the cradle argument deserved to be reinforced where its empirical basis was concerned. On some important points, the description of infant behaviour allowed imprecise areas which the opponents of the school were not slow to exploit. This, it would seem, is the conclusion to be drawn from the discussion instigated by Cicero, in Book II of the *De finibus*, on the question of the famous distinction between pleasure in motion (kinetic) and static pleasure (katastematic). Epicurus had apparently seen no need to make clear which of these two forms of pleasure the child sought by nature. The text, unfortunately, is not very clear on this point, and we must examine it more carefully. The only objection launched against the cradle argument (II 31–2) consists precisely in an attempt to extract from Epicurus an answer to this question: which of the two pleasures, static or kinetic, is the one that the example of the 'wailing child' allows us to designate as the sovereign good? The question is put in the most open terms (*stante an movente*, picked up later by *si stante, . . . si movente*); if Epicurus' text gave a clear-cut answer to it, this phrasing could not be accounted for. It is only from the Epicureans, at the end of relentless questioning (*quod tamen dicitis*), that we finally wrest a reply: it is kinetic pleasure that the child pursues. This is a reply that is both disastrous and inevitable for Epicureanism, at least in Cicero's view; for while he would not have objected at all if the Epicureans had opted for the other possible reply, their actual answer not only laid them open to the usual reproach of immorality (*nulla turpis voluptas erit, quae praetermittenda sit*), but also, more importantly, landed them in a contradiction; the cradle argument falls down if kinetic pleasure is what the child pursues, while static pleasure (here identified with absence of pain) is the supreme pleasure; the pleasure 'from which nature starts' is not the same as that put forward as the sovereign good. But this disastrous reply is, simultaneously, the only possible one, because Epicurus would lose all his credibility if he claimed that children and animals are attracted merely by the absence of pain; this negative pleasure cannot 'move the appetite of the mind' and does not possess sufficient 'force' (*ictus*) to shake the living being from its inertia.

So far Cicero's position is clear: Epicurus did not answer the question, but he could not have answered differently from the Epicureans. What follows in the text, however, blurs the image: 'That is why [*itaque*] Epicurus, in order to show that pleasure is sought by nature, always makes use of the fact [*semper hoc utitur*] that it is kinetic pleasure which attracts infants and animals and not the static pleasure which consists simply in freedom from pain.' It seems now that, contrary to first impressions, Epicurus has explicitly designated kinetic pleasure as the object of infant desires, and must himself have put forward, unambiguously and repeatedly, the very reply that we hoped for in vain at the beginning. How are we to resolve this problem? The simplest solution is to accuse Cicero, or his source, of having 'grossly distorted' Epicurus' thought;[34] but this would foist upon him, gratuitously, a particularly weak polemic position. We could also (bearing in mind the reproaches of 'tergiversation' directed in the *Tusculans* III 41 at the author of the *Peri telous*) assume that Epicurus' text was making a belated and reluctant reply to the question he is faced with; but if there is some excuse for tergiversation before embarking on a paradoxical thesis, like the identification of pleasure with the sovereign good, there is none when the thesis is not paradoxical, like the identification of kinetic pleasure with the object of infant desires. Short of

---

[34]　Cf. Rist (1972), pp. 104–6. According to him, it goes without saying that the new-born child wants the quiet and *ataraxia* provided by food and clothing; the first impulse assigned to it by Epicurus can only be the pursuit of a pleasure that consists solely in being neither hungry, thirsty, nor cold. Nothing but polemic distortion could burden Epicurus with the absurdity of deducing the identity of the sovereign good and *katastematic* pleasure, from the natural inclination of children and animals towards *kinetic* pleasure.

emending Cicero's text, which is hardly to be envisaged,[35] the most plausible explanation seems to me, despite first impressions, to reject the idea that Cicero's sentence credits Epicurus with an argument that is expressly based on kinetic pleasure. His method could be paraphrased as follows: in fact, only kinetic pleasure attracts the child; this is why, when he constantly reverts to the cradle argument, Epicurus relies on this very fact, even if he does not say so in so many words. The text as a whole then becomes compatible with my initial hypothesis: in the version he had given of the cradle argument, Epicurus had not identified the form of pleasure that he claimed children desired, thus bequeathing to his disciples the job of clarification and to his opponents the opportunity for criticism.

Unless I am much mistaken (or too gullible), all the documentation on Epicurus' treatment of the cradle argument can be neatly arranged as follows: the original version, in so far as it can be reconstructed from what Cicero says, allows us to understand, by what it contains and what it omits, the various additions that the Epicureans saw fit to introduce, the alterations it underwent in the course of the doxographical tradition, and the objections levelled at it by the opponents of Epicureanism.

III

Let us now turn to the Stoics. Cato's account in Cicero (*Fin.* III 16) also begins with a 'cradle argument' without mentioning a particular author:

Those whose views I share hold that as soon as a living being is born [*simulatque natum sit animal*] – for this must be the starting-point – it is appropriated to itself [*ipsum sibi conciliari*] and led to preserve itself [*commendari ad se conservandum*] and to love its own constitution [*suum statum*] and those things which preserve its constitution, and to be alienated from its death [*alienari autem ab interitu*] and from those things which seem to lead to death. They prove [*probant*] that this is so from the fact that (a₁) before either pleasure or pain has affected them, infants [*parvi*] seek what preserves them and (a₂) reject the opposite, something which would not happen unless (a′₁) they loved their own constitution and (a′₂) feared death. But (b) it cannot be the case that they desire anything unless (b′₁) they have a sense of themselves [*sensum sui*] and (b′₂) thereby love themselves. Hence it must be realised that the principle has been drawn from self-love [*principium ductum esse a se diligendo*].

[35] At first I was tempted to read the variant *utatur* that replaces *utitur* in the BE MSS.; this would mean that instead of *stating* that Epicurus ascribes the pursuit of kinetic pleasure to children, Cicero's text is *exhorting* him to do so, because he risks overlooking the psychological characteristics that accompany this type of pleasure. It is due to the thoughtful comments of P. Donini and P. Y. Chanut, whose arguments are individual but in agreement, that I abandoned this hypothesis.

The first thing that strikes us in this extract is that, if we are indeed dealing again with a 'cradle argument', where the observed data are carefully distinguished from the conclusions that follow from them, these conclusions have nothing to do with the sovereign good; it does not figure here at all.[36] If it remains necessary for the 'starting-point' of ethics to be the observation of the child (by virtue of an incidentally unexplained necessity), this observation does not provide by itself any truly ethical conclusion; the drift of the argument, briefly summarised, passes from the observable behaviour of the child to the combination of tendencies, ideas, and emotions which appears as the necessary condition of this behaviour. Since the Stoic moralist does not claim to draw an ethical conclusion from his initial observations, we may assume that he did not conceal this conclusion in his premises and may expect him to prove an observer who is attentive and, provisionally at least, disinterested.

There are however excellent reasons for expecting something quite different. Diogenes Laertius (VII 85) bequeaths to us another version of the first steps of Stoic ethics, explicitly borrowed from Chrysippus, where *a priori* argument is much more important than empirical data:

[The Stoics] say that a living being's first impulse is to preserve itself, nature appropriating this [*oikeiousēs hautōi*], as Chrysippus says in the first book of the *Peri telōn*, where he asserts that for every living being the first object of appropriation [*prōton oikeion*] is its own constitution and its knowledge thereof. For it was not likely [*eikos*] that nature would have made an animal inappropriate to itself [*allotriōsai*], nor that, having created it, it would have made it neither inappropriate nor appropriate. The only remaining possibility, then, is to say [*apoleipetai toinun legein*] that having constituted it, it makes it appropriate to itself; for in this way [*houtō gar*] it both wards off what harms it and embraces what is appropriate to it.

If we set aside the final sentence, we are faced with a train of reasoning by elimination, based on the enumeration of all possible attitudes of nature towards the beings it produces, and also on the improbable character of all the corresponding hypotheses except one. Without even a glance at a natural being (and, all the more, without charting the first moments of its life) we may assert that nature was unable, unless it contradicted itself, to endow it with hostility or even indifference to itself. This process suggests that the problem is not envisaged as one which can be solved by direct observation, either because the assertion to be proved is universal and

---

[36] The *telos* will only be reached, working from the *archē* of natural tendencies, at the end of the 'passage' movement, a process summed up by the famous metaphor of the letter of recommendation (*Fin.* III 23). On the central role of the concept of passage in Stoicism, cf. Goldschmidt (1953), pp. 55–60.

necessary, and we assume that experience would be unable to guarantee an assertion of this type, or because we presuppose that the relationships that a being has with itself are not open to external observation. It is striking indeed that at the end of the argument, once the assertion of *oikeiōsis*, which bears on the relationship a living being has *with itself* has been proved rationally, the text mentions, as confirmation, the choice of the useful and the harmful that it makes, visibly this time, among the *objects* around it. *Oikeiōsis* therefore seems to be demonstrable in two forms: rationally, *qua* relationship to oneself, and through its effects, *qua* creator of relations with the environment; but it is the first proof that is of prime importance here.[37]

Can the version of the *De finibus* be analysed in the light of these distinctions? It clearly reveals a proof through effects, and does not contain reasoning by elimination. But the distinction between premisses arrived at by observation, which ought to bear on our behaviour towards other people and objects, and the consequences that are rationally deduced from these premisses, which ought to bear on our relations to ourselves, is not as clear as one might wish. The theory is stated before the proof: it consists largely of statements bearing on oneself (the living being is appropriate *to itself*, inclined to *preserve itself*, to love *its own constitution*, to reject *its own death*), but consists also of some statements bearing on its relation to other things (it is inclined to love the things that preserve its own constitution, to reject those that threaten it with death); nothing suggests (except possibly, very inconclusively, the order of clauses within the sentence) that the first must be seen as more fundamental and recondite than the second. As for the *proof* (going from *id ita esse sic probant*) it clearly rests on the observation of the child's behaviour with regard to other things around him that preserve him (a_1) or harm him (a_2) (the restriction of the field of observation to the child is expressly intended to make it clear that the tendencies under discussion precede any experience of pleasure or pain, although there is no indication what precautions the observer should take to avoid any risk of error or uncertainty in this area). But the method of interpreting these observations is not plain. Twice, the text ventures to deduce necessary conditions without which the observed facts could not happen (cf. *quod non fieret nisi* and *fieri non posset* [...] *nisi*). These two successive applications of the same method (separated by *autem*) cannot however be interpreted in the light

---

[37] In spite of their connexions, it is important not to confuse the idea of *oikeiōsis* in relation to ourselves, which can, among others, be proved by its effect on the relations the living being has with its external environment, and the idea of *oikeiōsis* in relation to beings, or things, that are external to us. On the connexions between the relational and reflexive uses of the word *oikeios* and its associated terms, cf. the interesting discussions between Görgemanns (1983) and Inwood (1983).

of the schema that first comes to mind, to wit: P would not be possible without Q (i.e., if P, then Q) and Q, in its turn, would not be possible without R (i.e., if Q, then R); in fact, there is no identity between the consequent in the first conditional and the antecedent in the second; the consequent in the first conditional is that children love their own constitution and fear death $(a'_1 + a'_2)$; the antecedent on which the second conditional rests is that they are seeking something (b). The true relation between the two conditionals is that in the first instance we are identifying the conditions of the fact that children seek what preserves them and reject what harms them $(a_1 + a_2)$ and that in the second instance we are identifying the conditions of the simple fact that they are seeking something (b). In other words, we are trying to identify the conditions of a series of facts that do not vary but that are described in two different ways: firstly a complete description that refers to the desire and its object, then an abbreviated description that only retains the desire and does away with the object.

The text emerges, therefore, at first sight, as an analysis of the different conditions first for the desire for the thing that preserves (a_1) and then for this same desire, seen solely as a desire *simpliciter* (b). The logic of this operation would demand that there should be a difference between the conditions that corresponds to the difference between the facts, and which allows us to give an account of it. We might for example say that a being that desires something *simpliciter* must be able to imagine his own state and indeed to be aware *that* he is lacking something without which his state cannot be normal; then to attempt emotionally to fill this gap in order to restore the normal state. A being that desires a *specific* object must, furthermore, be aware of *what* is lacking and must therefore know in one way or another that such and such an object is suitable to fill this gap. It is therefore plausible to put forward a certain type of relationship to himself as the condition of a desire *simpliciter*, and a certain type of relationship to the outside world as the condition of a specific desire. But our text only half fulfils this expectation. It all goes as expected as far as the second conditional is concerned: the necessary condition of a desire *simpliciter* (b) is constituted by two reflexive relations, the awareness of self (b'_1) and the love of self (b'_2); the only deviation from our expectations is the link set up by the conjunction *eoque*, without apparent reason for our purposes, between awareness of self and love of self. But this no longer holds in the first conditional. What is offered as the condition of specific desire, directed at what preserves us and (in a negative way) at what harms us, is not a representation of the object, a foreknowledge of the world, but an emotional relationship with ourselves, the love of our own constitution (a'_1) and the fear of our own death (a'_2).

We may at least conjecture that the cause of this deviation lies in the irruption of a second line of reasoning which could have dislocated the ordinary development of the first. This second line would be inspired by the idea that a desire bearing on an object X can have as a condition a less overt and more basic desire for another object Y; for example, the desire for what preserves presupposes the desire for preservation itself (which is provided by what preserves), that is, the desire to maintain or restore the normal state; this desire to maintain oneself in an optimum state assumes in its turn that the agent loves himself. This line of reasoning corresponds to the first conditional of our text, which works from the desire for what preserves and which bases this desire on the subject's love for his own constitution, in other words, on his desire to maintain this constitution in or restore it to its optimum state. But the text does not see this operation through to the end: it does not deduce love of self from love of our own constitution; this last (a'_1) does not form the object of a new search for conditions. On the other hand, love of self reappears at the end of the argument (b'_2), this time in conjunction not with another kind of love, but with a representation, the feeling or awareness of self (b'_1), that appears as its condition (*eoque*).

This last stage heralds, it seems to me, the appearance in our text of a third line of reasoning, different from the two previous ones: it consists in isolating from a given emotional phenomenon the conditions of representation it assumes. The desire for an object has as necessary condition a representation of this object; no being can love itself without some awareness of itself. This method of arguing could in theory be applied to each of the emotional phenomena referred to in the text as a whole; if it is only put into effect with regard to self-awareness (which thus appears as the most basic condition of all those we returned to when discussing observable data), this is probably because, within the ethical barriers that form the boundaries of the excerpt as a whole, representative facts are not relevant. Rather, it is tendencies and emotions which are the motive force of practical behaviour. So we may understand the sentence, obscure as it is, which does duty for a conclusion: 'Hence it must be realised that the principle [sc. of Stoic ethics] is drawn from self-love.' The comment that the latter still presupposes self-awareness is one that may interest the psychologist but is not really relevant for a moralist.

To sum up, it seems to me that in this text observable data are subjected to three distinct types of treatment whose effects are interwoven in a complex way: an *abstractive analysis* (which, working from the obvious desire for what preserves, isolates desire *simpliciter* in order to extract its proper conditions), an *homonymous regression* (which passes from the desire for

what preserves to another desire, deeper and more fundamental, for preservation itself), and a *heteronymous regression* (which designates a representative fact, namely self-awareness, as the condition of an emotional
fact, the love of self).

To those who may object that this analysis shatters the unity of Cicero's
text, giving it an unconvincingly composite appearance, I would counter
with an argument that could back up the hypothesis of a concealed strati-
fication in this text. According to Alexander of Aphrodisias,

> the Stoics, though not all of them, say that the living being itself is the first thing
> appropriate to it [*prōton oikeion*] (for every living being, as soon as it is born, is
> appropriated to itself – and so too are men). Others, who are thought to be more
> subtle, and to give a sharper account of the matter, say that as soon as we are
> born, we are appropriated to our own constitution and preservation (*De anima*
> 150 28 Bruns = *SVF* III 183).[38]

Now the account of the Stoic theory, in Cicero, juxtaposes without reser-
vation the two statements that Alexander attributes to two different
groups of authors: appropriation to oneself (*animal ipsum sibi conciliari*,
cf. *zōion pros hauto oikeiousthai*) and concern for one's own preservation
(*commendari ad se conservandum et ad suum statum* [...] (*diligendum*),
cf. *pros tēn sustasin kai tērēsin oikeiōsthai*).[39] If the account of this thesis
is an amalgam, it is legitimate to suppose that the account of the argument
is one too.

If we now follow the line of thought that runs from Chrysippus, as summarised by Diogenes Laertius, to Cicero's sources, we discover that the
Stoic theory of *oikeiōsis* has changed its method of justification: the *a
priori* proof, founded on the logic of the behaviour of Nature towards its
products, has been replaced by a proof by observable effects. This development certainly seems to have continued subsequently, and it is in the
later Stoic texts that we come across the greatest number of subtle, sometimes indeed acute, remarks about child psychology. Such a development
is natural enough, for two reasons at least. On one hand, the Stoics found
themselves obliged to defend their own interpretation of child behaviour

---

[38] This 'subtlety' might arise from some reluctance to use the notion of *oikeiōsis* in a purely
reflexive sense. On the secondary, and even paradoxical, nature of this use, see Görgemanns (1983) again, p. 183.

[39] I do not think one can with any certainty say as much for Chrysippus' version in book I of
his *Peri telōn*, quoted by Diogenes Laertius, VII 85 (*pace* Inwood (1983), p. 192). The
quotation from Chrysippus perhaps only includes the phrase introduced by *legōn*, which
only refers to *oikeiōsis* as regards our own constitution; the references to *oikeiōsis* to ourselves, which precede and follow this clause, might not be taken textually from the same
source.

against the hedonists', which was the most obvious and widespread (even among those moralists who were opposed to pleasure). On the other hand, their theory involved certain paradoxical consequences, in particular the attribution to the child of a sort of self-awareness that should be encouraged if possible.

No immediate riposte was discovered to the hedonist reading of infant behaviour. We can pass quickly over the stratagem that consists in rejecting the premiss on account of the immorality of its consequences; Cato, who does not fail to avail himself of it, seems to emphasise that the idea is his own: 'Most Stoics[40] do not think that pleasure should be placed among the natural principles. For my part, I agree with them wholeheartedly, for if nature is thought to have placed pleasure among the things which are first desired, many vicious consequences follow' (*Fin.* III 17). Another solution, less crude, was to maintain that the child pursues what preserves him without having experienced the pleasure that accompanies its acquisition, or at least that he pursues it for the utility that it necessarily involves, and not for the delight that is associated with it. But how is either of these points to be proved? Cato, who adopts the first approach (*ante quam voluptas aut dolor attigerit*) does not seem to realise that it is possible to claim that no interval of time separates the beginning of life from the experience of pleasure and pain; besides, even if such an interval did exist, which the astute philosopher could exploit to devote himself to the requisite observations, it would hardly further the Stoic cause, because his enemies could always counter that the child instinctively anticipates this experience of pleasure, and that it is still plausible that this is what he is pursuing. We will therefore take refuge in the second solution; but this one is scarcely more impregnable. The Stoics, according to Diogenes Laertius (VII 86) say that 'it is false that the first impulse of animals is towards pleasure. For they say that pleasure comes (if it comes at all) as something supervenient [*epigennēma*] when nature by itself seeks and attains what is fitting for its constitution.' But the more we insist on the invariable link (even if it were 'supervenient') between the activity in accordance with nature and the pleasure that flows from it, the harder it is to be able to determine whether natural tendencies are directed towards that activity or towards that pleasure; why should not the living being aim at the *epigennēma* of pleasure as his true goal, to be reached via the acts or the objects that cannot fail to provide it? In the end, the Stoics are seen to be arguing, paradoxically, that behaviour is natural when it achieves a pleasure without being useful; this is why Cato (III 17), intent on proving

[40] This restriction might be justified by texts like Sextus, *M* II 73, and Aulus Gellius, *NA* XII 5, 8.

that acts of intellectual comprehension (*katalēpseis*) are naturally pursued for themselves, turns once again to children (children, it must be admitted, no longer in the cradle) to point out that we see them delight (*delectari*) in making discoveries by themselves, relying on their own reason, even if they do not gain anything by it (*etiamsi eorum nihil intersit*). It had been suggested, barely a page earlier, that they pursue what is useful to them (*salutaria*) without taking account of the experience of pleasure; here we see them now described as instinctively going in for an activity which brings them pleasure, independently of any usefulness. This pleasure is taken as an indication that the activity concerned is adopted for itself (*propter se*); but why should we not just as well conclude that it is adopted for the pleasure it provides?

What the Stoics had to discover in order to win the point that was important for them was not natural behaviour that was pleasant without being useful, but just the contrary. Does it happen that a child will adopt spontaneously a type of behaviour that is not accompanied by pleasure, or even that is accompanied by pain? Seneca attests (*Ep. mor.* 121 8) that in the end the Stoics put their finger on an observation that could justifiably be seen as crucial; it is true that it is not relevant to the newborn child, since it has to do with learning to stand upright and to walk, but these activities are still early ones, and precede the development of reason, as they should if they are to be used as an argument. This is how Seneca describes them: 'A child who is trying to stand upright, and is getting used to moving, immediately tries to test his strength; he falls down and gets up again, crying, until through pain he has managed to do what nature demands.' We may think, of course, that this description is noticeably distorted by its didactic purpose; the sorrows of a setback are unfairly emphasised in contrast to the joys of success, nor is anything said about the potential rôles of imitation, the help of the family environment, and its support when the child is learning to walk. But if pain is not an inhibiting factor, we may claim, in the interests of symmetry, that pleasure is not an inspiring one; the acquisition of new behaviour does not seem to be learning, properly speaking, but rather the effect of a maturing process that is purely endogenous. Nature fulfils its aims and obtains what it wants, both in the case when her demands bring pleasure as a reward and in the crucial case where they do not.

Letter 121, looking at it now as a whole, is also a central text as regards the second line of reasoning that I have just referred to: namely the reinforcement of the arguments that relate to the paradoxical attribution of a kind of self-awareness to the child (and to the animal). The whole letter is indeed devoted to a thorough investigation of the following question:

'Do living beings have the sensation of their own constitution?' (*constitutionis suae sensus*). It seems to me that several points should be brought out here.

(1) The moral bearing of this question is, at the beginning of the letter, the subject of a thoughtful and subtle discussion (which contrasts with the obscurity of Cicero's treatment of it).[41] To his correspondent, who objects that such a problem has no connexion with morals, intended as they are to improve behaviour,[42] Seneca allows that the connexion is fairly remote (*paulo remotiora*, 5); but ethics is not only composed of what will improve behaviour (cf. 1), but also encapsulates the physical study of human nature and of its goals ('How will you know what behaviour should be adopted unless you discover what is best for man and examine his nature? You will only understand what you should do and what you should avoid when you have learnt what your nature requires', 3). In the rest of the letter, the adult moral agent, to whom we direct prescriptions, is always carefully distinguished from the child and the animal, the subjects of the description (cf. especially 12); the question under discussion can and must be treated in an autonomous way, without its truly moral connotations, which are not referred to, having any part to play in its solution.

(2) The precise theme of the letter is the feeling living beings have about their own constitution. The idea of constitution is explained by a technical definition not found anywhere else; however, its authenticity seems proved by the terminology: constitution is 'the regent part of the soul related in a certain way to the body' (10).[43] Awareness of our own consti-

---

[41] At the beginning of his letter, Seneca quotes Posidonius and Archedemus as justification; but this seems to have more bearing on the relevance of the query about morals than on the specific content of the answer to it in the letter as a whole (we should note that the first paragraph is the only part of this letter to figure as *testimonium* in Edelstein-Kidd (1972), p. 26 = T 82). It is in any case hard to see a connexion, as much as regards method as content, between the theories set out in Seneca's letter and Posidonius' position on the natural tendencies of the child as they are put forward in Galen, *De dogm. Hipp. et Plat.* v 459–65, pp. 437–44 Müller (=Frag. 169 Edelstein-Kidd). This position consists in crediting children with three successive *oikeiōseis*, the first towards pleasure (the only one retained by Epicurus), the second towards 'victory', the third towards 'the beautiful' (which Chrysippus would allegedly have assigned to children 'from the beginning'). This construction is plainly intended to put Epicurus and Chrysippus on an equal footing, to re-introduce Plato's tripartite division of the soul, and thus to foreshadow the rehabilitation of the 'ancient philosophers'. As it deals with the whole development of the child right up to adolescence, like the texts on Antiochus, I consider it to be outside the scope of this article.

[42] Lucilius' objections (1) seem to have been provoked by previous letters that have not survived, where Seneca had already tackled the question of *oikeiōsis* in animals (18).

[43] *Principale animi quodam modo se habens erga corpus.* We have no trouble in identifying here a cumulative summary of the four Stoic 'categories' (*hupokeimenon poion pros ti pōs echon*).

tution is a complex idea, with a clearcut role to play as distinct from, on the one hand, forms of awareness directed at other things than our constitution, and on the other hand, forms of relationship to our own constitution that are distinct from awareness. The feeling for our own constitution, whose specific object is the presence of the soul in the body viewed as a whole, is separate from both the awareness of its own parts,[44] limbs and organs equipped with their individual functions (the latter, apparent in instinctive behaviour, acts as a sign of the former, cf. 6 and 9), and also distinct, it would appear, from self-awareness proper, that is from the awareness that the soul, or its major part, has of itself (cf. 12, where a parallel, though not an identification, is drawn between the feeling that *we* have of our *soul* and the feeling that *all living beings* have of their *constitution*);[45] *a fortiori* this awareness, which nowadays we should call proprioceptive, is distinct from the exterioceptive apprehension of useful or harmful objects, which is described further on (19). From another point of view, the feeling of one's own constitution, as a vague representation, is distinct both from a clearcut and intellectually articulated knowledge of this same object (cf. 11) and from the living being's attachment to its own constitution, which is not a representation, but a tendency, a guiding principle of our conduct, which is referred to in the classical terminology of the Latin versions of the theory of *oikeiōsis* (cf. *conciliari, commendat, commissus,* 14–18).

(3) This conceptual development is accompanied by a refined methodology. Seneca's efforts are directed at drawing a distinction between observable signs and the inferences that follow, at adjusting very precisely these inferences to these signs, and at listing rival hypotheses and the reasons for excluding them. We might look at, for example, the formula adopted (19) to show that animals have an understanding of what is useful or harmful to them: 'This is what appears from the fact that, if they possessed it, they would do nothing more [than what they do in fact do]' (*Ep.* 121 19). In this context, I have not come across any other examples of such concern to put forward a hypothesis, not just as *necessary* (cf. *fieri non posset nisi* in Cicero) but also as *sufficient* relative to the phenomenon it is setting out to explain. In Cicero's formula, the character of the expla-

---

[44] This *oikeiōsis* towards our own parts, as distinct from *oikeiōsis* towards ourselves, appeared in a formula which according to Plutarch (*Stoic. rep.* 1038b), Chrysippus reiterated in 'every book on physics and ethics' till his readers became bored with it. 'We have from birth an *oikeiōsis* to ourselves, to our parts and to our offspring.' This last item, so out of place for the moment of birth, makes me wonder if Plutarch has not conflated several different quotations.

[45] Cf. the parallel: *Qualis ad nos [pervenerit] animi nostri sensus, quamvis naturam eius ignoremus ac sedem, talis ad omnia animalia constitutionis suae sensus est.*

natory hypothesis must make it impossible to assume less than it does; in Seneca's, the hypothesis must further be such as to make it unnecessary to assume more than it does. As for the rival hypotheses, they are often cited as interventions from some anonymous detractor or in anticipation of a reaction from Lucilius; could not behaviour thought to be instinctive be explained differently, for example as a process of learning comparable to that which is found in the arts, whose ease and rightness it shares (5–6), or as a process of trial and error, controlled by experience of suffering and of danger (7, 19), or by imitating other members of the same species (23), or even simply by chance (20)? Seneca counters all these hypotheses with behavioural traits in children and animals which, he claims, invalidate them, and which figure instead as criteria for innate characteristics; to the classic criteria of the immediate mastery of behaviour (7, 20), of its precedence over all other experience (19), he adds that it is fixed in time (20) and identical in all individual members of the species (20, 23).

(4) *Letter 121* is also the repository of the only discussion to have survived on the problem of the identity of the *constitutio* through time (14ff.). The way here lay between Scylla and Charybdis; if we interpret *constitutio* as unchanging throughout all periods of human life, it is indeed difficult not to see rationality as one of its essential ingredients; but then we should credit the child as naturally possessing a *constitutio* which is not yet proper to it; if, on the other hand, we assign a different *constitutio* to each age, we run the risk of denying their owner any consistent nature. Seneca solves this problem ingeniously by using the distinction between *oikeiōsis* to oneself and *oikeiōsis* to one's own constitution. Instead of juxtaposing the two notions indiscriminately (like Cicero), or suggesting substituting the second for the first (like the 'subtler ones' quoted by Alexander of Aphrodisias), he keeps them both and incorporates them both into a general pattern. Each age possesses its specific *constitutio*, which is provided with a particular *conciliatio* (*omnes ei constitutioni conciliantur in qua sunt*, 15); but the *form* of this *conciliatio* remains invariable, and it is this that allows us to refer to permanent *oikeiōsis* by the individual to himself (*non enim puerum mihi aut juvenem aut senem, sed me natura commendat*, 16).

It is, I think, this type of remark that suggests that *Letter 121* makes an important step forward, both theoretical and methodological, in the handling of the notion of *oikeiōsis*. This idea is confirmed if we compare it with a later text, the *Ethikē Stoicheiōsis* of the Stoic philosopher Hierocles,[46] where I think I can identify a sort of disequilibrium in the economy

---

[46] This text of the 2nd century A.D. has been edited by von Arnim in 1906, from Pap. Berl. 9780. In addition to von Arnim's introduction, I have found the following helpful: Poh-

of the doctrine of *oikeiōsis*, as much as regards content as structure; between the various notions that make up the doctrine, and also between the various methodological devices that he resorts to in order to justify them, the links are shattered, become unsuitable or irrelevant; the different elements fall apart, like a necklace whose stones still sparkle with a peculiar brilliance, even though the string has broken. An analysis of some individual points will help me to bolster up this judgment.

Hierocles' treatise revolves round the theory of *oikeiōsis*; from the outset he asserts that the best point of departure when teaching the basic elements of ethics is to consider the *prōton oikeion* of living beings (1, 1–2); the later part of the text, increasingly fragmentary and corrupt, contains the debris of a commentary on the various forms of social *oikeiōsis* (9, 3ff.). The general shape of the commentary is based on the difference between the two characteristic properties of living beings, sensation and inclination (1, 31–3); in keeping with this distinction, Hierocles sets out to demonstrate separately that the living being perceives himself[47] and loves himself; the link is made at 6, 24ff., a passage unfortunately mutilated at several vital points. The order in which he establishes these two notions, *first* the one dealing with our perception of ourselves and *then* the one dealing with our attachment to ourselves, implies that we are abandoning the plausible principle that states that any feeling assumes a representation of the object involved. We are, rather, out to prove *directly* that living beings perceive themselves; the difficulty and the fascination of this exercise are increased by the way in which Hierocles couches his theory in this explicitly reflexive form (cf. 1, 37–9; 6, 22–4), instead of allowing living beings the feeling for their own constitution, which is more apparent by observing their external behaviour.[48]

The drawback to this approach is that the link between self-perception and self-love has to be forged in a new way. Hierocles solves this problem by cleverly adapting the reasoning by elimination that we have already met in Chrysippus (Diogenes Laertius VII 85). He states that self-representation, like any representation, is necessarily accompanied by some feeling, positive, negative, or neutral, and he concludes that the first

---

lenz (1940), Giusta (1964–7), Pembroke (1971), Inwood (1983) and (1984), the latter kindly sent to me by the author in advance of publication.

[47] Hierocles seems to use the terms *aisthēsis, sunaisthēsis* and *antilēpsis* almost interchangeably throughout his work. Like Seneca (*Ep.* 121 12–13), he only sees a difference in quality, not of nature, between the 'obscure', 'confused', and 'indeterminate' *aisthēsis* which children and animals possess themselves, and the adult version, 'clear', 'exact', and 'articulate'.

[48] The idea of *sustasis* appears in various remarks bearing on *oikeiōsis* (6, 52–3; 7, 49–50); but the connexion with oneself and with *sustasis* are set side by side without their relationship being explained.

hypothesis is the only acceptable one, because in the other two all nature's efforts would have been in vain (6, 40–9). But he runs into some difficulty in proving his point, that is, living beings' self-love, because his principle is that we cannot represent anything to ourselves without being affected to some extent by *this very representation*.[49] He would be better off adopting the principle that we cannot represent anything to ourselves without being affected to some extent by *the object of this representation*. In order to prove successfully that living beings love themselves, Hierocles is forced to slide from the representation to its object, as we can see in this formula: 'no one could say that a living being is displeased *with itself and with the representation it has of itself*' (6, 43–6). Having embarked on an attempt to establish the notion of self-awareness in an autonomous form, independent of the notion of self-love, he only reaches the latter by a treacherous tight-rope indeed.

Let us now return to the first part of his commentary which treats the representative aspect of things. He sets out to show that a living being perceives itself 'from birth' (1, 37–9); but instead of looking for evidence of this in the behaviour of the new-born child and of the young animal, he launches into a devious and elaborate chain of reasoning, at the end of which the theories connected to these particular categories of living beings emerge as the conclusions of an enormous syllogism, in which not a single premiss called for any observation of their behaviour. Here is the plan: (a) Hierocles shows first that the living being perceives itself, *without identifying when* (cf. 2, 1–3, 52–4); (b) then (2, 54ff.) he shows that this perception is absolutely uninterrupted; (c) finally (5, 40ff.), by applying to the actual moment of birth the remarks that he has made about all the moments of life as a whole, he shows that this perception is already present at birth (cf. the general conclusion of this section, 6, 22–4).

At stage (a), the first 'proof' (*pistis*, 2, 1) relies on the perception that the living being has of its own parts and of their function and use, just as Seneca did, but because Hierocles is not interested at this stage in the time when this perception appears, he feels justified in borrowing his arguments from the observation of animals whose age he does not specify, and of 'our' own behaviour, by which he means adults (cf. *hēmeis*, 1, 55–2, 1). He fails to notice, however, that this extension of the field of observation

---

[49] There is an important word missing on line 6, 26; 'It is clear that, having a representation of itself, the living being possesses (how could it be otherwise?) a [*s ... on*] about this representation.' As von Arnim indicates, the missing word must mean something like 'feeling'. In any case, the phrase *peri tēs phantasiās* shows that the object of this feeling is the *phantasia* itself, and not the object it represents; the words immediately following confirm this (*euarestai tēi phantasiāi, hēn heautou eilēphēn*).

ought really to be accompanied by further measures to identify the character, preceding all experience, of the behaviour that indicates that the living being's awareness of its physical potential, is natural and not learnt. The same is true of the other proofs he gives of the premiss (a) (2, 2–52): he retails many charming anecdotes about animals who know their own strong and weak points, as well as their enemies';[50] but he says nothing that might indicate that these marvels of adaptation owe nothing to acquired experience.

In section (b), which he devotes to a proof of the uninterrupted continuity of self-perception (3, 54ff.), we are first struck by a methodological peculiarity which does crop up elsewhere but which is particularly noticeable here. Hierocles sets theoretical arguments (drawn here from the nature of the soul and how it unites with the body, just as they figure in the Stoic system) alongside empirical arguments, and puts forward these two means of approach as independent until they converge on the results. Let us look at one or two transition formulae: 'The things that happen [ta sumbainonta] are reliable confirmation of the arguments [marturia pista ton logon]' (4, 53–4); 'it seems to me that the facts themselves [auta ta ginomena] reinforce the arguments [bebaioun ton logon]' (6, 53–4). These statements seem to show how observation and reasoning have become separated; the manoeuvre (so obvious in Cicero and Seneca) by which, on the base of an observation, reasoning extracts the necessary and/or sufficient conditions of the observed fact has no further role to play.

If Hierocles considers experience as able to act as immediate confirmation of the conclusion to a chain of reasoning, he nonetheless employs such a chain, a striking one, to establish in which area of experience we shall find 'reliable evidence' to assert the continuity of self-perception in living beings. He wonders at what point in time it would be plausible (*pithanon*) that this perception should vanish. If we can show that even at this point it does not vanish, we should have also shown thereby simultaneously that it never vanishes.[51] The conclusion is, of course, only valid if we can identify in the existence of a living being, a moment at which lack of awareness is more plausible than at any other moment. To play this part, Hierocles cannot select the moment of birth; he wants to reach the conclusion that the child itself perceives itself from birth and so there

---

50 Many of these stories may be found in the literature *de sollertia animalium* (Plutarch, Aelian, Pliny); cf. von Arnim's notes.

51 The course of this interesting argument is as follows: if S_1 is that S that has most chance of being P, and if S_1 is not P, then no S is P. Aristotle explained the principle (*Top.* III 119 b31–4); I have found at least one other clear example in Sextus (*M* VII 411).

is no question of allowing this to be a premiss; and in the last analysis we shall know what happens in cradles without needing to look into them. Hierocles cleverly opts for sleep as the time when lack of awareness is most plausible; this gives him the chance of regaling us with amusing anecdotes that illustrate how the sleeper continues to perceive himself (he pulls on the blankets if it turns cold, he wakes up, without an alarm-clock, at the time he decided on the previous day, etc.). But his argument is undermined by the speed with which he accepts that if this perception persists throughout sleep, it persists *a fortiori* all the rest of the time.

Once he has established (a) that the living being perceives itself and (b) that it does so continuously, the syllogistic method leads to the desired conclusion: since the moment of birth is 'a part of time' (5, 41), since we cannot isolate any moment in life which would be 'more remarkable' (*perittoteron*, 5, 48) than the first and all subsequent ones, and which would thus have a better claim to designate the beginning of self-perception, we may conclude that it does in fact begin with life itself.

We would, however, be doing Hierocles an injustice unless we emphasised that he is not satisfied with this indirect and somewhat mechanical proof whose conclusion relates to the child although none of its premisses do. He adds another proof, more specific and philosophically more interesting, which he takes upon himself to describe as 'perfect and irrefutable' (5, 61). Here is its structure: major premiss: the living being, from birth, perceives external things. Minor premiss: the perception of external things implies self-perception. Conclusion: from birth, the living thing perceives itself. The major premiss is put forward as an observed truth, which Hierocles is keen to refine by allowing that certain animals are born blind; if we are unwilling to grant new-born infants the faculties of sight and hearing, at least we can recognise that they possess those of taste and touch when we take into account their behaviour for feeding and self-protection. In view of its vital rôle, the establishment of the minor premiss ought to call for particular attention; it has to be said that Hierocles fails to provide it. He sets it in an explicitly universal form (*katholou*, 6, 1), but he draws it from an induction whose basis is unusually narrow: 'in connexion with the perception of whiteness, for example, we perceive ourselves as affected by whiteness [*heautōn aisthanometha leukainomenōn*]', and similarly in other cases.[52] Even if we admit that the introspec-

---

[52] Pembroke (1971), p. 118, describes this interesting passage as the reverse of the Sceptic argument in which the Cyrenaics maintained that we can be sure that we are affected by whiteness (*leukainometha*) but not that the object that has this effect on us is white (Sextus, M VII 191). In fact, Hierocles is not concerned with the epistemic value of sensory impressions; he is only interested in linking the awareness of this impression with the impression of whiteness, whatever its objective value may be.

tive experience may suffice to guarantee such a connexion between *our* external awareness and *our* internal awareness, he says nothing that would allow us to conclude that the same is necessarily true for *all* external awarenesses, including those of animals and of children; this is, however, the conclusion that he draws.

Throughout the first part of his treatise, he is attempting to give a rational demonstration of his dogmas of child psychology, without embarking on any child observation worthy the name; the only premiss of those I have mentioned which specifically refers to the new-born child is the one that attributes to it external sensations, and this does not need any special talents in an observer. In the second half, on the other hand, which Hierocles devotes to the emotional and active aspect of the living being's relationship to itself, we come across a splendid piece of observation on the fear of darkness and silence in the child of tender years, which, in its precision and realism, is a cut above most of the comparable texts of ancient literature: 'It is by nature', writes Hierocles, 'that young children seem to me not easily to tolerate being shut up in dark rooms where no sound of voices can penetrate. For they strain their sense organs, and yet can neither hear nor see anything; they gain from it the impression of their own destruction [*phantasian anaireseōs hautōn lambanei*], and this is why they are unhappy. This is also why nurses wisely advise them to close their eyes; if the removal of visible objects is done voluntarily, not under coercion, this dispels fear; besides, certain children shut their eyes without even being advised to.'

Two remarks should however be made on the doctrinal and argumentative context of this passage. We must first note how it fits into the section where Hierocles, in order to back up his theory of the attachment of the living being to itself, produces indications drawn 'from facts themselves' [*auta ta ginomena*, 6, 53]. After a few trite remarks on the instinct for preservation, he comments that this instinct is no less common in animals that are 'small and feeble' (7, 2–3) than in those which are outstanding in beauty, size, strength or speed.[53] Doubtless the latter seem to deserve more than nature gives them the means of preserving; the well-being of the former is only important to themselves. Through a significant association of ideas, Hierocles passes from these undistinguished creatures to children, which suggests not only that he does not think much of them, but also, and more importantly, that the child has stopped being the *paradigm* in which the phenomenon of *oikeiōsis* is in evidence, and has become a *borderline case* in which it is just distinguishable.

---

[53] An analogous expression occurs in Seneca, *Ep.* 121 24.

On the argumentative level, the observation on children's fear of the dark has been seen as out of place; according to von Arnim,[54] it would have been more relevant as evidence of the child's attachment to itself. It seems to me more accurate to say that these observations could be fitted into two lines of argument. One attempts to prove the doctrine of our attachment to ourselves, backed up by the doctrine of the connexion between internal and external awareness (deprived of external perception, the child feels threatened with destruction; if he feels fear in the course of this experience, it is because he loves himself). The other reverses *demonstrans* and *demonstrandum*; the child loves himself; if he is afraid of the dark, it is because this experience exposes him to the fear of his own destruction. Since Hierocles has already established to his own satisfaction the solid link between external and internal awareness, it is understandable that he opted for the first argument. The most we can say is that because he himself thinks that the *oikeiōsis* theory relies on 'an abundance of signs' (*periousia tekmēriōn*, 7, 15), while the point concerning the two awarenesses rests, as we have seen, on very narrow bases, he could with advantage have diverted an argument that supported the first and used it to reinforce the second. Hierocles is therefore sometimes capable of observation, but does not make the best use of it.

Here, for the moment at least, we must leave this account of the Stoic versions of the cradle argument.

[54] Von Arnim (1906), pp. XXXI–XXXII.

6 Discovering the good: *oikeiōsis* and *kathēkonta* in Stoic ethics

Troels Engberg-Pedersen

Virtue is the only good

1.1. Stoic ethical theory was famous in antiquity for making a radical claim, which outraged its opponents: only what has moral worth is good (*monon to kalon agathon*).

To people of a more Aristotelian cast of mind this seemed unintelligible in two respects:

(1) Even though it will no doubt be true that what has moral worth is good, why does the same not hold of other things that people ordinarily consider good, e.g. such 'natural' goods as one's health, a good wife, intelligent and flourishing children, etc.? The Stoics admit that these things are valuable (and they even coin a new word for them: *proēgmena*, preferable); so why not good? There is something counter-intuitive here.

(2) The Stoics start developing their claim about the good from a consideration of what accords with a man's nature and they maintain that viewpoint right through. But 'natural' goods of the type mentioned do accord with a man's nature (and the Stoics admit that when they start their account of the good precisely from those goods), and these goods continue to be in accordance with a man's nature no matter what more one will have to say later about man's nature and things that accord with it. So why are the natural goods eventually left out, in terms of goodness, at the end? This seems just inexplicable.

But the fact that the Stoic claim seems unintelligible at the intellectual level does not directly explain the highly emotional character of the opposition to Stoic ethics on the part of men like Plutarch, whose attack on their ethical system is nothing less than ferocious. This violent attitude is no doubt due to a number of features in that system, but foremost among these will be precisely the Stoic claim that only what has moral worth is good. Nor is there any doubt that this claim accounts for the fact that people of a different type than Plutarch became so strongly *attracted* to the Stoic ethical view that they would even take their own lives in the certain belief that they would not thereby lose anything, but would be doing the good.

1.2. In asking about the meaning of the radical Stoic claim we are there-

fore facing two different tasks. One is that of making sense in an intellectually satisfying way of the Stoic claim and its theoretical underpinnings.
This task has interesting ramifications for the history of philosophy. For
the Stoics shared with their immediate predecessors Aristotle and Plato
the basic framework for an ethical theory, according to which all
questions of value (whether moral or non-moral) fall under the basic
question of what things bring *eudaimonia* (happiness) to a man. They also
shared with Aristotle a specific view of the logical behaviour of the concept of *eudaimonia* in that rôle. But they differed from him with respect to
the role they assigned to moral virtue and natural goods respectively as
things that bring *eudaimonia*. How and why?

The second task is that of accounting for the attraction in emotional
terms of the Stoic claim. Perhaps the Stoics were on to something important in ethical theory – not just emotionally satisfying, but something that
corresponds to some deeply rooted moral intuition in such a way that it
should find its place in any ethical theory proper.

So a consideration of the radical Stoic claim should be of interest both
from the point of view of an 'internal' development in the history of philosophy and from an independently systematical point of view. Whether
the attempt to shed light on that Stoic position will actually succeed is a
different question. The textual material is too scant for comfort and the
matter is difficult.

Living in accordance with nature

2. The Stoics themselves certainly did not make things easier. Thus it is
not easy to find texts that develop in more detail precisely what they
meant by moral worth (*to kalon*, the noble) in their famous dictum. There
can be little doubt that they thought to include, in an entirely Aristotelian
way, virtue (*aretē*), even virtue of character (*ēthikē aretē*), and virtuous
acts, and it is clear that they wanted to include also the traditional moral
virtues (courage, moderation, etc.). But when it comes to answering the
question of what defines a state as a virtue, we are left in the dark in a way
not much different from what happens in Aristotle.

But then, of course, they do make a different, equally famous claim, viz.
that man's end (*telos*), i.e. the good, consists in living in accordance with
nature. While the fact that they talk of living in accordance with nature
more or less interchangeably with living in accordance with virtue raises
questions of its own, one may hope that consideration of the Stoic claim

about nature, which has a more prominent position in the texts, will throw light on the sense of their radical claim about moral worth and the argument behind it. So what is meant by living in accordance with nature in the sense adopted by the Stoics when they claim that to be the human end? And why should a man live like that?

The teleological view

3.1. One answer to the latter question refers to the teleological structure of nature. It is an answer that seems contained in a number of highly respectable sources, e.g. in a central passage in Diogenes Laertius (VII 85–8) to be quoted in a moment, and it pervades the whole of a text like Marcus Aurelius' *Meditations*.

The latter groups around the idea of living in accordance with nature such Stoic tenets as (A) that everything happens according to the providential plan of nature, (B) that man stands in a special relationship with nature since he (alone among animals) shares in nature's rationality, (C) that so-called external goods (Aristotle's natural goods) are in fact worthless, and (D) that a man should care for others, since he belongs in a special community with them. Marcus does not attempt to bring these ideas together in a systematic account of the sense of and argument for the claim about living in accordance with nature. Still it seems clear that (A) and (B) belong in an argument for that claim and that (C) and (D) express rather what living in accordance with nature consists in as maxims that will be justified by the argument incorporating (A) and (B).

3.2. The task of articulating more clearly the teleological basis of Stoic ethics according to this general line of thought has been undertaken in modern times in its most concentrated form in a paper by A. A. Long (1971). Long's aim is to develop as the logical basis of Stoic ethics the idea of nature's goodness, of cosmic nature (henceforth Nature) as 'a norm or principle of universal value' (p. 88). Thus he concludes that the points made in the central passage in Diogenes Laertius already referred to (VII 85–8) hang together logically in the following way (I paraphrase omitting a number of premisses and intermediate conclusions):

– living by sound reason, living in accord with human nature and living according to virtue is (a) advantageous to men and (b) right for them; for it is based in Nature, and Nature creates all living things and provides them with the means of securing what is *advantageous* to them, and that which accords with Nature is *right*,
– when men live by sound reason, in accord with human nature and according to

virtue, they live in accord with Nature in a special sense, since human nature is in a special sense part of Nature; from this it follows that when they live in the above way (as is advantageous and right for them), they will live in deliberate obedience to Nature's will; Long concludes that 'the Stoics held the pursuit of the goal referred to by the expressions "acting according to reason", "virtue" and "human nature" to be a moral imperative, a command of Nature (or God)' (p. 96); 'Nature stands to man as a moral law commanding him to live by rational principles, *viz.*, those principles of thought and action which Nature, a perfect being, prescribes to itself and all rational beings' (pp. 101–2).

The basis of this interpretation of Nature's rôle in Stoic ethics is the Stoic teleological view of Nature as divine, artistic, provident and right-reasoning (pp. 88, 94). We may present the basic line of thought as follows. (1) Nature is divine, artistic, provident and right-reasoning – and hence good. Living in accordance with Nature is good. (2) Humans (alone among animals) are rational. Since Nature itself is rational, humans stand in a special relationship with Nature. In virtue of this special relationship the good for humans, viz. living in accordance with Nature, consists in deliberately obeying Nature's will.

3.3. There can be no doubt that Long has articulated here what was taken to be the kernel of Stoic ethics in the centuries after Christ when Stoic ethics was amalgamated into the mainstream of Neoplatonic philosophy: Nature's providence, man's special relationship with Nature (and God) and the corollary of the worthlessness of ordinary human objectives and the fundamental unimportance of whatever happens to the individual as compared to the beneficient development of God's cosmic plan – all of these ideas turn up with a Stoic tinge in Neoplatonic texts.

There can be no doubt either about the emotional appeal of such a view of the world. A Stoic such as Marcus Aurelius is evidence of this.

Nor can there be any doubt that Long's account interprets correctly the central text in Diogenes Laertius on a number of important points, e.g. when Long claims that the teleological view of Nature is a vital premiss for the conclusion reached in section 85–6 that the human good is life in accordance with cosmic nature, and probably also when he claims that the same view of Nature is a premiss for the further conclusion that the good for man (living in accordance with cosmic nature) consists in deliberately obeying Nature's will.

Nor, finally, can there be any doubt that something like this view of Nature's role in laying the foundations of ethics is in fact old Stoic doctrine. Chrysippus is referred to in section 85 in Diogenes and the doctrine that is being described in sections 85–6 certainly goes as far back as him.

This is the famous Stoic doctrine of *oikeiōsis* ('appropriation', 'valuation').[1]

4. I shall not discuss the Diogenes passage in detail. But it is worth having it before us. The teleological basis of *oikeiōsis* in this account is quite clear.

The Stoics say that an animal's first impulse [*hormē*] is towards preserving itself, since nature makes it belong to itself[2] from the start, as Chrysippus says in the first book of *On Ends*. He says that the first thing belonging in any animal is its own constitution and an awareness thereof;[3] for it seems neither likely that nature should make the animal alien to itself, nor that having created it it should neither make it alien nor belonging; one must conclude, therefore, that having constituted the animal, nature has also made it belong to itself; for that is how things that damage are repelled and things belonging are sought for. [...] Furthermore, they say, nature did not behave differently with plants and with animals: plants too it manages [*oikonomein*] – without the use of impulse [*hormē*] and sensation (and in humans too certain things happen of a plant-like kind); and when in animals impulse is superadded, by which they move toward what belongs, nature's part is administered [*dioikeisthai*] for one type of animal via impulse; but for another type, viz. rational animals, to whom reason has been given as a more perfect guide, nature's part becomes rightly living in accordance with reason; for reason supervenes as a craftsman of impulse. That is why Zeno was the first to say, in *On the Nature of Man*, that the end is living in accordance with nature [...]

5.1. It is now time to ask whether a reference to the goodness of nature is the only thing the Stoics have to say in defence of their claim that the human good is living in accordance with nature. While this might of course be right, it would also be somewhat disappointing if it were. Furthermore, no argument has been developed to show that if living in accordance with nature is good because cosmic nature is good, then living in accordance with nature should be understood in such a way that it entails what is part of the radical Stoic claim: the total indifference of Aristotle's natural goods. So it would be satisfying if the Stoics have something more to say – and they should have. I believe that they do have.

---

[1] *oikeiōsis* is an abstract noun corresponding to the verb *oikeiousthai*. 'x *oikeioutai pros* y' means 'x comes to see y as belonging or his own' (medial sense) or 'x is made to see y as belonging or his own' (passive + medial sense). *oikeiōsis*, according to the Stoics, is a relation, but an intensional one. When in what follows I talk from time to time of *oikeiōsis* as a process, I am bringing in the Stoic idea that this intensional relationship may constantly be extended so as to incorporate new objects within itself.

[2] I accept the conjecture of Koraes: *auto* ⟨*hautōi*⟩, see *apparatus* in the OCT edition by H. S. Long (1964).

[3] It is immaterial to my purposes whether one reads, with the MSS, *suneidēsin* or, as favoured e.g. by Pohlenz (1940), p. 7 and Pembroke (1971), p. 142 n. 25, *sunaisthēsin*.

5.2. I propose to consider in some detail Cicero's account of *oikeiōsis* in *De finibus* book III.[4] Cicero introduces *oikeiōsis* in two contexts, one more general, which is that of impulse (*hormē*) and end (*telos*) – this is *oikeiōsis* towards nature (*Fin.* III 16–18, 20–1), and one more specific, connected with the virtue of justice – this is *oikeiōsis* towards other human beings (*Fin.* III 62–6). In these two passages the idea of nature as a conscious, provident agent is far less prominent than in Diogenes Laertius. It *is* present in some way, and to a greater extent in the later passage than in the earlier one. But Cicero also seems to point to a quite different account of why man's end is living in accordance with nature, and indeed of what this means. In order to explore this possibility I shall try to keep the teleological view at arm's length and to bring out ways of understanding what Cicero is saying that do not rely on or introduce the teleological view.

The explanation of impulse

6. First on *oikeiōsis* towards nature (*Fin.* III 16–18, 20–1).

III 16 runs as follows (tr. Rackham, Loeb edition (1931), with some changes and key-words added):

It is the view of those whose system I adopt, that immediately upon birth (for that is the proper point to start from) a living creature feels an attachment for itself [*ipsum sibi conciliari*], and a commendation [*commendari*] towards preserving itself and loving[5] [*diligere*] its own constitution [*status*] and those things which tend to preserve that constitution; while on the other hand it conceives an antipathy [*alienari*] to destruction and to those things which appear to threaten destruction. In proof of this they urge that infants desire [*appetere*] things conducive to their health and reject things that are the opposite before they have ever felt pleasure or pain; this would not be the case, unless they felt love for [*diligere*] their own constitution and were afraid of destruction. But it would be impossible that they should feel desire [*appetere*] at all unless they possessed self-consciousness [*sensus sui*], and consequently[6] loved themselves [*diligere se*]. This leads to the conclusion that it is love of self [*se diligere*] which supplies the starting-point.

---

[4] Teubner edition by Th. Schiche (1915).

[5] I employ 'loving' simply as a convenient stand-in for 'liking', 'being attached to', 'having a positive attitude towards', etc.

[6] *eo*: 'as a result of this'. I do not understand this nor have I seen any good explanation or emendation.

7.1. The topic of this passage is impulse (*hormē*), and the passage constitutes the first part of Cicero's account (running to the end of chapter 21) of what the end (*telos*) of man is. So far Cicero's account resembles the one in Diogenes Laertius, where chapters 85–6 are about *hormē* and chapters 87–8 about the *telos*. But the Cicero passage contains an analysis of what goes into a *hormē* that is far subtler than anything to be found in Diogenes.

Consider the first sentence, which may be analysed as follows.

(A) attachment for oneself	and
(B) commendation towards preserving	
oneself (*a*)	and
loving	
one's constitution (*b*)	and
the things that preserve that constitution (*c*).	

This sentence sketches a logical account of *hormē* to be understood as desire for certain definite objects (viz. those mentioned under *Bc*) based on *A*, attachment for an undescribed 'oneself', i.e. on what is at the end of the passage called love for self. The deduction is this. The basic pro-attitude towards oneself (*A*) engenders a derived pro-attitude (this is the point of 'commendation') towards preserving oneself (*Ba*). This is the first step in the process of 'relating the basic self-love to the world'. For the idea of preserving implies that of *acting*: doing something – in order that – one may oneself be in the state of being maintained. At the same time as the idea of preserving introduces that of acting it brings in the idea of *an end*, viz. that of oneself being in the state of being maintained. Thus *Ba* may be said to introduce the idea of *desiring*, and Rackham was in a way right to translate *commendari* as feeling 'an impulse to' something. But only in a way, for the point of *commendari* in the context is that of *explaining* impulse as a pro-attitude *derived* from self-love and connected with *action* and some *end*.

But *Ba* does not lead us far enough into the world. Although it brings in the ideas of acting and of an end, the implied end is only the highly formal one of oneself being maintained. What happens at *Bb* and *Bc* are two things, then. The first is that certain definite things are introduced that stand in a factual relationship to the hitherto entirely unspecified 'self'. That relationship is, for the idea of one's constitution introduced at *Bb*, that it *fills in* what the 'self' is, and for the things that preserve that constitution (*Bc*), that they stand in a special type of causal relation to that constitution, viz. the 'static' complement to 'bringing about': *preserving* what the self is taken to be.

The second thing that is being done by *Bb* and *Bc* is that the evaluative component of *A* is transformed, via what happens at *Ba* and the specification of the self performed under *Bb* and *Bc*, into a derived pro-attitude (commendation towards loving) towards certain definite objects. Here, then, is introduced the idea of certain concrete objects of desire to be handled in concrete acts aiming at the maintenance of oneself. And it is only at this point that we may speak of an impulse or desire proper, since that is an intensely concrete thing.

7.2. What we get from this sentence, then, are a number of points:

- the idea of a non-derivative pro-attitude towards an entirely unspecified self as the basis of acting and desiring, and hence
- the idea of deriving from this the pro-attitudes (towards acting as such and towards particular ends of action) that explain action in terms of desire,
- the idea of action's being for some end, and as a further development of this
- the idea of certain objects of desire being means to some end due to the fact that they stand in a special causal relationship with that end.

It will be immediately clear that this is not just more detailed than what we get in Diogenes, but an expression of a wider interest in *hormē*. The Cicero text is not only concerned to establish the objects and parentage of an animal's natural *hormai*, but also to account for the elements that go into these *hormai* and hence to provide an explanation of the concept of *hormē* in general.

7.3. The second and third sentences in the Cicero text, which contain a Stoic proof of the account of *oikeiōsis* given in the first sentence, also seem carefully constructed. In spite of the difficulty of drawing out of the text a fully satisfactory argument (see Jacques Brunschwig's analysis elsewhere in this volume), the general movement of the argument is clear enough. It is to argue from the observable fact that animals desire things that preserve themselves (i.e. *Bc*) to their love for their own constitution (*Bb*), and to argue from the fact of their desiring things at all (i.e. *B* as a whole) to their love of self (*A*). And in fact it seems noteworthy that the first of the two sentences takes up precisely one 'column' in the analysis I gave of the first sentence in the text, viz. the column that contains the development of the unspecified self in terms of its constitution (*Bb*) and the things that preserve that constitution (*Bc*), whereas the second of the two sentences takes up the other column, viz. the one that derives desire and impulse (*B*: via the ideas of commendation towards preserving and commendation towards loving certain definite objects) from the basic love of self (*A*).

So it is at least possible to see the second and third sentences as confirming the suggested interpretation of the first one. Similarly, of course, the last sentence in the quoted text deserves emphasis: it is love of self which supplies the starting-point.

Naturalism

8.1. The next two chapters (*Fin.* III 17–18), which I shall only paraphrase, introduce some important notions. Cicero first quotes the opinion of 'most Stoics' that pleasure does not belong among the *principia naturalia* or primary natural objects. As proof that we love those primary objects of desire *by nature* he then mentions the fact that there is no one who, given the choice, would not prefer to have all the parts of his body sound and whole, rather than maimed or distorted even if they were of the same use. In the rest of chapter 17 and the first part of chapter 18 he then brings in two more things to be included under the *principia naturalia*, viz. knowledge and the sciences. These things, he says, we believe to be worth having *for their own sake* (*propter se*). So we love the *principia naturalia* 'by nature' and we deem them worth having 'for their own sake'.

8.2. There can be little doubt that Cicero is here trying to make a single point: we consider the primary natural objects valuable irrespective of any *use* they may have (this point is made both in connection with 'loving by nature' and with 'believing to be worth having for their own sake'); and we consider them valuable 'by nature' (as is shown by the fact that we do it from childhood, cf. Cicero's suggestion that the intrinsic value of knowledge can be seen from the attitude of children, who take pleasure in discovering things for themselves methodically, even though they gain nothing by it) – *so these things are in fact valuable*. Cicero does not draw this conclusion explicitly, but it seems certain that it expresses the basic idea behind his whole account of man's end as starting in chapter 16. In other words, what animals take to be valuable when they are in 'the natural state', that *is* valuable. This is why, as Cicero said at the beginning of chapter 16, the proper point to start is from what happens immediately upon birth. This, of course, is a momentous move, but there is nothing strange about it. It is just a fairly clear-cut version of naturalism.

This means that there is no need to bring in an elaborate, teleological view of nature in order to understand what Cicero is saying when he considers whether pleasure is one thing that 'nature has placed' among the primary natural objects. He is just asking, with the Stoics, whether pleasure is something animals consider valuable 'by nature' (and he is denying that it is).

9.1. More important is the question of how we should understand chapters 17–18 in relation to chapter 16. Are the Stoics just introducing two more things that animals, or rather human adults (for knowledge and the sciences are distinctly rational things), consider valuable by nature? Or do they want to see these two things too in terms of the system of chapter 16? I prefer the second view.

In that case we should understand the Stoic naturalism as follows. There is one thing, and just one thing, that all animals (including humans) consider valuable by nature, viz. the animal's own self. There are also a number of other things that may be said to be considered valuable by nature (e.g. one's constitution, one's health, knowledge and the sciences), but they are considered valuable because they are taken to stand in some *factual* relationship with the animal's self, which is the only thing that is loved in a *non*-derivative way, and hence their actually being valuable is a function of that relationship actually obtaining. These things, then, *are* valuable, but not just because they are taken to be so, rather because they are in fact related to the animal's self in the way in which the animal takes them to be so.

9.2. If this interpretation is correct, then just after we have ascribed to the Stoics a substantial naturalist view in ethics, we shall have to qualify that ascription rather drastically. For if the only thing that has naturalist value is the animal's self, then the extent and character of Stoic naturalism are radically changed – for two reasons: first because it is reduced to concern a single thing, and secondly because that thing is in itself entirely unspecified.

I must confess that I do not feel absolutely certain about ascribing such a theory to the Stoics, nor am I quite clear what kind of theory it would actually be. But I do believe that the suggested interpretation fits best the whole of Cicero's account, including the further development in 20–1, and it also seems worth pointing out that this view of the basis of Stoic ethics fits very well with their general tendency to understand value judgments (e.g. 'passions') as *beliefs*. On the suggested view value judgments are precisely true or false *factual* beliefs about what 'belongs' or is 'alien'. Conversely, a main point of *oikeiōsis* will be that there is only one basic *evaluative* fact, viz. love of self.

Value

10.1. 'Let us proceed, then, since we have digressed from those first natural objects, with which what follows must be in accord.' Thus Cicero at the beginning of chapter 20.

There follows first this division: the Stoics term 'valuable' (for so I suppose we may translate it) what is either itself in accordance with nature or produces something that is, in such a way that it is deserving of selection [*selectione dignum*] due to its having a certain weight that deserves to have value attached to it,[7] i.e. what the Stoics call *axia*; and as against this they term 'valueless' what is contrary to the former.

10.2. The purpose of this passage in the context seems to be that of introducing a certain terminology as relevant to the concept of selection or choice (*selectio*): something's being 'valuable' (*aestimabile*) and having a certain 'value' (*aestimatio, axia*).

Two points should be made. First, it is noteworthy that the term valuable is stipulated for use for two categories of things: things which are themselves in accordance with nature and things that produce such things. Thus Cicero remembers the distinction drawn in chapter 16 between (*Bb*) one's constitution as something that fills in the self and is for that reason itself a thing of natural value and (*Bc*) things that have a causal relation to one's constitution as preserving it.

Secondly, it is worth noting that Cicero is fixing the reference for the term valuable from an 'objective' point of view: what is valuable, he intends to say, is either what is itself *in fact* in accordance with nature or what *in fact* produces something that is. Thus he is not defining 'valuable' in terms of the model of chapter 16, i.e. of what is taken by the animal to be valuable as being in accordance with his nature or producing something that is. Rather he is drawing on the basic idea behind chapters 17–18 that what is considered valuable by an animal 'in the natural state' and seen by the animal to be worth taking for its own sake *is* valuable – and the same goes, then, for what produces some such thing. It is not difficult to see why Cicero has dropped in the quoted passage the point of view of what the animal *sees*, which is the point of view of *oikeiōsis*. For he is just wanting to introduce the concepts of value and being valuable – and not even for immediate use, and doing that in terms of the precise mechanism of *oikeiōsis* would be unnecessarily complicated. What should be retained, however, is the need to do just that if one wants to bring out the logical underpinnings of the Stoic concept of value.

---

[7] This cumbersome translation is intended to bring out two points in what Cicero says of 'value' that may be worth remembering if one wants to get a clearer grasp of the Stoic concept of value: that there is more of a *nomen actionis* in *aestimatio* than in our 'value' (it goes more in the direction of 'valuation'), and that Cicero is often careful to talk of a 'certain' amount of value (*aliquod pondus* [...] *dignum aestimatione*), cf. *Fin.* III 41: 'everything that is deserving of a certain (or *some*) valuation' (*omne quod aestimatione aliqua dignum sit*) and similarly in *Fin.* III 44.

Towards discovering the good

11.1. Cicero continues as follows:

Next, on the basis of the principle that has been established, that the things in accordance with nature should be taken for their own sake and their opposites similarly rejected, the first duty [*officium*] – for so I translate *kathēkon* – will be to preserve oneself in one's natural constitution, the next to obtain the things in accordance with nature and to repel their opposites; when this [type of] selection and similarly rejection has been discovered, there follows next selection guided by a conception of duty [*cum officio selectio*], then such selection perpetually and then finally selection that is consistent and in accordance with nature, which is the point at which the good properly so called first starts to be present and to be understood in its true nature. For man's first attachment [*conciliatio, oikeiōsis*] is to the things in accordance with nature. But as soon as he acquires understanding etc.

11.2. The basic point of this passage is to bring us from *oikeiōsis* as it operates in animals in general (chapter 16) to *oikeiōsis* as it operates in adult human beings ending in an understanding of what is genuinely good. The sense of the individual stages in the development depicted by Cicero is not entirely clear, but its direction is beyond doubt in that it expresses a growing consciousness on the part of the person undergoing this development as to how, to put it vaguely, one should act. Correspondingly there is a change in point of view, in terms of my remarks on the immediately preceding passage, from the 'objective', 'external' one to the 'subjective' one of *oikeiōsis*. It is the former which is responsible for the principle (of chapters 17–18) from which Cicero starts, viz. that what is in accordance with nature should be taken for its own sake, and for the corollary that a man's first duty (this is 'objective' language) is to preserve himself and his next duty to obtain the things in accordance with nature and to repel their opposites. But this point of view gradually gives way to the 'subjective' one of *oikeiōsis*, which is responsible for the next stages: the 'discovery' of selection and rejection, selection guided by a 'conception' of duty, and finally an 'understanding' of what is truly good. And at the end of the quoted passage *oikeiōsis* is explicitly brought in.

What, then, is the good that a man finally comes to grasp? How does he arrive at that grasp? And why is that good alone to be properly so called?

12.1. Cicero provides some help (III 21).

Man's first attachment is to the things in accordance with nature. But as soon as he acquires understanding [*intellegentia*] or rather, perhaps, the capacity to form concepts [*notio*],[8] i.e. what the Stoics call *ennoia*, and sees the order [*ordo*] and as it were harmony [*concordia*] of acts,[9] he values this [viz. order and harmony] far more highly than all those earlier objects of his love, and he concludes by rational argument [*cognitione et ratione colligere*] that man's end, that highest something which is praiseworthy and desirable for its own sake – the good, lies in this [i.e. in this order and harmony]; this [good], since it consists in what the Stoics call *homologia* and we may call conformity [viz. with the order and harmony mentioned] – since in this [i.e. in conformity with the order and harmony] resides that good to which everything must be referred, noble acts and the noble itself, which alone is counted among things good, therefore though of subsequent development, still that [viz. the conformity mentioned] is the only thing desirable in and for itself, whereas among the first objects of nature none is desirable for its own sake [*propter se*].

12.2. There are two main points in this chapter:

(21A) When a man acquires understanding and sees the order and harmony of acts, he values that order and harmony far more highly than the things in accordance with nature that he loved first and he concludes by rational argument that man's end lies in this order and harmony – or rather in conformity with it.

(21B) Since conformity with the order and harmony of acts is the good to which everything else must be referred, even noble acts and the noble itself, which is the only thing reckoned good, such conformity is the *only* thing desirable for its own sake.

21A tells us what man's end is as he realises in *oikeiōsis* and it contains an elusive indication of how he comes to see that. 21B makes the further point that what the man has come to see as his end is the *only* thing desirable for its own sake, and it connects moral worth (the noble) with this end.

21B, then, introduces the radical Stoic claim, according to which there is only one thing that is good, whereas ordinary 'goods' (e.g. Aristotle's natural goods) are not after all *good*. This means that if the chapter hangs together, 21A should tell us not just what it is that a man comes to see in *oikeiōsis* as his end and how he comes to see this, but also *why* what he comes to see as his end is such that it will be the *only* end of his acts.

Section 21A will have a lot of work to do, then, and it should be clear from the start that it may be hoping too much to expect that it will prove

---

[8] I take it that Cicero is here talking of the general capacity to form concepts which is constitutive of the reasoning faculty, not of some specific concept or other. The argument for this reading cannot be detached from my overall reading of the passage.

[9] *rerum agendarum* may also be translated as 'acts to be done', but not necessarily with any gerundive sense of 'to be done'. The gerundive is most naturally taken here to have the sense of the passive participle in its non-perfect form (to be contrasted with *rerum actarum*).

capable of doing it. Still it seems worth trying to see whether the hope may be justified or not.

Argument or psychological account?

13. Before going into the details of the passage we should remind our-selves of what we should expect to find in it. Cicero is giving an account of *oikeiōsis* and he brings in *oikeiōsis* explicitly at the beginning of the pass-age. It follows, in terms of Cicero's account of the mechanism of *oikeiōsis* in chapter 16, that we should expect to be shown how when a man acquires reason he comes to see something new as *belonging*, i.e. as stand-ing in some factual relationship with himself, whom he loves.

Now Cicero clearly states that the man's new insight is a consequence of his having acquired reason and having seen something (by the use of his reason, I take it) and that his belief that man's end is conformity with the order and harmony of acts is a conclusion arrived at by reasoning. Since it is clear, as we have seen, even without this that in his account of *oikeiōsis* Cicero is constantly thinking only of insights into what belongs (in factual terms, as we know) that are *true* (for otherwise he could not move so quickly to the 'objective' language of chapters 17–18 and 20), we should take him to be saying in 21A that the insight reached by the man under-going *oikeiōsis* as described in that passage is true and that the reasoning on which this insight is based is also correct.

In that case, if we succeed in uncovering a chain of reasoning that shows that man's end is living in conformity with the order and harmony of acts (given that he loves himself), then we shall also have discovered an *argu-ment* for the Stoic claim that man's end is living in conformity with that order and harmony. And since living in conformity with this is identical, as will become clear, with living in accordance with nature, it will follow that once we understand 21A (if there is anything to understand), we shall also be in possession of a Stoic argument for the claim that man's end is living in conformity with nature.

Thus while 21A does not in itself *contain* an argument for that claim (since the reasoning by which a man reaches his new insight is not actually set out in the passage), still if it contains an indication of how a man will reach his new insight, then it will also contain an indication of a rational argument for the Stoic claim about man's end as formulated in 'objective' language. Correspondingly, when a man gains the new insight into man's end he will be making a genuine discovery of what is good.

14. This is worth stressing, since recently a different view of the passage has been presented with some force in a paper by Gisela Striker (1983a).

The traditional view is that Cicero's account in 21A is intended to bring out the elements in an argument proper for the thesis that life in accordance with nature is man's end. I believe that this view is correct, but that it should be held in the rather more complicated form I have tried to bring out.

Striker, however, has questioned the traditional view by asking what exactly the argument is. On her account *Fin.* III 21 makes two points (pp. 157–8). 'First, it comes out very clearly that the agent is to experience a change in interest such that he comes to uniquely value order and harmony, while before he had been pursuing things needed for self-preservation. [...] Second, the change seems to be explained by the consideration that *homologia* is the standard to which everything must be referred, and hence the only thing desirable for its own sake.'

Striker is willing to accept the explanation offered for the change in interest, along the following lines: if consistency and harmony are the only standard of valuation (cf. my 21B above), then only what conforms to this will be good. But things are desirable in so far as they are good. So they will be desirable because they are in accordance with nature (this being what is meant by consistency and harmony), i.e. accordance with nature is the only thing desirable in itself (cf. my 21A above).

But Striker reasonably complains, on the background of this reading of the passage, that 'taken as an argument for the thesis that accordance with nature is the human good, this argument begs the question by simply assuming that accordance with nature *is* the standard' (p. 158).

Perhaps, then, she suggests, we should rather take the Cicero passage as providing an account of *psychological development* that shows how man could come to adopt accordance with nature as his only goal although he starts out with an impulse towards self-preservation (p. 161): if he came to think that what made his former actions valuable was not that they contributed to self-preservation, but that they were in accordance with nature, he might cease to care about self-preservation as a primary goal, and try to achieve accordance with nature instead (p. 158). What the Cicero passage is doing, then, is trying to make psychologically plausible this crucial change of attitude (p. 161) – and if we want an argument proper for the Stoic doctrine of man's end we should go elsewhere, primarily to the argument in Diogenes Laertius from the design of nature (pp. 160–1).

It should be clear where Striker's approach to the passage differs from the one taken in the present paper – not in the view that Cicero (in contrast to Diogenes) is setting out the road to a certain view of man's end in 'subjective' terms (I agree, for *oikeiōsis is* about 'coming to see'), but in the view that it follows from this that Cicero will not be giving the elements in an 'objective' argument for the Stoic view of man's end. As I understand the mechanism of *oikeiōsis* he will also be giving that. But then, of course, he will not just be giving a 'psychological account' in the sense of an account of how a man may come to have certain beliefs *not* as a result of some reasoning, but to be explained 'psychologically' (and this must be the essence of Striker's suggestion).

Let us look at the passage in more detail.

The first two steps in self-reflexion

15.1. I shall set out in three steps the insight reached by a man when he comes to reason. The first step will consist in his seeing, as Cicero says, an order and harmony in certain acts. What order? Which acts?

The acts can hardly be other than those the man has himself been engaged in when as a child, in a way that is common to all animals (as we know from chapter 16), he has, in the words of chapter 20, been acting so as to preserve himself in his natural constitution, by trying to obtain what is in accordance with nature and repelling the opposite. The acts, then, are primarily his own earlier acts and secondarily the acts of other animals which he may care to notice.

But we also know that these acts exhibit a special order and harmony, viz. the one that Cicero describes in chapter 16. There are a number of things to be said about this order, which we shall have to bring in gradually. But surely the most obviously orderly feature about them is that they all fall under the description of the agent's trying to preserve himself. By seeing this our man will by a single stroke have imposed an order on a hitherto completely unstructured matter. This is already something, but clearly not enough, since seeing this order in one's own earlier acts (and in those of other animals) is very far from seeing conformity itself with that order as one's end (and indeed as one's single end). It is precisely only a first step.

15.2. Note, however, the special character of even this kind of seeing. It is what Epictetus in a comparable passage (1 vi 12–22) calls *parakolouthēsis* or self-reflexive understanding based on a capacity for such understanding (*parakolouthētikē dunamis*) which is special to humans. It seems highly likely that this capacity is also an important element in the general capacity for forming concepts that Cicero is talking of in our passage. But then it will also seem that we are free to ask what more (of an ordered and harmonious kind) reflexion on the system of action described in chapter

16 may discover. This will be the second step in *parakolouthēsis*.

16.1. Now one clearly does not come to reflect on one's own earlier acts out of the blue, as it were, but in a special context. That context may be described as the one of asking 'the practical question': what shall I do? Or in ancient terms: What are the proper *hormai*? What are the proper *telē* or 'the *telos*'? So at the same time as one is coming to reflect on one's earlier acts, one will be operating within this context. One will be asking what to do in terms of what *telē* one should adopt for one's acts.

What answer to this question, then, will one get from reflexion on the facts described by Cicero in chapter 16?

16.2. One answer might be this: one should oneself, i.e. it is proper that one should, set up preservation of oneself as one's *telos* – for reflexion on one's own earlier acts and those of other animals shows one that all living beings act in that way; that is something they do by nature; and what is natural is good. The order and harmony of our passage would then reside, as Nicholas P. White suggests in a recent study (1979), in the fact 'that one is so constituted by nature as to seek by impulse the very things that will preserve one's natural state' (p. 156) and that there is 'a fit between one's natural impulses and one's best chances for survival' (pp. 156–7). Note, however, that this is really just the old teleological view. What is orderly about acts of preserving oneself is not an internal feature of the system of acting itself that is described by Cicero in chapter 16, but something external to that system, viz. the *fact* that the system is there – due to the way things are structured by nature. But we have decided to keep the teleological view at arm's length and in fact there is nothing in Cicero's chapter 16 to suggest such a reading.

16.3. A different answer to the practical question would be this.

> Action of the kind engaged in by all animals is orderly and harmonious in that in the case of each individual animal it falls under the single heading of trying to preserve oneself.
> Such action is *itself* orderly and harmonious, in the sense of intelligible and justifiable, when it is seen to be based on the self-love of each individual animal.
> I am an animal and I have myself been acting like that all along; and I do love myself.
> So the thing for me to do is act so as to preserve myself.

This reading is closer to Cicero's text than the other one in that it locates the order and harmony of the acts under discussion *within* the system of action described by Cicero and takes into account the precise relationship of self-love, action so as to preserve oneself and derived definite objects of pro-attitude and acts in relation to them that we saw to be contained in Cicero's chapter 16.

It also has the advantage (as I take it) of understanding the order and harmony somewhat more formally than on the first reading. On the second reading this order and harmony does not consist in the admittedly striking fact that animals are so constituted by nature as to have the best chances for survival (this is an order and harmony of the 'external' kind I spoke of), but rather in the logical appropriateness of certain acts in a special context. It is because action so as to preserve oneself is *itself* orderly and harmonious in the sense specified that it is proper for one to act in that way.

But precisely this idea of an intrinsic order of acts of preserving oneself raises new questions. And this is as well. For if there were no further room for reflexive analysis of the order and harmony of acts of self-preservation, it would be impossible to understand the radical shift of interest that the Stoics talk of in the second part of Cicero's chapter 21 (21B above). In fact, however, what is impossible is stopping at the second step in reflexion that we have been considering. There is a third step in *parakolouthēsis*.

The third step in self-reflexion: rationality and the unimportance of the self

17.1. At the same time as one engages in reflexion on one's earlier acts and becomes aware of the context (viz. the one of asking the practical question) in which one's reflexion is being conducted, one also becomes self-reflexively aware of *oneself as* being engaged in that kind of activity. This means that one becomes aware of oneself *as rational* and that the property of acts that one is looking for is *rational justifiability*. I shall now try to develop the consequences of seeing oneself in this way as rational and as looking for rational justifiability.

17.2. Note the genuinely self-reflexive character of the third step in *parakolouthēsis*. The second step was also (in a sense) self-reflexive in that it consisted of reflexion on one's own instinctive acts (as a child). But one might also call it just reflexive because what it did was to bring in the idea of discovering by reflexion, i.e. reason, what to do, as against just acting instinctively. The third step, by contrast, is genuinely self-reflexive: it presupposes the reflexive understanding of level 2, which it leaves intact, but considers that understanding itself, as expressed in the argument of

§ 16.3, so as to illuminate its interior working. The argument will be left to stand, and so will the fact of its concluding in 'the justifiable act' of my acting so as to preserve myself; but it is *understood* in a way that has important consequences.

18. The first thing that is grasped at level 3 about the argument of § 16.3 concerns the two first premises in that argument. Once one turns self-reflexively to consider that argument, it will become clear to one what one was in fact after (even though one did not quite understand it) in accepting the two first premises as premises in an argument about what to do. The 'order and harmony of acts' that is mentioned in those premises will now be seen to be the rational order of deriving objects of desire from a more basic value and of acting so as to bring about some end based on the same more basic value – and to be that order applied to the case at hand: the rational order of deriving objects of desire from a love of self which is taken as basic, in the context of acting so as to preserve oneself. At this level of reflexion, then, the very mechanism of *oikeiōsis* as I developed it from Cicero's chapter 16 will become clear to one, and the intrinsic order and harmony of acts of self-preservation as indistinctly glimpsed at level 2 will be seen to be the one of rational acceptability and hence true rational justifiability – based on something which is taken as a fact, viz. the animal's love of self.

Note that this means that whereas the fact of self-love is not a *part* of what is rationally justifiable, it *is* a *presupposition* of the rational justifiability of acting so as to preserve oneself. Action so as to preserve oneself is rationally justifiable – given the fact of self-love; and at level 3 one grasps the concept of rational justifiability and sees that it applies to acts of preserving oneself – because of the fact of self-love.

So the self-reflexive consideration of the two first premises of § 16.3 results in a grasp of the concept of rational justifiability and of the existence of the system of self-preserving behaviour based on self-love from which that concept may be read.

This understanding of certain premises in an argument one accepted already at the second level implies an acceptance of applying the concept of rational justifiability in one's search for an answer to the practical question and of finding that answer within the terms of the system of self-love, derived objects of desire and action so as to preserve oneself. This acceptance, then, is the first thing 'added' to the argument of § 16.3 as a result of self-reflexive consideration of that argument.

19.1 The second thing that is grasped at level 3 about the argument of § 16.3 concerns the third premiss of that argument and indeed the point of the argument as expressed in the conclusion. That point is the one of subsuming an individual (myself) under some general law-like description contained in the two first premisses – a description which one might try to express in a set of if-then clauses. Now the grasp that this is the point of that reasoning has important implications due to the way the Stoics understand the concept of the individual. In order to see this it will be helpful to make a brief excursion into Stoic metaphysics and its Aristotelian background.

19.2. In Aristotelian metaphysics the concept of the individual has an insecure place. It falls under Aristotle's concept of (indistinct and unknowable) *matter* to be contrasted with *form*, which occupies the centre of gravity of Aristotelian metaphysics. On the other hand Aristotle's concept of a 'this something' or 'this whatever it is' (*tode ti*), although it applies to the form-side of the disjunction between form and matter, still seems designed to do justice in some way to the concept of the individual.

Stoic metaphysics develops Aristotle's position in a number of ways and reaches a clearer view of the individual. In Stoicism the form-side of Aristotelian metaphysics is captured in the concept of *lekton* ('what is said', 'meaning'), while the role of Aristotle's matter is played by the Stoic *tunchanonta* (objects, literally perhaps 'recipients', viz. of predicates). The Stoics then account for the concept of the individual in terms of the concept of pointing (*deixis*), in a way that shows the distinction between the level of *lekta* and the one of *tunchanonta* to be the distinction between a level of description and one of fact.

The special role of *deixis* in connection with the concept of the individual and with the two levels of fact and description comes out in what the Stoics have to say about a division of certain *lekta*, which they called simple propositions (*hapla axiōmata*), into definite (*hōrismena*), e.g. 'this man is walking', 'this man is sitting', and indefinite (*aorista*) or intermediate (*mesa*), e.g. 'someone is sitting' and 'a man is sitting' or 'Socrates is walking' respectively (S.E. *M* VIII 96–7, SVF II 205).

Definite simple propositions, they said, are 'utterances accompanied by some *deixis*' (*ta kata deixin ekpheromena*, ibid.), and the connexion of this with the distinction between a concept of fact and one of description seems to come out when Sextus says the following of the Stoics (*M* VIII 98 and 100):

They say that the indefinite [simple proposition], e.g. 'someone is walking' or 'someone is sitting', becomes true when the definite [simple proposition] is found to be true, e.g. 'this man is sitting' or 'this man is walking' ... and furthermore the definite proposition we spoke of, 'this man is sitting' or 'this man is walking', they declare to be true when what is predicated, e.g. sitting or walking, applies to that which falls under the *deixis*.

So individuals, on the Stoic theory, are things (*tunchanonta*) falling under some *deixis* and having certain things (*lekta*) predicated of them. And we can only speak properly, viz. definitely, of an individual once there *is* something to which the predicate applies. This follows from tying the concept of the individual to pointing.

19.3. This is highly relevant to the argument from which we started. For the point of this argument was seen to be that of subsuming an individual under some general description and it does this by using the term 'I', which is precisely, in modern parlance, indexical in such a way as to refer to an individual in the Stoic way, by pointing.

So what happens when the argument of § 16.3 is self-reflexively seen on the background of the Stoic understanding of the individual, is that the I that constitutes the subject of the conclusion of that argument is seen to contain two components with different functions. One component is the descriptive content of the I, i.e. the I *as* something or other (the level of *lekton*), whose function it is to deliver that in virtue of which the subsumption of the I under the general description may proceed.

The other component is the indexical element in the I, i.e. the I just as this thing rather than that. This element brings in a dimension that is wholly different from that of description, viz. the one of fact, and it is 'brute' or 'naked' in the sense of having no descriptive content whatever. Correspondingly, its function is entirely different from that of the descriptive component of the I. It is that of locating the application of that description (and of the further descriptions that are deduced in the argument to apply also) *here*.

Now seeing this also means seeing that the function of the I in the argument of § 16.3 is in fact not different from what would have been the function of 'this man'. For the descriptive content of the I (the level of *lekton*) might equally well apply to another man, and as for the force of the indexical element in the I it is the same as that of 'this man' with the only difference that 'I' has the meaning of 'this man' *as applied to the speaker*. Important as this difference will no doubt be in other respects, in the present context it will only mean that in the case of the 'I' the object of the pointing is very clearly fixed in advance, as it is not in the case of 'this man'. (In the case of the 'I' we know exactly where to look.) So the point will stand that the *function* of the I in the argument of § 16.3 is the same as what would have been the function of 'this man'.

I shall discuss in a moment what the consequences are of this understanding of the argument of § 16.3.

19.4. First, however, I will try to show that we do not in fact have to turn to Stoic metaphysics for drawing the distinction between the two components of the I in the conclusion of the argument of § 16.3. There is an element in the Cicero text itself that we are discussing that points in the same direction. This is fortunate, since it means that I can justifiably continue to claim that I am merely spelling out what 'seeing the order and harmony of acts' in Cicero's chapter 21A consists in.

We know already that third level reflexion on this order, as it was expressed in the second level reasoning of § 16.3, leads to an understanding of the mechanism of *oikeiōsis* as I have developed it on the basis of Cicero's chapter 16. But now this mechanism, as I developed it, contains an element that seems to indicate that the Stoics were alive to the special indexical force of the I. The point is that in Cicero's chapter 16 the fact of self-love was explicitly set apart in a way that seems highly relevant in the present context. There, as we know, the self as the object of love was distinctly implied to be completely undescribed and logically separable from its descriptions. This idea is further developed by Seneca in a letter analysed by Jacques Brunschwig elsewhere in this volume (Seneca, *Ep. mor.* 121). But the idea is clearly present in Cicero and lies behind his singling out self-love as the basis of Stoic ethics.

Now I have contended that the concept of self-love brings in the idea of an irreducible *evaluative* component in the concept of *hormē*. This seems to follow from the idea of a *love* for something which is completely *undescribed*. For if such love were to be reducible, it seems that its object would have to be described at least in some way.

But consider then further this idea of love of a completely undescribed self. Even if the self is completely undescribed, there must be *something* to say of it. But since we are after all talking of an undescribed *self*, what else could one possibly say of it than this: that the term may only be appropriately used by any given speaker of a single thing (viz. 'him')[10] and that whenever the term is appropriately used there necessarily *is* some living being or other who may appropriately apply the term to 'him' (no matter how exactly we should define what counts as a 'him')? But it seems precisely the point of the indexical I to bring in these two ideas. So the Stoic talk of love of an undescribed *self* seems to indicate that they were in fact alive to the complex behaviour discussed in § 19.3 of the I in the argument of § 16.3.

---

[10] Though the speaker may of course always speak at a meta-level of 'selves' without necessarily referring to himself.

19.5. What, then, is the point of seeing that the I in the argument of § 16.3 has (also) the indexical force which belongs to a level of non-described fact and that as far as this element goes the function of the I is not different from that of 'this man'? The answer is that by seeing this one comes to understand that it plays no rôle whatever, when one is giving a rational answer to the practical question, whether the predicates that enter into that answer refer to oneself or to somebody else. (More concretely one will see that as long as one is operating within the horizon of rationality no valid reason can be given for paying any special attention to oneself just because it is oneself one is thinking about.)

Now this means two things. It means, first, that by accepting the argument of § 16.3 one also accepts the appropriateness of inserting other individuals than oneself in that argument. So one will also accept the conclusion when *you* apply it to *your* case. But understanding the function of the I in the argument and seeing that in accepting the argument at level 2 one was accepting it with the implications of that function which one has now come to recognise also means understanding and accepting that what one was trying to discover in answering the practical question along the lines of the argument of § 16.3 was not only an answer of direct practical import to the practical question of what one should do, but at the same time *the rational and true answer* to that question as pertaining to all the individuals to whom it may apply.

There is nothing strange about this insight. One was using one's reason at level 2 for answering a question pertaining to oneself. One continues to accept the argument as leading to an answer to that question. But one *also* comes to see that trying to answer that question by rational means, as one did, implies the acceptance of rational canons for answering such a question which have nothing to do with the fact that it is oneself, i.e. just this man rather than this one, who asks the question.

So seeing the argument of § 16.3 from the self-reflexive third level will have as its two consequences that one understands and accepts first, that one's reasoning will be just as valid when applied to somebody else and secondly, that the question to whom it applies is in a sense immaterial, since the point of engaging in reasoning of the type of § 16.3 lies in discovering the truth irrespective of where it has application.

The grasp, and acceptance, of both implications of using one's reason for answering the practical question, as one did at level 2, is a grasp of *the objectivity of reason* and an acceptance of applying the objective point of view, which requires that one lays oneself open to *all* those considerations (be they evaluative or factual) that will be relevant to answering the practical question. As opposed to this we may speak of a subjective or parochial point of view which distorts one's view of the facts because of its restricted basis.

The acceptance of the objectivity of reason is the second thing 'added' to the argument of § 16.3 as a result of self-reflexive consideration of that argument.

19.6. We may try to bring out the scope of the objective, rational point of view by contrasting it with the subjective point of view as it is found in human beings during their development from childhood to adulthood.

A child is non-rational and so, on this view, necessarily subjective. And in fact, of course, children *are* subjective. They lack, as we say, the capacity for 'self-objectivisation', for seeing that what holds for themselves will also hold for anyone situated like themselves (in the relevant respects) – the first of the two implications mentioned in § 19.5.

Adults, by contrast, do have the capacity for 'self-objectivisation', but they may often fall back on the subjective point of view. This, of course, is an indefensible lapse since adults may in fact do better (as children may not – but of course we do *teach* them to consider what they would think if they were in another child's shoes). But adults may also err, the Stoics would say, in that although they may have the capacity for self-objectivisation which is implied in the ability to deliberate, they may still fail in their reasoning to lay themselves open to an undistorted view of all the relevant facts about the world; they may still not be prepared to 'let the facts speak'. This is an error of a different type, corresponding to the second of the two implications mentioned in § 19.5. It is the error of adults who although they are prepared to reason about what to do, reach a false answer to that question, not (necessarily) because of any faulty use of reason (in a formal sense), but because their appreciation of the facts about what has value is wrong. Still, this may also fairly be said to be an error that is due to an insufficient capacity to give up the subjective point of view. For in many cases, at least, the faulty understanding of such adults of what has value is derived from their evaluative attitudes as children or from a false appreciation of those attitudes – e.g. if they think that the good for man is pleasure.

Both types of error, then, may be referred back to an incapacity to go beyond or give up the subjective point of view. Conversely, as soon as one engages in reasoning about the practical question, as at my level 2, the correct appreciation of the rôle of one's self and of the objectivity of reason will be implied in the reasoning, and at the third level that appreciation will become explicit.

20. So to sum up so far, reflexion at the third level on the argument of

§ 16.3 will give one a grasp of the concept of rational justifiability and of the system of self-preserving behaviour based on self-love that is operating in animals in general (§ 18). It will also give one a grasp of the unimportance of any given individual just as that in a rational answer to the practical question and of the objective character of reason, directed as it is towards the discovery of truth (§ 19.1–6).

Grasping these points as implied in the argument at level 2 will imply accepting them as guidelines for what further practical inquiry one may have to engage in. This implies that one accepts *giving up* any subjective point of view based on either an incapacity for self-objectivisation or an incapacity to include all relevant considerations, even those that do not immediately present themselves in a favourable light, in one's deliberation about what to do (§ 19.1–6). Conversely one will *embrace* the requirement to act in a way that is rationally justifiable and in accordance with the system of self-preserving behaviour based on self-love, the objective status of which one has come to recognise (§§ 18 and 19.1–6).

21. Suppose these are the insights one acquires by seeing the reasoning of level 2 from the self-reflexive level 3. In that case there is one more insight one will acquire, viz. a grasp of the unimportance of the act's being successful or not in terms of actually contributing to the preservation of the agent. The reasoning is this.

Till now we have considered the question of what a man comes to see in *oikeiōsis* in terms of the general context of asking the practical question and looking for an act that is justifiable. We have been induced to this by the way we have found it necessary to develop Cicero's remark of an acquired insight into the order and harmony of certain acts. We might also say, of course, that we have been concerned with the value of certain acts, using 'value' in a general modern sense, which is less specific than the Stoic one.

Now seen from the rational point of view that value was expressed in the idea of rational justifiability. But the justifiable act as expressed in the conclusion of the reasoning of level 2 evidently contains one more value element, precisely that of the success of the act. For the idea of acting so as to preserve myself makes no sense unless it is taken to imply that the success of the act has value.

Here, however, we must repeat the distinction between the rational content of the conclusion of the argument of § 16.3 and the sheer fact of its being tied to a certain individual (here: myself). In terms of the rational content of that conclusion, viz. the rationality of acting so as to preserve oneself (given the fact of self-love), and also in terms of the conclusion's being tied to *some individual or other*, the value of the success of acting on the conclusion, i.e. of actually preserving the given individual, is part of what makes the act rationally justifiable (given the fact of self-love):

But in the case of *my* acting so as to preserve myself, i.e. in terms of any given individual's tying the conclusion to *himself*, the value of the success of the act acquires additional importance in a quite different way. It is no longer just something to be noted dispassionately as logically implied in what makes the act rationally justifiable. Rather it is the 'felt' importance of this act of mine reaching the end for which I have designed it. This emotional element is tied, I suggest, to the indexical force of the I-element of the justifiable act at level 2. The fact that it is *my* action is connected with the *drive* behind the act, and this drive is connected with the 'felt' importance of the success of the act.

But now we know that once a man has reached the third level of reflexion, he will have come to see and accept that he must not, indeed cannot consistently let himself be influenced by any consideration that is subjective. It follows that when a man has reached that level of reflexion, the special importance for him of the success or failure of any act of his so as to preserve himself falls completely out of view. It does not enter into the determination of the value of the act.

This does not mean, of course, that he no longer accepts the conclusion of § 16.3 as action-guiding, speaking as it does about what is the thing to do for *him*. On the contrary, he started out asking the practical question in terms of what *he* should do and the conclusion of the argument of § 16.3 constitutes an answer to that question. What, at the third level, he has come to understand in addition does not make it less appropriate that he should ask and answer the practical question on his own behalf and indeed act on his answer. What he has come to see at the third level is only that the value of his act is an objective one and hence unconnected with the fact that his act is *his* act rather than somebody else's.

On this reading the Stoics will be seen to connect together the following items: the fact of someone being engaged in the whole investigation and the action that may follow from it, the felt importance of the investigation and the ensuing action and hence the value for the agent of success rather than failure, and finally 'desire' (*hormē*). All these items the Stoics will derive from the I or self which is the object of love in self-love.

In addition, as we know, their idea of self-love also introduces as a basic component of *hormē* the element of valuation, viz. the notion of a basic *love* for the undetermined self. But this element should be clearly distinguished from the element of 'desire' in *hormē*: whereas the latter is a function of the indexical force of the I-element and hence based on the fundamental love for *oneself*, the former is an independent element, which also enters into the analysis (in the form of a basic presupposition) of the rational content of the conclusion of the argument of § 16.3.

But the present point is that by deriving the items I mentioned from the I or self the Stoics effectively deny the relevance of any of these items to a determination of the value of any given act. These items cannot enter into the objective evaluation of the act.

22. When this is seen, the process of *parakolouthēsis* has reached its end, and at this point the reflecting person will have performed the famous shift of allegiance from natural goods to conformity with nature. Once a man has come to reason, he will have come to see that the importance to him of the success or failure of any justifiable act of his belongs with a number of other things (including his whole emotional attitude to the act) to a wholly separate dimension, viz. the one of fact, which is completely irrelevant to the terms in which he is conducting his investigation. His view of the value of the justifiable act will not, therefore, be in the least influenced by its eventual success or failure.

23. But if this is the result, why should a man be at all willing to undergo the process of *parakolouthēsis* to its final conclusion? Would it not be preferable for him to remain in the innocently selfish state of animals and children before the advent of reason? Now this is not something a human being can choose for himself, since he does acquire willy-nilly the reasoning capacity at the appropriate point in time. But though capable of seeing what reason tells him about how to act, he could perhaps choose to think that that is not relevant to himself, since he does not wish to conform to reason. While capable of entertaining certain rational beliefs, he will not be prepared to make them his own. *He* is attracted to that clear-cut innocent state of animals and children.

Here, however, the basic mechanism in *oikeiōsis* becomes important again. A man loves himself. But this means that he loves whatever he takes himself to be. Now a grown up man is (also) rational and he cannot but see that he is. So he will come to love 'his' reason. And from this it follows that he will come to adopt any insights reached by reason as his own: he will necessarily *believe* them as being valid for himself too.

Conformity with the order of acts, with nature, and with moral virtue

24. I now wish to single out two points connected with this reading of *oikeiōsis* in adult human beings. I am moving back from living in conformity with the order and harmony of acts to living in accordance with

nature and from there to living in accordance with moral virtue (cf. § 2 above).

25. The first point concerns the relation between living in conformity with the order and harmony of acts and the official Stoic phrase 'living in accordance with nature'. Cicero implicitly identifies the two, but how can he?

I have argued that we should understand 'living in conformity with the order and harmony of acts' as 'living rationally – on the basis of the natural fact of self-love'. This will correspond in two ways to living in accordance with nature:

(1) By 'nature' the Stoics, at least certainly Chrysippus (D.L. VII 89), meant both man's own nature and universal nature. In either case they clearly meant to refer to one and the same thing: reason. This needs no proof in the case of man's nature. But the Stoics were equally unhesitating in affirming the rationality of universal nature. They did this, of course, when they spoke of cosmic nature as provident. But this should presumably be understood as one side of a coin whose other side is cosmic nature as exhibiting the inexorable pattern of causal determinism (*fatum*). And it may be precisely this feature of nature which is relevant to the order and harmony of acts. For the means–end structure of acts of trying to preserve oneself, which is what accounts for the rational justifiability (given the fact of self-love) of such acts, precisely presupposes nature's causal structure. So living rationally will be living in accordance with nature.

(2) But the very fact of self-love also fits well with the concept of nature. It introduces, as we know, an evaluative component that is basic, and it is taken by the Stoics to be a natural fact. So here we may well speak of a 'norm of nature'.

I conclude that one can well understand how the Stoics could identify living in conformity with the order and harmony of acts (as I have interpreted it) with living in accordance with nature.

26.1. The second point concerns the relation between living in accordance with nature and living in accordance with moral virtue. We have seen that the Stoics are asking in the Cicero passage about the *telos*. They find it in conformity with nature in the sense I have specified. But they also connect this with a life in accordance with moral virtue: how can they?

It is reasonable to expect that the Stoics started out, like their immediate predecessors Aristotle and Plato, wanting to show that the exercise of moral virtue as this concept is ordinarily understood is (at least) a necessary condition for *eudaimonia* and hence is a constituent element in the *telos*. They then conclude, as we have seen, that there is only one thing going into the *telos*, viz. conformity with nature, and this will therefore be both a necessary and a sufficient condition for *eudaimonia*. But then they also assert that a life in accordance with nature is a life in accordance with moral virtue. Do they mean here moral virtue as it is ordinarily understood? In that case they will have some work to do in order to show that living in accordance with nature as they understand this amounts to the same thing as living in accordance with moral virtue as ordinarily understood. Or do they propose a revisionary account of moral virtue? In that case they will still have some work to do in order to show why moral virtue as ordinarily understood is *not*, after all, genuine moral virtue.

I believe that the Stoics took the first road. Life in accordance with nature in effect amounts to the same thing as life in accordance with the moral virtues as ordinarily understood. But we only get a glimpse of how they would defend this position.

26.2. It will clearly be relevant to look at passages that bring together the various moral virtues under some description that tells us what it is about them that makes them moral virtues. Perhaps we can then see some connexion between this supposed element and living in accordance with nature as I have interpreted this. A number of passages collected by von Arnim might seem relevant: *SVF* III 264, 265 and 280. Unfortunately they do not bring us very far. There is more to be got once more, I believe, from Cicero, who concludes a discussion of wisdom (*sapientia*, which translates either *epistēmē* or *phronēsis*) in *Fin.* III 23–5 as follows:

... Wisdom alone [as compared to certain arts like medicine or seamanship] is totally turned towards itself [*in se tota conversa*], which is not the case with the other arts. [...] For wisdom comprises both magnanimity and justice and the fact that one believes that everything that may happen to a man is beneath one [*infra se*], which is not the case with the other arts. But no one can possess those same virtues I have just mentioned unless he has decided that nothing is different from anything else other than noble and base things.

This passage seems to contain an attempt to bring together three things which should initially be distinguished: Stoic wisdom understood as the insight that man's end is living in accordance with nature in the sense I have developed on the basis of Cicero's chapter 21, ordinary moral virtue as represented by magnanimity and justice, and Stoic moral virtue as represented by the noble as against the base.

26.3. Note first that Cicero is hardly just saying, in the second sentence of the quoted passage, that wisdom comprises, chosen at random, magnanimity, justice and the fact that one takes everything that may happen to a man to be beneath one. Rather he is picking out two especially important moral virtues (magnanimity and justice) and suggesting that what is common to them and hence makes them moral virtues is the fact that both the magnanimous man and the just man believes that everything that may happen to a man is beneath him.

I cannot argue properly here for this suggestion. A few remarks must suffice. First, magnanimity (Greek *megalopsuchia*) is defined by the Stoics as 'knowledge or a state that makes a man superior to what may happen to morally good and bad people alike' (*SVF* III 265, cf. also 264, 269, 270, 274 and 275). Thus Cicero's point about believing everything that may happen to a man to be beneath oneself seems to be part of the very definition of magnanimity.

Secondly, in spite of the very different attempts to fit magnanimity into a system of virtues and connected commendable states of mind (*hexeis*) contained in the passages referred to, it seems a fair guess that magnanimity does have a special status, not least on the background of Aristotelian ethics, in which magnanimity has in fact a special rôle to play in relation to the other virtues in spite of the fact that it is also just mentioned by Aristotle as one virtue among others.[11]

My suggestion is that corresponding to the fact (and this, fortunately, is a fact) that the Stoics spoke of *oikeiōsis* in two contexts, viz. the one we have already considered and the one to be considered later, which concerns justice, they will have tried to connect all the ordinary moral virtues they wanted to account for in two columns, one of which has 'magnanimity' as its title while the other is called 'justice'. And they will have put forward as a way of seeing all ordinary moral virtues together the suggestion that what makes them moral virtues is that they make a man believe that the external things or events that may happen to him are beneath him.

26.4. If this is correct, our passage may be seen to contain an argument of the following form:

> Wisdom (understood as the insight that man's end is living in accordance with nature) brings in the idea of believing external things and events to be beneath oneself.
> But this idea is what brings ordinary moral virtues together as represented by magnanimity and justice.
> So living in accordance with nature and living in accordance with moral virtue as ordinarily understood go together.

---

[11] I argue for this in Engberg-Pedersen (1983), pp. 75–81.

(The arts, by contrast, differ from wisdom in that external things and events do have relevance: in their case, as Cicero says a little earlier in the text (*Fin.* III 24), the point of the art does not lie, as it does in the case of wisdom, in the act itself, but must be sought from without.)

Now having those ordinary moral virtues as implying the belief that external things and events are beneath oneself presupposes the belief that the only difference (in value, presumably) between things is in terms of noble and base, i.e. of moral virtue as the Stoics conceive it.

It follows that Stoic wisdom (living in accordance with nature), ordinary virtue and Stoic virtue go together.

On this reading the passage contains a simple argument with the belief of the unimportance of external things acting as middle term. Even if the argument is not very tidy (which is why I have been speaking of 'going together' in a number of places), and even if the premiss about what holds ordinary moral virtues together may not seem obviously right, the passage does seem to contain a serious attempt to answer the question from which we started. Living in accordance with ordinary moral virtue is in fact captured in living in accordance with nature (as I have interpreted it).

Oikeiōsis *towards other humans: justice*

27. So much for *oikeiōsis* in its first version, towards nature. By this type of *oikeiōsis* a man comes to see that his end lies in acting rationally (within the naturally given context of self-love) in such a way that his own desire for preservation and his own interest in the successful outcome of his acts add nothing at all to the value of those acts. But the Stoics also talk of *oikeiōsis* in a second version, towards other humans. The best evidence for this is Cicero, *Fin.* III 62–71. I will not go into detail, but will present the salient points.

28.1. Let us first ask: Why should the Stoics need to talk of *oikeiōsis* a second time?

As I have explained the way the Stoics understand reason (its objective character) and its relation to the objects of action, the moral insight reached in *oikeiōsis* has remained completely self-centred in the sense that in acting on the basis of the insight reached so far a man will continue to act on his own behalf only. In relation to the moral insight itself this is accidental, but it is a fact. Reason has not provided one with any more justification for acting on one's own behalf than for acting on the behalf of any other individual, but neither has it provided one with any justification for acting on behalf of any of *them*. So if one is to care for anybody other than oneself, the Stoics must have something more to say.

28.2. And they do have more to say. It has two stages.

The first stage concerns the basic step away from natural self-centredness. Just as in its first version *oikeiōsis* starts from a single basic evaluative fact, viz. one's attachment for oneself, so in its second version *oikeiōsis* starts from a basic evaluative fact which is one's love for one's offspring.[12] This love constitutes a step away from self-centredness because it is love for one's children for *their* sake, in proportion to their needs, in order that *they* may survive, and the Latin word for it is *cura* (e.g. Cicero, *Off.* I 11, 12). It is not a result of *oikeiōsis* in its first version precisely because it is truly other-regarding. Nor is it a result of *oikeiōsis* in its second version, but its starting-point.

28.3. The step that follows, then, is the extension of this basic feeling of care for one's offspring (or whoever else it may be) to human beings as such. The mechanism is not spelled out in the texts, but it should be the following.[13] When a man comes to reason, he will self-reflexively notice that he has been caring all along for other beings (for their sake) because he has seen them as belonging to himself: they were *his* offspring or *his* associates. But he now also comes to see himself as rational with the consequence that whatever else is rational will belong to him and be his just as much as, nay even more than, his offspring or other associates. So his basic other-regarding attitude of care (for their own sake) for others who were seen to belong to him must needs be extended to cover all rational beings. *They* are now seen to belong to him to the highest degree since in so far as they partake in rationality, which is common to them all, they are identical with him on the point which has by far the most important rôle to play for determining *what he himself is* (i.e. for determining his 'constitution' as we know it from Cicero, *Fin.* III 16).

Thus the Stoics can speak in a very Kantian way of a 'city' of men and gods and connect the fact that each of us is a member of that city with a utilitarian type of altruism (*Fin.* III 64):

The Stoics believe that the universe is governed by the power of the gods and that it is a sort of city or state that is common to men and gods and that each of us is a

---

[12] It need not, of course, be one's offspring, but might also be one's associates in a number of connections etc. The reason why the Stoics speak so emphatically of one's offspring is presumably that here it is easier to see how love for oneself may extend outside oneself towards others – for in a quite concrete sense, of course, one's offspring *is* an extension of oneself.

[13] Cf. Kerferd (1972), pp. 195f. Also relevant is the aporetic discussion in Pembroke (1971), pp. 121–32.

part of this universe; from which it follows by nature that we set the common advantage [*utilitas*] before our own. For just as the laws set the safety of all before the safety of individuals, so a man who is good, wise, law-abiding and conscious of his civic duty will care for the advantage of all rather than of some single individual or himself.

The second version of *oikeiōsis* then, produces justice, or at least the basic attitude underlying justice, as the texts repeat.

Happiness

29. What, then, does *oikeiōsis* in its two forms give us? What will the Stoic do in fulfilling his end? What will his happiness consist in?

The Stoic will be concerned to get for himself those primary things in accordance with nature that are required to keep him alive and in proper physical form. But he will also be concerned that other people with whom he is living shall get those things. This clearly gives him as many things to do (duties) as, e.g., Aristotle's morally good man has. The Stoic will also marry and rear children. And with respect to his children (in bringing them up) as well as his fellow-citizens he will be concerned to instil in them the principles of wisdom (Cicero, *Fin.* III 65). This will require, e.g., that he engages in philosophy, and he may communicate his wisdom in poetical form (as Cleanthes did) or in hortatory letters (like Seneca), always taking care to speak to others in the way that suits *them* best. In short, the Stoic who has seen the light will lead a rich and varied life, mixing and engaging with others and trying to extend the good.

What he will *not* do is do whatever he does just because he fancies doing it. He may write poetry that makes use of all the blandishments of poetic style in order to influence men's minds, but just for that reason, because they *are* the appropriate means to influence them, not simply because he happens to have a poetic urge. For anything that he does will be constantly transfigured by the insight he has acquired by undergoing *oikeiōsis* in its two forms that whatever may happen to a man is beneath him, and hence that whatever desires he happens to have, as the individual that he is, will have no rôle to play in determining the value of his acts.

As long, therefore, as he lives among men needing his care, and as long as he is himself a human being with bodily needs, he will have plenty of things to do which, one may suppose, will be high on the list of what goes into happiness on almost any modern account thereof.

The Stoics did not distinguish between questions of happiness and questions of morality. On the contrary, morality would have to find its proper place within an overall framework defined in terms of happiness.

Furthermore it did this, as we have seen, in such a way that morality came to be seen as the *only* thing relevant to happiness. But the result of this was not disastrous, since applying the moral view does not in the least prevent a man from engaging in a wide variety of activities. What the Stoics could not, and would not, accommodate was the view that questions of happiness relate crucially to the idea of each individual's being free to pick and choose (within certain limits set up by morality) the activities that *he* finds satisfying, *outside* the moral point of view, that is. No act, in Stoicism, that is relevant to happiness will fall outside that point of view.

Kathēkonta *and the content of the good*

30. This concludes the first part of the paper. In the second part I shall be concerned to define the exact rôle of *kathēkonta* (the *officia*, a man's duties) in Stoic ethics with special reference to the picture of *oikeiōsis* in its first version that I have sketched.

31. In Cicero's account in *Fin.* III *kathēkonta* play a rôle already in chapter 20, in the account of the pattern of behaviour that is exhibited by a man *before* he comes, by *oikeiōsis*, to the final insight into what is good. Here the idea is that a man may perform all his duties, do everything that is required by reason or morality, but without himself having the final insight that accounts for their being his duties. He may do the 'what', in Aristotelian terms, without knowing the 'why' or 'how'.

Later in the book, then (chapters 5 off.), Cicero introduces a 'difference among things', which is captured in the concepts of being 'preferred' (*proēgmenon*) and being 'relegated' (*apoproēgmenon* – perhaps 'dispreferred'). He states (ibid.) that unless this difference be admitted, no function (*munus*) or task (*opus*) could be found for wisdom nor would there be any choice (*dilectus*) among things.

This claim should come as no surprise. Among the 'preferred things' (or 'advantages') will be the primary natural objects that we know from Cicero's chapters 16–20, and the man who has acquired the final insight into what is good will continue to consider valuable all the things that belong to him objectively as the being that he is (viz. both a rational one and one with a bodily and animal nature). For the point of his insight is not that these things no longer have value. His insight (acquired as a result of *oikeiōsis* in its first version) is that he should live rationally based on the natural fact of self-love, and this means two things. It means, first, that things have value to the degree that they preserve a man as the being that he is: this value is 'rational' because it is based, first on an evaluation which is taken to be a basic natural fact, viz. the self-love of living creatures, and secondly on there being a factual relationship of a determinable kind between the valuable thing and the self that is loved. But secondly the sense of the man's insight is the one I have spent most time on bringing out, viz. that what counts in a rational answer to the practical question is the objective status of self-love and of such rationally derived objects of desire, a status that is independent of the fact that the man loves his own self and the things that preserve that.

So wisdom will in fact consist in choosing the 'advantages', but always in such a way that the wise man considers 'everything that may happen to a man' beneath him. He chooses (for himself, if we are talking only of *oikeiōsis* in its first version) natural 'advantages' because he is a being for whom such things are in fact objectively valuable, not because he happens to want to get them for himself. He does want to get them for himself, but this fact, which is a fact, has no rôle to play in the justification of his action; it adds nothing to a consideration of the act's value.

But just as wisdom will consist in choosing 'advantages' rather than 'disadvantages', so the *kathēkonta* too will operate in the same area. Cicero makes the point in *Fin.* III 58–9, where he connects the *officia* with the 'intermediates' (*adiaphora, media*), i.e. precisely the area of things lying 'between' things noble and base. Still, the exact sense of what Cicero says of *officia* in the two chapters referred to should be scrutinised; for it adds to the earlier picture according to which a man may do *all* that is required in the intermediate area just lacking the insight into the why. As we shall see, the final insight reached in *oikeiōsis* will make a difference even with respect to the what.

32. Cicero defines *officium* in chapter 58 as 'something which is such that a reasonable ground can be given for putting it into action'. He is translating the Greek definition, according to which *kathēkon* is 'following [sc. nature] in one's life' and 'something the putting into action of which can be reasonably justified' (*SVF* III 494, 493).

We should first note that the Stoics wanted to claim the term *kathēkon* for acts in accordance with nature not only of rational beings, but also of non-rational animals (ibid.). So their definition is well chosen. For a reasonable or well-grounded justification may be given for acts in accordance with nature of non-rational as well as rational animals.

But it also seems that the Stoics had a more specific idea in mind when they spoke in the definition of *kathēkon* of a reasonable or well-grounded justification (*eulogos apologia*). This seems indicated by the Stoic definition of a proposition that is *eulogos* (*eulogon axiōma*) as 'one that has to start with more chances of being true than not', e.g. 'I shall be alive tomorrow' (D.L. VI 76, *SVF* II 201). If we transfer this to the case at hand, the result will be that an *officium* is something of such a kind that if one puts it into action (cf. the talk of putting into action in the quoted definitions of *officium* and *kathēkon*), it is more likely than not that one's act will be *right*.

Now in chapter 59 Cicero distinguishes between a type of *officium* which is perfect (*perfectum*) and one which is just 'starting' (*inchoatum*). The former, he says, is a right act (*recte factum, katorthōma*), the latter, we may infer, not necessarily so. And Cicero exemplifies the distinction by the case of handing back a deposit justly (a right act) as against just handing it back: the latter, he says, is an *officium*, meaning, we may suppose, an *officium* proper.

Here Cicero is in effect saying that *officia* proper are those *not* necessarily right, precisely those captured by the definition of *officium* when this is interpreted on the basis of the more restricted sense of *eulogos* contained in D.L. VII 76. Conversely a perfect *officium*, which is always right, is an act that has escaped the relative instability of *officia* proper.

But now perfect *officia* are the acts performed by the wise man, who is the one who has reached the final insight into the good that one may acquire in *oikeiōsis*. It follows that his insight may make a difference, not just in motive, but also *in the act*: in some cases the wise man will perform an act which will be right, but which is also such that at the level of the insight had by the not yet wise man, no *eulogos apologia* for doing the act could have been given in advance of doing it.[14]

I shall try to develop in a moment why this is important for the understanding of the proper place of *kathēkonta* in Stoic ethics.

33.1. First I will try to work towards the conclusion I have just drawn by a different route.

Diogenes Laertius has preserved two distinctions relating to *kathēkonta* which it will be worth considering (D. L. VII 109): some *kathēkonta* are 'without circumstance' (*aneu peristaseōs*), some are 'with circumstance' (*peristatika*). Examples of the former are 'taking care of one's health and of one's sense organs'. Examples of the latter are 'maiming oneself' and 'sacrificing one's property'. Furthermore, among *kathēkonta* some should be done always (*aei kathēkei*, e.g. 'living in accordance with virtue'), some not always (*ouk aei*, e.g. 'conversing', 'walking around').

Let us start from the latter distinction. Note here that both types of action (living in accordance with virtue and engaging in conversation etc.)

---

[14] The best work on the question of 'difference in motive only versus difference in motive + difference in the act' is two papers by I. G. Kidd (1971 and 1978). In the later paper Kidd redresses the balance in the direction of 'difference in the act as well as in motive'. He is right.

are kathēkonta, it is just that the former type should always be done, the latter not. They are *kathēkonta*, we may suppose, because a *eulogos apologia* may be given of them. This seems also true of the latter type of act: it is in fact natural for humans to engage in conversation as it is not, e.g., for non-rational animals.

But it should not always be done: here it becomes clear that *kathēkonta* are action-*types* that may be well-grounded as such, but the *apologia* (unless given by the wise man) is *eulogos* in the more restricted sense we have already met that if one acts *in a particular situation* in accordance with an action-type of the form in question, it is only more likely than not that one's act will be right.

Note also that *kathēkonta* which are always to be done are act-types under such a description that they should necessarily be done always: living in accordance with virtue is empty as far as descriptive content goes and for that very reason, because it *mentions* virtue, always to be done.

By contrast, conversing etc. are action-types that are rich in descriptive content – which is why, in spite of being *kathēkonta* they should *not* always be applied in the particular situation. *Kathēkonta* that should always be done are in fact those 'right acts' we have already met (*katorthōmata*), *kathēkonta* that should *not* always be done are neither right acts nor wrong acts (*hamartēmata*, SVF III 501, note the examples).

Here the point of *kathēkonta* proper (those that should not always be done, i.e. in any given particular situation answering to the description; those for the putting into action of which a justification can be given that is only *eulogos* in the restricted sense) becomes clear. They serve to produce a fit between on the one hand the empty account of the good as living in accordance with virtue and nature and on the other hand the factual world; they are *elements in the progressive clarification of what the good actually consists in*.

33.2. However, before developing this further, let us turn to the other distinction in Diogenes. It has recently been studied by Nicholas P. White (1978), who argues (p. 111) that *kathēkonta* 'without circumstance' are not 'actions which are *kathēkonta* under all circumstances', but 'actions which are, in the absence of special circumstances, *kathēkonta*'.

This is both right and wrong. *Kathēkonta* 'without circumstance' are evidently not 'actions which are *kathēkonta* under all circumstances' as the point of Diogenes' examples shows, so they should not be done (they do not *kathēkein*) under all circumstances, i.e. in every particular situation. But in spite of that they are and remain (in all circumstances, if you like) *kathēkonta*. They are act-types for which a *eulogos apologia* may be given, no matter whether their application in a given particular situation would give the wrong result. So the point of calling them 'without circumstance' *kathēkonta* will be that they do not in their description *mention* any specific circumstances.

This, by contrast, is what the *kathēkonta* 'with circumstance' do. They are act-types whose descriptions mention specific circumstances, e.g. maiming oneself in a situation where by so doing one will rescue one's country. In so doing these descriptions move us one more step in the direction of establishing the perfect fit between acting virtuously or in accordance with nature and some act-description in descriptive terms; but the point of the distinction I discussed first, between *kathēkonta* that should always be done and *kathēkonta* that should not always be done, is, I suggest, that the fit will never be perfect: one can always think of a situation in which the application even of a very specific *kathēkon* 'with circumstance' will not yield a *katorthōma*. So, and this is the point I made earlier, the wise man's insight makes a difference even as regards the what.

Kathēkonta *and the wise man*

34. So what is the rôle of *kathēkonta* in Stoic ethics with special reference to the process of *oikeiōsis*?

Cicero implied that one could do everything right before knowing the why. We have seen reason to think that this picture should be supplemented. It is true that the insight one acquires at the final stage of *oikeiōsis* is of a new kind (and this is what Cicero's picture brings out so well) – it is insight into the why and it belongs to a higher level of reflexion than the thinking that goes into accepting the *kathēkonta* proper: in relation to that thinking it is genuinely self-reflexive, it illuminates the *kathēkonta* from within. But it also makes a difference as regards the what. Still, if the insight one acquires at the final stage is one of an instant recognition of the good (viz. a grasp that one should live in accordance with nature in the sense of rationally, based on the natural fact of self-love), and if this insight will not presuppose total knowledge of what concretely is in accordance with nature; if, furthermore, it seems reasonable to say that acquisition of the latter piece of knowledge *depends* on the grasp of the good (plus, I would say, *experience*, cf. Chrysippus' 'living in accordance with experience of what happens by nature', D.L. vii 87), then although *kathēkonta* will still, as Cicero has it, play a rôle in the deliberation of the *un*-wise man (who has not yet reached insight into the why – Cicero's final stage), they will *also* play a rôle in the deliberation of the person who *has* reached Cicero's final stage, viz. in his progressive deliberative clarification of what, in detail, the end and the good consists in. This person, too, will build on *kathēkonta* when making the final and complete discovery of the good.

35. Is this person the Stoic sage, is he wise? In one way yes, in another no.

He *is* wise because he has undergone the conversion I spoke of, having come to see that the end lies in living in accordance with nature (in the sense I have attempted to specify) and that this is the only good. This is a finite insight with the character that Ariston claimed basic philosophical tenets should have (Seneca, *Ep. mor.* 94 15–16). Indeed, it is *the* 'dogma', according to the Stoics, in ethics.

On the other hand he is not yet *quite* the wise man, since he has not reached the perfect fit between his evaluative insight on the one hand and the filling in of it in descriptive language on the other hand. This immense task cannot, in fact, be performed by men, so the Stoics should say – and I suppose they do say it when they speak of the wise man as just as rare as the bird Phoenix – since it requires that one becomes one with the world.

So, should we say that the Stoics operate with two types of wise man?[15] I think not, for although I have done my best to develop the picture of a human being who is wise in that he has acquired the basic evaluative insight into what is good, I believe that the Stoics would also insist that that insight may be deepened, though not changed, when it is spelled out completely in descriptive language, i.e. when the total fit is being achieved. The demand that we should talk of types of wise man or settle on placing the wise man at some particular point in this continuum is unreasonable. The basic evaluative insight remains the same, but its descriptive content may be refined *ad infinitum*.[16]

---

[15] For a similar question see Kerferd (1978).

[16] This is an extensively revised version of the paper I read at the conference. The basic idea is the same, but the orchestration is different. I am grateful to the participants in the conference for making me see the inadequacies of the original version. A later version of the paper was read to the Copenhagen Aristotelian group. I should like to thank all members of the group, in particular Johnny Christensen and Finn Collin, for helping to clarify a number of points.

7 Antipater, or the art of living

Gisela Striker

In reading the doxographical reports on Stoic philosophy, one gets the impression that the Stoics had a singular, and often irritating, predilection for identity-statements. The best known case is undoubtedly that of nature, which is at the same time reason, *fatum*, providence and Zeus himself (Plut. *Stoic. rep.* 1050b). But in ethics, too, one finds such series of identifications, which do not always make understanding the texts any easier. The goal of life, for example, *eudaimonia*, is supposed to consist in a life in agreement with nature, which is ostensibly the same as a life in accordance with virtue. And this in turn seems to be a life which is determined by the rational selection of that which accords with nature. Virtue, for its part, is designated as a 'consistent attitude' (*diathesis homologoumenē*, D.L. VII 89), as 'knowledge of what is good, bad and neither of these' (S.E. *M* XI 170, 184), and finally as 'the art of living' (*technē peri ton bion*, ibid. 170, 181, 184). These claims are not at all self-evident, and hence obviously require justification. But the explanations are mostly omitted, or merely hinted at by the doxographers, so that part of the task of interpretation, a part unfortunately sometimes neglected, consists in finding the justifications.

As long as one does not know how an identity-statement is justified, one can hardly judge arguments in which it appears. Identity-statements can of course have totally differing epistemological or argumentative status – they can be definitions or empirical propositions, they can be definitions in the Socratic sense, i.e. statements regarding that which makes a thing what it is, and they can also be conclusions from such definitions combined with other premises which do not necessarily say anything about the essence of a thing. The consequences of giving all identity-statements the same status can be illustrated by an example of Plutarch's (*Comm. not.* 1072a, cf. S.E. *M* XI 186): if medicine is the science of health and sickness, then it follows that health and sickness are the subject

I am grateful to Ansgar Beckermann and Wolfgang Carl for discussion and comments on the first version of this paper, and to the participants of the conference for their critical remarks on the second version. Thanks are also due to Christopher K. Callanan, not only for the translation, but also for pointing out a number of ambiguities in the German, which hopefully have disappeared in the English.

matter of medicine. It would, however, not be a good idea to use both statements simultaneously as definitions.

Identity-statements can of course also be used to replace one expression with another, for if A and B are identical, then all that holds of A must hold of B. It is however well known that there is a whole range of contexts in which such a substitution changes either the status or the truth value of a statement. If this fact is ignored, one can easily derive more or less absurd consequences. That the ancients were already aware of this possibility, is shown by the following argument of Alexander of Aphrodisias: 'if someone who wonders whether virtue is sufficient for happiness, is not asking an absurd question, yet someone who wonders whether virtue is sufficient for virtue, is asking an absurd question, then the two questions are not identical. But if these are not identical, then virtue and happiness are also not identical. The first, therefore the second.' (*De an.* II 159 22–26).

A statement concerning the goal of life must be handled with care in two respects at once. One cannot immediately tell what status the statement should have, and it might also be viewed as an intentional context, precisely because it is a statement concerning the goal of an action. If it were, for example, my goal to acquire the most beautiful painting of an exhibition, one could not immediately conclude that it was my goal to acquire the most expensive painting of the exhibition, even if it should be true that the most beautiful painting is identical with the most expensive. If after learning this fact, I were with a heavy heart to decide to buy, one would be justified in saying that I wanted to buy the most expensive painting because it was the most beautiful, but not that I wanted to buy the most expensive painting because it was the most expensive, let alone that I wanted to buy the most beautiful painting because it was the most expensive.

Statements concerning the goal of life thus offer a variety of opportunities for misunderstandings, and it seems to me that some of the arguments that have been handed down to us from the second-century controversy about the Stoic definitions of the goal of life depend on the improper use of identity-statements, which however the Stoics, by their predilection for such propositions, seem practically to invite. These arguments are usually merely paraphrased by commentators – perhaps because the fame of the 'sharp-witted dialectician' Carneades, to whom the arguments are with greater or lesser justification generally attributed, has secured them greater respect than they deserve. Consequently the substantive core of the controversy between Antipater and Carneades has tended to remain unclear, hidden behind the web of intellectual tricks. Yet if one takes the trouble to put aside the superficial paradoxes that result from substitution or status-confusion, there remains, I believe, a serious dispute, in which neither of the opponents was satisfied with mere verbal tricks or sophistical hair-splitting (*heurēsilogiai*, cf. Plut. *Comm. not.* 1072f).

I

Since Hirzel (1882), pp. 230ff., much has been written on the Stoic '*telos*-formulae', above all from the point of view of the question whether and how far the second-century Stoics, Diogenes of Babylon and Antipater of Tarsus, departed from the view of the older Stoics, Zeno, Cleanthes and Chrysippus. As is well known, Zeno, Cleanthes and Chrysippus taught that the goal is a life in agreement with nature.[1] Diogenes and Antipater, however, are said to have defined the goal of life as 'rational behaviour in the selection of what is natural'; Antipater additionally as 'doing everything in one's power, constantly and unwaveringly, to obtain the primary natural things'.[2] The difference between the first and the latter two formulae is greater than it might perhaps appear at first sight. I have attempted to suggest the terminological difference between the phrases *homologoumenōs tēi phusei* and *kata phusin* by the expressions 'in agreement with nature' and 'natural'. By 'agreement with nature' the Stoics apparently understood consciously adapting one's life to the order of universal nature. That which corresponds to the nature of a species in the sense of being necessary or helpful for, say, the unimpeded development of a creature, they called 'natural things'. Hence for men such things as health, physical strength and beauty are 'natural'.[3] The possession of

---

[1] ὁμολογουμένως τῇ φύσει ζῆν. This is by far the most frequently used formula, which was evidently viewed as the official doctrine of the school. Almost as much has been written about the various formulations of Zeno, Cleanthes and Chrysippus as about the divergent formulations of the later Stoics. Fortunately the differences, should they be of consequence, are unimportant for the questions dealt with here.

[2] εὐλογιστεῖν ἐν τῇ τῶν κατὰ φύσιν ἐκλογῇ καὶ ἀπεκλογῇ or πᾶν τὸ κατ'αὐτὸν ποιεῖν διηνεκῶς καὶ ἀπαραβάτως πρὸς τὸ τυγχάνειν τῶν προηγουμένων κατὰ φύσιν cf. *SVF* III Diogenes 44–6; Antipater 57–8. On the word προηγουμένων see Hirzel (1882), Excursus V, pp. 805ff., esp. pp. 823–5. Hirzel thinks – it seems to me correctly – that the word, if it is not a later interpolation to begin with, could also be omitted, as e.g. in Cic. *Fin.* V 19. Cf. also Bonhöffer (1894), p. 169f.

[3] On the concept of natural things see Long (1967), p. 65f.; on the difference between τὰ κατὰ φύσιν and πρῶτα κατὰ φύσιν, which I disregard in the following, cf. Bonhöffer (1894), pp. 175–6 and Madvig (1876), Excursus IV, pp. 815ff. Cicero (*Fin.* III 22) gives the impression that the expression πρῶτα κατὰ φύσιν was at least occasionally used to distinguish morally indifferent natural things from virtue, which was also 'natural'. However, the expression τὰ κατὰ φύσιν is often used without further qualification for morally indifferent things.

these things does not yet mean that one consciously conforms to nature. A 'natural life' (*kata phusin bios*) is not therefore eo ipso a life in agreement with nature, and it is not trivial to claim that it is natural for a man to want to live in agreement with nature, or that a life in agreement with nature consists in choosing what is natural.

Nevertheless it hardly seems possible to me to doubt Diogenes' or Antipater's orthodoxy. If they said that the goal of life was the rational selection of what is natural, then this can be justified by the fact that life in agreement with nature is supposed to consist precisely in rationally[4] choosing what is natural and rejecting what is not. This is the behaviour that nature prescribes for man, and one finds oneself in agreement with nature if one seeks to follow its commandments. Antipater's second formula is treated by Plutarch (*Comm. not.* chap. 26–7) as being equivalent to the first, and probably was not intended to replace, but rather to clarify the first.

It is often assumed that the divergent formulations of the later Stoics are to be attributed to the criticism of the Academics, especially of course that of Carneades (cf. e.g. Pohlenz (1970) I, p. 186f.). But for historical reasons it is unlikely that Diogenes introduced his formula under the influence of Carneades. Diogenes was considerably older than Carneades, who is supposed to have been his pupil in logic, and as far as arguments survive which either originate with Carneades or can plausibly be attributed to him, they assume the selection-formula or the second formula of Antipater.

It is probably no longer possible to determine precisely why Diogenes spoke of rational selection of what is natural rather than agreement with nature. A connexion could be made between this change and Chrysippus' polemic against Aristo of Chios.[5] However if one wished, against Aristo, to insist that virtuous action must be guided by the standard of what is natural, one was not yet forced to declare the selection of what is natural to be the goal of life. Still, this interpretation is more plausible than the presumption that Carneades talked Diogenes into using his formulation in order to pounce upon him all the more easily. Since Antipater is said to

---

[4] The expressions εὐλογιστεῖν and εὔλογος ἐκλογή are clearly related to the definition of καθῆκον, appropriate action, as ὃ πραχθὲν εὔλογον ἴσχει ἀπολογισμόν (D.L. VII 107). The goal is reached only if one not only chooses what is natural, but is also able to give a rational explanation for one's every act. The explanation will generally consist in showing that what one wants to do corresponds to man's nature. With διηνεκῶς καὶ ἀπαράβατως Antipater presumably wished to express the same thing: only he who knows why he acts as he does will be able to exhibit constancy without any wavering. It is not entirely clear why Antipater preferred to speak of constancy. This could have something to do with his conscious description of the goal of life as the goal of a craft (τέχνη). Constancy and unwavering procedure are also characteristic of an accomplished craftsman (cf. S.E. M XI 207).

[5] As e.g. by Reiner (1969), p. 342 n.25.

have also used the selection-formula, the simplest assumption is that the arguments we find in Cicero, Plutarch and Alexander of Aphrodisias all stem from the controversy between Carneades and Antipater (cf. Plut. *Comm. not.* 1072f.). For there are in fact good reasons for supposing that Antipater's second formula was meant to serve in defence of the Stoic position against Carneades' objections. Not only is it documented that Antipater spent a good deal of time on the polemic against Carneades (cf. *SVF* III Antipater 5,6), but Cicero even tells us which objection he was trying to refute. In *Fin.* III 22 the archer simile, which belongs to Antipater's second formula, is cited in order, as Cicero says, to avoid the misunderstanding that the Stoics had assumed two goals instead of one.[6] Cicero says nothing about how this misunderstanding could come about. Precisely this 'misunderstanding' is put forward in Plutarch (*Comm. not.* 1070f.) as an objection to the Stoic *telos*-formulae, although here the difference between the selection-formula and Antipater's second formula does not appear to be taken into account.

It is likewise clear that Antipater's second formula was also criticised by Carneades: one of the arguments in Plutarch refers to the archer simile; and the so called Carneadea divisio, reported by Cicero, *Fin.* V 16ff., presupposes this formula.[7] In order then to reconstruct the course of the controversy, one should begin with the arguments against the

[6] It seems to me that M. Soreth (1968) did not take this reference into account. She assumes merely that Antipater was attempting to refute an objection to the selection-formula, and thinks this to be found in an objection of Al.Aphr. (Soreth p. 70f). Alexander claims that virtue cannot be sufficient for virtuous action, and hence not for happiness either. For virtuous action consists, according to the Stoics, in the selection of natural things, but in order to be able to make this selection the natural things must be present. In Soreth's view, Antipater attempted to avoid this objection by speaking of 'doing everything etc.', rather than of 'selecting'. While selection presumes the presence of things to be selected, the same cannot be said of mere effort towards these very objects. This interpretation does not seem plausible to me, above all because Antipater's alleged escape route seems to offer little promise of success. Contrary to Soreth's views, Alexander's argument can also be applied to the second formula: to do everything in one's power [...], one must at least be alive. Hence virtuous action presupposes life, and consequently virtue is not sufficient for virtuous action [...]. Moreover, doubtless due to a misunderstanding, Soreth has failed to notice that Alexander also reports the Stoics' answer to this argument (Soreth, p. 71 n. 60. Alexander writes (160 12) οὐδὲ γάρ, ὥς φασιν [...]. As the parallel passage 161 31–2 shows, we must translate: 'For it is not the case, as they say, that [...]', and not: 'For it is, as *they* say, not the case, that [...].'). As can be inferred from the terminology of the whole section, the question is, in Stoic terms, whether virtue is the 'perfect' (αὐτοτελής) cause of virtuous action. Alexander claims that natural things, as the material (ὕλη) of selection, are at least contributory causes (συνεργός), the Stoics on the contrary believed them to have only the status of necessary conditions (ὧν οὐκ ἄνευ), as do heaven and earth, space and time. (On the terminology of the Stoic theory of causes cf. Frede (1980), pp. 227ff.). I do not see why Antipater should not have concurred with this response.

[7] Hence Soreth (1968) is correct in pointing out that the divisio, or the argument contained therein, cannot, as it has often been, be viewed as the objection that induced Antipater to adopt his second formula.

selection-formula, which are found in Plutarch and in Alexander's reper-
toire of arguments against the self-sufficiency of virtue (*De an.* II, 159ff.).

II

Plutarch begins his criticism of the Stoic *telos*-formulae with the claim
that the Stoics become entangled by their definitions in a dilemma: they
must either assume two goals, or claim that the goal is distinct from the
reference-point of all actions. Either alternative, he says, is paradoxical
(*para tēn ennoian*).

In the following passage, in which Plutarch explains the dilemma, the
text is so corrupt that it hardly seems capable of proper reconstruction.[8] It
is, however, at least clear what the two goals, or rather the goal and the
reference-point of all actions, are supposed to be: namely on the one hand
the selection, on the other the obtaining of natural things. The dilemma
evidently arises from the Stoics' claim that the selection, not the obtaining, of natural things is the goal of life.

The paradox is derived from the Stoic definition of '*telos*' as 'that to
which everything done in life should be referred, while it itself is not to be
referred to anything else'.[9] The definition seems to presuppose that there
is at least one goal which one seeks to attain by all one's actions, and in relation to which these actions are judged as right or wrong. If there were
two such goals, it would have to be the case that all actions must be
referred to both at once. Why this is paradoxical is not said; but it might
be that the definitions were understood in such a way that there must be
exactly one goal. That the second possibility is paradoxical is easier to see.
For if all actions were to be referred to something other than the goal, then
this would have to be simultaneously the goal (by definition) and not the
goal (by hypothesis).

---

[8] On the various attempts at reconstruction see Soreth (1968), p. 59f. and Cherniss' edition
(1976). Whether Plutarch mentioned just one or both possibilities, he did not in any case
indicate how the dilemma was reached. One cannot therefore view this section as a complete argument, but rather as an announcement, which is meant to be supported by the following arguments. It seems to me that this is in the event the case, although Plutarch does
not explicitly point it out. The argument at the start of chapter 27, 1071f–1072b does not,
however, belong in this context, but it also does not refer to the *telos*-formulae.

[9] cf. Stob. *Ecl.* II p. 46, 5–10 w.: ἐφ' ὃ πάντα τὰ ἐν τῷ βίῳ πραττόμενα καθηκόντως τὴν
ἀναφορὰν λαμβάνει, αὐτὸ δ'ἐπ'οὐδέν. The other two definitions, οὗ ἕνεκα πάντα
πράττεται καθηκόντως, αὐτὸ δὲ πράττεται οὐδενὸς ἕνεκα and οὗ χάριν τἆλλα, αὐτὸ
δ'οὐδενὸς ἕνεκα, are both evidently meant to say the same thing. For the translation of
καθηκόντως by 'should', cf. Cic. *Fin.*III 21 quo omnia referenda sint; *Fin.* I 29 oporteat. In
this way it is laid down that we are dealing with that goal which nature has provided for
man, as opposed to a goal that a man has chosen for himself.

Now if, as Cicero says, Antipater's second formula was intended to meet the objection that there would have to be two goals, then it is reasonable to suppose that the dilemma was part of an argument against the selection formula.

However, our sources offer no exact account of how the paradox of the two goals was thought to come about. Plutarch seems in the following chapters to have forgotten the dilemma he announced. But at the end of chapter 27 he does produce an argument which refers only to the selection-formula and in which the explanation of the paradox can perhaps be recognised (1072e–f).

As usual, Plutarch is trying to make the Stoic theory look absurd, and claims that by their selection-formula the Stoics blunder into a circle of explanations. The circle-allegation is easily refuted; nevertheless, the argument can show what the actual difficulty consisted in. Plutarch argues as follows: according to the Stoics, the goal of life is rational behaviour in the selection of what is natural. They choose what is natural, insofar as it is of value for the goal of life. But the goal of life is precisely this rational behaviour. It follows, then, that the goal of life, according to the Stoics, consists in rational behaviour in the selection of that which is of value for rational behaviour. As I have said, the Stoics were easily able to refute the accusation of a circle – they would of course, as the commentators point out, not have accepted the second premiss. In Stoic theory natural things are of no value for the goal of life, but at most for a natural life (*kata phusin bios*; cf. Al.Aphr. *De an.* II, 167.18; Stob. *Ecl.* II 80.9–13, 81.4 W., D.L. VII 105). One could then only conclude that according to the Stoics the goal consists in rational behaviour in the selection of what is of value for a natural life, and that does not produce a circle. But this does not yet do away with the argument. For the second premiss rests on a thesis which Plutarch has already advanced against the Stoics a number of times (1071e, 1072c); namely that a selection can only be called rational if it is made in reference to a goal which itself has a value and contributes to a happy life. But notoriously the Stoics claimed that natural things were indifferent as far as the goal of life is concerned. Alexander attacks precisely this assumption (*De an.* II 164 7; 167 13–17). He also shows why the Stoics would not gain much ground by pointing to the natural life: it is after all possible to ask in the case of the natural life, whether it is to be considered good or merely indifferent, albeit 'preferred' (*proēgmenon*). And in the latter case it will again be asked, in reference to what it is supposed to be preferred. If not in reference to the goal of life, but rather to something else, then the argument will be directed at this, and so on ad infinitum (ibid. 167 18–168 1).

As can be seen, both Plutarch and Alexander claim that the value of that which is selected must consist in its contributing to the goal of life. Now if in Stoic theory natural things contribute only to a natural life, then it could be concluded that this is a second goal, which the Stoics must assume next to their declared goal of rational selection.

Aside from the alleged paradoxicality of such an assumption, it is clear that the Stoics could not accept it. After all, they insisted that the obtainment of what is natural is irrelevant for happiness.

To refute this argument, the Stoics had to show that it is not absurd to choose something, the obtainment of which is indifferent for the goal of life.

And this seems to be exactly what the archer simile was meant to do. This context has, however, been obscured by the fact that Plutarch presents his arguments in what is historically probably the reverse order, and that he tries – evidently successfully – to give the impression that by his second formula Antipater took the Stoics out of the frying pan and into the fire.

Antipater's second formula ran: doing everything in one's power ... in order to obtain the natural things. Plutarch proclaims (1071b–c) this to be just like claiming that an archer does everything in his power – not to hit the mark, god forbid, but rather in order to do everything in his power. The absurdity arises from Antipater's declared goal being itself a purposeful activity. If it is assumed that men's behaviour can in general be described as an effort to obtain natural things, then it must be possible to insert the expression describing the goal of life in an explanatory final clause, and this would produce the sentence: 'Man does everything in his power to obtain the natural things, in order to do everything in his power to obtain the natural things.' Admittedly this may sound absurd, but if looked at carefully, it isn't. This can be clarified by using the example of the archer. For the corresponding sentence should not run the way Plutarch gives it, but more precisely: the archer does everything in his power to hit the mark, in order to do everything in his power to hit the mark (cf. Cic. *Fin.* III 22). This is, to be sure, complicated, but not absurd – it is simply meant to say that the archer is not concerned with hitting the mark, but only with shooting skilfully. This could for example be explained by assuming that the archer is undertaking a task, but is personally little interested in its fulfilment – he does what he does in order to carry out his orders. Or he could have shot merely to practise shooting: if a gust of wind diverts his arrow from its path, this need not bother him much, as opposed, say, to the case that he wants to shoot a rabbit and would presumably be angered by failure, even if he were not responsible.

Of course it has long since been seen that this is the point of the archer simile.[10] But it is also possible to do away with the complicatedness and vagueness of this formulation, if one considers that Antipater's formulation 'doing everything in one's power...', is only meant as an interpretation of the older 'living in agreement with nature'. If in the sentence mentioned above, we substitute for Antipater's formula in the second position the older formula, then we get: 'doing everything in one's power to obtain what is natural, in order to live in agreement with nature'. This, it seems to me, expresses more clearly what the Stoics' main concern really was. But it also lets us see that Diogenes and Antipater were themselves not entirely free of responsibility for the emergence of the rather superficial paradoxes.

If the goal of life is to be that for the sake of which everything is done, then a definition of this goal will be expected not only to give a correct description of what the goal consists in, but at the same time to make clear what makes this goal worth striving for. But neither Diogenes' selection formula nor Antipater's second formula accomplishes this. The selection of what is natural can be viewed as the goal only because the life truly worth striving for, that in agreement with nature, is supposed to consist in precisely this selection. The *telos*-formulae of Diogenes and Antipater are to be sure proper and orthodox statements of what the Stoics saw as the goal of life, but they cannot rank as definitions, and they do not contain that description of the goal of life according to which it is supposed to be the goal of all human endeavours. Hence the insertion of the expression 'selection of what is natural' in '[...] is the goal of life' is just as problematical as the substitution of 'the most expensive painting' for 'the most beautiful painting' in the example discussed initially. And the claim that man does everything in his power [...] in order to do everything in his power, is just as false as the corresponding statement that one acquires the most expensive painting in order to acquire the most expensive painting.

Posidonius seems to have pointed this out in his often quoted criticism of Antipater's second formula (ap. Galen, *De dogm. Hipp. et Plat.* p.450M; fr.187 Edelstein/Kidd). He complained about some people reducing life in agreement to doing everything possible for the sake of the primary natural things. This formulation is, he said, self-contradictory[11] and names nothing that is noble (*kalon*) or conducive to happiness (*eudai-*

---

[10] See especially Reiner's excellent article (1969).

[11] It is not clear to me why Posidonius considered the formula to be self-contradictory. Perhaps Hirzel's guess is right (1882), p. 245, that the contradiction was thought to lie in the fact that a specification is included in the definition of the highest goal which points to a goal that lies beyond the highest goal. Cf. Cic. *Fin.* IV 46.

monikon). To be sure, this (scil. the contents of the definition in question) is a necessary consequence of the goal, but it is not itself the goal. Posidonius demands, it would seem, that a proper definition of the goal of life state what makes the *telos* what it is. Antipater's formula does not do this, any more than the – correct – description 'the most expensive painting' describes the goal of my longings as something worth desiring. It is therefore understandable that Stoics after Antipater returned, as far as can be seen, to the older formula.

III

As long as only the interpretation of the archer simile is considered, it is difficult at first to see why Carneades should have insisted that the real goal of the actions of an archer must be hitting the mark, and not shooting correctly. Even if archers normally do shoot in order to hit the mark, it is at least not absurd to assume that in special cases professionally correct performance, and not success, is the goal of an action. The example can at least show that it is not absurd for one to strive for something, the possession of which is of no consequence to him. Hence Reiner, (1969) p. 347, flatly declared such objections untenable. It could perhaps be said that these are cases in which the goal striven for is different from the reference-point of the individual actions. But it would still not be patently false to say that the archer bends his bow, for instance, in order to practise archery, not (or not only) to hit the mark. Why should anyone wish to deny that such cases are possible?

The reason for Carneades' objection does not become clear until one considers that his dispute with Antipater was not about the goal of individual actions, but rather about the goal of a craft, namely the art of living, which in the view of the Stoics is identical with virtue. The goal of this craft is of course supposed to be at the same time the goal of life (cf. Al.Aphr. *De an.* II 159 34: *hē aretē technē kat'autous eudaimonias poiē-tikē*). But if one is of the opinion that this goal is to be achieved by the proper practice of a craft, then one will have to presume that the goal of this craft stands in the same relation to it as the goals of other crafts to their practice. According to Stoic theory, the art of living is practised by choosing in a rational way what is natural, or, according to the second formula, by doing everything in one's power to obtain the natural things. Carneades argued, it seems, that such a craft must have as its goal the obtaining of the natural things and not its own practice.

That this was the background of the controversy is not stated in Plu-

tarch, but it is shown almost conclusively by the other sources. The Carneadea divisio, in the form in which Cicero *Fin.* v 16ff. presents it,
proceeds from the assumption that *prudentia (phronēsis)* is the art of
living. The goal of this art is clearly whatever the individual schools
declare to be the goal of life. Alexander of Aphrodisias, in his arguments
against the self-sufficiency of virtue, refers constantly to the fact that
virtue is supposed to be a craft that according to the Stoics consists in the
selection of what is natural. And finally, this assumption also explains
why Antipater chose a formula which, as Rieth (1934), p. 28 n.1 (cf.
Alpers-Gölz (1976), pp. 66–8), has shown, describes the function of a stochastic craft – i.e. a craft in which the result is not solely dependent upon
the correct performance of the craftsman.

In dealing with the question of what the goal of an entire craft is, however, it is not sufficient to point out that this craft can in a particular case
be practised in order to achieve a certain goal. Rather, one would have to
say that the craft is normally practised with this goal, and that it was
invented for this purpose. Regarding the archer, it may well be entirely
plausible to allege that under certain circumstances he does everything to
hit his target only because he wants to practise archery or to fulfil his
duty; but it would be paradoxical to claim that archers normally view
shooting properly as the purpose of their activity, and thoroughly absurd
to say that archery was invented for the sake of shooting.

There were, however, according to Alexander of Aphrodisias (*Quaest.*
II 61 1ff.), people who defended the theory that the goal of all stochastic
crafts consists in 'doing everything in one's power to achieve the intended
result [*to prokeimenon*]'. I assume these unnamed people were Antipater,
or at least Stoics influenced by Antipater. Von Arnim will presumably
have thought the same when he included the entire passage in his collection of Stoic fragments.[12] We can also infer, it seems to me, from Alexander's explanation, how Antipater presumably justified his thesis (ibid.
11–23): in other crafts, that for the sake of which they are practised, results from technically correct performance, and if the goal is not achieved,
then it can be assumed that a technical error was made. Here, therefore,
correct performance and the achievement of the intended result coincide.
In the stochastic crafts, on the other hand – medicine and navigation are
standard examples – the result is not solely a matter of mastering the corresponding craft, but rather depends on quite a number of external factors. Therefore in these crafts the goal is not the achievement of the

---

[12] For the text of this passage, see the heavily emended version in von Arnim, *SVF* III 19,
which is, at least as concerns the meaning, evidently correct. Lines 23–8 are not included
in von Arnim.

intended result but the complete execution of that which pertains to the craft (*to apoplērōsai ta tēs technēs*).

This line of argument is at least not entirely implausible. Whether someone is a good shoemaker can be judged by the shoes he produces; but whether someone is a good doctor is not judged solely on the basis of successful recoveries, which, as everyone knows, often come about even without his intervention, but rather by whether he knows the rules of medicine and acts accordingly. If the goal of an art is supposed to be what makes someone who has learned the craft a good craftsman, then one could be inclined to agree with Antipater. It is also clear why Antipater wanted to take this view regarding virtue as the art of living, for it seems characteristic for judgments of actions as morally right or wrong that one is not guided by their success, but – to put it as analogously as possible – by whether the agent followed the rules of morality. The analogy between virtue and the stochastic crafts seems, then, at first glance to have some merit.

In contrast to other crafts, success is in the stochastic crafts not simultaneously the standard for judging the capabilities of the artist or even the correctness of his action in an individual case. Whether a therapy is in general correct depends on whether it is successful in most cases, but it may in an individual case be correct, even though the patient is not cured. This demonstrates that in the stochastic crafts the intended result does not coincide with the standard of judgment of individual actions: to justify the rules of a craft, one must to be sure refer to the intended result, but in judging the actions of the craftsman, one must refer to the rules themselves, and only indirectly, by way of these, to the result.

Since in the stochastic crafts it is also possible to act correctly, or even admirably, without achieving the intended result, it is possible that someone who is only interested in, say, doing his job, is satisfied with his action, although he has not achieved the intended result. For this reason, examples taken from such crafts are particularly suited for showing that it is possible to work for something, the obtaining of which is a matter of indifference. This may in principle also be the case in practising other crafts: for example, if someone manufactures souvenirs in order to make money, then the objects he produces may be of no interest to him at all, as opposed to the money that he can earn with them. Nevertheless, he can only be satisfied with his activity if he has also produced the objects which are supposed to make money for him. Only in the case of the stochastic crafts can it be said that the result may be not only indifferent to oneself, but also irrelevant for judging one's achievement.

On the other hand, however, one might also be inclined to agree, regarding the stochastic crafts, with Alexander's opinion, according to which the achievement of the intended result is the goal in these crafts too – this is after all that for the sake of which one 'does everything in one's power' (Al.Aphr. *Quaest.* II 11.23–4) – while it is the specific function (*ergon*) of the craftsman to do everything in his power to achieve the result.

For if we assume the Stoic definition of the *telos*, which must hold mutatis mutandis for other crafts too, certainly for the art of living – 'that for the sake of which everything should be done', or 'what all actions should have as their point of reference' – then it would have to hold, e.g. of medicine, that it is only practised to comply with the rules of the art. This is implausible, not only because patients at least, and also most doctors see the purpose of their activity in curing the patients, but also because the rules of this activity itself can only be explained with reference to this intention. Even if in a particular instance one could correctly say that the doctor gave the patient cough syrup because he wanted to abide by the therapeutic guidelines, still the instruction to give the patient cough syrup under certain circumstances can only be justified by the fact that this can contribute to a cure. If then the formula 'to which all actions should be referred' also means that rules regarding actions should be justified with reference to the goal, then the goal of stochastic crafts must be seen as being the result intended, and not the fulfilment of the rules of the craft or the technically correct performance.

Moreover, in most cases one would certainly say that the craft was invented for the sake of the intended result – medicine for the sake of health, archery for hitting targets, navigation because one does not want merely to sail around on the high seas but also to arrive safely in port. To be sure, one need not say with Plutarch (*Comm. not.* 1071c–d) that according to the Stoic view health exists for the sake of treatment and not the other way around; for to be precise it is not the success of the therapy, but rather the activity of the doctor by which he in the Stoic sense achieves his goal. Still it would be reminiscent of the old doctor-joke, 'operation successful, patient deceased', if one wished to claim that the success of the cure was of secondary importance compared to the correct therapy.

Still, there are a few types of crafts that one would probably call stochastic and of which it would at least be said that they were not invented for the sake of the intended result. If for example it is assumed that sport serves to strengthen the body and not to set records, then it is true for this case that the intended result of winning the race is indifferent compared with the physical performance: the runner who loses the race has built up his strength just as much as has the winner. This relationship is of course particularly clear in the case of games – certainly one plays to win, but the important thing is the enjoyment, and one can have this even if one loses. Accordingly, various authors have pointed out that the Stoics' attitude towards obtaining natural things can be compared to that of people playing games towards winning the game.

However, it is nevertheless true of games too, that rules of strategy must be justified by reference to the intended result. A good move in a game of chess is one which brings the player closer to victory, not one which he finds especially entertaining. Even if it should be true that the purpose of the game is enjoyment or perhaps intellectual training, still in this sense each particular act must be referred to the intended result. For these cases it is true that the goal of the crafts is different from the reference-point of the individual acts. But compared to the real purpose of playing, the intended result is a subordinate goal, and it is only for the sake of enjoyment or training that one makes an effort to achieve this goal. Hence one could claim concerning the individual acts, that in the final analysis they are directed towards the main goal. We see then that there is a type of stochastic crafts in which the intended result is not identical with the goal of the entire craft, and in which one can achieve the goal even without achieving the result.

It must be admitted though, that the example of the archer is hardly suitable for illustrating this fact, should it be meant. The connection between the goal or purpose of a craft in general and the motive of a particular activity seems to consist in the fact that the agent normally wants to achieve what would be seen as the purpose of the craft, or that for which it was invented. For this reason one expects of a doctor that he is interested in curing the patient, of a person playing a game on the other hand, that having fun, and not winning, is his object. As can be seen in the example of the archer, this connexion need not hold for each individual case. On the other hand, this example seems at first implausible precisely because a motive other than the expected one is supposed to be presumed. For this reason, one might be inclined to think that Carneades originally introduced the simile as a counterexample against the Stoic theory of virtue as a stochastic craft.[13] For the Stoics too seem to assume that a master of the art of living strives after the goal of this art and does not practise it for some other reason. While other men, that is to say fools, are concerned about natural things because they wish to possess them, it is supposed to

---

[13] If, as is usually assumed, Antipater used the terms σκοπός and τέλος in his interpretation, in order to distinguish between the intended result – hitting the mark – and the purpose of the activity, then this will presumably only have gotten him into deeper trouble; cf. Alpers-Gölz (1976), p. 72 and Irwin, this vol., p. 228 n. 25.

hold for the Stoic wise man that he only seeks to obtain natural things because he wishes to abide by the commandments of nature. But the reason for this is not that the wise man merely wants to exercise himself in the art of living, as the archer perhaps does in that of archery, but rather that the fools have not recognised the real goal of striving after natural things.[14] That the most common motive need not necessarily be the correct one, can perhaps be shown by the example of sport: even if all athletes were only interested in records, one would still not want to concede that the purpose of sport was setting records. That is why it is considered wrong if an athlete ruins his health due to exaggerated ambition, and if a player gets angry about losing, he is called a poor sport. In the case of an athlete, one would perhaps concede that he was a good athlete if he was successful, but in a certain sense, one would also be inclined to deny this. A good athlete should after all be a good sport, just as only somebody who does not get angry about losing is a truly good athlete, and just as a good player is not a poor sport. So too the Stoic wise man is supposed to be the one who is untouched by the failure of his endeavours to obtain natural things, because even without them he achieves his real goal.

If we assume that Antipater was thinking of such examples, then his thesis could be thought to be true at least for a sub-class of the stochastic crafts. But strictly speaking, his formulation is still too narrow even for these cases. For according to it, we would have to claim that it is the goal of a person playing a game to do everything in order to win. This in turn is understandable in an individual case – we play to win, but the game's the thing – but not for the game in its totality. The purpose of football is not scoring goals, but neither is it playing football itself or the effort to score goals, but rather, as one might say, just the enjoyment. Even if the enjoyment in this case consists in nothing other than playing, it is not correct to conclude, from the claim that the purpose of playing is the enjoyment, that the purpose is the playing itself.

But this is a difficulty that Antipater could easily have avoided, if instead of 'doing everything [. . .]' he had spoken of 'complete execution of that which pertains to the craft', as e.g. Alexander did in the passage quoted above.[15] After all, in interpreting his theory I constantly used expressions like 'doing his job', 'technically correct performance' or 'abiding by the rules'. Technically correct performance or doing a job consists in the case of the stochastic arts of course in doing everything in one's

---

[14] This can, it seems to me, be shown e.g. from Cicero's description of the development of perfect wisdom in *Fin.* III 21.

[15] Cf. the formula attributed to Archedemus: πάντα τὰ καθήκοντα ἐπιτελοῦντα ζῆν, *SVF* III Archedemus 19,20.

power in order to achieve the intended result; but what makes this the goal of the individual actions is precisely the fact that it is doing the job or following the rules. In short, with their formulation Diogenes and Antipater set themselves, so it would seem, a trap by which they offered at least their less benevolent critics such as Plutarch the opportunity for a whole series of essentially unnecessary objections.

But even if these objections are ignored, there remain a few arguments that form the background of both the dilemma cited in Plutarch and the criticism of Antipater's second formula which seems to be summed up in the argument of the so-called Carneadea divisio. In the context of the controversy concerning the goal of the art of living, this criticism can be seen to make good sense.

IV

The Carneadea divisio is introduced in Cicero *Fin.* v 16ff. as a complete classification of all possible goals of life. After this announcement, Cicero turns without further explanation to a determination of the possible goals of the art of living (*prudentia*). Cicero does not appear to distinguish the question of the goal of this art from that of the goal of life. This is of course quite correct as far as the Stoics are concerned, but not so in the eyes of philosophers who had not asserted even the existence of such an art, or had at least not identified it, as had the Stoics, with virtue. It seems as if Cicero wanted to include an anti-Stoic argument about the goal of the art of living in his classification, without stopping to think that it doesn't really belong in this context. In this way, the argument about the art of living is on the one hand presumably truncated, while on the other hand the classification has become incomprehensible.[16] If one views the passage

---

[16] If Cicero's report is accepted, then the Peripatetics, for example, should have held the theory that happiness consisted in the obtainment of the primary natural things together with the art of obtaining them. The reason for this is that virtue was introduced shortly before only as an art of living which must be concerned with one of the objects of the primary impulse. But according to the version of Peripatetic ethics that Cicero, following Antiochus, presents in this book, virtue is not the art of selecting what is natural in the Stoic sense. Rather, as a 'psychic good', as opposed to external and corporeal goods, it belongs itself to the objects with whose obtaining and development wisdom is supposed to concern itself (cf. *Fin.* IV 16f.). Madvig (1876), Excursus IV p. 820, has quite correctly, it seems to me, pointed out that the range of what is in accord with nature is much more extensive in the 'Peripatetic' theory of books IV and V of *De finibus* than that of the Stoic πρῶτα κατὰ φύσιν, which comprises only those things that are supposed to be indifferent as regards the goal of life. Therefore, no place can be found for the theory of Antiochus in the schema used here, which assumes three possible objects of the primary impulse. But it can also not be simply appended as a combination of two or three of the previously mentioned possibilities.

Fin. v 16–20 as a self-contained argument which does not belong to the classification of the goals of life, then one can interpret it as a summary of Carneades' position in the controversy about the goal of the art of living. In this way we can with a certain degree of probability reconstruct the arguments he used to support the thesis, advanced avowedly only for polemical reasons, that the greatest good must consist in the enjoyment of the primary natural things.

He proceeded from the assumption that there is no craft which refers exclusively to itself. This does not imply, as is often assumed, that every craft must refer to an external object, which it seeks to produce or obtain – it is hardly to be thought that Carneades would have overlooked the well-known cases of those crafts whose object is an activity, e.g. playing the flute. Carneades only made the claim that a craft and its object (*propositum*) must in each case be different; and this also holds for the examples with which some Stoics evidently tried to refute him (*Fin.* III 24), namely the arts of dance and acting. Both are, at least in the view of the ancients, forms of the representation of behaviour or feelings (*mimēsis*), and the representation or imitation of behaviour is not the same thing as the art of acting, even if the activity of an actor consists in the representation of behaviour. So those Stoics apparently ended up saying that wisdom was the only craft which referred wholly to itself (ibid.).

Since then every craft must have an object different from itself, Carneades, evidently referring back to the Stoic *oikeiōsis*-theory, counted off the possible objects of the art of living. The art which refers to one of the three possible objects, is supposed – again according to the Stoic view – to be virtue, and this can be viewed either as a stochastic craft in the sense Antipater has given the term, that is, as having its goal in doing everything in one's power to obtain the natural things, even if one does not obtain them, or in the normal sense of a craft whose goal is the achievement of a specific result. The goal of this art must of course be identical with the goal of life. If Carneades defended in this context the thesis that the *telos*

The parallel passage *Tusc.* v 84, which contains only the classification, not the argument about the art of living, does not assume the derivation of the *honestum* from the primary impulse, but rather divides the theories simply from the point of view of whether they assume one or more types of goods. The Peripatetic theory can of course be integrated into this framework without further ado. It seems fairly clear to me that the connection of the passage on the possible goals of the art of living with the classification of the goals of life is a mistake, which should probably be attributed to Cicero or Antiochus rather than to Carneades. It could, for example, have been caused by the fact that there were not one but two divisions: one for the goals of the art of living and one for the goals of life. (On the two divisions cf. Lévy (1980).) The fact that no place can be found in the first divisio for Antiochus' theory could perhaps indicate that the connection of the οἰκείωσις-theory with Peripatetic ethics was first made by Antiochus.

must consist in the enjoyment of the primary natural things, then it can be assumed that he adopted the Stoic theory concerning the object of the primary impulse, but then tried to demonstrate that the goal of the corresponding art must lie in obtaining what is in accord with nature, and not in the mere effort to obtain this. His arguments have not been transmitted to us explicitly, but they will probably not have been much different from those which are hinted at in Alexander's quaestio on the goal of stochastic crafts: that for the sake of which these crafts are practised is usually the intended result, and this both in the sense that the entire craft was invented for this purpose, and that the correctness or incorrectness of actions is judged according as they contribute to the intended result or not. Hence, if the Stoics wanted the art of living to consist in endeavouring to obtain the primary natural things, then to be consistent, they would have to have said that the goal of this art consisted in the obtainment or possession of these things.

But we have just seen that this line of argument is not of itself conclusive. It does seem to hold for most stochastic crafts that their purpose lies in attaining the desired result, but there are still some types of stochastic crafts in which this is obviously not the case, such as sports or competitive games. One would therefore have to attempt to decide to which type the art of living belongs. One could then ask, for example, why nature has set us the task of making an effort to obtain the natural things if their possession is ostensibly of no concern to us and is supposed to contribute nothing to our happiness. This question was indeed already raised by Carneades in regard to the selection of what is natural, if the Sorites argument cited by Alexander (*De an.* II 163 32–164 3) originated with Carneades. It is not clear to me how the Stoics reacted to this. But it should perhaps be stressed that it is not necessarily legitimate to rely for support (as Epictetus, *Diss.* II 5 4–5 does) on the claim that happiness can only consist in something that is in our power. For this is a thesis that the Stoics should prove and not assume.[17]

Be that as it may, by appealing to cases like sports and games, it was in any case possible to show that the Stoic view of the art of living is not absurd. Still, even in these cases it cannot be denied that in a certain sense all individual actions are to be referred to the intended result – namely insofar as the type of actions performed is determined by the fact that one

---

[17] That this thesis played a rôle is shown by Alexander's comment, *in Top.*34 3–5: ἐπὶ δὲ τῶν στοχαστικῶν οὐκέτι τὸ τέλος ἐπὶ τοῖς τεχνίταις, ὡς οὐδὲ τὸ εὐδαιμονεῖν ἐπὶ τοῖς σπουδαίοις, εἰ μὴ μόνον τὸ καλὸν ἀγαθόν. (Wallies prints εἰ μὴ μόνον τὸ καλὸν καὶ ἀγαθὸν εἶναι: he takes εἶναι from l.1 where it is superfluous, καί is added in P by a second hand.)

is seeking to achieve this result. It would therefore seem that what Plutarch cites as the second half of his dilemma holds for the second type of stochastic crafts: the goal is different from that to which all actions must be referred. But as it is only in view of the real goal that one seeks to achieve the result, this reference-point of all actions remains a subordinate goal. The observation that there is a reference-point of all action which is not identical with the highest goal, does not then lead to the absurd consequence that something must at the same time be the highest goal and not be the highest goal. It is simply wrong to assume that there can be only one reference-point of all action. Hence the Stoics had no reason to defend themselves against this description of their position, and there is in fact some evidence that they accepted it.

We have no precise information concerning the reaction of Antipater or his successors to the arguments of Carneades just discussed, because it is often difficult to decide whether an opinion attributed to 'the Stoics' originates with an older or a younger member of the school. It would also seem that the controversy about the goal of the art of living was not, or at least not very energetically, pursued after the death of the two approximately coeval opponents Antipater and Carneades.[18] But a number of comments can be found in Cicero's *De finibus* which suggest that some Stoics rejected Antipater's classification of virtue among the stochastic crafts, while others explicitly stressed that the point of reference for appropriate actions (*officia*) was different from the goal of life.

As has already been mentioned, some Stoics evidently declared it a mistake (*inscite*) to compare the goal of wisdom with that of medicine or navigation (*Fin.* III 24–5). Wisdom, they said, must rather be compared to the art of acting[19] or that of dance, which have their goals in, and not outside of themselves. This is of course plausible, insofar as these arts, just as, in the Stoics' opinion, virtue, achieve their goal through technically correct performance alone. But with these comparisons, the point of Antipater's argument is abandoned. It is also hard to deny that in Stoic theory the art of living refers to an 'external' object. If it is nevertheless supposed to achieve its goal through mere technically correct activity, then the reason

---

[18] Professor Donini points out to me that there is an echo of the debate in Seneca (*Ep.* 85 31–41). Seneca presents it as a controversy between Peripatetics and Stoics. Perhaps some later Peripatetics found it convenient to use some of the Academic arguments against the Stoics. It is then not surprising to find the same material used by Alexander of Aphrodisias. It is not clear whether the arguments of Sextus (*M* XI 168ff., *PH* III 239ff.) on the question whether such a thing as an art of living could even exist originated at the same time or not.

[19] On the use of the comparison with acting, which was evidently popular among Stoics, cf. Ioppolo (1980), pp. 188ff. and 197ff.

for this is not that it does not refer to anything external, but rather that obtaining the external object is supposed to be unimportant. It is perhaps worth noticing that it is apparently nowhere stated that the art of living should rather be compared to sports or games than to medicine. Still, Epictetus does use the comparison with games once (*Diss.* II 5 1–23), though without pointing to the contrast to medicine or similar cases.

Whether or not they noticed this analogy, some Stoics in any case continued to hold that it was not absurd to refer appropriate action to something other than the goal of life.[20] Cicero's justification for this in *Fin.* III 21 is remarkably weak though: the obtaining of the first things of nature cannot be the highest goal, because virtue is not involved in it ('It cannot be the highest goal, because the highest goal is something else.'); but in another passage he expresses himself more precisely albeit with polemical intent: it is the consideration that this is the proper course of action (*officii ratio*) that leads one to strive after the things which accord with nature, not the fact that they attract us and awaken our desire. The Stoic wise man acts out of duty, not inclination, even if duty should consist in doing what he is inclined to do.

After reviewing the controversy about the goal of the art of living, one will not, I think, wish to say that Antipater, as is so often claimed, was not equal to his eloquent opponent. It is true that the Stoics brought unnecessary difficulties upon themselves by the incautious formulation of the *telos*-definition, which however Antipater had probably already inherited from his teacher, Diogenes. But the more important objections to the Stoic theory, according to which something should be selected or striven for, the possession of which is irrelevant for a happy life, are independent of these difficulties. By comparing virtue to the stochastic crafts, Antipater pointed out the decisive difference between the planned result and the standard for good or right action. The analogy between virtue and stochastic crafts is of course not sufficient to demonstrate that the Stoic theory is correct, but it can serve to show that it is not absurd. Carneades' criticism seems, in this as in other cases, to have led the Stoics more clearly to formulate and better to understand their own theory.

---

[20] Among these were undoubtedly the unnamed Stoics who introduced the expression ὑποτελίς as a term for the πρῶτα κατὰ φύσιν; cf. Stob. *Ecl.* II 47 12ff.. But the expression seems to have been first used by Herillus, cf. D.L. VII 165. What the connexion might be, is not clear to me.

8 Stoic and Aristotelian conceptions of happiness

T. H. Irwin

1. *The Stoic dilemma*

The young Jeremy Bentham suffered a rather disagreeable introduction to Stoic doctrines on virtue and happiness:

> I had not completed my thirteenth year, when at Queen's College, Oxford, the task was imposed on me [...] of rendering into English that work of Cicero which is known by the title of The Tusculan Questions or Tusculan Dissertations. Pain, I there learnt, was no evil. Virtue was, and is, of itself sufficient to confer happiness on any man who is disposed to possess it on these terms. What benefit, in any shape, could be derived from impregnating the memory with such nonsense? What instruction from a self-contradictory proposition, or any number of any such propositions?[1]

Other readers have been less vehement but equally firm in their rejection of these central Stoic doctrines, agreeing that the Stoics have nothing to say on these issues that is both interesting and plausible.

If we take seriously the Stoics' claim that virtue is identical to happiness, then, in the view of some ancient critics, we cannot distinguish them from Cynics. They cannot be describing happiness for a human being. A human being has a body; but the Stoics pay no attention to its welfare; they must, then, neglect some part of a human being's good (Alexander, *De an.* 162 3–16; Cicero, *Fin.* IV 36; *Ac.* II 139).

The Stoics have an answer. Unlike the Cynics, they believe that bodily advantages and other alleged goods besides virtue deserve attention. Though these advantages are indifferent in relation to happiness, neither parts of it nor means to it, they deserve the virtuous person's attention. Here the critics reply that the Stoics fail to distinguish themselves from Aristotle. For though they deny, and Aristotle affirms, that these advantages are parts of happiness, their denial reflects a purely verbal disagreement (Cic. *Fin.* III 41; IV 72; V 74, 89; *Tusc.* V 32, 120). No substantive disagreement underlies the Stoic view that happiness consists entirely in virtue.

These criticisms that deny the Stoics any defensible position between Aristotle and Cynics are reflected in our frequent immediate reactions to

[1] Bentham (1834), I, p. 300.

Stoic ethics. Sometimes the Stoic sage seems radically detached from concern with the vicissitudes of the world, because his virtue is self-sufficient for happiness. Sometimes he seems zealously and eagerly concerned with the world around him. These two sides of the Stoic may strike us if we read *De officiis* immediately after reading Book v of the *Tusculan Disputations*.

From the Stoic point of view, our reactions betray our failure to understand Stoic ethics. The belief that virtue is identical to happiness separates them from Aristotle; and the recognition of valuable indifferents separates them from the Cynics. Against the Peripatetics the Stoics urge that the alleged external goods contribute nothing at all to happiness (*Fin.* III 41–4); against the Cynics and such deviant Stoics as Ariston they urge that the indifferents must have some value if virtue is to have any intelligible task or content (*Fin.* III 50).

To decide whether the Stoics or their critics are more nearly right we may usefully examine Stoic views of happiness. The Stoics suppose that they have good reasons for rejecting Aristotle's view of happiness. They offer a series of related, but distinct, arguments against Aristotle; and we will find that these arguments are of unequal merit.

2. Formal conditions for happiness

Aristotle considers and rejects the claim that virtue is happiness (*EN* 1095 b31–1096 a2, 1153 b14–25). He rejects it as a striking paradox that conflicts with common beliefs. But he also has deeper reasons for rejecting it. The insufficiency of virtue follows from the formal conditions for happiness. The formal conditions are constraints that we can find good reason to accept even before we accept or reject any particular view of the content of happiness: and we can resolve disagreements about its content if we can agree on the formal conditions that any acceptable account must satisfy.

In *EN* I 7 Aristotle states the formal conditions for the highest human good, and claims that happiness evidently satisfies them. The conditions are these:

1.   The highest good is the ultimate end, 'for the sake of which the other things are done' (1097 a15–24).
2.   Since it is the ultimate end (*telos*) it must be complete (*teleion*) (1097 a24–b4).
3.   Since it is complete, it must be self-sufficient (1097 b6–16).
4.   Since it is self-sufficient, it must be incapable of increase by the addition of any other good (1097 b16–20).

For present purposes we need only notice three features of these formal conditions:

(a) They all depend on the claim that the highest good is the ultimate end of action. The ultimate end must be complete. If x is alleged to be the ultimate end, but it excludes our other ends y and z, then the ultimate end is not x, but (x+y+z). Happiness counts as the highest good in so far as it displays the appropriate completeness.

(b) Completeness is taken to require comprehensiveness. To illustrate self-sufficiency Aristotle remarks that the individual must include the happiness of family, friends and fellow-citizens; it must extend to all the goods that a rational person is justified in pursuing.

(c) Comprehensiveness must include all goods, not just the desired goods. When Aristotle speaks of an ultimate end, he does not refer to something that will satisfy all my actual desires. My ultimate end includes everything that is good for me, whether or not I happen to desire it. When Aristotle mentions the extended goods required by self-sufficiency, he does not claim that everyone's actual desires require these extended goods, but that everyone's good requires them. Someone could have satisfied his actual desires without achieving his happiness; this is what would happen to us if we acquired the desires of fools or children (1174 a1–4).[2]

These formal conditions seem to Aristotle to show that happiness must include not only virtue, but also the external goods that are not infallibly secured by virtue, and are vulnerable to good and bad fortune. Since happiness is complete, it requires a complete life (1098 a16–20); and a complete life requires a sufficient supply of external goods in addition to virtuous action (1099 a31–3).

The complete good requires external goods for two main reasons:

(a) Happiness requires virtuous actions, since the state not expressed in action is less complete (1095 b31–2). But virtuous actions require external goods; as Aristotle says, these are instrumental and cooperative in virtuous actions (1099 a31–b2). The virtuous person aims to do actions that require, e.g., money; and so the fulfilment of his aims requires the appropriate external goods for him to use.

(b) The happy person needs other external goods that are necessary for happiness even though they are not used as instruments of virtuous action (1099 b2–6). The virtuous person is not simply a rational agent; he also wants the other goods that realise his whole nature as a human being. He does not want to be ugly or solitary; he wants friendship, honour and suc-

---

[2] In this account of Aristotle I have not asked whether *EN* x 6–8 is or is not consistent with these formal conditions as I understand them. For different views see Keyt (1983), White (1981).

cess. These are legitimate aims; but they are vulnerable to external conditions.[3]

If we tried to exclude either type of external goods from happiness, we would allow that happiness could have external goods added to make a greater good. But then we would violate the fourth formal condition. Once we admit the formal conditions, Aristotle sees no escape from the further admission that happiness includes more than virtue, and therefore depends on external goods.

If the Stoics have sound objections to Aristotle's view, they should prove at least one of these claims:

1.   Aristotle's formal conditions are wrong. Happiness need not be complete.
2.   Aristotle's inference from his formal conditions is unwarranted; a complete good need not include external goods, and is fully achieved by virtue.

I will argue that the Stoics follow the second line of argument. They do not challenge Aristotle's formal conditions, but attempt the apparently difficult task of showing that these conditions allow, indeed require, the identification of virtue with happiness. They argue from Aristotelian premises, and try to show that someone who accepts them must draw a non-Aristotelian conclusion.[4]

3. Stoic methods

The Stoics have some reason to follow Aristotle's method, even if they disagree with his use of it. When he has set out the formal conditions for happiness, Aristotle remarks that he will probably appear to have simply stated something that is generally agreed (1097 b22–3); and the Stoics try in the same way to argue from what is agreed. They appeal to preconceptions (prolēpseis), innate tendencies to interpret perceptions and

---

[3] I hope to discuss Aristotle's views on these questions at more length elsewhere, and so will not defend these claims further here. I have understood the issues better, and have been able to formulate some issues more sharply, as a result of reading Cooper (1985).

[4] The fact that the Stoics offer these arguments does not show that the arguments provided the Stoics themselves with their original reasons for believing their claims about virtue and happiness. I have not discussed the relation between the 'Aristotelian' arguments that I examine and arguments that might be derived from the place of human beings in cosmic nature. See n. 39 below. I doubt, however, if the appeal to cosmic nature solves many problems about Stoic ethics. Kidd (1971), p. 158, argues from the divine nature of the logos in human beings that 'the logos in man as in the universe is all-important, and happiness depends on it alone', and cites D.L. VII 88 = SVF III 260 (cf. Sen. Ep. 92 1–3). But Stoic physics does not show clearly that virtue and reason are the only things that matter, or that adapting myself to my place in cosmic nature counts as happiness (cf. Epict. Diss. II 5, 24; 6, 9–10).

experiences in particular ways (Plu. *Stoic. rep.* 1041e–f = *SVF* III 69; *Comm. not.* 1060a).[5]

Epictetus claims that preconceptions are universally shared, and all consistent with each other, though their consistency is not always obvious to us (Epict. *Diss.* I 22, 1–8; IV 1, 41–5). They appear to be inconsistent because we have not thoroughly articulated them (*diarthroun*; II 17, 7; 17, 10), and so apply them wrongly to particular situations. 'Preconception does not conflict with preconception, but [sc. conflict arises] when we come to apply them' (IV 1, 44). We suppose that we are happier if we gain power or influence, because we believe truly that happiness is our ultimate good, and believe falsely that happiness requires external goods. Our false belief is not a genuine preconception, because it conflicts with firm preconceptions about happiness (illustrated in IV 1, 46).

Even if it is not certain that the earlier Stoics all accept Epictetus' methodological principle, it is still useful to ask how they can argue against Aristotle if they accept it; for an answer to this question will show us whether Aristotle could reasonably be persuaded, from premises that he accepts, to change his views about virtue and happiness.

The Stoics think that their belief in the identity of virtue with happiness is important enough to deserve defence from two directions:

1. They begin from the concept of the fine (*kalon* = *honestum*), and argue that (a) nothing is good except what is fine; and hence (b) the happy life is included (*contentam*) in virtue (Cic. *Tusc.* v 18).

2. They also argue from the highest good to show that virtue is identical to it. 'For they treat the fine and the highest good in separate books; and when they prove from the fine (*ex eo efficiatur*) that virtue has enough power for living happily, none the less they argue for this claim separately (*hoc agunt separatim*). For each subject, especially one of such importance, must be treated by its own appropriate arguments and forms of instruction' (*Tusc.* v 19).[6]

---

[5] The innate character of *prolēpseis* is discussed over-sceptically by Sandbach (1971), p. 28; Todd (1973), pp. 53f., 67, 73; Rist (1969), p. 34. Epictetus' view is discussed by Bonhöffer (1890), pp. 188–99, and the rôle of preconceptions in Stoic argument by Schofield (1980), pp. 293–8.

[6] In '*ex eo efficiatur*' Dougan and Henry (1934), ad loc., take '*eo*' = 'the identity of the *honestum* and the *summum bonum*', and King in the Loeb takes it as = 'the nature of the good'. To have two clearly different directions of argument we need to take '*eo*' = '*honestum*', and '*hoc*' = '*satis magnam in virtute ad beate vivendum esse vim*'.

The two directions may be indicated, as Dougan and Henry suggest, by the division of Stoic books, D.L. VII 84. The Stoics write (a) *peri aretōn*, D.L. VII 127, 175, and *peri kalōn*, 175, and also (b) *peri agathōn*, Plu. *Stoic. rep.* 1048a. *Peri telous*, D.L. VII 85, 87, 102, should also be included in (b). The claim that only the fine is good is defended both in *peri tou kalou*, D.L. VII 101, Plu. *Stoic. rep.* 1038c, and in *peri agathōn*, D.L. VII 101, indicating the two directions. There is no evidence of such a division in Zeno's books, D.L. VII 4.

This argument in two directions is reasonable if the Stoics follow Epictetus' principle. When they argue in the first direction, they rely on our preconceptions about the fine and about virtue; they argue that we assign to virtue a status that excludes anything else as a component of happiness. When they argue in the second direction, they rely on our preconceptions about goods and about happiness; they argue that these preconceptions rule out most of the generally-favoured candidates for being components of happiness, and leave nothing except virtue as a successful candidate.

These two directions of argument impose a worthwhile and non-trivial task on the Stoics; for they must succeed with both directions of argument if they are to show that our preconceptions are consistent, and that the claims of virtue do not conflict with the claims of happiness. We might find that we accept the claims of virtue to be the whole of happiness, but at the same time we conceive happiness in a way that makes virtue insufficient for it. The Stoics need to show that preconceptions do not suffer this sort of conflict; and they try to show this by arguing in the two directions.

Let us, then, turn to the Stoic arguments, to see how far the two directions can be distinguished, and how far the Stoics have reasonable objections to the Aristotelian views of happiness.

4. The fine and the good

The Stoics argue that only the fine is good (Cic. *Ac.* I 7, 35; *Fin.* III 27 = *SVF* III 37; IV 48; *Tusc.* V 43–5; Plu. *Stoic. rep.* 1039c = *SVF* III 29; D.L. VII 101 = *SVF* III 30).[7] Their typical form of argument tries to connect prudential concepts related to good with the moral concept of fineness, which embraces the virtues (D.L. VII 100). The connexion relies on the assumption that the good deserves praise, pride or commendation; when this assumption is granted, it turns out that the fine is the only good, since only the fine is praiseworthy and commendable.

These Stoic arguments are meant to prove not only that (1) being fine is necessary for being good, but also that (2) something is a good only in so far as it is fine – its goodness consists in its fineness. The arguments are taken to show that the fine and the good 'have the same force' (*isodunamein*, D.L. VII 101).[8]

---

[7] The concise and formal character of these arguments (*brevia et acuta*, Fin. III 26) suggests that some may derive from Zeno. See Sen. *Ep.* 82 6; Schofield (1983), p. 32f.

[8] This claim, and the claim that virtue is identical to happiness, must be understood so that the Stoics can distinguish properties that belong to happiness qua happiness and qua end from those that belong to it qua virtue. Qua happiness, e.g., it is the end of goods; qua

The second claim conflicts with Aristotle's position. Aristotle himself insists that happiness is the finest thing, as well as the best and pleasantest; this is the very first claim in the *EE* (1214 a7), and it is defended in the *EN* also (1099 a24–31). He agrees with the Stoics to the extent that he regards fineness as a necessary condition for the final good. But he must reject their second claim. He does not believe that happiness is good only in so far as it is fine. Besides the goods that are fine it also includes external goods that are good but not fine (*EE* 1248 b17–25). Contrary to the Stoics Aristotle claims that 'being good and being fine-and-good differ not only in their names but also in themselves' (1248 b17).

Can the Stoics show that Aristotle is wrong to regard fineness as a part, but not the whole, of the goodness of the final good? One obvious reply to Stoic arguments will deny the claim that every good is praiseworthy (Cic. *Fin.* IV 48–9). Aristotle will certainly disagree with the Stoics on this point; but he cannot reject the narrower claim that any final good must be praiseworthy and fine, since he accepts this claim about happiness. The Stoics must show that if Aristotle concedes this much to them, he must agree that happiness is good only in so far as it is fine.

Aristotle raises a difficulty for himself when he claims that happiness is the finest thing. We might take 'finest' to mean 'finer than anything else', and hence 'more praiseworthy than anything else'; in particular, if virtue is not identical to happiness, happiness must be more praiseworthy than virtue. But here the Stoics will correctly insist that the external advantages added to virtue do not result in a good that is more praiseworthy than virtue. As Aristotle agrees, what is praiseworthy is an agent's voluntary action or voluntarily-produced state, in so far as it is voluntary (1109 a31); and we do not achieve anything more praiseworthy if we combine voluntary actions with external advantages that do not depend on voluntary actions. Chrysippus argues that what we praise someone for is not his achievement by itself, but the achievement as an expression of his will and choice. The results of virtue may well be quite trivial; if a temperate man happens to meet only ugly old women, the results of his temperance will be quite unimpressive; but if he is really temperate, the expression of his temperate state in these results is still praiseworthy.[9]

---

virtue it is good and beneficial (S.E. *M* XI 22 = *SVF* III 75; 30 = *SVF* III 73; D.L. VII 98 = *SVF* III 87). Qua happiness it is a good flow of life; qua virtue it is temperance, justice etc.

[9] At *Stoic. rep.* 1038e–1039d, *Comm. not.* 1060e–1061a Plutarch alleges that Chrysippus is inconsistent in saying both that (a) not everything done according to virtue is praiseworthy, 1038e, and that (b) whatever is good is praiseworthy, 1039c. Since (c) everything done according to virtue is good, but (d) things done according to virtue, e.g. temperate abstention from an ugly old woman, are sometimes not praiseworthy, it follows that (e) such a thing both is and is not praiseworthy. Plutarch seems to rely on an equivocation in

If the Stoics are right to argue that the addition of external advantages to virtue makes the result no finer than virtue alone would be, then Aristotle cannot be right to claim that happiness is the finest thing; for it turns out to be no finer than virtue alone. Aristotle makes his view consistent again once he concedes that happiness is identical to virtue. Once he concedes this, however, he has conceded that only the fine is good. For if there were any other goods besides virtue, happiness, being comprehensive, would have to include them; since virtue and happiness are identical, there can be no other goods.[10]

The Stoic arguments, then, point to an apparent difficulty in Aristotle's conception of happiness as both the finest thing and yet not identical to virtue. And if 'finest' means 'finer than anything else', the difficulty is real and serious. Aristotle has an answer, however, if he understands 'finest' differently. If the finest thing, virtue, is a part of happiness, then happiness includes the finest thing as a part, but need not be finer than this part of it. (If I make a meal in which the main course is the most nutritious food there is, and the other courses are non-nutritious, but one is the saltiest thing there is and the other the sweetest, I can say that the meal is the most nutritious, saltiest and sweetest thing there is, without saying that the whole meal is more nutritious than the main course alone would be.)

It is fairly plain that Aristotle needs to understand his claim about happiness in this way. For just after he has said that happiness is the finest thing, he goes on to deny that it is the sort of thing that is praiseworthy; it is a matter for honour and congratulation, not for praise (1101 b21–34). If he denies that happiness is praiseworthy, but agrees that whatever is fine is praiseworthy, and that happiness is fine, then his view seems grossly inconsistent. It is consistent, however, if it is carefully explained. Since happiness includes the finest thing, virtue, it is finest, and to that extent appropriately praised. But since it includes more than virtue, happiness as a whole is not praised, but honoured; Aristotle relies here, as he usually does when he extends happiness beyond virtue, on the completeness of happiness (1101 b35–1102 a1). If he explains his position this way, it is invulnerable to the Stoic attack.

'things done according to virtue'. In (c) it refers to (i) actions, as expressing virtue; but in (a) and (d) it refers to (ii) the results of (i) – hence *tōn sumbainontōn ap'aretēs*, 1039a. Chrysippus' point may be that (ii) are never praiseworthy, while (i) always are. The results are more and less preferred, but not good. (In 1038f. the best reading is perhaps *esti ta proachthenta* [i.e. *proēgmena*] *kai toutōn*, where Cherniss in the Loeb reads *ta mē prosenechthenta*.) Chrysippus discusses these questions in his work *On Zeus*, 1038e, and *On the Gods*, 1039a, where he is perhaps trying to undermine Aristotle's objections to praise of the gods, in 1101 b18–21, 1178 b16.

10 Alexander remarks that if the Stoics are right to claim that only the fine is good, then neither fortune nor the gods contribute any good to happiness, *Quaest.* 26, 16–27 = SVF III 32. The view about the role of the gods is different from the view in *EN* 1099 b14–18.

On this issue, then, we should neither dismiss the Stoic argument as a 'leaden dagger' (Cic. *Fin.* IV 48) nor agree that it deals a fatal blow to the Aristotelian position. The Stoics have a powerful objection to Aristotle, under one reasonable interpretation of his position. The force of their objection shows that his position needs another interpretation; and another interpretation is available to meet the Stoic objection. The objection is important because it shows how Aristotle's position has to be understood if it is to be consistent and plausible.

5. Happiness as a mixed end

When Aristotle insists that virtue is not identical to happiness, he must allow that happiness is a mixture. While being virtuous is one of our ends, it is not the only end; we also want to succeed in our virtuous actions, and want to secure the external goods apart from virtuous actions. Happiness will be the end that we achieve by achieving this mixture of ends.

At the same time Aristotle insists that virtue and the fine predominate in this mixture over all other parts of happiness. (For predominance see Cic. *Fin.* V 91–2; *Tusc.* V 51.) A virtuous person is expected to sacrifice his life and his happiness if virtue requires such sacrifices of a brave person defending his friends or his country (*EN* 1117 b7–15, 1169 a18–29). Aristotle needs to say that in such cases we are still doing the best we can for our own happiness; we are not sacrificing the prospect of future happiness to fulfil the demands of virtue, since we cannot be happy if we neglect its demands, and we will always be happier if we fulfil them. None the less the demands of virtue require the sacrifice of some genuine goods, and by sacrificing them the virtuous person makes it impossible for himself to achieve happiness.

The Stoics believe that Aristotle cannot consistently maintain both that happiness is a mixture and that virtue is its dominant component. Since we accept the dominance of virtue, we must deny that the end is a mixture.

Chrysippus apparently concedes that a mixed end, including virtue as one component, is logically possible. He argues that justice and fineness would be abolished if we regarded pleasure as the end, but would not be abolished if we regarded pleasure as simply a good (Plu. *Comm. not.* 1070d = *SVF* III 23; *Stoic. rep.* 1040c; Cic. *Fin.* V 22).[11] Here Chrysippus

---

[11] In *Stoic. rep.* 1040c *telos* must be the ultimate end (as in Stob. *Ecl.* II 46 5–10 = *SVF* III 2), not the sort of end that is mentioned in the Stoic definition of a craft (see Part 12 below). The optative in the passage quoted from Chrysippus by Plutarch suggests that Chrysippus might be making a counterfactual suggestion; 'if [contrary to fact] the status of virtue as intrinsic good allowed pleasure to be an intrinsic good also [...]'.

recognises the possibility of allowing other goods besides virtue, but assigning them less weight; other external advantages can be treated as he treats pleasure.[12] To treat pleasure as the end is to abolish justice and fineness; for a hedonist can assign only instrumental value to virtuous actions, but Aristotle and the Stoics agree that a virtuous person must regard virtuous action as fine and valuable in itself. Chrysippus admits that Aristotle's mixed end allows logical room for the intrinsic value of virtue.

None the less the Stoics insist that the virtues and the fine are abolished if we allow a mixed end (Plu. *Stoic. rep.* 1040d). The happy life must be composed of parts that are uniform with each other and with the whole that they compose, as a heap of corn is composed only of grains of corn. 'If they [sc. the goods composing the happy life] are mixed from dissimilar things, nothing fine can be achieved from these; and if this [sc. the fine] is taken away, how can anything happy be taken to survive?' (Cic. *Tusc.* v 45). The final good must be simple, and cannot be the result of mixing dissimilar elements (Cic. *Off.* III 119; *Fin.* II 34–5 = *SVF* III 14; Sen. *Dial.* VII 15 1). By adding pleasures or external advantages to virtue we are trying to combine a human being with a beast (*Off.* III 119; *Ac.* II 139). The result will be a Scylla, a monstrous hybrid composed of 'disparate and dubiously compatible members' (Sen. *Ep.* 92 9).

Are these attacks on a mixed end compatible with the admission that a mixed end does not abolish the virtues? Some of Epictetus' objections explain more precisely what is meant by calling the mixed end an intolerable hybrid. How, he asks, can we maintain the right relations with others if we admit goods other than virtue? We cannot:

For I have a natural tendency towards my own interest. If it is in my interest to possess a field, it is in my interest to deprive my neighbour of it also; if it is in my interest to possess a cloak, it is in my interest to steal it from a bath-house also. Hence wars, conflicts, tyrannies, conspiracies. (Epict. *Diss.* I 22, 13–14.)

This argument is meant to show that we have no preconception that external advantages are goods; for the belief that they are goods conflicts with my preconception about the value of virtue. We learn from this case how we must apply preconceptions (I 22, 1–3).

When the Stoics seem both to affirm and to deny that the recognition of

---

[12] See Cic. *Ac.* II 138; for these theoretical purposes Chrysippus thinks it does not matter whether we regard pleasure, or freedom from pains, or natural advantages, as intrinsic goods to be combined with virtue in happiness.

a mixed end 'abolishes virtue', what status is assumed for virtue? Two claims need to be considered:

1. Virtue is an intrinsic good, even the greatest single intrinsic good (cf. *meizon agathon apolipontes*, Plu. *Stoic. rep.* 1040c).
2. Virtue is the dominant component of happiness.

Both Aristotle and the Stoics accept the second claim, which is considerably stronger than the first. The Stoic objections to a mixed end are much stronger if they rely on the second claim than if they rely only on the first. If we allow a mixed end, we allow that sometimes a large combination of other components might be secured by vicious action. In that case why should I be virtuous? The Stoics challenge Aristotle's right to maintain the dominance of virtue.

Aristotle should admit that a mixed end allows these conflicting reasons. But he might see nothing wrong in this. A just person sees that he has a prospect of some benefit from cheating his neighbour, and that he therefore has some reason to do the unjust action. But, being a just person and recognising that virtue predominates in happiness, he will always see that he has better reason to do the just action. The recognition of reasons that count against virtue need not weaken his commitment to virtue.[13]

We might say that this reply is consistent but impractical. If we allow that we have reason to pursue external advantages as goods, we will develop desires for them; and can we control the strength of these desires? If not, our belief that virtue predominates may be ineffective, and may eventually fade.

It is hard to see why this argument should move Aristotle. It assumes that the strength of desires is uncontrollable if and only if we believe that their objects are goods. To see whether this sort of argument might appeal to the Stoics we would need to examine their view of affections (*pathē*) more fully. But in any case it scarcely seems to be a serious threat to Aristotle.

To present a plausible objection to the mixed end the Stoics need to challenge Aristotle on a more basic claim. Once we allow that external advantages are goods, and are needed as components of happiness, can we any longer maintain that they never outweigh virtue? We might think that we can describe cases where a vicious action will secure a huge

---

[13] We would ascribe a much more Stoic view to Aristotle if we accepted the suggestion in McDowell (1980), p. 369f., that the conflicting considerations are supposed to be 'silenced'.

increase in external goods; perhaps I can steal my stingy neighbour's lottery ticket, win the first prize, and spend the money on a magnificent scale, both for my own benefit and for other people's. A Stoic critic might argue that once we allow external advantages to count against virtue, we cannot plausibly maintain that they never dominate over virtue.

This sort of challenge implies, quite correctly, that Aristotle needs to explain why virtue is dominant, and what actions it requires or allows. He needs to explain this in enough detail to show why these sorts of examples need not damage his claim. A demand for this sort of explanation is quite fair. But the Stoics should not assume that Aristotle cannot find it. If he cannot, perhaps we should conclude that virtue is not dominant in happiness; should we instead agree with the Stoics in identifying virtue with happiness? The Stoics may not be able to undermine Aristotle's position without also undermining their own at the same time. This point will be clearer when we consider further Stoic arguments for identifying virtue with happiness; we will see that these arguments allow Aristotle some possible ways to support his claims about the predominance of virtue.

6. Mixed motives

Whether or not the mixed end results in the sort of conflict that undermines virtue, it will certainly imply that we often have more than one desire for the same action. Often the virtuous action brings the agent pleasure or honour; the agent knows this in advance, and, in Aristotle's view, he does the action for the sake of the pleasure or honour. At the same time he does the action for its own sake because it is fine. He acts on mixed motives.

The Stoics may think that Aristotle offers here a ground for objection to his belief in a mixed end. If we believe both that a rational person acts for the sake of happiness, and that the virtuous person's motive must be pure and unmixed, choosing virtue for nothing but itself, then the virtuous person must identify virtue with happiness; and if his beliefs are true, virtue must be identical to happiness.

There is some reason to suppose that the Stoics accept this demand for unmixed motives in a virtuous person. If we aim at pleasure, then, in their view, we destroy

[...] community with the human race, affection, friendship, justice and other virtues, none of which can exist unless it is for no reward [*gratuita*], since what is urged to a fitting action by pleasure as a sort of reward is not virtue, but some sort of deceptive imitation and pretence of virtue. (Cic. *Ac.* II 140.)

The Stoics

[...] most strongly deny that justice or friendship is approved because of its usefulness; for in that case the same usefulness will be able to overthrow and distort them. In fact neither justice or friendship will be capable of existing at all, unless they are sought for themselves. (*Fin.* III 70.)

Epicurus' actual behaviour and attitudes showed, contrary to his ethical theory, that he had 'a good character not pursuing reward (*probitatem gratuitam*), not responding to pleasures or induced by the gain of rewards' (*Fin.* II 99; cf. Sen. *Dial.* VII 9 4).

These Stoic demands are imprecise on the very point that concerns us here. Sometimes they seem to be part of the Stoics' criticism of those who make the end consist in something that excludes virtue – pleasure or external goods; these people make virtue impossible by requiring us to regard it as purely instrumental (*Fin.* V 22; *Off.* III 118). If this is the only point, then the Stoics have no ground for objection to Aristotle. But they have a ground for objection if they require unmixed motives. If we act 'for no reward' only when we are not aiming at any gain other than virtue itself, then Aristotle's account of the good person's motive cannot pass the Stoic test.

If the Stoics reject mixed motives, it is easy to see why they reject Aristotle's conception of happiness, which plainly allows mixed motives. And if the Stoics are right to reject mixed motives, they have a good reason for rejecting Aristotle. But are they right?

It is fair to expect that the virtuous person will do what virtue requires even if he gains no other reward; his concern with virtue should be sufficient by itself to move him to action. If this demand is fair, then a counterfactual about his motives must be true; he must have the sort of concern for virtue that would move him to do the virtuous action even if he could expect no other reward from it. But the truth of this counterfactual does not imply that the virtuous person does not in fact aim at any other reward. Aristotle's virtuous person satisfies the counterfactual, as Aristotle is careful to point out (1097 b3–4, 1174 a7–8); and it is not clear why the demand for a purer, less mixed motive should be accepted.[14]

Apparently, then, the Stoic claims about the virtuous person's motive face a dilemma. Understood one way, they are reasonable, but raise no difficulty for Aristotle. Understood another way, they are inconsistent with Aristotle, but not clearly reasonable.

[14] It is tempting to compare the Stoics' demand (if they make it) with Kant's claim (*Grundlegung*, Academy edition, pp. 397–9). I believe, however, that Kant is committed to no more than the counterfactual than Aristotle also accepts. For discussion see Beck (1960), p. 119f.; Henson (1979); Herman (1981).

7. Virtues and external goods

The arguments considered so far appeal to the nature of virtue and of the fine in general. The Stoics add some closely related arguments that appeal to our beliefs about specific virtues. They argue that the types of desires and motives included in these virtues leave no room for counting external goods as parts of happiness.

The Stoics argue for their view by appeal to bravery, and to magnanimity, one of the virtues subordinate to bravery (Stob. *Ecl.* II 60 21–2 = *SVF* III 264; D.L. VII 92 = *SVF* III 265). The brave person must be entirely unafraid (Cic. *Fin.* III 29; *Tusc.* V 41–2, 51–4). The magnanimous person must be superior to all the vicissitudes of fortune; but he will be superior to them only if none of them affects his happiness; 'hence virtue will be sufficient in itself for happiness, since it despises even the things that seem to cause trouble' (D.L. VII 128). The virtuous person regards his virtue as good, but does not fear its loss, since it is in his power. If he regarded any external advantage as a good, he would fear its loss, and hence would not be brave or magnanimous (Sen. *Dial.* VII 15 3–4).[15]

The first controversial point in this Stoic argument is the claim that the virtuous person must be free from fear. A Stoic reader might certainly argue that Aristotle is committed to a position very close to his. For Aristotle allows that the brave person should be fearless (1115 a16), and even imposes an apparently Stoic condition on the extent of the brave person's fearlessness: 'Presumably one must not fear poverty or disease, or, in general, anything that is neither the result of vice nor caused by oneself' (1115 a17–18).[16] We might infer that the brave person is fearless in these cases because he thinks that nothing except vice is really bad for him.

The rest of Aristotle's argument shows, however, that he does not accept this extreme view. The brave person is afraid to the extent that is right (1115 b17–20), and someone who has no fear at all of external conditions is said to be 'mad, or incapable of feeling pain' (1115 b24–8). Some objects of fear are beyond human strength not to fear; and even those that are not beyond human strength will be objects of fear for the brave person too (1115 b7–13). Here we might think that the brave

---

[15] Here the issue is complicated by the Stoics' doctrine of affections, *pathē*, which partly rests on arguments that are distinct from the dispute with Aristotle over virtue and happiness. But in so far as the Stoics think we should be free of affections because they involve the false belief that some indifferents are goods or evils, they cannot use the desirability of freedom from affections as an independent argument against Aristotle.

[16] Gauthier and Jolif (1970) quote Colle: 'Et voilà, chez le Stagirite, le paradoxe du Stoïcisme'. They explain: 'Noter cependant que la formule Aristotélicienne veut dire qu'il ne faut pas craindre ces malheurs au point d'en omettre de faire ce que l'on doit; cf. 1115 b10–13.'

person is afraid, but overcomes his fear when he sees that it is fine to over-come it and stand firm; but if that is what he does, is he not continent rather than strictly virtuous (cf. 1228 b9–17)? Here the Stoics might claim to have found that Aristotle's account violates his own conditions for virtue unless it is thoroughly Stoic.

Probably, however, Aristotle wants to maintain his view that the brave person acts fearlessly when he acts bravely. The brave person regards death, poverty and earthquakes as evil and dangerous, and normally fears them; he will be careful crossing the street, will not waste his money, and will not thoughtlessly build a skyscraper where there are frequent earth-quakes. But when he sees that fine and virtuous actions can expose him to these evils, he will not be afraid of them; he sees that it is reasonable to face them, and his feelings follow reason (1229 a7–9). When nothing fine is at stake, he regards external disasters as evils, and fears them enough to take reasonable precautions; when fine action is at stake, he regards them as evils, but no longer fears them.

Aristotle would be right, then, from the point of view of his theory, to deny the Stoic assumption that the brave person must be free from fear (Cic. *Ac.* II 135). But he accepts the Stoic assumption that the brave person has no fear of death when he bravely faces death. It is easy to see how a Stoic, failing to distinguish the second assumption from the first, might think Aristotle is committed to the premiss of the Stoic argument. Here, as often, the Stoic argument neither ignores nor totally misrep-resents Aristotle; to show that he can avoid the Stoic argument Aristotle must either explain or revise his views. We have tried to explain them by arguing that the brave person is fearless towards the same evil on some oc-casions but not on others. If we think this is an arbitrary or unjustifiable distinction, we will demand more thorough revision from Aristotle.

Related questions arise about Aristotle's view of magnanimity. He cer-tainly thinks that the magnanimous person will be calm and undisturbed about the loss of external goods. He will be calm because he regards them all as small in comparison with virtue (1123 b32, 1124 a12–20). But, in Aristotle's view, this attitude does not require the magnanimous person to think external goods are valueless. When they do not conflict with virtue, he cares about them and fears their loss. He is not prone to lament the loss of external goods, because he does not take them seriously (*spoudazein*, 1125 a9–10); but he can value them to some degree without taking them seriously.

Study of Aristotle's account shows us why the Stoics might think they are entitled to their premiss; they think Aristotle himself is committed to it. But the same study of Aristotle's account shows that he can avoid the

Stoic premiss if he is entitled to a further distinction. The Stoics might well challenge his right to this further distinction; but the argument we have considered so far does not contain the necessary challenge. The Stoics have not offered Aristotle a convincing reason for agreeing that the virtuous person's outlook requires the rejection of external goods.

8. *Genuine goods*

So far we have been following the Stoics' first direction of argument. They rely on our convictions about virtue and fineness; and once we understand the nature of virtue or fineness, we are expected to see that it leaves no room for any other component of happiness. This direction of argument must rely on some beliefs about happiness. But it tries to prove positively that virtue absorbs the whole of happiness. The other direction of argument, to which we must turn now, proceeds differently; it relies on our views about happiness and the good, and argues from these to show that happiness must exclude anything apart from virtue. Without considering the claim of virtue to expel all other candidates for being components of happiness, we see that these candidates cannot in any case be allowed if we have the right views on happiness and goods.

The Stoics attack Aristotle's views about the composition of happiness by assuming, quite fairly, that happiness must be composed of goods, and then attacking the claim of anything besides virtue to be a good. Here they rely on an argument of Socrates. Socrates observes that among the goods normally recognised some can be misused, so that they produce bad results; only virtue, identified with wisdom, cannot be misused (Plato, *Euthyd.* 280 e3–281 e5; *Meno* 87 e3–88 e2). He infers that wisdom is the only good, and folly the only evil (281 e3–5). Aristotle rejects Socrates' conclusion, and insists that goods allowing misuse are still goods (*EN* 1129 b1–6, *EE* 1248 b27–34, *MM* 1183 b28–35).

Here the Stoics agree with Socrates, claiming that nothing liable to misuse is a genuine good (D.L. VII 103 = *SVF* III 117; S.E., *M* XI 61 = *SVF* III 122; Cic. *Tusc.* V 45; Plu. *Stoic. rep.* 1048cd = *SVF* III 123). Since happiness must be composed of genuine goods, none of these alleged goods that are liable to misuse can be a component of happiness. The Stoics infer that virtue must be the only component of happiness.

The Stoic inference is open to doubt. Let us concede that health by itself is not a good. We are still free to claim that health regulated by virtue is a good (cf. *Euthyd.* 281 d6–8); for this condition cannot be misused. But this regulated health seems to be distinct from virtue alone; hence virtue cannot be the only component of happiness.

The Stoics disagree. For they take 'regulated health' to mean 'the regulation by virtue of whatever degree of health we may have'; and for this virtue is sufficient, since no particular degree of health is required. But we might instead take it to mean 'a high degree of health regulated by virtue'; and for this condition virtue is not sufficient, since our degree of health does not depend on virtue alone. The Stoics' argument about misuse does not justify them in ruling out the demand for a high degree of health regulated by virtue. Hence this argument, despite its prominence in the sources, does not achieve its purpose. To exclude such alleged goods as regulated health from happiness, the Stoics must appeal to some further features of happiness or of genuine goods.

9. *Chance*

When the Stoics reject a mixed end that includes goods of fortune, they remark that on their view happiness turns out to be in our power; and they regard this as an advantage of their view against the Aristotelian view (Cic. *Fin.* IV 15; V 82). Theophrastus is often attacked for having left happiness exposed to good and ill fortune (*Fin.* V 12, 77, 85; *Tusc.* V 24, 85; *Ac.* I 33). To the extent that Aristotle counts external goods as necessary for happiness, he is open to the same objections.[17] We have already considered those Stoic objections that rely on the assumption that genuine virtue allows nothing beside itself to be a genuine good. But even apart from this sort of objection, the Stoics seem to think that Aristotle is wrong to allow happiness to be out of our control.

It is hard to find the premiss and the conclusion here. Do the Stoics simply assume that an acceptable account of happiness must show that happiness is in our power? Or do they rely on some more basic feature of happiness, and argue from this to the conclusion that happiness must be in our power?

They should not simply assume that happiness must be in our power, if they want to argue against Aristotle. For Aristotle rejects the assumption. He agrees that it is desirable to show that happiness is to some significant

---

[17] At *Fin.* V 12 Cicero contrasts Theophrastus' belief that wisdom itself does not provide a happy life with the view of 'Aristotle and his son Nicomachus'. Madvig (1876) comments appositely: '*Si tamen Ciceroni illa* [...] *Ethica Nicomachea aeque nota ac pertractata fuissent atque Theophrasti liber, nec de Aristotele Antiocho credidisset, vim fortunae ab Aristotele minime excludi vidisset.*' He cites *EN* I 10–11, x 9. Antiochus distinguishes Aristotle from Theophrastus because he thinks that in Aristotle's view virtue is sufficient for the *beata vita*, not for the *beatissima vita*, *Fin.* V 81; *Tusc.* V 22, 28, 76; *Ac.* II 134. I think Antiochus is wrong about Aristotle, and therefore Aristotle must face the objections aimed at Theophrastus.

extent in our power (1095 b25–6, 1099 b18–25); and he thinks he satisfies this demand if he shows that virtuous actions control happiness (1100 b7–11). But in saying this he plainly does not mean to claim that happiness is entirely in our power; for at the same time he insists that human life needs the appropriate external goods added to virtue (1100 b8–9).

Aristotle assumes here that the completeness of happiness must be assumed before we consider the extent to which happiness is voluntary. And here the Stoics disagree. If we assume that it is a complete and comprehensive good, we must make sure that it includes all the genuine goods; only then can we decide how far it is in our power. If we could first assume that happiness is voluntary, and then consider what is needed to make it a complete good, we would have to say that the external goods, not being voluntary, are not genuine goods, and therefore are not genuine parts of happiness at all.

This order of argument will suit the Stoics better (cf. Epict. *Diss.* III 24 17). But they seem to give no good reason for preferring it over Aristotle's order of argument. Epictetus claims that the universe would be badly ordered if Zeus did not take care for his fellow-citizens to be happy like himself (III 24 19). But how do we know this? Aristotle can reply, without contesting Stoic cosmology as a whole, that the universe is well ordered if each of us can secure the dominant component of happiness. Zeus does not actually provide happiness for everyone, and the Stoics do not explain why he must even make it in everyone's power. To decide whether it is in everyone's power we must apparently consider the most plausible views of the composition of happiness; the Stoics do not seem to be entitled to assume its voluntary character from the start.

If the Stoics use the voluntary character of happiness as a premiss of their argument, they are begging an important question against Aristotle. If they try to argue for it, then either they must rely on the arguments about virtue (returning to the first direction of argument), or they seem to have nothing convincing to offer against Aristotle's claim that happiness is only partly voluntary.

10. *Fear and incompleteness*

Aristotle's demand for completeness seems to him to imply that happiness cannot be purely voluntary. The Stoics argue that if he is right about this, he makes happiness not merely more difficult, but actually unattainable.

Let us suppose that someone is virtuous and has all the external goods that Aristotle takes to be necessary for happiness. Aristotle seems to think that such a person will be happy if this condition lasts for the proper length of time (1101 a14–16). But the Stoics argue that this condition not only fails to secure happiness, but actually prevents it. If my happiness includes external goods, then I realise that it is possible to lose these components of happiness, and hence to lose my happiness. Realising this, I will fear the loss of these goods. But if I am afraid, I will not be happy (Cic. *Fin.* ii 86–7; *Tusc.* v 40–1; Epict. *Diss.* ii 17 17–18). The conditions for Aristotelian happiness destroy each other.

Where should Aristotle try to resist this argument? It seems only realistic to recognise the practical possibility of losing external goods; and, for reasons we have seen, Aristotle cannot safely deny that this prospective loss is an appropriate object of fear. For present purposes we may concede that such fear need not undermine a person's virtue. All that the Stoics need is the claim that we would be better off if we lacked this justified fear and the grounds for it. If our life lacked these grounds for fear, it would be better than our present life; and if we can add some good to make our life better it cannot have achieved the complete good, and hence cannot be happy. If the Stoic argument works, then it shows that happiness is impossible if it must be complete and completeness requires external goods.

To reply to this argument Aristotle needs to explain more clearly what is assumed in the attempt to add goods so as to produce a better good. Suppose we say:

1.   If (a) x were added to life L, then (b) L + x would be a better good than L alone.

We might understand this claim in two different ways:

2.   If (a) x were added to L, and the effects of x on the rest of L were considered, then (b) ...
3.   If (a) x were added to L, and L were assumed to remain otherwise the same, then (b) ...

Here (2a) directs us to consider the possible loss of goods that might result from adding x to L. It leaves open the possibility that x might be a gain, but the consequential losses might be serious enough to make L+x worse than L alone. (It would be good for me to learn the *Iliad* by heart, but it would take too much time from more important things.)[18] In (3a) we

---

[18] If (2) is Aristotle's intended interpretation, then the requirement that nothing can be added to happiness is an analogue of Pareto-optimality (discussed by, e.g., Barry (1965), pp. 49–51). Aristotle requires some further principles to assign different weights to different components of happiness.

ignore these effects of the addition of x to L; the situation that (3a) requires us to assume may be impossible.

The Stoic argument about fear shows that Aristotle's virtuous person cannot be happy, if (3) specifies the right test for the completeness of a complete good. But if (2) specifies the right test, then Aristotle may have a reply. For he can argue that the price of removing fear would be the removal of the external goods that both contribute to happiness and occasion fear; hence the removal of fear would produce a worse, not a better life, and the bad effects of fear do not show that a life including fear fails to achieve the complete good.

Here as elsewhere, the Stoic objection raises a useful question about the meaning and the plausibility of an Aristotelian claim. When Aristotle offers (1) as a test for a complete good, does he intend (2) or (3)? This may not be easy to decide.[19] But at first sight (2) seems more reasonable than (3). For the sorts of effects that are considered in (2) and ignored in (3) seem to be crucial for the design of a life; and if our test for happiness ignores these effects, it will probably mislead us in the task that Aristotle has undertaken, the designing of a life.

On this point, then, we have good reason for rejecting the Stoic objection. But even if we allow this objection, it need not by itself undermine the Aristotelian conception of happiness. For the objection shows at most that in many realistically-conceived conditions we cannot achieve happiness. Aristotle might not welcome this conclusion; but he need not admit that it refutes his conception of happiness. Why not simply agree that happiness is often unattainable? If we agree to this, we are still free to claim that we should try to attain happiness to the extent that it is attainable; it may still be a goal that deserves our attention. The Stoics seem to rely on the disputable assumption that happiness must be attainable; and we have previously criticised Epictetus' defence of that assumption. Aristotle might fairly refuse to accept it.

11. Happiness and tranquillity

The previous Stoic arguments in the second direction have tried to show that Aristotle's conception of happiness violates some necessary condition for happiness. Some Stoics argue positively that the Stoic conception satisfies clearly sufficient conditions for happiness, and that we can see

---

[19] It is not easy to say, e.g., which facts about external conditions or normal human psychological limitations should be taken for granted when the truth of the counterfactual is considered.

this even if we do not already accept Stoic claims about the supreme value of virtue.

The main Stoic argument is as follows:

1.   Happiness is (identical to) a good flow of life (*eurhoia biou*).
2.   A good flow of life is (identical to) a tranquil life, undisturbed by fear or anxiety, in which we achieve the purposes we form, and need not fear the loss of the resources for achieving them.
3.   The virtuous person has a tranquil life.
4.   Therefore the virtuous person is happy.

The first premiss is Stoic. It is one of the formulae of happiness associated with all the three founders of the school (Stob. *Ecl.* II 77 20–4 = *SVF* I 184, 554; S.E. *M* XI 30 = *SVF* III 73; D.L. VII 88; cf. M. Aurel. II 5; V 9; X 6; S.E. *M* XI 110; Sen. *Ep.* 120 11).[20] 'Good flow' is interpreted, most clearly by Epictetus, as the condition of calm and freedom from fear; we have a well-flowing life if we attach no value to anything whose loss we have any reason to fear (Epict. I 4 1, 3, 6, 27–9).[21] Plainly the Stoic sage has the right beliefs and attitudes for tranquillity. He values nothing besides his virtue as a good; hence he faces the loss of external advantages without fear; and since he has no fear of losing his virtue, he is entirely free from fear and disturbance. To some Stoics this seems to be sufficient for happiness (Cic. *Tusc.* V 16, 40, 43, 48, 81; Sen. *Ep.* 85 2, 24; 92 3).

Why should Aristotle agree that tranquillity is sufficient for happiness? The Stoics defend their claim by arguing that tranquillity satisfies the demand that happiness should be complete and lacking in nothing: 'When someone is placed outside longing for anything, what can he lack? When he has gathered all that is his into himself, what need has he of anything external?' (Sen. *Dial.* VII 16 3). 'Completeness' and 'lacking in nothing' are taken to refer to the agent's desires; since the Stoic desires nothing outside him for his happiness, he lacks nothing external that he needs for his happiness, and so has a life lacking in nothing, which is just the sort of life that Aristotle counts happy. If the Stoics understand the formal conditions for happiness in this way, they might agree with the surprising

---

[20]   *Eurhoia* is associated with Zeno's conception of happiness as an internal state by Pohlenz (1938), p. 202, and (1970), p. 116. But it is not clear what Pohlenz takes to constitute *eurhoia*.

[21]   Epictetus associates *eurhoia* with happiness, II 19, 29, and with freedom and magnanimity, II 16, 41, and treats it as the end of desire, IV 4, 4. He associates it with a purely subjective state of tranquillity, I 1, 22; IV 1, 46; 4, 22; 36, 7. His view is less clear in I 28, 30; II 16, 47; II 10, 10; 14, 8; 17, 9; 20, 14; IV 4, 36–7, 39; 6, 35; 12, 2; *Ench.* 8. Bonhöffer (1894), e.g. p. 47, regards it as a subjective state, and actually takes it to be synonymous with *eudaimonia*, p. 254.

claim that Democritus' identification of happiness with 'good spirits' (*euthūmia*) is uncontroversially correct (Cic. *Fin.* v 23; cf. 88).

Should Aristotle agree, though, that this is the right account of completeness? He does not define completeness with reference to an agent's desires. He does not suggest that if I have no unsatisfied or unsatisfiable desires I will be happy. Completeness seems to be defined by reference to the agent's nature and capacities, not his desires. When Aristotle insists (in explaining his formal conditions) that the complete good must extend to friends, family and fellow-citizens, he does not mean that everyone's desires extend this far, but that a human being's nature requires this conception of his good. When happiness is taken to be complete in this way, the Stoic claim that tranquillity is sufficient for happiness should not convince us.

While the Stoic argument should not convince Aristotle, it perhaps should not convince the Stoics themselves either. For it wins them an easy victory only by assuring them of a more serious defeat. If tranquillity is sufficient for happiness, the Stoics' belief in the sufficiency of virtue for happiness is one way to secure tranquillity, and hence one way to secure happiness. But why should it be the only way? We could perhaps secure tranquillity by being Epicureans or Sceptics, or by equipping ourselves with the right sorts of foolishly optimistic expectations and the right sort of forgetfulness about their disappointment. Once we agree that tranquillity is our aim, the Stoics seem to offer us no reason to follow them rather than those who offer different recipes for the same sort of tranquillity.

If the Stoic sage's belief about virtue is valued for the tranquillity that it produces, what matters is only that he holds the belief, not whether the belief is true or not. Epictetus sees and accepts this consequence:

> If one had to be deceived in order to learn that nothing external to us and outside our decision is anything to us, I would be ready to undergo this deception, from which I would live a well-flowing and undisturbed life. (1 4, 27.)

Epictetus' choice is quite reasonable if tranquillity is the end to be pursued.

But this very feature of Epictetus' argument raises some doubt about its earlier Stoic credentials. Epictetus quotes in his support a passage from Chrysippus:

> So that you can know that these things are not false from which flowing well results and from which freedom from emotion reaches us, take my books, and you will know how conforming and concordant with nature are the things that make me free from emotion. (1 4, 28.)

To Chrysippus, as opposed to Epictetus, it seems to be important that the beliefs producing a well-flowing life are true, not simply that they are believed. Either he has not seen that he is committed to Epictetus' view about deception, or he does not take mere tranquillity by itself to be happiness.

The Stoics who identify tranquillity with happiness also appeal to the Stoic conception of magnanimity. Seneca claims that the happy life is

freedom from care and uninterrupted tranquillity. This is produced by magnanimity, by constancy that sticks to a judgment that has been formed well. How is this reached? If the whole truth is discerned. (*Ep.* 92 3.)

Seneca suggests that the truth results in a sufficient condition for tranquillity. But when he identifies tranquillity with happiness, he fails to explain why the sage needs true beliefs; it seems to be the fact that he believes them, not the fact that they are true, that ensures his happiness by ensuring his tranquillity. Seneca's arguments might appeal to Hecaton's claim that magnanimity is sufficient for happiness because it leads us to despise things that seem troublesome (D.L. VII 128). The Stoic definition of magnanimity insists that it is *knowledge* of the triviality of apparent troubles (see *SVF* III 264 (p. 64.37), 265, 269, 274, 275). But if a Stoic accepts Seneca's argument, the magnanimous person's belief apparently need not rest on knowledge.

A Stoic can connect magnanimity with happiness in two different ways:

1.   It is sufficient for happiness because it is the knowledge that virtue is the only good; since this belief about virtue is true, the virtuous person is happy.
2.   It is sufficient for happiness because it is the belief that virtue is the only good and this belief is sufficient for the tranquillity that is identical to happiness.

It is clear that the early Stoics are committed to the first claim. It is less clear if they are committed to the second claim, presented in Cicero, Seneca and Epictetus. We do not know exactly how the early Stoics understand 'well-flowing life', whether a 'good flow' is just a tranquil condition, as it is for Epictetus, or includes more. And we do not know whether the description of happiness as a well-flowing life is meant as a definition of happiness or as a description of one of its constituent or concomitant features. Posidonius accuses the Stoics of confusion on this point, and his charge may be justified (Galen, *De dogm. Hipp. et Plat.* v 6, 10–12 = *SVF* III 12).[22]

---

[22] This passage is discussed by Rieth (1934), pp. 35–7; Edelstein (1936), p. 313f.; Long (1967), p. 8of.; Striker (this vol. p. 193f). Posidonius thinks that Antipater's second

We can say with some confidence, however, that the conception of happiness as tranquillity does not seem to be excluded by the early Stoics. If the argument we have discussed is not their argument, it is at least a reasonable way to interpret and to combine some Stoic claims.[23] But though it is reasonable, it is none the less disastrous for the Stoics. It leaves them defenceless against the Epicurean and Sceptic views of happiness; and they should be far more eager to reject these views than to reject Aristotle's.

We may not realise how controversial a claim is made by Cicero, Seneca and Epictetus, when they identify happiness with tranquillity. It is easy for us, influenced by the fortunes of the term 'happiness' in English-speaking moral philosophy, to identify happiness with some subjective condition of the agent, with something in his attitude to his condition. The argument from tranquillity shows that such a view may also be tempting for Greeks thinking about *eudaimonia*.[24] But we must not fail to notice that such a view, while tempting, is disputable. Aristotle's conception of happiness correctly challenges such a view; and the Stoics give no reason for rejecting his challenge.

12. Happiness as the end of action

So far we have found that the Stoic objections to Aristotle are answerable, or answerable if Aristotle's position is suitably clarified. But one objection is more fundamental, and harder to answer.

The Stoics begin from the uncontroversial assumption that happiness is the end of our actions (*EN* 1097 a18–24, a34–b6).[25] If it is the end, it is the final cause of action, 'that for the sake of which' we act (1097 a21–2).

---

account of the end as 'doing all in one's power for the sake of the first things according to nature' commits the same fault, of confusing a necessary concomitant of the end (*parhepetai gar kata to anankaion tō(i) telei*) with the definition of the end (which, in Posidonius' view, ought to mention control by reason rather than the irrational part of the soul). Whether or not Posidonius' objection damages Antipater's account, it seems to damage Epictetus'.

23 The arguments from tranquillity provide Schopenhauer with evidence for his claim that 'Stoic ethics is originally and essentially not a doctrine of virtue, but merely a guide to the rational life, whose end and aim is happiness through peace of mind. Virtuous conduct appears in it, so to speak, only by accident, as means, not an end' (1819, I sec. 16, p. 86). He offers more evidence in II ch. 16, p. 158f.

24 Reasons for rejecting a purely subjective account of the English term 'happiness' are presented by Kraut (1979). The possibility of a purely subjective construal of *eudaimonia* tends to support his view that 'happiness' is the right way to describe *eudaimonia*.

25 The Stoics distinguish *telos* and *skopos* in a way Aristotle does not; they say that happiness is the *skopos*, and achieving happiness (the same as being happy, *eudaimonein*) is the *telos*, Stob. *Ecl.* II 77 25–7 = *SVF* III 16. I don't think that the observance of this distinc-

If it is the final cause, it is related to the efficient cause. The efficient cause of action is decision, which includes a desire and a conception of the end (1139 a31–3). Hence happiness will be that end the conception of which is part of the efficient cause of action.

In looking for the efficient cause of action the Stoics assume that Aristotle is looking for what they call the 'perfect' or 'principal' or 'containing' cause (see Clement, *Strom.* VIII 9, p. 95.22–96.5 = *SVF* II 346; Cic. *Fat.* 41). For present purposes the important point is that the relevant cause must be the proximate cause; it must be sufficient in the circumstances for the effect, not merely antecedent to some other cause.[26] It is quite fair of the Stoics to assume that Aristotle wants the proximate cause; they are simply following his maxim that 'we must state the most proximate causes' (*Met.* 1044 b1–2), and relying on his conception of the 'controlling origin' (*EE* 1222 b21–2).[27] What, then, is the proximate cause of rational action, and what is the end that is conceived in the proximate cause?

To answer this question the Stoics appeal to another Aristotelian distinction. Aristotle argues that the function (*ergon*) of rhetoric and dialectic is not to succeed in persuading, and the function of medical science is not to succeed in curing (*Rhet.* 1355 b8–14; *Top.* 101 b5–10, 149 b24–30). Rather, the function of rhetoric is to find the persuasive arguments that are available on each point, and the function of medicine is to lead someone as close to health as is possible; 'for it is possible to give fine treatment even to those who are incapable of a share in health' (1355

---

tion matters for the argument I discuss here. It would matter considerably if Rieth (1934), pp. 32–4, and Long (1967), p. 78, were right to suppose that the Stoics identify the external result (the *prokeimenon*) of a stochastic craft with its *skopos*, and the craftsman's action with the *telos*. But Rieth and Long offer no evidence to show that the Stoics use their distinction in this way; and such a use would conflict with their doctrine about happiness. For virtue is not sufficient for its preferred external results; and if these constitute happiness, virtue will turn out to be insufficient for happiness, but sufficient for getting happiness. These odd results suggest that Rieth and Long misuse the Stoic doctrine. Stoic views on *telos* and *skopos* are fully discussed by Alpers-Gölz (1976), pp. 68–100. Her interpretation of Antipater, p. 70, seems to me to be wrong in identifying the *prokeimenon* (*ta prōta kata phusin*) with the *skopos*.

[26] I am speaking of the 'proximate cause' in the way Cicero speaks of the '*proxima et continens* [i.e. principal] *causa*' at *Fat.* 44: '*Neque enim Chrysippus, concedens assensionis proximam et continentem causam esse in viso positam* [...]' Unfortunately, Cicero also applies '*proxima*' to non-principal causes, at *Fat.* 41. See further Frede (1980), esp. p. 245. In assuming that Stoic assumptions about causation are fairly applied to Aristotle I assume that the Stoics are less innovative than Frede suggests; see Irwin (1983), p. 130–3.

[27] The translation 'controlling' for *kuria* in 1222 b21 is defended by Woods (1982), pp. 126f., 207. Other passages he mentions seem to associate the *kuria* with the proximate cause; *Met.* 1048 a10, *EN* 1113 b17–21, 32–3, 1114 a2–3.

b13–14). The function of the craft also explains what the craftsman will deliberate about; he will not deliberate about success in making healthy, but about what contributes to health, i.e. about what he can do to bring someone as close to health as possible, since this is up to him (EN 1111 b26–30, 1112 b11–16). Aristotle defines the function of a craft narrowly, to exclude the chances and circumstances that may prevent a favourable result from the exercise of the craft. When we apply medicine or study rhetoric our aim is to find the type of action that will be competent and proper exercise of the craft; we are not thinking about the good or bad luck that makes the proper exercise turn out well or badly.

When Aristotle distinguishes the function from the external results of the craft, he identifies the result, not the function, with the end (1111 b26–30, 1112 b11–16). But here the Stoics have some reason to disagree. The conception of the end of the action should appear in the efficient cause of the action; but Aristotle himself shows that it is the conception of the function, not the conception of the external result, that appears in the efficient cause of the craftsman's action. When we think about what to do now, we will guide our decision by what we think is required by competent practice of the craft; hence this competent practice will be our end. There is no point in thinking about the external result; for that depends on circumstances that cannot be controlled by our action.

The Stoics seem to see that Aristotle is open to objection on this point. For they use his distinction between the function and the external result, and draw from it conclusions that contradict his. They recognise a class of 'stochastic' crafts; these are stochastic (i.e. 'aiming') because all the craftsman can do is to aim at an external result; the successful performance of his function does not ensure success in getting the external result. In these cases they call the external result the 'objective' or 'work proposed' (*pro-keimenon ergon*, Latin *propositum*; Alex. *in Top.* 33 15), and the competent practice of the craft the end (*telos*, Alex. *in Top.* 33 17–22; *Quaest.* 61 12–23 = SVF III 19). In reporting this Stoic doctrine Alexander expresses his own preference for the Aristotelian terminology, which the Stoics reverse (*in Top.* 33 23–34 5; *Quaest.* 61 23–8).[28]

The distinction between end and objective explains the Stoics' use of their favourite example of the archer (Cic. *Fin.* III 22 = SVF III 18; Plu.

---

[28] The *Quaest.* passage does not show which solution Alexander accepts. But *in Top.* 34.3–5 shows that he accepts the Aristotelian solution, taking it to conflict with the Stoic claims about virtue: 'In the case of stochastic crafts it is no longer true that the end is in the craftsman's power, just as being happy [*eudaimonein*] is also not in the virtuous person's power, if it is not the case that only the fine is good.' (I agree with Striker (this vol. p. 202) in reading *ei mē monon to kalon agathon* in 34.5, rather than Bruns's emendation.) Alexander's use of *eudaimonein* follows the Stoic conception of the *telos*; see n. 25 above.

Comm. not. 1071b–d). The normal, expected result of the archer's aiming is the hitting of the target; but his end when he takes aim is to make a good shot, to do what a good archer does. It is irrelevant to his attaining his end if a gust of wind blows the arrow off course or someone moves the target after he has shot at it.

The Stoics are severely criticised for their description of the end pursued by a stochastic craft. Plutarch links the distinction to an alleged attempt by Antipater to respond to a criticism by Carneades (*Comm. not.* 1071a–e, 1072e–f). Carneades may have been criticising the Stoics by arguing that they neglect the role of external results in determining the nature of a craft. We would not have a craft of medicine, and it would not prescribe what it prescribes, if we were not concerned about health, the external result of the craft (Cic. *Fin.* v 16–17).

If Carneades intends this remark about crafts to be an objection to the Stoic position, it is adequately answered by the distinction between the end and the objective of a craft. Zeno already defined a craft as 'a system composed of apprehensions trained together for some end that can be used well in life' (*SVF* i 73, ii 93–7); and his definition is plausible if it construes 'end' in the Stoic way that contrasts ends with objectives. The craft of medicine is a system of apprehensions concentrated on the end that is competent practice of the craft; and this end can be used well in life. The apprehensions are not concentrated on the external result, health; that involves so many chances that there is no systematic way to concentrate the apprehensions and the craft on it.

Carneades suggests that the craft must have some concern with the external result, not just with (what the Stoics call) the end. But the Stoics can quite easily agree. The end of the craft – competent practice – is useful to us in life because we are concerned about the external result. But this does not mean that the external result is the end. We would not have the end if we were not concerned with the external result; hence the concern for the external result is an antecedent cause of our action. But it is still not the proximate and principal cause of the action. Similarly, appearance (*phantasia*) is a necessary condition and antecedent cause of an action, but only our assent is the principal and proximate cause. If the conception of the end is part of the proximate efficient cause of the craftsman's action, his end must be the competent performance, not the external result.

I have described the Stoic distinction between the end and the objective of a craft to make it clear that the distinction is neither arbitrary nor contrived nor a mere device to defend their claim about virtue and happiness. Zeno's account of a craft may already reflect Stoic criticism of Aristotle's claims about ends; and even if it does not, the distinction is quite defensible within the Stoic account of the different types of causes. The Stoics suggest that Aristotle's remarks about ends reflect loose thought about causation; had Aristotle thought more carefully about the proximate efficient cause of action, he would not have identified the end of a stochastic craft with its external result.

Once these points are accepted, the Stoics can apply them to show that if happiness is the end of action, it must be virtue, not the external results of virtue. Virtue is a stochastic craft, in so far as virtuous action does not guarantee the preferred external results;[29] hence the efficient cause explaining our action will include our conception of the action required by virtue, not our conception of the external results that might or might not be achieved. Since Aristotle agrees that this conception will be the conception of the end, virtue itself, not the external result, must be the end of virtuous action. The external result will be considered in an antecedent cause of the action, but not in the proximate cause; it will not, therefore, be the end of action.

When the Stoics criticise Aristotle for identifying the end with the external result, they offer their own conception of the end to avoid Aristotle's mistake. They define the end as reasonableness in the selection of things according to nature (Plu. *Comm. not.* 1071a, 1072c–d), and as doing all we can to achieve them (Epict. *Diss.* II 6, 9; Plu. *Comm. not.* 1071a; *SVF* III 12; III Ant. 56–8).[30] The natural advantages are the external results; the appropriate and reasonable action is the end; and this is where we must find happiness. Since happiness is the complete good, none of the external results of virtue can be a good.

On this point the Stoics have a convincing objection to Aristotle's position. And once they carry this point, they can use it to reject a further rôle for external goods. In Aristotle's view, we need external goods for virtuous action; and so we need them even if virtuous action is agreed to be the whole of happiness. For Aristotle there will be an important difference between the claim that virtue is happiness and the claim that virtuous action is happiness; though I can remain virtuous even if I lose external goods, there are some virtuous actions that I can no longer do. For the Stoics this difference will not matter in the same way. For the virtuous person's end will not be virtuous action, described as e.g. 'spending large amounts of money for the public good'; that is an external result that might concern

---

[29] [Ar.] *MM* 1190 a26–8 describes virtue as *stochastikē tou telous*, thinking of the *telos* in Aristotle's way rather than the Stoic way. For the Stoics virtue will be stochastic for its *prokeimenon*, not its *telos*.

[30] These definitions of the end are discussed by Long (1967) and Striker (this vol.). For the reasons given above I doubt if they should be regarded as primarily responses to Carneades' criticisms. A Stoic could easily reach them by his own reflexion on Aristotle.

him, but it involves too many chances to be the right guide for his action. His virtue will be concentrated on doing what he can to spend large sums of money for the public good; and he can achieve this end even if he has no money to spend at all. In Aristotle's view, the action required by the virtue of magnificence requires possession of wealth; but the Stoics suggest that we can see the error in this view once we see the end that the virtuous person really aims at. Aristotle believes that if happiness requires virtuous activity, and not just the state of being virtuous, it requires external goods; but the Stoics reply that he is mistaken about the nature of the virtuous activity that is the virtuous person's end.[31]

If the Stoics are right to reject Aristotle's position, given Aristotle's conception of the end and of happiness, it does not follow that Aristotle should agree with the Stoics. He could restore consistency to his position by accepting any one of these claims:

1. Happiness is not the end, but the external result.
2. The conception of the end need not be part of the proximate efficient cause of action.
3. Happiness is not the complete good; the complete good also includes the external results of virtuous action.
4. Happiness is the complete good, but not our only object of rational concern.

If Aristotle chose (2), he would not need to alter the rest of his ethical theory very much; we would just need to understand when he is talking

---

[31] The Stoic conception of virtuous action allows us to explain the rejection of Aristotle's view that virtue requires an appropriate *chorēgia* of external goods.

(a) The Stoic view identifies virtuous action with the right use of *whatever* external advantages and disadvantages may be present in any situation (see Horace, *Carm.* IV 9.46–9).

(b) The Aristotelian demand for *chorēgia* identifies virtuous action with the right use of a *suitably large amount* of external advantages; the suitably large amount is what is needed for achieving the objective (in Stoic terms) of virtuous action; see *Top.* 152 a5–30; *Pol.* 1325 b40–1326 a5, 1332 a19–25. The Stoic can count on the existence of some external advantages and disadvantages as long as he is alive; hence his need for them does not challenge the claim that virtue is in his power. (These points allow the Stoics to answer Alexander's objections at *De an.* 161 3–16, 26–40.)

If Posidonius and Panaetius are correctly reported in D.L. VII 128 (cf. 103) as reviving the Aristotelian demand for *chorēgia*, understood in its Aristotelian sense, then they depart sharply from orthodox Stoicism; and Kidd (1971), p. 158f., points out clearly how hard it would be to count them as Stoics at all if we accepted D.L. Rist (1969), pp. 8–10, tries to explain D.L. by referring to Antipater's account of the end. But such an explanation blurs the distinction between (a) and (b). The self-sufficiency of virtue for happiness is not compromised by (a); virtue is self-sufficient, *autarkes*, for happiness in the way that the principal cause is self-sufficient (*autoteles* or *autarkes*, Clem. *Strom.* VIII 9, p. 96.1), a way which still allows other necessary conditions (Alex. *De an.* 161 27). There is no evidence to show that Antipater accepts (b), rather than the orthodox Stoic (a).

The difference between Aristotelian and Stoic views is also blurred by Long (1968), p. 75f., who does not stress Aristotle's commitment to (b).

about a principal and proximate cause, and when about an antecedent cause.

The Stoics assume, however, that the only reasonable choice is (4), and they construct the rest of their position on this assumption. We need to know why this is a more reasonable choice than any of the others would be. They might argue that a clear account of the causation of actions requires their conception of an end, if the end is to be a final cause at all. Moreover, if we maintain the identity of virtue with happiness, we maintain a reasonable account of the end, and we maintain Aristotle's formal conditions for happiness; it remains the complete good and the ultimate end. All the preconceptions are preserved once we reject external goods as components of happiness or means to it.

13. *The incompleteness of happiness*

We ought to concentrate on this last Stoic argument for the identity of virtue with happiness. For it forces on the Stoics a problem that their previous arguments might conceal. When we look at the previous arguments, we might take the Stoics to mean that nothing but virtue is a fit object of a rational person's concern; they seem to suggest that, e.g. the brave person who is killed loses nothing that he has any reason to value at all. The last argument makes it plain that the Stoics ought not to mean this. For any plausible account of stochastic crafts should recognise that concern for the external result of the craft shapes our conception of the craft. Hence the Stoics ought to explain how their conception of happiness still allows rational concern for external advantages. The belief that they cannot explain this is the basis of the charge that they cannot distinguish themselves from Cynics.

The Stoic answer to this charge is the doctrine of indifferents.[32] The external advantages are called indifferent because they make no difference to happiness, but they are certainly not indifferent altogether (D.L. vii 104 = *SVF* iii 119; Stob. *Ecl.* ii 79 1–17 = *SVF* iii 118; S.E. *M* xi 59–63). Some indifferents are reasonably preferred and selected (though not strictly 'chosen', *haireta*) over others. Whatever reason Aristotle gives for treating external goods as parts of happiness or means to it provides a reason for the Stoics to select these advantages as parts of or means to the life according to nature (Stob. *Ecl.* ii 83 10–84 17 = *SVF* iii 124–5, 128; D.L. vii 105–6 = *SVF* iii 126–7). The action that is reasonably calculated to secure a preferred indifferent is an appropriate action (*kathēkon*; Cic.

---

[32] This doctrine is well explained by Kidd (1971), pp. 155–7.

Fin III 58; D.L. VII 107; Stob. *Ecl.* II 85.12–86.4 = *SVF* III 494; S.E. *M* VII 158; Cic. *Off.* I 8, 101).[33]

Appropriate actions are the material of virtue (Plu. *Comm. not.* 1069e, 1071b; Alex. *De an.* 160 1–8; Cic. *Fin.* III 61), since virtue is also concerned with the selection of natural advantages. Every virtuous action is first of all an appropriate action; it becomes right and successful by being done from the right aim and motive, the one that values the rational choice for its own sake (Stob. *Ecl.* II 93 14–18 = *SVF* III 500; *SVF* III 510–12). In their choice of the term 'successful action' (*katorthōma*) the Stoics follow Aristotle (*EN* 1106 b26, 1107 a14, 1142 b30, *EE* 1247 a4). But they want to correct his view about the type of success that is to be demanded. Aristotle might be taken to demand success in achieving the external objective (Stoic *prokeimenon*) of the virtuous action, and the Stoics think his demand is unreasonable.[34] We can demand success in attaining the end, not the objective. An appropriate action may fail to achieve its objective (D.L. VII 177); but if it is done with the right motive it still succeeds in achieving its end.

When the Stoics explain the relation of preferred indifferents to virtue, they make it clear that the virtuous person is rationally concerned with these indifferents, and attaches value to them (D.L. VII 105 = *SVF* III 126), even though he thinks they are indifferent in relation to virtue and happiness. Critics suppose that the Stoics undermine their own position here. For the critics assume that if something has value, it must have the value in relation to some end; but the value of ends is relative to the ultimate end, and happiness is the ultimate end; hence all value must be relative to happiness. This is the sort of argument that Alexander, on Aristotle's behalf, advances to show that the Stoics must recognise happiness as the ultimate end to which the preferred indifferents are related (Alex. *De an.* 167 13–168 1).[35] The Stoics will reply that value does not depend on relation to an end; it may also be conferred by relation to an objective; and the life according to nature is the objective that confers value on preferred indifferents. The opponent can then ask about the value of the life according to nature; must it not be valuable only in re-

---

[33] The sense of 'reasonable', *eulogon*, in the definition of appropriate action is discussed by Tsekourakis (1974), p. 25, answering Rist (1969), p. 107f. See also Sedley (1982), p. 250f., Burnyeat (unpub.). We ought to translate 'reasonable' rather than 'probable', to make clear the connexion with 'being reasonable', *eulogistein* (i.e. not merely doing what is in fact reasonable, but exercising reason in selecting it) in Plu. *Comm. not.* 1072c–d = *SVF* III Ant. 59. But consideration of probabilities seem to be relevant in deciding what is *eulogon*.

[34] See Tsekourakis (1974), p. 44. His suspicion of Stoic influence in the use of *katorthōma* in *MM* 1199 a13 is unjustified; the use is similar to the *EE*, not to the Stoic use.

[35] Following Bruns (1887) (apparatus) I read *peri ekeinou logos* in 168.1.

lation to happiness (Alex. *De an.* 167 17–33)? The Stoic must reply that the life according to nature is valuable in relation to itself, not in relation to any end.

Is this an intelligible reply? Aristotle must say that the life according to nature is good in itself, and that its goodness is not wholly derived from any further end – otherwise this life would not itself be a component of happiness. Whatever reason Aristotle offers to defend his claim will be a reason for the Stoics to say that the life according to nature is valuable in itself, not with reference to any more ultimate end.

To this extent the Stoics separate themselves sharply from Aristotle's account of rational action. In Aristotle's view, every object of rational concern and value must be related to happiness. The Stoics reject this view. They do not recognise two ends; but they recognise two objects of ultimate concern, virtue and the life according to nature, and identify only virtue with happiness. Happiness, identified with virtue, is an object of rational concern, but not the only ultimate object. It is not clear that the Stoics have the worse of the argument here.

14. *Virtue and the indifferents*

Once we grasp the Stoics' position, however, we may wonder if it is what they need to meet their own objections to Aristotle. For they allege that when Aristotle allows other goods besides virtue he saps the strength of virtue by allowing possible conflicts. We could see how the Stoics would remove the possibility of conflict if they attached value to nothing except virtue. But in fact they attach value to the preferred indifferents also. Must they not face the same possible conflicts that they criticise in Aristotle?

The problem arises if we assume, reasonably, that virtue and the preferred indifferents together constitute a valuable result (call it the Total) that is more valuable than virtue alone:

> For [sc. the Stoics] say that some things are preferred by the sage, and have value, and are proper and attractive to him, but also that if virtue together with these things and virtue alone lay apart, the sage would never choose [*helesthai*] virtue separated if it were possible for him to select [*labein*] the virtue that is with other things. (Alex. *De an.* 163 4–8.)[36]

Alexander uses this argument to show that happiness, being complete and

---

[36] Alexander distinguishes *hairesis* (choice, applied only to virtue) from *lēpsis* (selection, applied to indifferents and to the Total). His argument assumes that virtue has selective value (the second kind distinguished in D.L. VII 105 = *SVF* III 126.) The assumption is correct, since every *katorthōma* is also a *kathēkon*; the same assumption is made in *Fin.* III 44.

self-sufficient, must include the preferred indifferents (162 25–163 4). The Stoics can resist his conclusion if their previous argument about happiness as an end is accepted. But even if virtue is identical to happiness, it is not identical to the Total; apparently the Stoics must allow that the Total is more valuable than virtue, and is therefore worth selecting in preference to virtue alone.

The Stoics, however, boldly deny that this problem even arises; for they insist that the value of the Total is no greater than the value of virtue alone. In their view, 'there is no value so great that it can be placed before virtue' (Cic. *Fin.* III 44). To explain their claim the Stoics offer a series of analogies. A drop of honey makes the Aegean no sweeter; a penny is not worth adding to the wealth of Croesus; just one step on the road to India is not worth taking; the light of a lamp is obscured by bright sunlight (Cic. *Fin.* III 45; IV 29; V 71; Sen. *Ep.* 92 5, 17).

In denying any greater value to the Total the Stoics may seem to have undermined their own attempt to distinguish themselves from the Cynics. For if the Total has no greater value, why should we select the preferred indifferents rather than their absence? Our selection seems to result in no added value in our lives. The Stoics need to show that their doctrine about the equal value of virtue and the Total does not conflict with their doctrine of preferred indifferents.

To see what the Stoics have in mind, we need to ask what is meant by 'selective value'. One way to understand it is to attend to the rôle of selection; we might say that x has greater selective value than y if and only if we have reason to select x over y. Then the question for the Stoics will be: have we any reason to select a life of virtue plus health (or any other preferred indifferent) over a life of virtue alone?

We might construe this selection as a selection of one or the other of two policies, one requiring the pursuit of virtue and the other requiring the pursuit of the Total. But what is required by the policy of pursuing virtue alone? A virtuous action must be an appropriate action; and an appropriate action is one that is best calculated to secure the preferred indifferent that is needed for the life according to nature. The virtuous person must have the rational aim of doing what he can to achieve the Total. If, then, we make virtue our aim, we must also make the Total our aim. If we are selecting one or the other of two policies, 'Pursue virtue' and 'Pursue the Total', there is nothing to distinguish them; we have no reason to select the Total, rather than virtue alone, as our object of pursuit, since the pursuit of virtue already requires the pursuit of the Total.

It is easy to see that the Stoics' disputes with Aristotle about ends also affect their argument about the Total. If we think of selecting one policy over another, we will want the policies to affect our thought and action in different ways. They must affect our thought and action by affecting our conception of the end, or of the means to it, since these will be part of the proximate efficient cause of our action. But concern with virtue and concern with the Total will in fact give us the same end, and will affect our thought and action in the same way. We are merely confused if we think there is some reason for selecting one policy over the other.

If this is the Stoics' argument, it is fairly easy to justify their claims about the Total, and the analogies they use to illustrate their claims. The main point of the analogies is that the addition of preferred indifferents is foolish and ineffectual, because it achieves nothing that virtue does not achieve by itself. This point is expressed best in the analogy of the sun and the lamp; in bright sunlight we have all the illumination we need, and it is foolish to add a lamp, since it adds no extra useful illumination. The other analogies suggest that it is futile to add a penny to the wealth of Croesus, because it will make him no better off (though it will make him wealthier by a penny), and futile to add a drop of honey to the Aegean or to take one step towards India, because it makes no significant contribution to our aims. If they are understood this way, the analogies support the Stoics' main point; when we see that virtue already pursues the Total, we see that it is futile to select the pursuit of the Total rather than virtue alone. If this is the Stoics' point, they are right to claim that virtue and the Total have equal selective value.

But if the Stoics are right about this, they must at the same time grant that from another point of view the Total has greater selective value. If we are not selecting one policy over another, but selecting one or another possible result of the same policy, then we may say that one result has greater value than another, even though just the same policy is needed to aim at both results. The Stoics agree that they would select a life of virtue plus a preferred indifferent over a life of virtue without it (Cic. *Fin.* IV 30), and so must recognise that the life including the Total has more value than the life of virtue alone. Indeed, they must say this if they are to explain why the virtuous person is right to calculate ways to secure the preferred indifferents. If one result had no more value than another, there would be no reason to aim at it over the other; and if there were no reason to aim at it over the other, there would be no reason for the virtuous person to try to get this result rather than the other.

Here again the Stoics' position appears consistent and reasonable if we attend to their views on causation. The Total is a result to be selected in so far as it has greater selective value than virtue alone has; hence the virtuous person will do what he can to achieve the Total; hence the policy of pursuing the Total will have *no* greater selective value than the policy of pursuing virtue alone. It is precisely because the Total is a more valuable result than virtue alone that the virtuous person tries to achieve it; and this is why the policy of pursuing virtue alone has no less value than the policy of pursuing the Total.[37] Our views about the external result are anteced- ent causes of our action, because they affect our view of the end; but it is our view of the end that is part of the principal cause of the action.

It would be wrong, then, to follow those ancient critics who claim that the Stoics can give no reasonable account of the preferred indifferents that makes them irrelevant to happiness (Cic. *Fin.* IV 30). The Stoics have reasonable grounds for claiming that happiness cannot be an external result of virtuous action; and so they must infer that happiness does not include everything valuable, if they are to justify the selection of preferred indifferents. Their rejection of the view that happiness includes all value is not clearly mistaken; indeed, Aristotle has often been criticised for accept- ing the view that the Stoics reject; and his critics should regard the Stoics with some sympathy.

15. *The dominance of virtue*

Does the Stoics' position on happiness and the Total allow them a defence against the charges that they urge against Aristotle? When Aristotle allows components of happiness beyond virtue, he is alleged to undermine virtue. Why do the Stoics not undermine virtue when they allow compon- ents of the Total beyond virtue?

We thought the Stoics' belief in the equal selective value of virtue and of the Total might avoid a conflict between virtue and the rest of the Total. But now we can see that this belief, understood in the sense that makes it true, does not avoid conflict. If I want to form a rational policy for pursuit of the Total, then perhaps the best I can do is to be virtuous. But still it may often happen, because of external conditions outside my control, that I need to select either virtue or some other component of the Total. (Perhaps, e.g., the opportunity for dishonest wealth suddenly arises.) The Stoics expect us to select virtue in this case; but why? They may assure us that virtue is identical to happiness. But why should we assume that hap- piness predominates over other components of the Total? Once we agree

---

[37] Alexander's wording at *De an.* 163 5–8 (quoted, Part 14, init.) is careful; the Stoic is com- mitted to the truth of a counterfactual conditional similar to that in *Fin.* IV 30, which is consistent with the claim that the policy of pursuing virtue has in fact as much selective value as the policy of pursuing the Total.

with the Stoics' claim that there is value outside happiness, we must apparently ask for proof of the dominance of happiness.

The Stoics criticised Aristotle's mixed end because it allowed possible conflicts between virtue and the other components of happiness. We now see that they must recognise a mixed objective, the Total, and allow possible conflicts between virtue and the other components of the Total. The Stoics can show that this possible conflict leads to no actual conflict if they can show that virtue is the dominant component of the Total. But if they can show this, can Aristotle not also show that virtue is the dominant component of happiness? The same questions seem to arise for both theories, and the same answers seem to be available.

Similar arguments seem to apply to Stoic criticisms of Aristotle's virtuous person for feeling fear and acting on mixed motives. The criticisms can apparently be restated in Stoic terms, and seem to have as much or as little force against the Stoics as they have against Aristotle.[38]

In noticing these points we should not endorse the ancient criticism that takes the Stoic position to be only verbally different from Aristotle's. The Stoic argument from the nature of final causation requires Aristotle to change some of his views, not merely to rephrase them. But though the differences between the two positions are more than verbal, it still seems fair to ask whether the differences really solve the problems that the Stoics see in Aristotle.

To answer this question we need to focus the issue more exactly. Aristotle wants to keep potential conflicts within happiness, and to solve them by making virtue a dominant component of happiness. The Stoics want to free happiness from any conflicting elements, and to solve the conflicts by making happiness a dominant component in the Total. Is there any reason to think that one strategy will be better than the other for proving the dominance of virtue? This is too large a question to allow an adequate treatment here; but it is worth suggesting some of the other questions it raises.

In one way the Stoics might claim to be explaining what Aristotle needs to show if he is to maintain the dominance of virtue. For he argues that happiness requires the realisation of a human being's nature. The dominant place of rational agency in human nature is intended to secure the dominance of virtue in happiness. The Stoics see this when they identify the Total with the life according to nature; for they want to argue that it is

---

[38] Here again (see note 15 above) the Stoic doctrine of affections complicates the issue. Though the sage is free of the affection of fear, he has the *eupatheia* of caution, *eulabeia*, about indifferents. Why might this not be as disturbing as fear? If the Stoic replies, 'Because the sage keeps it in proportion, knowing the predominance of virtue in the Total', an analogous defence seems to be open to Aristotle.

the nature of human beings as rational agents that justifies us in regarding rational agency, and hence virtue, as dominant.

On the other hand, the Stoic conception of the Total seems to support Aristotle's belief in the insufficiency of virtue for happiness. The Total is exactly the sort of compound, involving the full realisation of human nature, that Aristotle identifies with happiness. When the Stoics make this clear, they cannot plausibly maintain that the loss we suffer if we lose the other components of the Total besides virtue is no loss at all, or a trivial loss. If virtue is dominant, we may say that the loss is too small to justify the sacrifice of virtue. But if we say this, we need not also agree that the loss is insignificant.

In this comparison of the Stoic with the Aristotelian view we have assumed that the Stoics regard the life according to nature as a total or maximum, in the way Aristotle regards happiness, so that it requires the fullest possible realisation of human nature and capacities. They would distinguish their position more sharply from Aristotle's if they did not interpret 'according to nature' this way. We might say that we live according to nature if we are not living against nature; we are living against nature if we are actually violating some natural needs – for a minimal degree of health, nourishment, freedom from pain etc. If we have the basic minimum, then we are living according to nature, and anything above that will be absolutely indifferent. If I find myself with more than the basic minimum I have no reason to get rid of the surplus, since a virtuous person will not be harmed by being wealthy or vigorously healthy; but I have no reason to want to raise myself above the basic minimum. On this view, the Stoic sage will always achieve the life according to nature. If the life according to nature meets Aristotle's more demanding conditions for happiness, the sage will not always achieve it, though he will always achieve the dominant component of it, by being virtuous and living in agreement with nature.[39]

The Stoics, however, would be ill advised to adopt this minimal interpretation of 'life according to nature'. They have powerful reasons for adopting the maximal interpretation that keeps them close to Aristotle:

1.   Without the maximal interpretation the Stoics give us no ground for thinking that the Total is as reasonable an ultimate objective as Aristotelian happiness is.

---

[39] Here a large question arises about the significance of references to nature in Stoic accounts of the good and of virtuous action. Different views are discussed by White (1979), pp. 170–7. For present purposes I assume that the Stoics claim at least that the sage acts in accordance with human nature. This claim is consistent with the further claim that in doing so he also thereby acts in accordance with the wider, cosmic nature and his place in it. But unless he is acting in accordance with human nature, he can hardly claim to be meeting Aristotle's demand that happiness should be complete.

2.   The maximal interpretation is needed for a reasonable account of appropriate action. The Stoic will find it hard to convince us that the sage meets our preconceptions about the virtues if he cares only about securing a basic minimum.

3.   Most important, it is hard to see how we can justify the pursuit of virtue if we do not accept a maximising interpretation of the life according to nature. For everyone to some minimal degree realises his capacities as a rational agent. The Stoics need to ascribe dominant value to the *full* realisation of this capacity. But it is hard to see how they can do that without attaching value to the full realisation of human nature as a whole.[40]

For these reasons a minimal interpretation of the life according to nature raises more difficulties for the Stoics than it solves. They seem to be required to accept a maximal, Aristotelian interpretation, and therefore seem to face those very problems that they offer as reasons for rejecting Aristotle's views on virtue and happiness.

16. Conclusion

At the beginning I mentioned an apparent dilemma for the Stoics; their position seems to collapse either into the Cynics' or into Aristotle's, if it is a consistent position at all. We can now see how they should react to the apparent dilemma.

They should firmly reject the Cynic interpretation. It relies on a mistake about the importance of indifferents. Moreover, they can reasonably claim that their position is non-trivially distinct from Aristotle's. Their criticism of his claims about happiness as an end expose a fault of his account, and show that some change is needed.

Still, the Stoics' criticisms do not lead them as far from Aristotle as they seem to hope. The identification of virtue with happiness may appear to meet some of their criticisms of Aristotle, but really it does not. When we think about any plausible account of the Total, we can see that the same criticisms can easily be adapted so that they apply to the Stoic position as well.

This does not mean either that the Stoic criticisms of Aristotle are mis-

---

[40] This argument might be supported by appeal to the Stoic doctrine of *oikeiōsis*, if we take it to involve some appeal to the realisation of human nature. This view of *oikeiōsis* is ascribed to Antiochus, and rejected as Aristotelian and un-Stoic, by White (1979), pp. 153–9, supported by Striker (1983a), p. 156n. I am more sympathetic to the Antiochene view. It shows how the Stoics could fairly claim to be satisfying Aristotelian conditions; and it does not necessarily expose the Stoics to Antiochus' criticisms, once they are able to distinguish happiness from the Total by distinguishing the end from the objective.

guided or that the Stoics' own position is misguided if it is open to the same criticisms. The Stoic criticisms show that Aristotle is committed to the belief that virtue is dominant in happiness, and show that he needs to defend this view more carefully and fully than he defends it in his ethical works. Moreover, the Stoics show more clearly than Aristotle shows where we must look for a defence. The Stoic conception of happiness as an end associates virtue and happiness with rational agency itself, as distinct from the results that the rational agent properly takes as his objective. The dominance of virtue is secured if we can show why the exercise of the agency is dominant over success in obtaining the objective. The task of showing this is a common task for Aristotle and the Stoics. The Stoics perform the valuable service of showing that this is the common task. They do not see that success in this common task will allow Aristotle to answer Stoic objections to the compound character of happiness.[41]

Our conclusion will disappoint us if we expect the Stoics to be radical innovators on these basic questions about ethics. They do not reject the basic structure of ethical argument derived from Plato and Aristotle; and their Stoic paradoxes are in fact less Socratic than they seem (cf. Cic. *Parad.* 4; *Ac.* II 136). Though the Platonic and Aristotelian questions about happiness become questions about the Total, they do not go away. If we think that the Platonic and Aristotelian project of defending virtue as the dominant component of happiness, but not the sole component, is a waste of time, we will regret the Stoics' pursuit of essentially the same project. In that case we will welcome any tendencies that seem to challenge the assumptions of the Platonic and Aristotelian project. When the Stoics deny that the Total has any selective value greater than the value of virtue, we might think they are groping for some conception of the incommensurability of non-moral and moral values; and we might regret that their groping has so little effect on their general theory.

If our previous argument has been correct, there is nothing to regret here. By associating the value of virtue with the value of rational agency, the Stoics show how Aristotle might have defended the dominance of

---

[41] A different moral is drawn by Striker (1983a), p. 167: 'The paradoxes they [sc. the Stoics] were willing to accept rather than giving up their view of the supremacy of morals may indeed have helped to show that justifying moral standards and finding out what human happiness consists in are different, though certainly not independent tasks.' I don't think the Stoics are committed to any intolerable paradoxes, or that the difficulties raised for the Aristotelian project require Striker's conclusion ('that justifying [...]'). I have left undiscussed many questions about the plausibility of the Aristotelian project (e.g. the one raised by Plato's *Republic*, briefly mentioned by Striker, p. 150f.).

virtue within an Aristotelian conception of happiness. The Stoic criticisms of Aristotle should encourage us to believe that Aristotle's strategy is essentially sound.[42]

[42] I am very grateful to those who discussed versions of this paper read at Bad Homburg; the Institute of Classical Studies, London; the University of California, Riverside; and a seminar at Cornell. I am especially conscious of having benefited from remarks by Julia Annas, Jonathan Barnes, Myles Burnyeat, Pierluigi Donini, Gail Fine, David Furley, Harry Ide, Susan Sauvé and Malcolm Schofield. For the leisure to write some of the paper I am indebted to Cornell University, the American Council of Learned Societies, and the Warden and Fellows of All Souls' College, Oxford.

9 Epicurus – hedonist malgré lui

Malte Hossenfelder

Epicurus has gone down into history as the archetype of the sensual hedonist, interested only in pleasures of the flesh and willing to eschew an opportunity for pleasure only for a greater pleasure. It has long been clear to anyone who has had any closer acquaintance with Epicurus that this picture is distorted, but nevertheless no one will deny that it is correct to describe Epicurus as a hedonist. In my view, however, hedonism was a last resort for him; he would have preferred to be a Stoic if he had regarded Stoicism as a tenable position. I deduce this above all from the ambivalence of his concept of the highest good, from the difficulties he encounters with the traditional concept of pleasure, and from the paradoxes of his own doctrine of pleasure. All these peculiarities lose their oddity as soon as we accept that Epicurus' point of departure was not really hedonism at all.

I

Cicero begins his criticism of Epicurus in the *De finibus* with the reproach that Epicurus was ambiguous in his definition of the highest good. When he called it 'pleasure', he understood it to mean two quite separate things, things which he not only characterises with the same word, which would be acceptable, but which he actually identifies with each other, which is not. On the one hand, Cicero says, Epicurus did really mean pleasure when he spoke of the highest good, but on the other he meant freedom from pain, not, however, as though we should imagine two equal highest goods, but as though both consisted of one and the same state. This is completely incomprehensible (II 3–30). Epicurus himself bears out this accusation to some extent in his *Letter to Menoeceus*. Here freedom from pain (in body and soul) is at first cited as the highest good, when he says: 'The aim of the happy life' is 'health of the body and *ataraxia* of the soul'; 'for that is why we do everything, so that we have neither pain nor disturbance'. A few lines later, pleasure is set up in the highest place: 'We say that pleasure is the beginning and end of the blissful life.' Finally, freedom from pain is described as pleasure: 'If we now say, pleasure is the highest good, we do not mean the pleasures of the dissipated and of enjoyment

[...] but freedom from pain in the body and disturbance in the mind' (*Ep. Men.* 128, 131).

Cicero's criticism is founded on the threefold division of states of feeling which already occurs in the Cyrenaics. It distinguishes between pain, pleasure, and an intermediate state in which we feel neither pleasure nor pain. These states are compared with conditions at sea, so that pain corresponds to a storm-lashed ocean, pleasure to a smooth swell, and the middle state to a flat calm (Euseb. *Praep. ev.* XIV 18, 32). Epicurus also uses this metaphor. In *Ep. Men.* 128 he speaks of the 'storm of the soul', in Us. fr. 411 of the 'smooth movement of the flesh', and in *Ep. Hdt.* 83, with reference to the desirable condition of freedom from pain, he speaks of a 'flat calm'. In the Cyrenaic schema of things, however, this middle state of calm is sharply distinguished from pleasure, since one property of its definition is that in it we feel *no* pleasure. And Epicurus himself admits implicitly that pleasure and freedom from pain are in fact two different states. While, he says, it is true that both are concerned with pleasure, in one case it is with 'pleasure in motion', in the other with 'static [*katastēmatikē*] pleasure' (D.L. X 136).

How does this ambivalence in the concept of the highest good come about? Why does Epicurus become entangled in imprecisions on this decisive point, and attempt to unite two things that are distinct in themselves? I consider this an important question, for it seems to me to lead us to the core of Epicurus' philosophy and to provide us with the key to understanding his hedonism. The answer will emerge if we interpret Epicurus against the Hellenistic background he shared with the Stoics and Sceptics, and so I should like to give a rough outline of my view of this background.[1]

Historians of ideas of all kinds agree that an essential characteristic of the Hellenistic period is its concern with the individual; historians of philosophy as well as of literature, art, and customs make it clear that at that time man as an individual became the centre of attention, so that we are dealing with a fact well-attested in all facets of intellectual life. Hellenistic ethics, too, in so far as we can identify a position common to all the schools, can be explained with reference to this basic notion. They are eudaimonistic, like the ethics of all antiquity. On this point commentators are united, even though the Hellenistic terminology is occasionally misleading and obscures the true character of this eudaimonism. Thus, the Stoics commonly describe virtue as the *telos* while the Epicureans identify

---

[1] A more detailed explanation will soon appear in: M. Hossenfelder, *Die Philosophie der Antike* 3: *Stoa, Epikureismus und Skepsis* (München 1985) (Gesch. d. Philosophie, ed. W. Röd, vol. III).

it as pleasure. This, however, is a somewhat imprecise expression, for the *telos* in the strict sense – as something for whose sake everything else is done, while it itself is not sought for the sake of anything else – is always *eudaimonia*. Virtue or pleasure are the qualities in which we may see and attain *eudaimonia*, but they are subordinate to it, and their only value derives from their relationship with it. Their occasional appearance *as* the *telos* is linked to the unquestioning acceptance of eudaimonism in antiquity, so widespread an assumption that it is often simply not discussed; its prevalence is what makes us think that the dispute about virtue or pleasure is concerned with the supreme goal.

Of course, the concept of *eudaimonia* did not remain unaltered throughout the course of antiquity, but underwent certain changes. For this reason it is not easy to find a definition that encompasses all its nuances. I think, however, that we can represent to some extent the element common to all periods if we say that *eudaimonia* represents the attainment of all our aims; a happy man is therefore one who achieves all his aims. The particular character of the Hellenistic concept is the result of individualism. If the crucially significant factor is no longer the happiness of society, of the *polis*, but of the individual, then he must set for himself the goals he has to achieve. For since *his* happiness is the highest aim, all other goals must be set with this in view. If they were then in fact set with it in view, but not *by him*, his happiness would be the supreme goal only within the confines of a pre-established order; this order would be the end that it is essential to achieve, a final goal that ranks above the individual. To put it another way: if the order of aims is established by an external authority, the happiness of the individual is dependent on the wishes of this authority; it is only the highest aim because this is what the authority wants, and this means that the wishes of the authority are what we should above all strive to fulfil. It is this consideration that illuminates the Hellenistic idea of happiness. Aims are no longer prescribed for man within a teleologically structured cosmos, but *eudaimonia* consists in reaching all the goals he has chosen *for himself*. In this way, a wholly new path to well-being opens up in front of us. Since the choice of aims is the responsibility of the individual, *eudaimonia* can be guaranteed by setting ourselves as few aims as possible, indeed only those that we can realise completely on our own, without being helped or influenced by others. In order to interpret the world, it therefore becomes necessary to explain it in a way that restricts the truly valuable to something which is readily attainable but that condemns what is unattainable as valueless and indifferent.

This is the common doctrine of the Hellenistic schools, a doctrine which they developed very fully and in considerable detail; indeed, those with similar tendencies today would be well-advised to see if perhaps the Hellenistic philosophers can provide them with short cuts. The Hellenistic philosophers were convinced that their doctrine could be established by showing that the only true values were the so-called 'internal goods', the qualities of the soul, because the individual, if he were to attain anything, could attain them alone; all outward things on the other hand were more or less unattainable and so had to become *adiaphora*. The Hellenistic belief that *eudaimonia* could be reached only by achieving a certain inner state was made possible because individualism had as a further consequence a radical internalisation of *eudaimonia*. If we ask for more precise information about the source of *eudaimonia*, given that it consists in the realisation of all the aims which the individual has set himself, it cannot be the thing that is realised. If for example someone's wish to own a horse is fulfilled, possession of the horse cannot be *eudaimonia*. If *eudaimonia* were to be found exclusively in the things realised, then the question whether or not we desired them would be meaningless, and it would always have to be the same things that made us happy. It so happens, however, that we are made happy now by one thing, now by another, and that this is dependent on the state of our own desires. Equally, the same thing can make us both happy and unhappy. Thus it is quite possible that the same man who at first is happy in the possession of a horse later becomes unhappy, when he would like to sell it and cannot find a buyer. Consequently the thing realised just in itself cannot be the thing that provides *eudaimonia*; nor, however, can it be the mere desire, whether or not it is realised, because then we should be content with our desires. It must be something that arises from a combination of both these things: in other words, the consciousness that a desire of our own is reaching fulfilment and that an aim we have set ourselves is becoming reality. This consciousness, however, is not an external but an internal human condition, a particular state of the soul, and thus *eudaimonia* does not lie in the realisation of a certain order in the world, as in classical thought, but is solely a creation of our own internal workings. It is not to be attained by contemplating the world but by contemplating our own mind within. The external world is in itself neutral as far as happiness is concerned; it becomes significant for happiness only in so far as we focus our strivings for happiness upon it. This inspires the Hellenistic belief that everyone can become happy in no matter what circumstances; that the slave toiling in chains or the man tortured in Phalaris' bull has exactly the same prospects of happiness as the rich landowner. As long as we can control our own mental life, external circumstances are immaterial for happiness, nor do they give any indication of a person's happiness. *Eudaimonia* therefore becomes a strictly private phenomenon. Only I can decide whether I am happy or not; no one else can judge.[2]

From a psychological point of view, the Hellenistic philosophers interpreted circumstances as making man unhappy if he does not reach his aims, because the inner tensions of his efforts are not relaxed but become ever tauter, so that his soul constantly becomes more excited and disturbed. Correspondingly, happiness is that inner peace and acceptance born from the awareness that all our aims are being fulfilled and that all our desires are being satisfied.

So much for this short summary or outline of the Hellenistic background. The resulting programme – the devaluation of everything unattainable – emerges clearly both in the fundamental Stoic doctrine that all things except virtue should be considered as *adiaphora* and in the Pyrrhonian requirement that everything, even our own indifference, must be indifferent to us. To the same extent it was decisive for Epicurean philosophy, and if we take this as a starting point, we can explain many of its peculiarities and difficulties. If this interpretation is correct, Epicurus must have seen *eudaimonia* as consisting in inner peace and calm. The correctness of this assertion is borne out when Epicurus calls *ataraxia*, peace of mind, the *telos*: precisely the same condition that he compares with the calm mirror of the unruffled sea. On the other hand he does suggest pleasure as the highest good, so certain misgivings are in order. If we consider, however, which is the real focus of Epicurus' ambivalent concept of the *telos*, pleasure or peace of mind, we must conclude that for him happiness resides in peace of mind and in the final analysis comes down just to this.

---

[2] Certainly even in classical times happiness no longer simply consists in external well-being, but principally in the right constitution of the soul. But this internalisation is in a way 'chance' – just a consequence of the fact that the soul is an inner organ; however, it is seen as part of the cosmos as a whole, and it is the outward world order that determines its right constitution. In Plato the dependence is on social order, in Aristotle on the order of concepts (*EN* 16). That implies, although this idea has perhaps never been explicitly mooted, that someone can be happy without noticing it himself, and that someone else can be better informed about my happiness than I myself. In the Hellenistic period it is quite different. Here, our own consciousness is the final absolutely autonomous criterion of *eudaimonia*; it can no longer be deduced from world order. Epicurus' sentence: 'All good and evil are in perception' (*Ep. Men.* 124) would have been impossible in the classical period, nor must we misinterpret in the classical sense the Stoic formula of 'a life in accordance with nature'. If we ask why the Stoic wants to live in harmony with nature, the answer will run that this is the only way to achieve his own aims. (For a more detailed account I would refer the reader to the book mentioned in the previous note.) It is only in the literal spatial sense that we can speak of an internalisation of *eudaimonia* in the classical period; the extended meaning only applies in the Hellenistic period. Thus it was here that the prevailing Western concept of happiness as being a private matter, a subjective feeling, originated.

Doubts as to the consistency of Epicurus' hedonism must arise as soon as we examine his doctrine more closely. From a hedonist, we would expect a polished technique in the maximisation of pleasure, along with a subtle analysis of how we come to have the needs whose satisfaction engenders pleasure. In Epicurus, however, the opposite occurs. One of his main theses is that beyond the removal of pain no increase of pleasure is possible, and that all needs that do go beyond this point are meaningless.[3] And if we look at the practical consequences of his doctrine, the concrete rules for life that he provides, we can establish that they are almost identical with those of the Stoics, opposed to pleasure as they were, and that only their basis is different. Any American Women's Lunch Club of the fifties might have adopted wholesale Epicurus' advice for living as their official constitution. Even a formal examination of his concept of the *telos* argues against hedonism. If Epicurus had been a true hedonist, he could not have had any problems with the concept of the *telos*. He determines the state of peace and calm as the complete freedom from pain. His requirement for freedom from pain can legitimately be deduced from his requirement for pleasure, since pain injures pleasure. If, therefore, pleasure is the highest good, freedom from pain can easily be established as a relative value, as a means to pleasure. Conversely, pleasure cannot be deduced from the requirement for freedom from pain. It is incomprehensible why someone who does not feel pleasure cannot all the same be free from pain. In this case, pleasure would have to figure as an independent value, distinct from freedom from pain, and if we want to avoid two highest goods side by side we must try to combine the two, just as Epicurus does; in this way we have yet another confirmation of the idea that he was originally concerned not with pleasure but with inner peace.

This entails the question why he ever made pleasure the *telos*. In my view this can be explained by seeing his thought in the light of the Hellenistic assumptions I have referred to, taking as our basis the notion that, since *eudaimonia* consists in the realisation of all the aims we have set ourselves, we should only aim at those goals that can be attained, while disregarding everything unattainable. A critical point for practising this doctrine is the problem of how to judge our capacity for setting our own goals. The Stoics were convinced that reason could choose absolutely any aims at its own discretion, and that this freedom was the only really

---

[3] The concept of the maximisation of pleasure unquestionably deserves wider investigation. This is because there has hitherto been no real examination of the phenomenon of pleasure. However that may be, the notion that freedom from pain is the highest level of pleasure is so plainly false that anyone who espouses it cannot be advocating pleasure simply and solely for his own sake, but is accommodating his hedonism to other interests.

attainable thing. So they stipulated that we should not recognise any value other than rational insight, which constitutes virtue. The consequence was that they were forced to reject the immediate assessments that underlie the emotions of pleasure or pain; and this led to the famous paradoxes and finally to the admission of the founders of the school, that not even they themselves were wise and happy. Epicurus on the other hand had a more realistic appreciation of human capabilities. In my view, his philosophy may have evolved from the following fundamental notion. The aim is the rejection of everything unattainable. Yet the sensations of pleasure and pain contain immediate assessments that everyone carries out and that no one can avoid. Their immediacy quite prevents us from arguing them away. Here, then, is an established fact. We can give a rationale of it which leaves reason as a purely formal faculty, with no content of its own. Reason can, it is true, deduce one value from another, but it is not in a position to make original assessments that might serve as a basic starting-point for deductions. Rather, since one value depends on another, reason is threatened with an infinite regress – unless it is provided from outside itself with some absolute value not in turn dependent on a further value. Providing such an absolute value is a role that is discharged by sense perception; it furnishes the original values which are implied in the sensations of pleasure and displeasure, so that not only our theoretical notions, but also our practical predilections, are in the final analysis irrational at source.[4] The effect of this idea on the Hellenistic programme of the devaluation of everything unattainable is that it is hard to deny the force of all apparently mistaken values just by an edict of reason. We must take another less radical path and concentrate all our efforts on two things. For one, we must make sure that pleasure and pain remain the only absolute values, which entails in particular that reason

---

[4] The dependence of reason on sensation is confirmed in D.L. x 32: *pās logos apo tōn aisthēseōn ērtētai*; in connection with practical value Cic. *Fin.* I 30: *itaque negat [Epicurus] opus esse ratione neque disputatione, quam ob rem voluptas expetenda, fugiendus dolor sit. sentiri haec putat, ut calere ignem, nivem esse albam, mel dulce, quorum nihil oportet exquisitis rationibus confirmare, tantum satis esse admonere [...] etenim quoniam detractis de homine sensibus reliqui nihil est, necesse est, quid aut ad naturam aut contra sit, a natura ipsa iudicari* (that is, the final, absolute values, the *phusei agatha*, are given to us by sensation). The notion of infinite regress is proposed at ib. 41: *quod si vita doloribus referta maxime fugienda est, summum profecto malum est vivere cum dolore [...] nec enim habet nostra mens quicquam, ubi consistat tamquam in extremo, omnesque metus et aegritudines ad dolorem referuntur, nec preaterea est res ulla, quae sua natura aut sollicitare possit aut angere.* The idea that absolute values are given to us, that we play a passive rôle and do not form them for ourselves, is attested at Stobaeus, *Ecl.* II p. 46, 17: *touto d' hoi kat' Epikouron philosophountes ou prosdechontai legein "energoumenon", dia to pathētikon hypotithesthai to telos, ou praktikon; hēdonē gar.*

shall not introduce any other 'apparently basic values', thus distorting its own capabilities. For the other we must take care to make pleasure and pain attainable.

If we accept this as Epicurus' point of departure, his teachings become coherent. Firstly, it is clear how they actually relate to hedonism. If pleasure and pain are to be the only absolute values, pleasure must be seen as the highest good and pain as the greatest evil. Secondly, we understand why pleasure is equated with peace of mind, which is in its turn equated with freedom from pain. For, as the highest good, pleasure must be what constitutes bliss. Yet for the Hellenistic age, *eudaimonia* is inner peace, which is defined as the absence of any disturbance caused by unfulfilled desires. Consequently, pleasure must consist in just this inner peace, and the disturbance whose absence results in peace must, as the greatest evil, be pain. This means that pleasure equals peace of mind and thus freedom from pain. Two considerations may have facilitated this identification for Epicurus, rejected as it had always been by classical philosophers. In the first place, a Hellenistic philosopher had to ask himself why man is happy if he reaches his goals and unhappy if he does not. In the end, the answer could obviously be no more than that he felt the inner peace of the former situation positively and the disturbance of the latter negatively. That, however, implies that we can give no reasons for these assessments any more, that they are therefore irrational; and that in its turn means that they stem from sense perceptions, on which one state has a pleasant and the other an unpleasant effect; we are therefore dealing with pleasure and pain. Accordingly, anyone working out Hellenistic thought to its conclusion will sooner or later, because of the frontiers of reason, come up against pleasure and pain as basic values. In the second place, the equating of peace of mind with pleasure afforded the possibility of a positive definition of happiness. Elsewhere, it was only described in negative terms as *ataraxia* or apathy. This was only a definition of what constituted unhappiness; happiness was only expressed in terms of that definition, as freedom from it. Freedom from unhappiness, however, is not in itself a positive but primarily an indifferent state. But happiness as the highest value cannot be something indifferent. We have therefore no answer to the question of what happiness *is* in itself positively speaking; the concept remains largely meaningless, so that we cannot tell just what aim, in concrete terms, we should strive for if we strive for happiness. Such a goal is also urgently required for logical reasons. For we can only derive prohibitions from a negative goal, prohibitions which often cannot offer any positive rules of conduct. We do indeed then know what we should not do but not, once faced with several possible courses of action, what we in fact should do. And here pleasure, as a readily identifiable and concrete sensation, can come to our aid.[5]

II

Considerable difficulties naturally arose when Epicurus attempted to define pleasure as peace of mind and freedom from pain; however, he was not disheartened by them, although in his efforts to solve them he had to stretch the meaning of the phenomenon of pleasure, at least to some extent. This is a further indication that he was concerned not with pleasure but with *ataraxia*. The Greeks connected the word *hēdonē* first and foremost with the sensual enjoyments of eating, drinking, making love, and so on, and in philosophical literature they had been interpreted, as Aristotle among others reports, as the liberation from pain.[6] Hunger, for example, represents a feeling of pain that is assuaged by eating, and the emotion engendered by this same assuagement is what constitutes pleasure. The theory that we feel the one positively and the other negatively was further reduced to the idea that pain is the sense that some natural element is lacking, while pleasure is the sense of 'fulfilment', a return to a state that is in accordance with nature. Pleasure, then, is the *transition* from a state of pain to one of freedom from pain; it is a *kīnēsis*, a movement or change. Now Epicurus could not simply identify this concept of pleasure with that of freedom from pain, because the latter was intended to be a state of rest, but above all because pleasure as a transition can never be free from pain, but is always accompanied by it; if all pain vanishes, pleasure vanishes too.

To this dilemma there were two solutions. Either Epicurus rejected the traditional concept of pleasure outright, and asserted that all happiness was freedom from pain, or he attempted rather to define *eudaimonia* in such a way that it became compatible with the standard concept of pleasure. The first solution was not viable because it was indisputable that we feel the satisfaction of our natural needs – in ancient terms, the process of transition from deprivation to a natural state – in a way that is immediately and inevitably positive. Besides, it was precisely this concept of pleasure that was well-fitted to complete in a positive way the concept of

---

[5] Cicero passes on this view in *Fin.* II 32: *nec tamen argumentum hoc Epicurus a parvis petivit aut etiam a bestiis, quae putat esse specula naturae, ut diceret ab iis duce natura hanc voluptatem expeti nihil dolendi. neque enim haec movere potest adpetitum animi, nec ullum habet ictum, quo pellat animum, status hic non dolendi. itaque in hoc eodem peccat Hieronymus. at ille pellit, qui permulcet sensum voluptate. itaque Epicurus semper hoc utitur, ut probet voluptatem natura expeti, quod ea voluptas, quae in motu sit, et parvos ad se adliciat et bestias, non illa stabilis, in qua tantum inest nihil dolore.*

[6] *EN* 1173 b7 sqq. For the contemporary meaning of *hēdonē* cf. ibid. 1153 b33 sqq.

happiness. It was envisaged as a precisely assignable and familiar feeling, so that everyone could have a clear picture of happiness and would know what he was striving to achieve. If, on the other hand, pleasure were simply equated with freedom from pain, the result would again be a merely negative concept, so that in this respect we would have gained nothing. But the second solution, whereby *eudaimonia* is adapted to the concept, is also ruled out. It is true that happiness could have been defined under Hellenistic presuppositions in such a way as to include a kinetic element, thus allowing us to make use of the traditional concept of pleasure, by re-identifying happiness as the *process* of the *fulfilment* of our aims. That, however, would have contradicted one idea that was central to the concept of happiness, the idea of perpetual duration. The Hellenistic programme of the reduction of aims, which was supposed to guarantee this very perpetuity and security of happiness, would have been turned on its head. Their slogan would have had to advocate not as few aims as possible, but as many. For in one case the fleeting happiness we experience only for the brief moment when we reach our goals would have to be constantly renewed, while in the other case it would be impossible not to think that we can rise to greater and greater heights by having ever more numerous aims, which entails the suspicion that we had not yet tasted true happiness at all. The pursuit of happiness would have perpetually aroused new needs but would itself have remained fruitless, because our dependence on the unattainable would have increased constantly. The traditional concept of pleasure was not well suited to an idea of happiness just because happiness was supposed to be permanent, not transitory. This is why Epicurus had to abide by the notion that man is happy once he *has* achieved what he wants, and knows for sure that he must not undertake anything unless he is certain he can attain it.

The means and methods that Epicurus resorted to in order to escape from the dilemma can best be reconstructed as follows: Epicurus defines happiness as 'the stable condition of the flesh' (*sarkos eustathes katastēma*, Us. p. 122, 15), by which we must obviously understand the natural and healthy disposition of all the vital functions. Pleasure is therefore the sensation of this healthy condition.[7] This leads to two achievements. In the first place we can envisage pleasure as permanent, and secondly we have an absolute limit to its possible extent, for nothing can be healthier than healthy. Epicurus now seeks to link this concept of

---

[7] It is hard to tell whether Epicurus distinguished the state itself and the sensation of it or whether he equated pleasure with the state. Myself, I think that the distinction between state and sensation was consistent with his line of thought; but a thorough examination of this view would side-track us too far.

pleasure with the traditional one, by interpreting the phenomenon of transition contained in the latter concept to fit in with the former. He appears to think: that which we experience positively while eating, drinking, and so on, is manifestly the return to the natural state. It is therefore this that is the true reward, the truly pleasurable. The value, on the other hand, of the *transition* from pain to freedom from pain, the process of liberation, is only derivative, a means to an end. We eat because the liberation from the pain of hunger has *as its consequence* feelings of pleasure. The pleasurable is therefore what follows liberation: that is freedom from pain. An intermediate state, in which we feel neither pleasure nor pain, therefore does not exist, because freedom from pain constitutes pleasure. So Cicero has:

[...] doloris omnis privatio recte nominata est voluptas. ut enim, cum cibo et potione fames sitisque depulsa est, ipsa detractio molestiae *consecutionem* adfert voluptatis, sic in omni re doloris amotio *successionem* efficit voluptatis. itaque non placuit Epicuro medium esse quiddam inter dolorem et voluptatem. illud enim ipsum, quod quibusdam medium videretur, cum omni dolore careret, non modo voluptatem esse, verum etiam summam voluptatem. quisquis enim sentit, quem ad modum sit affectus, eum necesse est aut in voluptate esse aut in dolore. omnis autem privatione doloris putat Epicurus terminari summam voluptatem, ut postea variari voluptas distinguique possit, augeri amplificarique non possit (*Fin.* I 37 sq.).

Metrodorus explains it thus: good has no place unless evil yields, allowing good to occupy its place. In other words, disturbance must be banished so that a healthy state can take over, a state that consists indeed in freedom from disturbance, 'so that just this is the good: avoidance of evil' (*hōste tout' auto to agathon esti, to phugein to kakon*, Plutarch, *Non posse* 1091 a. Cf. Epic. *KD* 3). According to Epicurus, then, a more careful examination of the transition phenomenon reveals that pleasure is a permanent state rather than a passing emotion. Of course the natural state does not return suddenly, but continually over a period of time; as time passes pleasure gradually increases until it reaches its zenith when all pain has vanished; it may then decrease if yet another new disturbance appears. Because of this rise and fall we can say that pleasure is 'in motion', in contrast to 'static pleasure', the katastematic *hēdonē* of freedom from pain. Here, however, we are not dealing with two different types of pleasure, but with one and the same emotion that only varies occasionally in intensity (Us. fr. 417, *KD* 18, D.L. x 136).

If this analysis of Epicurus' justification of his thesis, that freedom from pain is pleasure, is correct, then the common interpretation, that he understood two qualitatively different kinds of pleasure by kinetic and katastematic pleasure, must be incorrect. This interpretation seems to be considered self-evident, and the sources back it up, but the evidence is in no way cogent. To support my contrary view I should like to draw attention to three places which probably all originate with Epicurus himself. The first is *KD* 9: 'If all pleasure were to be condensed [locally] and temporally and existed in the whole compound or the most essential parts of nature, pleasures would never differ from one another'. This suggests that if pleasure were always to hand everywhere at the same level of intensity, there would be no variations; and from this it follows that Epicurus allowed that pleasures could vary only in their intensity. Secondly I refer to the *Letter to Menoeceus* 128. Here, Epicurus informs us that we only need pleasure when we suffer pain through its absence, but that in the absence of pain we have no need of it. This assertion, strange as it is, would lose all its difficulties if Epicurus had distinguished here between the pleasures and had confined his remarks to *kinetic* pleasure. Yet he is speaking of pleasure *tout court*, a fact which, like the rest of the context, indicates that in his eyes there is only one kind of pleasure, the freedom from pain. His sentence '*tote gar hēdonēs chreian echomen, hotan ek tou mē pareinai tēn hēdonēn algōmen; [hotan de mē algōmen], ouketi tēs hēdonēs deometha*' can only make sense if we understand the '*chreian echein*' and '*deisthai*' as 'feel the want of' and translate thus: 'We only suffer the lack of pleasure when we suffer pain from the absence of pleasure; but if we have no pain, we do not feel the want of pleasure any more.'[8] The sense is now: as long as we are free from all pain, we are in complete possession of pleasure and need not trouble further to acquire pleasure. We only have to seek it if we suffer pain, because pain is nothing more than lack of pleasure, just as, conversely, pleasure is nothing more than the freedom from pain, so that there is no second kind of pleasure. Finally, this is confirmed at *KD* 3, where to counter the claims that pleasure is insatiable and that it is always mingled with pain, Epicurus establishes that it reaches its apogee in complete freedom from pain and that pain can never occupy the same place as pleasure. These theses, too, are convincing only for someone who equates pleasure with freedom from pain and accepts no other different pleasure. For if there existed another kind of pleasure on a par with freedom from pain, it would no longer be immediately plain why no pleasure is stronger than the feeling of freedom from pain, nor indeed why pleasure is never to be mingled with pain. That

---

[8] Hicks and Mewaldt also translate thus, as does Bollack; he, however, sees a distinction in meaning between '*chreian echein*' (avoir l'usage de) and '*deisthai*' (être dans le manque de), and gives an individual and unconvincing explanation. The usual translation, using 'benötigen, bedürfen' (Apelt, Gigon), 'to need' (Bailey), 'avere bisogno' (Arrighetti, Gigante), gives the impression that we can relinquish pleasure if we are free from pain. This makes nonsense when pleasure is described as the *telos* in the next sentence.

would have demanded empirical investigations that Epicurus did not have at his command and which would certainly have produced different results. Epicurus' strategy consisted in establishing his theses a priori through a particular interpretation of the *concept* of pleasure, and this is why he could not allow any other concept of pleasure.

This seems to be contradicted by Cicero's report in *Fin.* I 56:

Non placet autem detracta voluptate aegritudinem statim consequi, nisi in voluptatis locum dolor forte successerit, at contra gaudere nosmet omittendis doloribus, etiam si voluptas ea, quae sensum moveat, nulla successerit, eoque intellegi potest, quanta voluptas sit non dolere.

It appears here that kinetic pleasure is not identical with that of the transition from pain to freedom from pain, but could be present or absent independently from it. This, however, runs absolutely contrary to Cicero's own version elsewhere (e.g. *Fin.* II 9), just as the first sentence of the quotation is a clear contradiction of *Fin.* I 38, because it implies that there is an intermediate state of freedom from both pleasure and pain, an implication that is explicitly disputed there (see above, p. 255). This is all the more striking because, as Usener correctly observes (p. 271n.) and Cicero does not seem to realise, the quotation belongs to the Epicurean critique of the Cyrenaics and because the point of this critique is to demonstrate that, in contrast to the Cyrenaic claim, *no* intermediate state exists, but freedom from pain is pleasure. The quotation hardly reproduces the Epicurean doctrine correctly. Perhaps Cicero (or his source) is merely being inexact, for one error could easily be eliminated if we rewrote it thus: 'at contra gaudere nosmet *omissis* doloribus, etiam si voluptas ea, quae sensum moveat, nulla *iam adsit*'. This change would restore kinetic pleasure to one of transition, which no longer survives as such once freedom from pain has been achieved.

In his analysis of the phenomenon of transition, Epicurus is trying to lay claim to the traditional positive concept of pleasure and to use it for his own concept of inner peace, freedom from pain, by turning the tables and reducing kinetic pleasure to static pleasure, so that the positive sensation everyone has is in all cases the sensation of the possibly permanent state of freedom from pain. If we interpret him like this, the contradictory elements in his oft-quoted remarks simply vanish. On one hand he emphasises (*Ep. Men.* 131sq.) that when he calls pleasure the *telos*, he does not mean 'the pleasures of the dissipated', not 'drinking and continuous parties nor sexual pleasures nor the enjoyment of fish and other delicacies of a wealthy table', but 'the freedom from pain in the body and disturbance in the mind', and in Us. fr. 423 he sees the 'nature of the good' in 'evils we have avoided'. But on the other hand he exclaims 'I at any rate do not know how I should imagine good, if I set aside the pleasures of taste, of love, and of hearing, along with pleasurable reactions to the sight of a human form and with all the other pleasures, that men, with whatever sense, constantly experience.' And: 'The origin and root of all good is the pleasure of the stomach, for even wisdom and refinement only come down to this' (Us. fr. 67, 409). It seems to me perfectly obvious how this all fits together. If we take into account Epicurus' point of departure as I have outlined it here, it is apparent that for him the ultimate source of value could only be sensual pleasure; for while reason can only establish relative values, sensual pleasures contain an immediate irreducible sensation of values. It is therefore surely out of place to try to 'intellectualise' Epicurus' *telos* by translating it not by pleasure but by joy, Freude, and so on. This falsifies his basic idea that sensual enjoyments contain assessments that simply cannot be argued away, because reason cannot set any absolute values. Whatever activities we choose to label pleasure, whether it be the enjoyment of works of art or theoretical contemplation, pleasure itself always remains an irrational and sensual feeling. This was what Epicurus wanted to point out with his colourful and startling examples, which were certainly intended to shock us. It is true that he also distinguishes between sensual and intellectual pleasure, and indeed he prefers the latter. But the sources leave us in no doubt as to how we should understand this. Intellectual pleasure is by no means an independent experience, different in content from sensual pleasure; it is merely the reproduction, the intellectual representation of a sensual pleasure. Its pre-eminence does not lie in the notion that it represents a qualitatively superior sensation, but is based on quantity, because the mind is, differently from the senses, not limited to feelings of the immediate present but can also anticipate future pleasurable sensations and remember those that are past (Us. fr. 429sqq. 452). Pleasure is therefore always sensual, but is not therefore a transient *kīnēsis*; on closer examination it always reveals itself as the sensation of a state that may be permanent, that is the freedom from pain. So Epicurus was not contradicting himself when he placed good now in the pleasures of the stomach, now in the freedom from pain. Both examples are illustrating the same emotion, because the pleasure of eating, drinking and so on is nothing more than the sensation of increasing freedom from pain.

III

It is naturally understandable that such an interpretation as this should have encountered frequent incomprehension or even rejection, for it ascribes to the sensual feeling of pleasure properties that run counter to general human experiences that arise every day. It was above all the idea that pleasure can be permanent that met with opposition, for it was part of the unanimous opinion, subscribed to even by the Cyrenaics, that it was transitory, because sensation always wearies at some time or another; and this is why pleasure does not qualify as a true bringer of happiness. It cannot therefore be identical with freedom from pain. But Epicurus' theory contained still more paradoxes, which were difficult to reconcile with emotional data. If pleasure is the same as freedom from pain it follows that all methods of banishing pain engender equal pleasure. But the plain truth is that wine tastes better than water, or at any rate that not all food or drink tastes the same to individual people. Moreover, it was hardly plausible that pleasure was to reach its zenith with the complete eradication of pain. Everyday life supports the opposite idea that enjoyment of food dwindles as our hunger becomes satisfied. The fact that Epicurus took these difficulties in his stride, although he could not eliminate them, confirms our interpretation of his real interests. He was concerned not with an unprejudiced investigation of the sensation of pleasure, such as we have come to expect from a true hedonist, but rather with conquering this phenomenon within the context of Hellenistic reductionism. The paradoxes I have referred to could contribute something to this, and if we can look at them against this background, it will at once become apparent how they came about.

As I have already shown, Epicurus' first duty under these preconditions was to prove that pleasure was the *only* absolute value and therefore the *telos*; for an absolute value was, in his view, always irrational, always a product of sense perception; the more such values there are, the greater the risk that we cannot attain them. (To say nothing of the danger that having several ends may evoke a conflict of norms.) Epicurus strengthens his proof by citing the new-born infant, who is still uncorrupt and quite free from the influence of reason. It therefore embodies purely sensual nature. Since from the moment of birth the infant strives for pleasure and avoids pain, it follows that pleasure is the only true absolute value: the only one, because the infant's whole behaviour is dictated by the desire for pleasure and the rejection of pain; the true one, because reason has as yet no footing, so that there is no question either of a merely invented apparent basic value or of a derived value, because it is only reason that can invent or derive (Cic. *Fin.* I 30, D.L. x 137).

The second requirement for a Hellenistic analysis of pleasure was to prove that it was attainable. Now in Epicurus' eyes this was achieved by reason. Reason cannot, it is true, originally establish our aims, but it can show us the path we must follow in order to reach them by providing us with the means to do so – those same derived values. Hence the almost crusading belief of the Epicureans in reason; this belief is expressed in the Proems of Lucretius and in Epicurus' dictum: 'It is better to have misfortune with understanding than good fortune without' (*Ep. Men.* 135). It was simply on the strength of his faith in the powers of our reason that Epicurus could accept the viability of *eudaimonia*, for while pleasure appeared attainable through reason, it was possible to envisage a permanent and therefore real state of happiness. It is not debauchery and luxury, says Epicurus, that 'make for a pleasurable life, but the sober reckonings of reason [*nēphōn logismos*], which search out the reasons for all our choices and rejections and which dispel the vain beliefs that cause great disturbance in the soul' (*Ep. Men.* 132). Epicurus and the Stoics are therefore agreed on belief in reason; both see rational understanding as the true and only way to happiness, and this is why *phronēsis* is rated equally highly in both schools. But their belief rests on different bases. For Epicurus, reason is not the clinching principle of nature, but merely the compass to guide us through a world that is in itself irrational.

How, then, are we to understand the attainability of pleasure? Since pleasure equals freedom from pain, it is attainable if we can avoid all pain. But, as we have seen, pain is unsatisfied need. We must therefore avoid all unsatisfiable needs. Such needs have three sources: desire, fear, and pain. It therefore comes down to controlling these three sources. This is how we can reconstruct the Epicurean version of the general Hellenistic programme. The schools even have the classification of negative factors in common, for when Epicurus sees fear, pain, and desire as a threat to happiness, he is plainly adopting the same schema as the Stoics used in their division of the emotions into fear, trouble, desire, and pleasure, except that pleasure does not of course figure on Epicurus' list of negatives (*KD* 10, 11). Of his other three headings, fear and desire, directed at future events as they are, are controlled by reason and can therefore, as the Stoics also thought, be conquered by purely rational understanding. Of course the sort of understanding demanded by the two schools is not the same.

Epicurus' treatment of desire is particularly interesting in this connexion. Desire, he thinks, can only be directed at the further acquisition of *pleasure*. But then he has to contradict the view that pleasure is capable of unlimited intensification, because this view necessarily leads to the formation of insatiable desires. His concept of pleasure provides excellent counter-arguments. For one thing, it contains, in the total absence of any pain, an absolute limit to the intensification of pleasure. For another, it follows that this limit, or supreme pleasure, had to be easily attainable;

for since, according to Epicurus' concept, pleasure does not lie in the method of eliminating pain but in the ensuing freedom from pain, all methods of eliminating pain are equally valid, and none creates more pleasure than the other, so that we can be content with the simplest readily available method without any detriment to our pleasure. 'Simple enjoyments bring the same pleasure as dainty fare' (*Ep. Men.* 130).

These achievements of the concept of pleasure are, however, connected with the paradoxes I have already referred to. If complete freedom from pain represents the highest limit of the intensity of pleasure, it follows that the sensation of pleasure becomes weaker and weaker with increasing pain, that for example the greater the hunger, the less the enjoyment we feel in eating. This conception has also the advantage for Epicurus of avoiding a problem that crops up with and bedevils all the hedonists who adopt the inverse scheme, the problem that pleasure is greatest when pain is also greatest, and that when the pain vanishes, so does the pleasure. There is therefore no pleasure unmixed with pain, and thus no pure happiness, and the absurdity results that we must seek out greater unhappiness in order to increase our happiness. This problem Epicurus solves; however, his conception contradicts the common experience that hunger is the best cook, and the sources do not reveal how Epicurus coped with this difficulty. He himself seems to use the experience that pain intensifies pleasure in order to show that it comes down to freedom from pain alone and that therefore every method offers the same pleasure, when he says: 'Bread and water produce the highest pleasure when someone who needs them serves them to himself' (*Ep. Men.* 131). But we do not discover how this argument otherwise relates to his concept of pleasure.

We do at all events know a little more about the way he approaches the second paradox. Experience teaches us that *not* all methods of eliminating pain are equally effective, as his concept of pleasure implies, but that fish and wine taste better than bread and water, so that anyone who has the choice would naturally prefer the former. Epicurus tries to do justice to this phenomenon with the concept of 'variation': no intensification of pleasure is possible over and above freedom from pain, and if we choose fish rather than bread, pleasure is not increased, but only 'varied' (*poikilletai, KD* 18). The sources have nothing to tell us about the exact way we should interpret this concept, or indeed whether it was pinned down at all; we can only speculate. But it should certainly not be understood to mean that alternation in its turn became the path to pleasure, as the proverb would have it (cf. Aristotle, *EN* 1154 b28sq.). That would have resulted in the very thing Epicurus sought to avoid, the possibility of an intensification of pleasure beyond the freedom from pain. Similarly, the explanation that various pleasures are prompted by various foods, drinks, etc., will not stand. We have seen that there could be just one unique kind of pleasure for Epicurus, precisely because the absolute limit of pleasure was otherwise not to be proved. If he had accepted that differing pleasures would be engendered by various pleasurable methods, the endless throng of resultant pleasures would have stretched out beyond the eye of man, making it impossible to decide if perhaps it might include some pleasures that surpass freedom from pain. It is plain from Cicero's attack in *Fin.* II 10 that this explanation really will not do:

[...] voluptas etiam varia dici solet, cum percipitur e multis dissimilibus rebus dissimiles efficientibus voluptates. eam si varietatem diceres, intellegerem, ut etiam non dicente te intellego; ista varietas quae sit non satis perspicio, quod ais, cum dolore careamus, tum in summa voluptate nos esse, cum autem vescamur iis rebus, quae dulcem motum afferant sensibus, tum esse in motu voluptatem, qui faciat varietatem voluptatum, sed non augeri illam non dolendi voluptatem, quam cur voluptatem appelles nescio.

This only makes sense if Epicurus did not accept that 'many and various things prompt various pleasures'. Cicero, on the other hand, seems to understand him to mean that he ascribed the variety to 'pleasure in motion', i.e. the transition from pain to freedom from pain, and that bread brings satisfaction in a different way from fish (cf. ib. 75). But this would only lead to the trivial notion that we can assuage our hunger in various ways. It is important to remember, however, that all methods result in the same pleasure, that is in freedom from pain, that none is more pleasurable than the other, and that even alternation brings with it no increase of pleasure in itself, but is quite insignificant, so that it is pointless to pursue new and more extravagant enjoyments. Those who nonetheless do so are misinterpreting their feelings, because they have failed to grasp the true nature of pleasure.

Epicurus' concept of pleasure leads therefore to consequences that do not tally with experience but which Epicurus allows, even though he does not manage to explain convincingly how they fit in with experience. This confirms the suggestion that he was not a heart-and-soul hedonist, and that he was not out to achieve the greatest possible abundance of pleasure, because otherwise he would have paid more attention to the realities of this sensation. His paradoxical views on pleasure, the apparent ambiguity of his concept of the *telos*, and the difficulties he encounters with the traditional concept of pleasure are more readily understood if we see him in the light of his own times, sharing the Stoic and Pyrrhonist goal of making the individual independent from everything unattainable. Thus, he only became a hedonist because he admitted that we could not deny the happiness-restricting force of sensual feelings and then cast sidelong glances at the Indian ascetics, as Zeno the Stoic did. He wanted to make allowance for this view, and all his efforts were directed at interpreting the Hellenistic programme so as to underline the immediate and irrevocable values of sensual feelings. The result was that he tried to guarantee the individual's chances of happiness by elevating pleasure to the status of exclusive source of value and by interpreting it so as to make it attainable. I cannot of course prove that this explanation is the only possible one; there would in any case be little chance of that when we are engaged in reconstructing the background to a philosophy. I am just suggesting it as a method of forging plausible links between the evidence we have inherited; a mere hypothesis that looks for further confirmation.[9]

---

[9] I should like to thank the participants in the conference for countless suggestions and contributions during the discussions and in private conversations. I am especially indebted to Jacques Brunschwig, whose detailed written criticism alerted me to many mistakes and imprecisions. My thanks are also due to Jennifer Barnes for translating this paper.

Bibliography

Ancient authors

The main sources for Hellenistic ethics are all well-known authors who are readily available in standard editions, notably those of the Loeb Classical Library with original text and facing English version: here will be found (besides Plato and Aristotle) Cicero, Diogenes Laertius (who in Book x includes Epicurus' *Letter to Menoeceus* and *Kuriai Doxai*), Epictetus, Lucretius, Marcus Aurelius, Plutarch, Seneca and Sextus Empiricus. Note also the Teubner texts of Cicero, Diogenes of Oenoanda, Epictetus, Epicurus' letters, Plutarch and Sextus, as well as editions of Diogenes Laertius, Lucretius and Seneca in the Oxford Classical Text Series. Other editions, translations and commentaries cited in this volume are:

Annas and Barnes 1985. J. E. Annas and J. Barnes, *The Modes of Scepticism: Ancient Texts and Modern Interpretations*, Cambridge 1985.

Arrighetti 1973. G. Arrighetti (ed.), *Epicuro: Opere*, second edition, Turin 1973.

Bailey 1926. C. Bailey, *Epicurus, the Extant Remains*, Oxford 1926.

Bollack 1975. J. Bollack, *La Pensée du Plaisir. Epicure: Textes Moraux, Commentaires*, Paris 1975.

Bruns 1887. I. Bruns (ed.), *Alexander Aphrodisiensis, De anima liber cum mantissa*. Supplementum Aristotelicum II 1, Berlin 1887.

Bruns 1892. I. Bruns (ed.), *Alexander Aphrodisiensis, Quaestiones*, Supplementum Aristotelicum II 2, Berlin 1892.

Diano 1974. C. Diano (ed.), *Epicuri Ethica et Epistulae*, Florence 1974 (first edition 1946).

Diels and Kranz 1951. H. Diels and W. Kranz (eds.), *Die Fragmente der Vorsokratiker*, sixth edition, Berlin 1951 (later editions reprint the sixth).

Dougan and Henry 1934. T. W. Dougan and R. M. Henry (eds.), *Cicero, Tusculan Disputations*, Cambridge 1934.

Edelstein-Kidd 1972. L. Edelstein and I. G. Kidd (eds.), *Posidonius. I The Fragments*, Cambridge 1972.

Gauthier and Jolif 1970. R. A. Gauthier and J. Y. Jolif (eds.), *Aristote, L'Éthique à Nicomaque, Introduction, traduction et commentaire* (4 vols.), Paris and Louvain 1970 (first edition 1959).

Giusta 1964–7. M. Giusta (ed.), *I Dossografi di Etica* (2 vols.), Turin 1964 and 1967.

Hershbell 1981. J. P. Hershbell (ed.), *Pseudo-Plato, Axiochus*, Chicago 1981.

Hossenfelder 1968. M. Hossenfelder (trans.), *Grundrisse der pyrrhonischen Skepsis*, Frankfurt 1968.

Humphries 1968. R. Humphries (trans.), *Lucretius, The Way Things Are,* London and Bloomington 1968.
Joachim 1951. H. H. Joachim, *Aristotle: the Nicomachean Ethics,* Oxford 1951.
Kenney 1971. E. J. Kenney (ed.), *Lucretius, De Rerum Natura Book III,* Cambridge 1971.
Madvig 1876. J. N. Madvig (ed.), *Cicero, De finibus,* third edition, Copenhagen 1876 (first edition 1839).
Usener 1887 (abbreviated as Us.). H. Usener (ed.), *Epicurea,* Leipzig 1887.
Usener 1977. H. Usener, *Glossarium Epicureum,* edited by M. Gigante and W. Schmid, Rome 1977.
von Arnim 1903–24 (abbreviated as *SVF*). H. von Arnim (ed.), *Stoicorum Veterum Fragmenta,* Leipzig 1903–24.
von Arnim 1906. H. von Arnim (ed.), *Hierokles, Ethische Elementarlehre* (Pap. 9780), Berlin 1906.
Wachsmuth 1884. C. Wachsmuth (ed.), *Ioannes Stobaeus. Eclogae Physicae et Ethicae,* Berlin 1884.
Wallies 1891. M. Wallies (ed.), *Alexander Aphrodisiensis, In Aristotelis Topicorum libros octo commentaria,* Commentaria in Aristotelem Graeca II 2, Berlin 1891.
Woods 1982. M. J. Woods, *Aristotle, Eudemian Ethics I, II, VIII,* translated with introduction and commentary, Oxford 1982.

Modern works

Alpers-Gölz 1976. R. Alpers-Gölz, *Der Begriff* ΣΚΟΠΟΣ *in der Stoa und seine Vorgeschichte.* Spudasmata VIII, Hildesheim and New York 1976.
Barnes 1982. J. Barnes, 'The beliefs of a Pyrrhonist', *Proceedings of the Cambridge Philological Society* 208 (1982), 1–29.
Barry 1965. B. M. Barry, *Political Argument,* London 1965.
Beck 1960. L. W. Beck, *A Commentary on Kant's Critique of Practical Reason,* Chicago 1960.
Bentham 1834. J. Bentham, *Deontology,* ed. J. Bowring, London and Edinburgh 1834.
Bertier 1972. J. Bertier, *Mnésithée et Dieuchès,* Leiden 1972.
Blackburn 1971. S. Blackburn, 'Moral realism', in J. Casey (ed.), *Morality and Moral Reasoning,* London 1971.
Blackburn 1980. Id., 'Truth, realism and the regulation of theory', in *Midwest Studies in Philosophy,* vol. v, Minneapolis 1980.
Blackburn 1981. Id., 'Rule-following and moral realism' (reply to McDowell 1981), in *Wittgenstein: to follow a rule,* edited by S. Holtzmann and C. M. Leich, London 1981.
Bonhöffer 1890. A. Bonhöffer, *Epictet und die Stoa,* Stuttgart 1890.
Bonhöffer 1894. A Bonhöffer, *Die Ethik des Stoikers Epictet,* Stuttgart 1894.
Brandon 1980. E. P. Brandon, 'Subjectivism and seriousness', *Philosophical Quarterly* 30 (1980), 97–107.
Brunschwig 1964. J. Brunschwig, Review of Kleve 1963 in *Revue des Etudes Grecques* 77 (1964), 352–6.

Burnyeat 1980. M. F. Burnyeat, 'Can the sceptic live his scepticism?', in Schofield et al. 1980.

Burnyeat 1982. Id., 'Idealism and Greek philosophy: what Descartes saw and Berkeley missed', in *Philosophical Review* 91 (1982), 3–40.

Burnyeat 1984. Id., 'The sceptic in his time and place', in *Philosophy in History*, edited by R. Rorty, J. B. Schneewind and Q. Skinner, Cambridge 1984.

Burnyeat unpub. Id., 'Carneades was no probabilist', unpublished.

Cooper 1985. J. M. Cooper, 'Aristotle on the goods of fortune', in *Philosophical Review* 94 (1985) 173–96

DeWitt 1954. N. W. DeWitt, *Epicurus and his Philosophy*, Minneapolis 1954.

Dirlmeier 1937. F. Dirlmeier, *Die Oikeiōsis-Lehre Theophrasts, Philologus* Suppl. Bd. 30, Heft 1, 1937.

Edelstein 1936. L. Edelstein, 'The philosophical system of Posidonius', *American Journal of Philology* 57 (1936), 286–325.

Engberg-Pedersen 1983. T. Engberg-Pedersen, *Aristotle's Theory of Moral Insight*, Oxford 1983.

Frede 1979. M. Frede, 'Des Skeptikers Meinungen', *Neue Hefte für Philosophie* 15/16 (1979), 102–29.

Frede 1980. Id., 'The original notion of cause', in Schofield et al. 1980.

Frischer 1982. B. Frischer, *The Sculpted Word*, Berkeley 1982.

Gigante 1975. M. Gigante, '*Philosophia medicans* in Filodemo', *Cronache Ercolanesi* 5 (1975), 53–61.

Goldschmidt 1953. V. Goldschmidt, *Le système stoicien et l'idée de temps*, Paris 1953 (subsequent editions 1969, 1977).

Goldschmidt 1982. Id., 'La théorie épicurienne du droit', in *Science and Speculation*, edited by J. Barnes, J. Brunschwig, M. Burnyeat, and M. Schofield, Cambridge 1982.

Görgemanns 1983. H. Görgemanns, 'Oikeiōsis in Arius Didymus', in *On Stoic and Peripatetic Ethics. The Work of Arius Didymus*, ed. W. W. Fortenbaugh, London and New Brunswick 1983.

Hare 1963. R. M. Hare, *Freedom and Reason*, Oxford 1963.

Henson 1979. R. G. Henson, 'What Kant might have said', *Philosophical Review* 88 (1979), 39–54.

Herman 1981. B. Herman, 'On the value of acting from the motive of duty', *Philosophical Review* 90 (1981), 359–82.

Hirzel 1882. R. Hirzel, *Untersuchungen zu Ciceros philosophischen Schriften*, vol. II: *Die Entwicklung der stoischen Philosophie*, Leipzig 1982.

Inwood 1983. B. Inwood, 'The two forms of *oikeiōsis* in Arius and the Stoa' (reply to Görgemanns 1983), in *On Stoic and Peripatetic Ethics. The Work of Arius Didymus*, ed. W. W. Fortenbaugh, London and New Brunswick 1983.

Inwood 1984. Id., 'Hierocles: theory and argument in the second century AD', *Oxford Studies in Ancient Philosophy* 2 (1984), 151–83.

Ioppolo 1980. A. M. Ioppolo, *Aristone di Chio e lo Stoicismo antico*, Naples 1980.

Irwin 1983. T. H. Irwin, Review of Schofield et al. 1980, in *Nous* 17 (1983), 126–34.

Isnardi-Parente 1961. M. Isnardi-Parente, 'Un discorso consolatorio del Corpus Platonicum', *Rivista critica di storia della filosofia* 16 (1961), 33–47.

Jaeger 1957. W. Jaeger, 'Aristotle's use of medicine as a model of method in his ethics', *Journal of Hellenic Studies* 77 (1957), 54–61.

Kerferd 1972. G. B. Kerferd, 'The search for personal identity in Stoic thought', in the *Bulletin of the John Rylands Library* 55 (1972), 177–96.

Kerferd 1978. Id., 'What does the wise man know?', in *The Stoics*, ed. J. M. Rist, Berkeley 1978.

Keyt 1983. D. Keyt, 'Intellectualism in Aristotle', in *Essays in Ancient Greek Philosophy*, vol. 2, edited by J. P. Anton and A. Preus, Albany 1983.

Kidd 1971. I. G. Kidd, 'Stoic intermediates and the end for man', in *Problems in Stoicism*, ed. A. A. Long, London 1971.

Kidd 1978. Id., 'Moral actions and rules in Stoic ethics', in *The Stoics*, ed. J. M. Rist, Berkeley 1978.

Kleve 1963. K. Kleve, *Gnosis Theon. Die Lehre von der natürlichen Gotteserkenntnis in der epikureischen Theologie*, Oslo 1963.

Kraut 1979. R. Kraut, 'Two conceptions of happiness', *Philosophical Review* 88 (1979), 167–97.

Lévy 1980. C. Lévy, 'Un problème doxographique chez Cicéron: les indifférentistes', *Revue des Etudes Latines* 58 (1980), 238–51.

Long 1967. A. A. Long, 'Carneades and the Stoic *telos*', *Phronesis* 12 (1967), 59–90.

Long 1968. Id., 'Aristotle's legacy to Stoic ethics', in the *Bulletin of the Institute of Classical Studies* 15 (1968), 72–85.

Long 1971. Id., 'The logical basis of Stoic ethics', *Proceedings of the Aristotelian Society* 71 (1970–1), 85–104.

Long 1978. Id., 'Timon of Phlius', *Proceedings of the Cambridge Philological Society* 204 (1978), 68–91.

Long 1981. Id., 'Aristotle and the history of Greek scepticism', in *Studies in Aristotle*, ed. D. J. O'Meara, Washington D.C. 1981.

McDowell 1980. J. H. McDowell, 'The role of *eudaimonia* in Aristotle's ethics', in *Essays on Aristotle's Ethics*, ed. A. O. Rorty, Berkeley 1980.

McDowell 1981. Id., 'Non-cognitivism and rule-following', in *Wittgenstein: to follow a rule*, edited by S. Holtzmann and C. M. Leich, London 1981.

Mackie 1977. J. Mackie, *Ethics*, London 1977.

Mackie 1980. Id., *Hume's Moral Theory*, London 1980.

Marrou 1948. H.-L. Marrou, *Histoire de l'éducation dans l'antiquité*, Paris 1948.

Midgley 1981. M. Midgley, *Heart and Mind*, Brighton 1981.

Miller 1976. F. D. Miller, 'Epicurus on the Art of Dying', *Southern Journal of Philosophy* 14 (1976), 169–77.

Nagel 1979. T. Nagel, 'Death', in his *Mortal Questions*, Cambridge 1979.

Nussbaum 1979. M. C. Nussbaum, 'The speech of Alcibiades: a reading of Plato's *Symposium*', *Philosophy and Literature* 3 (1979), 131–72.

Pembroke 1971. S. G. Pembroke, 'Oikeiōsis', in *Problems in Stoicism*, ed. A. A. Long, London 1971.

Platts 1980. M. Platts, 'Moral reality and the end of desire', in *Reference, Truth and Reality*, ed. M. Platts, London 1980.

Pohlenz 1938. M. Pohlenz, 'Zenon und Chrysipp', *Nachrichten der Akademie der Wissenschaften zu Göttingen* (phil.–hist. Klasse), N. F. 1 2 (1938), 173–210 (reprinted in his *Kleine Schriften*, ed. H. Dörrie, Hildesheim 1965).

Pohlenz 1940. Id., *Grundfragen der stoischen Philosophie*, Abhandlungen der Gesellschaft der Wissenschaften zu Göttingen (phil.-hist. Klasse), 3, 26 (1940).

Pohlenz 1970. Id., *Die Stoa*, fourth edition, 2 vols., Göttingen 1970.

Pritzl 1983. K. Pritzl, 'Aristotle and Happiness after Death: *Nicomachean Ethics* I 10–11', *Classical Philology* 78 (1983), 101–11.

Reiner 1969. H. Reiner, 'Die ethische Weisheit der Stoiker heute', *Gymnasium* 96 (1969), 330–57.

Richter 1902. R. Richter, 'Die erkenntnistheoretischen Voraussetzungen des griechischen Skeptizismus', *Philosophische Studien* 20 (1902), 246–99.

Richter, 1904. Id., *Der Skeptizismus in der Philosophie*, Leipzig 1904.

Rieth 1934. O. Rieth, 'Über das Telos der Stoiker', *Hermes* 69 (1934), 13–45.

Rist 1969. J. M. Rist, *Stoic Philosophy*, Cambridge 1969.

Rist 1972. Id., *Epicurus: an Introduction*, Cambridge 1972.

Rorty 1983. A. O. Rorty, 'Fearing Death', *Philosophy* 58 (1983), 175–88.

Rorty 1982. R. Rorty, 'Philosophy in America', in his *The Consequences of Pragmatism*, Minneapolis 1982.

Sandbach 1971. F. H. Sandbach, 'Ennoia and Prolēpsis', in *Problems in Stoicism*, ed. A. A. Long, London 1971.

Schofield 1980. M. Schofield, 'Preconception, Argument and God', in Schofield et al. 1980.

Schofield 1983. Id., 'The syllogisms of Zeno of Citium', *Phronesis* 28 (1983), 31–58.

Schofield et al. 1980. M. Schofield, M. Burnyeat and J. Barnes (eds.), *Doubt and Dogmatism*, Oxford 1980.

Schopenhauer 1819. A. Schopenhauer, *The World as Will and Representation*, in the translation of E. F. J. Payne, New York 1965.

Sedley 1982. D. N. Sedley, 'On Signs', in *Science and Speculation*, edited by J. Barnes, J. Brunschwig, M. Burnyeat and M. Schofield, Cambridge 1982.

Silverstein 1980. H. S. Silverstein, 'The evil of death', *Journal of Philosophy* 77 (1980), 401–23.

Soreth 1968. M. Soreth, 'Die zweite Telosformel des Antipater von Tarsos', *Archiv für Geschichte der Philosophie* 50 (1968), 48–72.

Striker 1980. G. Striker, 'Sceptical Strategies', in Schofield et al. 1980.

Striker 1981. Id., 'Über den Unterschied zwischen den Pyrrhoneern und den Akademikern', *Phronesis* 26 (1981), 153–71.

Striker 1983a. Id., 'The role of *oikeiōsis* in Stoic ethics', *Oxford Studies in Ancient Philosophy* 1 (1983), 145–67.

Striker 1983b. Id., 'The ten tropes of Aenesidemus', in *The Skeptical Tradition*, ed. M. F. Burnyeat, Berkeley 1983.

Sudhaus 1911. S. Sudhaus, 'Epikur als Beichtvater', *Archiv für Religionswissenschaft* 14 (1911), 647–8.

Taylor 1976. C. Taylor, 'Responsibility for Self', in *The Identities of Persons*, ed. A. O. Rorty, Berkeley 1976.

Taylor 1970. C. C. W. Taylor, Review of Hare 1963, reprinted from *Mind* 74 (1965) in *The Definition of Morality*, edited by G. Wallace and A. Walker, London 1970.

Todd 1973. R. B. Todd, 'The Stoic common notions', *Symbolae Osloenses* 48 (1973), 47–75.

Tsekourakis 1974. D. Tsekourakis, *Studies in the Terminology of Early Stoic Ethics, Hermes* Einzelschrift 32, Wiesbaden 1974.

Warnock 1978. G. Warnock, 'On choosing values', in *Midwest Studies in Philosophy*, vol. III, Minneapolis 1978.

White 1978. N. P. White, 'Two notes on Stoic terminology', *American Journal of Philology* 99 (1978), 111–19.

White 1979. Id., 'The basis of Stoic ethics', *Harvard Studies in Classical Philology* 83 (1979), 143–78.

White 1981. Id., 'Goodness and human aims in Aristotle's ethics', in *Studies in Aristotle*, ed. D. J. O'Meara, Washington D.C. 1981.

Williams 1973. B. A. O. Williams, 'The Macropoulos case: reflections on the tedium of immortality', in his *Problems of the Self*, Cambridge 1973.

Index of Passages

We are grateful to Thomas Haussmann for help with this and the following indices.

Glossary of Greek and Latin terms

ἀγαθόν   *agathon*   **bonum**   good   145, 215, 255
ἀδιάφορος   *adiaphoros*   indifferent   179, 248f
αἵρεσις   *hairesis*   choice   236n. 36
αἱρετόν   *haireton*   chosen, choiceworthy   120n. 22, 125, 234
αἴσθησις   *aisthēsis*   perception   121, 139n. 47
ἀλλοτριῶσαι   *allotriōsai*   **alienari**   to alienate   128, 129
ἁμαρτία   *hamartia*   error   49
ἀναισθητεῖν   *anaisthētein*   to be insensate   75
ἀναισθησία   *anaisthēsia*   lack of sensation   78, 79
ἀντίληψις   *antilēpsis*   awareness   139n. 47
ἀξία   *axia*   **aestimatio**   value   154n.7, 155
ἀξίωμα   *axiōma*   proposition   103, 164
ἀπαθής   *apathēs*   unaffected   19, 93
ἀταραξία   *ataraxia*   peace of mind, tranquillity   17, 39, 45, 46, 48, 68, 127n. 34, 245, 249, 252f.
αὐτάρκης   *autarkēs*   self-sufficient   223n. 31

βούλησις   *boulēsis*   desire   101

διαρθροῦν   *diarthroun*   to articulate   209
δόξα   *doxa*   belief, judgment   121, 122

ἐκλογή   *eklogē*   **selectio**   selection   188n. 4
ἔννοια   *ennoia*   **notio**   concept, notion   156
ἐπιγέννημα, ἐπιγιγνόμενον   *epigennēma, epigignomenon*   supervenient   118n. 4, 134
ἔργον   *ergon*   function   197, 229
εὐαρεστεῖσθαι   *euaresteisthai*   to rejoice   124
εὐδαιμονία   *eudaimonia*   happiness   56, 61, 86f., 146, 172, 185, 194, 225n. 21, 228n.24, 247–53, 260
εὔλογος   *eulogos*   reasonable, probable   179f., 188n.4, 235n.33
εὐπάθεια   *eupatheia*   state of being well affected   93, 240n.38
εὔροια βίου   *euroia biou*   good flow of life   225,nn.20,21

ἡδονή   *hēdonē*   pleasure   253n.6, 255f.

ἰατρεία, ἰάτρευσις   *iatreia, iatreusis*   medical treatment   65

καλόν   *kalon*   **honestum**   fine, noble   145, 146, 193, 201n.16, 202n.17, 209, 230n.28
καθῆκον   *kathēkon*   **officium**   appropriate action, duty   145, 155, 178–83, 188n.4, 190n.9, 199n.15, 203f., 234, 236n.36
καταστηματικός   *katastēmatikos*   static   126f., 246, 255
κατόρθωμα   *katorthōma*   **recte factum**   right act   179, 235n.34, 236n.36
κίνησις   *kinēsis*   movement, change   253, 258
κύριος   *kurios*   controlling   229n.27

λῆψις   *lēpsis*   selection   236n.36
λόγος   *logos*   argument; reason   32–73 passim, 208n.4

μετριοπαθής *metriopathēs* moderate in emotion 93

οἰκειοῦσθαι *oikeiousthai* **conciliari** to appropriate 128, 129
οἰκείωσις *oikeiōsis* **conciliatio** appropriation 130–44 passim, 148–82 passim,
201n.16, 242n. 40
ὁρμή *hormē* impulse 149–52, 160, 166, 170

πάθος *pathos* affection, emotion, feeling 32, 42, 59, 60, 66, 67, 93–110 passim,
118n.13, 121–5, 215
παρακολούθησις *parakolouthēsis* self-reflexive understanding 160, 162, 171
περιστατικός *peristatikos* with circumstance 180
πραότης *praotēs* gentleness 23n.26
προηγμένον *proēgmenon* preferred, preferable 145, 178, 191, 212n.9
προκείμενον *prokeimenon* **propositum** intended result 195, 201, 229n.25, 230,
232n.29, 235
πρόληψις *prolēpsis* preconception 123, 125n.32, 208, 209n.5
προσκρούειν *proskrouein* to dislike 117n.12, 124n.30
πρῶτα κατὰ φύσιν *prōta kata phusin* first things in accordance with nature 187n.3,
200n.16, 204n.20, 229n.25
πρῶτον οἰκεῖον *prōton oikeion* first thing appropriate 129, 133, 139
πρωτοχρονεῖν *prōtochronein* to be antecedent 84

σκοπός *skopos* target 198n.13, 228n.25
στοχάζεσθαι *stochazesthai* to take aim 57, 65
στοχαστικός *stochastikos* aiming; stochastic 57, 202n.17, 232n.29
συναίσθησις *sunaisthēsis* consciousness 139n.47, 149n.3
συνείδησις *suneidēsis* consciousness 149n.3
σύστασις *sustasis* **constitutio** constitution 133, 136, 137n.45, 138, 139n.48

ταραχή *tarachē* anxiety 18
τέλος *telos* **finis** end, goal 34n.4, 54, 116, 129n.36, 146, 149f., 160, 172, 187, 190,
193f., 197, 198n.13, 201, 202n.17, 204, 206, 213n.11, 227n.22, 228n.25, 230n.28,
232n.29, 249f., 256n.8, 257, 258, 259, 262
τέχνη *technē* **ars** art, craft, science 42, 56, 57, 185, 188n.4, 194, 202n.17

ὑποτελίς *hupotelis* subordinate end 204n.20

φαντασία *phantasia* impression, appearance 106, 140n.49, 143, 231
φρόνησις *phronēsis* **sapientia** or **prudentia** wisdom 173, 195, 260
φύσις *phusis* **natura** nature 14, 115, 187
κατὰ φύσιν *kata phusin* natural, in accordance with nature 119, 187, 191

General Index

Academy, 78, 114, 117, 188
Aenesidemus: his interest in ethics 4n.2;
tenth Mode 4ff.; confusing moral realism
with moral absolutism 9n.13
Aeschylus, 52
affections (*pathos*); of the soul, Stoic
doctrine of 93–110; part of human nature
or not? 93–9; passive 97; judgments of
reason 98, 100, 102f.; diseases of reason
99; *see also* emotion, feeling
Alexander of Aphrodisias: 186, 212n.10;
on *oikeiōsis* 133, 138; his arguments
against the self-sufficiency of virtue for
happiness 189–92, 195, 235, 236,
239n.37; on the goal of stochastic crafts
195, 197, 199, 202, 203n.18, 230n.28
Antiochus of Ascalon: 113, 114, 136n.41;
his version of Peripatetic ethics 200n.16;
distinguishes between Aristotle's and
Theophrastus' views on happiness
222n.17; on oikeiōsis 242n.40
Antipater of Tarsus: his defense of Stoic
ethics against Carneades' objections
185–204 passim; 229n.25, 231, 233n.31
Antisthenes, 9
appropriate action (*kathēkon*): Stoic
doctrine of 178–83; definition of 179,
188n.4, 234, 235n.33; objective of,
different from goal of life 203f., 235f.;
material of virtue 235
Arcesilaus, 74; on the inactivity argument
22f.; criticising the Stoic theory of
judgment 103f.
Archedemus, 136n.41; his definition of the
end 199n.15
archer simile, 192, 231
Aristocles, 14, 23; his attack on scepticism
19f
Aristo of Chios, 182, 206; Chrysippus'
polemic against 188
Aristotle: on the analogy between medicine
and ethics 31–74 passim; on education
67f.; his contribution to metaphilosophy
of ethics 70–2; on happiness affected by
events after death 85–7; his theory of the
emotions 93–9; on forms of desire 101,
102; on the natural state of human beings

119, n.18; his ethical theory compared
with Stoic 205–44 passim, 146f., 149,
157, 172, 174, 177; contrasted with
Hellenistic ethics 249n.2, on pleasure
253n.6; his metaphysics developed by
Stoics 164
Arius Didymus, 114, 116
Arnim, H. von, 144, 173, 195
art, *see* craft

belief: and desire 33; and emotion 94, 98,
121f.; voluntary 98f.; Stoic theory of
103f.; and impulse 107; value judgments
as factual beliefs 154; *see also* judgment
Bentham, J., 205
bravery, Stoic vs. Aristotelian view of, 218f.

Carneades: his critique of Stoic ethics
185–204 passim; 231, 232n.30
chance, and happiness 69, 221f.
child: child psychology 113–44 passim;
natural creature not corrupted by
education 33f., 119f., 121f., 259; lacks
the ability to be happy, acc. to Aristotle
and Plato 119, n.18; naturally strives for
pleasure 117f., 124–6, 259, or not 134–5
Chrysippus: 11, 118n.14, 229n.26; on
affections of the soul 102; on *oikeiōsis*
129f. 133, 136n.41, 137n.44, 139, 148f.;
uses 'nature' both of human and of
universal nature 172; his definition of the
end 182, 187; argues against Aristo of
Chios 188; his arguments for the thesis
that only the fine is good 211–13;
concedes that a mixed end is logically
possible 213–14; on the relation between
happiness and tranquillity 226f.
Cicero: 40, 65, 81, 97f., 116, 123; on
Epicurus' theory of pleasure 126–8; his
account of Stoic *oikeiōsis* 128–33,
149–77; compared with Seneca's 136–8,
141; his account of *kathēkonta* 178–80,
182
Cleanthes, 177, 187
Colotes, 47
confession, in Epicureanism, 48ff.
craft: philosophy as a curative art 31–74

283

Hume, D., 9

identity: of the human constitution 138; statements, Stoic use of 185f.
impression: Stoic theory of, 103–9 passim; often distorted by judgment acc. to Epicurus 121–2
impulse (*hormē*): a form of judgment acc. to Stoics 106–7; Stoic explanation of animal's natural impulses 150–2
indifferents (*adiaphora*), Stoic doctrine of, 234–9; *see also* appropriate action
individual: Stoic vs. Aristotelian concept of 164; centre of attention in Hellenistic ethics 246f.
insulation, of morality 22f., 26ff.
Isnardi-Parente, M., 78, 80
Isocrates, 52

Joachim, H. H., 86f.
judgment: Stoic theory of 103–7; may distort impressions acc. to Epicurus 121–2; *see also* belief

Kant, I., 217n.14
Kenney, E. J., 76

Long, A. A., 147f., 229n.25
Lucretius: 47, 260; on sexual desire and love 35n.5, 42; on the fear of death 76–82

Mackie, J. L., 7, 13, 24
magnanimity: has a special place among the virtues in Stoicism 174; excludes fear? 218f.; sufficient for happiness acc. to Hecaton 227
Marcus Aurelius, 147f.
medicine: as an analogue to philosophy 31–74 passim; as a stochastic craft 195ff., 229, 231
Moore, G. E., 7, 26

Nagel, T., 87f., 90
naturalism, Stoic form of, 152–4
nature: normative meaning of 119; teleological view of 147–8, 161; refers to both human and universal nature 172; in Stoic definitions of the end 187f., 241n.39, 249n.2; emotion (not) a part of human nature 93–9; life in accordance with nature, how connected with order and harmony 157–9; and virtue 146f., 171–5; distinguished from life in agreement with nature 187, 241; objective of rational selection 191f., 202–4, 232, 235f.; as realisation of human nature and capacities 241f.;

natural, as a term used by sceptics 20n.22; desires, in Epicureanism 34f.; impulses, Stoic vs. Platonic–Aristotelian view of 108–9; natural state of human beings acc. to Epicurus 34f.; and Aristotle 118–20; objects of natural inclinations, valuable because natural? 99, 153, 161

oikeiōsis: different forms of 130n.37, 133n.38, 136n.41, 137n.44, 149f., 175; directed towards oneself, or one's constitution? 133n.39, 138, 139n.48; in relation to oneself, proofs for 130–4; Seneca's account of 135–8; Hierocles' account 139–44; Cicero's account 149–75; Antiochus' interpretation of 242n.40; in relation to other humans, foundation of justice 175–6

Panaetius, departing from Stoic orthodoxy? 233n.31
Parmenides, 47
peace of mind (*ataraxia*): attained by suspension of judgment 17f., 23; attained through dogmatic belief 46; desired by new-born children? 127n.34; sufficient for happiness according to some Stoics 224–8; as a subjective state, constitutes happiness acc. to Hellenistic philosophers in general 248–9; identified with pleasure by Epicurus 252f.
perception: as a criterion of truth 121f.; of oneself 139–44; source of value-judgments 251–2, 259
Philo of Alexandria: his treatment of the Modes of scepticism 4n.5, 5n.6; his arguments for moral scepticism 6f., 10f.
Philodemus: on therapeutic argument 37f., 40–52; objects to Aristotelian use of medical analogy 65f.
philosophy: analogous to medicine 31–74 passim; purpose of acc. to Epicurus 31, as a curative art 36f., 43f., 51
Plato: 15n.17, 53, 54, 65, 78, 84, 136n.41, 146, 172; the Cave as an illustration of unreal desires 90; his theory of emotion 93–9 passim; identifies one's true self with reason 98; on desire 101; on the disturbances of childhood 119n.18; his conception of happiness contrasted with Hellenistic 249n.2
pleasure: Epicurus' theory of 245–63 passim; not increased by length of time acc. to Epicurus 81; recognised as the supreme good through the criterion of emotion 115; desired by children from birth, acc. to Epicurus 117–28; not

Made in the USA
Lexington, KY
27 April 2011